Frank Gruba-McCallister's *Radical Healing: No Justice Without Wellness* provides a rigorous and timely critique of neoliberalism's oppressive impact on human suffering while offering a compelling framework for radical healing. Drawing on critical psychology, existential and humanistic approaches, and spiritual practices, the book situates healing within both individual and collective contexts, arguing that liberation from suffering must engage with the structural sources of oppression—most notably, the intersections of neoliberalism and fascism. This comprehensive analysis challenges the depoliticized and commodified models of mainstream mental health care, calling for a more holistic approach that recognizes the spiritual, social, and psychological dimensions of suffering.

The book's strength lies in its ability to integrate various theoretical perspectives, from critical theory to liberation theology, to provide a model of healing that is not only radical but practical. By emphasizing the interconnectedness of compassion and justice, Gruba-McCallister addresses a critical gap in the literature, highlighting how the commodification of care often strips away the deeper moral commitments required for genuine healing. His call for personal transformation, particularly among healers, is a welcome reminder that healing cannot happen without self-examination and an ongoing commitment to confronting one's complicity in oppressive structures.

One of the most compelling aspects of the book is its attention to spirituality, particularly the role of contemplative practices and the idea of the "wounded healer." In contrast to the often-fragmented focus of mainstream therapeutic practices, Gruba-McCallister weaves together spiritual, psychological, and social understandings of suffering, offering a truly integrative approach to care. This emphasis on spirituality as a necessary dimension of healing brings much-needed attention to the often-neglected existential concerns of those seeking care, while also grounding the work in traditions that emphasize humility, openness, and moral responsibility.

Ultimately, *Radical Healing* makes a powerful case for rethinking both the purpose and practice of healing. By centering healing within the broader struggle for justice, the book offers a path forward that is both politically engaged and spiritually grounded. Gruba-McCallister's work challenges us to not only understand suffering differently but to take action toward liberation—both personal and collective. This book is a must-read for those in the fields of psychology, social work, and critical health studies who are seeking a more just and compassionate way forward.

Justin M. Karter, PhD
Instructor/Advisor, Center for Psychological
Humanities & Ethics, Boston College
Executive Board, Society for Theoretical and Philosophical
Psychology (American Psychological Association Division 24)
Research News Editor, Mad in America

I am beyond grateful for Dr. Gruba-McCallister and this astonishing, extraordinary book, which has been sorely needed for a very long time and is exactly what our world needs now in this time of unprecedented global psychospiritual crisis. We are all suffering in the same storm, though not in the same boat, in the wake of the global pandemic and volatile de-stabilization of global geo-political relations. This book not only restores the integrity of the foundational aspects of existential and humanistic psychology as prosocial, emphasizing the critical importance of the relational and profoundly interconnected nature of the self; it also manages—with respect and cultural humility—to illuminate the place of psychotherapy and related work in the global and historical context of how human beings have evolved together to heal each other through social means and contexts. It also celebrates spirituality as a life-giving source of awe, healing, and transformation in our lives, as opposed to reducing it to an artifact of human culture and interaction. In service of facing life directly and with courage, it undertakes a ruthless and relentlessly honest exploration of the phenomena that fracture and divide us, forces that have perniciously instilled internalized oppression, neo-liberal hegemony, and fascism. Dr. Gruba-McCallister invites us, from our individual places of cultural embeddedness, to explore how we might identify and dispel the illusions that keep us in a state of fragmentation, alienation, separation, and isolation from each other and the natural world. He also passionately advocates for the necessity of compassion and justice, showing us that it is long past the time where expressing individuality for its own sake, in its own inflated privilege, can be considered to be sufficient. Perhaps it is time to eschew the narcissistic limits of the Golden Rule in favor of radical healing, which draws us into embodied, authentic empathy and relationship.

Drake Spaeth, PsyD
Director, Existential and Humanistic psychology Specialization, Humanistic Clinical Psychology Faculty, Saybrook University
Past President (2019-2020), The Society for Humanistic Psychology (Division 32, The American Psychological Association)

I've been waiting for a book like this for years. Through its expansive synthesis of critical social theory, existential and psychoanalytic psychology, Buddhism, humanistic and transpersonal thought, and spiritual wisdom, *Radical Healing: No Wellness Without Justice* offers a profound, courageous, compassionate, and insightful examination suffering.

Building on insights from critical psychology, Gruba-McCallister presents a compelling case for healing that integrates personal liberation with societal transformation. He challenges mainstream psychological approaches that individualize and pathologize suffering, exposing oppressive systems like unchecked capitalism, neoliberalism, and fascism as significant contributors of harm.

Grounded in values of compassion and justice, *Radical Healing* delves deeper into the psychological and spiritual mechanisms that sustain oppression and hinder both personal and collective liberation. Included in this exploration are dynamics such as fear, ego, alienation, self-deception, and the innate longing for transcendence.

Gruba-McCallister implores healers to embrace the dual obligation of supporting individuals through pain and growth while also answering a sacred and moral call to challenge the systems of oppression and inequity that perpetuate human-caused suffering.

This book challenges readers to envision what healing could be: a personal, moral, spiritual, and societal endeavor that restores our connection to ourselves, one another, and something greater. Bold and idealistic in its vision, *Radical Healing* provides a practical path for healers to become transformative agents of revolutionary change, advancing a more just, compassionate, and joyful world. It is an essential resource to be revisited time and time again.

Sebastienne Grant, PhD
Associate Professor
PhD in Psychology with a Concentration in Integral Transpersonal Psychology
California Institute of Integral Studies

Radical Healing is a most remarkable book that boldly discusses how we can help ourselves and others with the totality of the suffering that we experience in life. This book seriously addresses the question of how we can serve as healers in a society that is often sicker than the individuals that we are called to help. Frank Gruba-Mccalister's analysis of the nature of suffering includes the role of systemic forms of oppression and spiritual factors that are commonly left out of many other theories in clinical psychology. His goal is to help people with a radical form of healing that includes how we can become de-mystified, empowered, and embodied in healing from the sicknesses not only within ourselves as individuals, but also within our societies and cultures. His writing provides an astonishing integration of many disparate fields of humanistic, existential, transpersonal, and critical psychology along with insights from historical, political, economic, and spiritual sources. *Radical Healing* is designed to help people to awaken to the nature of their suffering, so that they travel down pathways to a radically complete form of holistic healing.

Ian Wickramasekera II, PsyD
Fielding University

Radical Healing:
No Wellness Without Justice

Frank Gruba-McCallister, PhD

University
PROFESSORS PRESS

Colorado Springs, CO
www.universityprofessorspress.com

First Published in 2025, University Professors Press.

Hardcover ISBN: 978-1-955737-60-9
Paperback ISBN: 978-1-955737-59-3
ebook ISBN: 978-1-955737-61-6

University Professors Press
Colorado Springs, CO
www.universityprofessorspress.com

Cover Design by Laura Ross
Cover Image by Marguerite Laing

To my wife, Sandra,
who helped me to understand the meaning of radical
and has been a source of support and inspiration
in my pursuit of compassion and justice.

Table of Contents

Acknowledgments

My thanks first to my like-minded colleagues for their insights and support for the vision of radical healing that I advance in this book. Likewise to my family and friends, particularly my wife, Sandra, for their steadfast encouragement. This includes my departed mother and father, who each in their own way helped me to recognize and understand the ways in which injustices do egregious harm to the marginalized and oppressed. I feel that I am accompanied by all of these fellow-travelers in my commitment to provide compassion and advocacy for victims of injustice. I also wish to thank those who were kind enough to provide positive endorsements for my work. Finally, my gratitude to Dr. Louis Hoffman and his colleagues at University Professors Press for their guidance, feedback, and support in bringing this book to press.

Preface

It has been over six years since I wrote the Preface to my first book, *Embracing Disillusionment: Achieving Liberation through the Demystification of Suffering.* In it I highlighted the principal themes of the book, with particular focus on the significant role that oppression plays in inflicting suffering on human beings. Oppression is a social practice in which one group uses its power and privilege to dominate a subordinate group in order to advance their interests and exploit the oppressed. As Isaac Prilleltensky asserts, oppression has both political and psychological elements. The political is evidenced in the ways in which power and authority is used to define what is normal and desirable in a society by means of the imposition of a dominant ideology. This ideology permeates every aspect of society and is so pervasive that it is rendered invisible and so resistant to criticism and change. All individuals are indoctrinated into this ideology by major social institutions. Any alternative worldview is demeaned, pathologized, and, if necessary, violently repressed. This political element of oppression leads to a range of material harms that include economic impacts such as deprivation, exploitation, and poverty, as well as physical impacts—the most extreme due to systematic violence.

The psychological dimension of oppression encompasses its impacts on mental states such as emotions and beliefs. Those who are oppressed essentially are made to feel inadequate, inferior, undeserving, immoral, and despised. This leads to a number of deleterious psychological consequences rooted in the internalization of oppression, including anxiety, shame, guilt, helplessness, depression, and self-hatred. These psychological impacts not only inflict suffering on the oppressed but are also used to maintain the status quo by promoting their consent to their oppression. The essence of oppression is the dehumanization of its victims. Depriving individuals of their dignity and worth is the cause of systemic injustice and is morally condemnable.

Sadly, the terrible legacy of oppression is not new. It can be traced historically to the earliest civilizations. The historian of religion Karen Armstrong, describes what she calls the development of structural violence in agrarian societies in which there existed a fixed hierarchy of status and power. A small elite that is not more than two percent of the population, assisted by a small group of retainers, exploit the masses by appropriating their labor in order to support their aristocratic lifestyle and maintain their power. Armstrong asserts that this oppressive system was inevitable in premodern civilization and provided certain advantages despite also inflicting terrible costs. In order to maintain control, the ruling class devised an overarching worldview or ideology that portrayed the existing social arrangement as not only natural and inevitable but desirable and moral. In premodern societies religion often played a notable role in supporting and even enforcing this ideology. However, powerful critiques of the absence of compassion and justice for the downtrodden can also be found in in a number of religious traditions that began in this era.

It is unfortunate, as I detailed in my earlier book, that little has changed regarding the magnitude of suffering inflicted on human beings by systematic and structural oppression. Unjust hierarchies persist in which a very small class of powerful elite individuals possess the vast majority of wealth and exercise tremendous power. This is evidenced in the growing number of oligarchies throughout the world and ever-widening disparities in income and wealth. Moreover, as I detail in my previous book, the workings of oppression and its harmful impacts continue to be justified, sanitized, and obscured by means of socially manufactured illusions (e.g., the process of mystification). These illusions are based in the dominant ideology or hegemony and are used to keep the subaltern classes frightened and submissive. I identified this dominant ideology as neoliberalism—an extreme form of capitalism. This ideology fosters an extreme individualism that, in turn, promotes selfishness, greed, unbridled consumption, and competition. All of these contribute to oppressive practices that are detrimental at every level of life.

This book continues to argue that it is imperative for healers to address suffering by both extending compassion to those who are oppressed and advancing justice to remove its preventable causes. However, to be faithful to this goal healers must acknowledge the roots of oppression in neoliberal ideology and take measures not only to oppose it but to establish a counter-hegemony that promotes human liberation. My earlier critique of mainstream psychology's and other health care disciplines' adoption of neoliberal ideology continues in this present work. This leads those whose charge it is to provide care not only to employ this ideology but to enforce and impose it on those seeking help. It is utterly self-defeating to try and end oppression by engaging in acts of oppression—even if such actions are "good intentioned." Those who do so are engaging in a dangerous form of self-deception that is based on a failure to engage in sincere and rigorous critical examination of their ideological illusions.

While this book builds on my previous one, it is devoted to providing more comprehensive and detailed practical guidance to those who provide care to the suffering. As I argue previously, healing must recognize the interdependent relationship between the values of compassion and justice. Assuming the vocation of healer means that one must first engage in a process of personal and professional transformation that then parallels the process of assisting others to achieve liberation. And that process must be radical in that it must get down to the basic roots from which the dehumanization of oneself and others arises. This needs to be followed by uprooting dehumanizing beliefs and values first in oneself and then in society.

Thus, the early part of the book is devoted to examining the meaning and purpose of being a radical healer by discussing what radical healing is and outlining its essential elements. My approach integrates elements of humanistic/existential psychology, critical psychology, and an understanding of spirituality from a mystical viewpoint in order to provide a truly holistic perspective. These same elements are then used to elucidate how radical healing is a vocation in which one must respond to a higher calling. This discussion is framed based on the historical roots of this vocation in the earliest healers, including shamans and other indigenous practitioners. This illustrates how healers must align their work in the service of a higher power as well as actualize the transformative potential of their own suffering to awaken that potential in others.

The discussion then moves from the personal transformation of the healer to a model of the practice of radical healing based on an integral understanding of human beings. In light of this, chapters are devoted to explaining the three fundamental causes of suffering: personal, spiritual, and social. Moreover, in keeping with this integral perspective, these three causes are understood as intertwined with one another and share a number of common elements. In exploring these forms of suffering, the role played by neoliberal ideology continues. However, unlike my first book, the present book considers a second significant ideological factor responsible for suffering—fascism. This addition is based first on the recognition of the prominent role that capitalism has historically played in slavery, colonialism, imperialism, and other forms of oppression. These are all aspects of fascist ideology. The work of a number of early critical psychologists, such as Adorno, Horkheimer, and Fromm, also described the interrelationship that exists between capitalism and fascism, often employing a Marxist theoretical framework. Contemporary authors, such as Thomas Teo and Naomi Klein, continue this important work, noting how greed, commodification, patriarchy, racism, colonialism, and fear of difference continue to be substantial factors responsible for oppression.

The final three chapters utilize the theoretical framework developed in the earlier chapters to lay out a model of radical healing presented as an alternative to current models that suffer from being grounded in neoliberal ideology. The first of these chapters describes a method of assessment that takes into account both the individual and societal dimensions of human beings. It is patterned on Ken Wilber's ground-breaking work on integral psychology, which offers a truly multidimensional and multifaceted understanding of human beings. The next two chapters then challenge the highly individualistic nature of current models of psychotherapy, while arguing that psychotherapy itself still has value as one means of promoting healing. Nonetheless, the role of the radical healer must be an expanded one in which there is a commitment to constantly engage in a critical examination of the assumptions and values guiding one's work. Radical healing is a commitment to promoting not only individual emancipation but also collective liberation. The prominent social causes of suffering thus must not be neglected. This means that radical healing needs to advocate a counter-hegemony that better enables optimal human flourishing. That counter-hegemony is proposed in the form of democratic socialism.

The challenges to what it means to be a human being extend far beyond what is occurring "inside" of those who seek our care. Restricting our focus may seem to be safer and more manageable. It may give us the illusion that we are making a difference in the lives of those who are suffering. It may allay our own fears about what is the matter with the world. However, it is a guarantee that we will ultimately fail in the commitment to compassion and justice required for our vocation. What is needed is healing that is genuinely radical. There can be no wellness without justice. My hope is that in this book I have provided clarity about what this means and about how it can be achieved.

Frank Gruba-McCallister, PhD
Park Ridge, Illinois
September 18, 2024

Chapter 1

Laying Down the Foundations for Radical Healing

The Dialectic of the Individual and the Collective

This is a book about radical healing. But before I explain what I mean by radical healing, it is important that I first provide some preliminary discussion of foundational assumptions regarding how I understand the process of healing. This includes a number of themes or guiding principles that will consistently run through my subsequent discussion of what makes healing radical. In addition, in this chapter I introduce a number of concepts pertinent to radical healing that will be more fully elaborated in later chapters. This preliminary material provides a useful background for my analysis in two ways. First, by introducing what I believe are elements essential to situating healing within broader social, economic, political, and cultural contexts, I will be challenging the overly individualistic dominant perspective. That is, it is critical to ensure that any understanding well-being and what impairs it includes not only looking within persons but also looking from the outside in. Those who practice healing never do so within a vacuum. The multiple contexts within which they practice shape their understanding of what healing is, the nature of their role as healer, and how they understand and treat the various problems and afflictions that individuals suffer from.

Second, while making this important correction to the current one-sided perspective, it is nonetheless true that radical healing still recognizes and values the importance of acknowledging and responding to what is happening within individuals. Thus, equal consideration must be given to the imperative of according absolute respect to the lived experiences of both those who are seeking healing and those who have committed themselves to the vocation of healing. This serves to underline and highlight the centrality of relationship to healing.

From the outset, it must be made clear that there can be no serious discussion of healing without a corresponding discussion of its principal aim. And that is to address and respond to the universal experience of suffering with the utmost respect and care. The etymological roots of the word "healing" come from the Old English and Old Norse "to be whole, sound, or well." Common elements of the experience of suffering are feeling broken, separated, isolated, and out of harmony (Gruba-McCallister, 2019). One experiences that his or her sense of integrity and wholeness has been damaged or threatened. These reactions are all natural and predictable responses to a common element of the experience of suffering: loss. As expressed in existential philosophy (Gruba-McCallister & Levington, 1995; Spinelli, 2014) and Buddhism (Rahula, 1974), loss is an inescapable part of human life due to its transience and the sense of insecurity that follows. Each loss is a reminder of the ultimate loss, death, and thus triggers a deep fear and sense of dread (Becker, 1973). As Frank and Frank (1991) observe, the common prelude to individuals seeking therapy is the shattering of their worldview. This worldview plays a very important role in providing individuals with a sense of order, predictability, and control, which is among the most powerful of human needs.

Moreover, an individual's worldview is inextricably bound up with their powerfully held beliefs about who they are or their "ego" (Gruba-McCallister, 2019). Thus, loss of one's worldview is experienced as the loss of one's very self—again giving rise to extreme anxiety and terror. This experience of loss highlights another central feature of the experience of suffering, alienation. This can be expressed as a sense of no longer feeling at home in the world and feeling estranged from ourselves, others, and the world around us. Less extreme experiences of alienation occur at those times when we act in ways that are out of character or contrary to what we intended (Gruba-McCallister, 1993). This internal sense of being at odds with oneself and the experience of estrangement and isolation are central features of all forms of disease and a key aspect of the problem of self-deception, as will be described in a later chapter.

Existential theory provides a useful framework for understanding how the dialectical continuum of wholeness (health) vs. alienation (dis-ease), in which health and dis-ease mutually define each other, can be used to describe the process of healing. This continuum can be further described along four dimensions that characterize human existence. The philosopher Martin Heidegger (1962) sought to convey the essential relatedness of human beings with the world by using the term *Dasein* which literally means "being-there." However, this is more typically expressed as "being-in-the-world" in order to convey the point that humans cannot be abstracted from their total environment as they are aware of it. The world to which human beings are inextricably related consists of the aforementioned four distinct spheres. Each provides a means of distinguishing between different forms of relationships that human beings are constantly engaged in as they live out their existence. The first three come from the work of Heidegger. The fourth is proposed by van Deurzen (1997, 2002).

The first is the *Eigenwelt*, which is the relationship that individuals have with themselves. This is made possible by the human capacity for self-reflection or their ability to be aware of themselves. The second is the *Mitwelt,* which is the relations individuals have with other human beings—the inherent social nature of human existence. The third is the *Ümwelt*. This is the relationship persons have with the natural world but also includes our relationship with our body as it constitutes a crucial part of the physical realm. This accounts for the material nature of human existence. The fourth realm is an important facet of human life that is often neglected. It relates to the etymological roots that healing shares with "holy," that is, to be whole. To acknowledge this equally relevant facet of healing, van Deurzen proposed the inclusion of the *Überwelt*. This is our relationship with a higher or transcendent order (e.g., spirituality). This can refer to values, ideals, or some overarching philosophy of life but also can characterize spirituality as a search for and commitment to a transcendent Reality. Spirituality will be a very central element of the model of healing that I present in this book.

Following from the assertion that suffering is an experience of alienation, another major theme of this book is that the central telos or purpose of healing is to respond to alienation by promoting wholeness and restoring a sense of relatedness to those who suffer. As noted above, wholeness can be conceptualized as one side of a continuum that stands in a dialectical relationship to alienation. Human existence is constantly negotiated moment by moment along this continuum. This is because human existence is an ever-unfolding, dynamic process. Individuals are a work in progress. They are engaged in an on-going journey in which loss, conflict, and challenges to their sense of harmony and integrity must be continually navigated. This view is consistent with existential thought, which sees human beings as characterized by their possibilities. Through the exercise of freedom and choice, they are constantly engaged in realizing certain possibilities, while simultaneously negating countless others. Thus, the process of becoming or growth inevitably brings with it the experience of loss since for every possibility realized, many more are negated. This has been described as giving rise to *existential anxiety*, which is rooted in the experience of loss. Each loss is a "little death," a constant reminder of one's mortality (Gruba-McCallister & Levington, 1995).

Sartre (1953) calls this process of freely choosing certain possibilities the fundamental project. In the face of existential anxiety, individuals must nonetheless assume the task of making and remaking themselves moment by moment through their choices. Alan Watts (1951) described the futility of eliminating insecurity from our existence, given that we are called upon to engage fully in the perpetual flow of life and, in doing so, relinquish our resistance to change. Living with a certain degree of uncertainty comes with being immersed in a perpetual process of becoming. Wholeness gives direction and meaning to this process as a recognition that our brokenness can lead us to the next step in a developmental process oriented toward growth. The movement toward wholeness is rooted in an ever-expanding embrace of what it means to be human. Healing requires assuming a broader and more inclusive perspective from which to understand and live life, and a wider capacity to embrace the paradoxes inherent in human existence based on a healthy tolerance for ambiguity.

Compassion, Justice, and Two Forms of Suffering

Healing must also be situated within an ethical framework and thus firmly grounded in two guiding values. These core values are compassion and justice.

These two values are inseparable and, as I argue later, are both central to making healing radical. The distinction between these two values is also useful in elucidating a necessary and useful distinction between two forms of suffering (Gruba-McCallister & Levington, 1995). Because healing, at its heart, is devoted to addressing suffering, understanding the roots of these two forms of suffering, how they are related to each other and how they require very different responses to promote wholeness, is pivotal. This distinction has been frequently described in theological writings on the problem of evil and suffering. One way in which this difference is expressed is in terms of two kinds of evil, natural and moral.

The first form of suffering is rooted in the workings and laws of the physical world and so is inherent in the human condition (natural evil). This suffering occurs due to the unavoidable experiences of illness, aging, and death and so is linked to the inevitable losses that are part of life's dynamic, ever-changing process. This suffering will be described as *inescapable* because it is outside of our control. The second form of suffering arises from the exercise of free will and the destructive impact of the choices one makes (moral evil). It is described as moral evil because human beings are seen as responsible agents who are accountable for the consequences of their behavior. A broad range of motives and underlying factors for these choices have been proposed, including ignorance, selfishness, anger, and greed. Because this suffering is under our control, it is called *self-created*.

One other feature of self-created suffering is important to note. An illusion widely held by human beings is that all suffering is evil and without value or benefit and thus should be avoided and resisted at all costs. However, as we have seen, there is a form of suffering inherent in being alive that is thus unavoidable. The illusory nature of this belief provides an understanding of how the two forms of suffering are often linked to each other. Another, and common, form of self-created suffering results when human beings seek to evade or resist this inevitable suffering. This suffering is rooted in a particularly harmful form of self-deception and gives rise to a self-defeating pattern in which individuals suffer even more *because they are suffering.* A discussion of these two forms of suffering and the necessary interrelationship between them is revisited often in my examination of radical healing.

Compassion and justice are related to these two forms of suffering as they form the basis of how best one responds to each of them. Compassion is the ability to be fully open and present to one's own suffering as well as the suffering of another. This attitude is based on the ability to suspend judgment regarding experiencing this suffering. This is essential when nothing can be done to remove the cause of the suffering, as it prevents the desire to resist or deny the necessity of experiencing it. One can at least "suffer with" (the root meaning of compassion) the one who is afflicted out of love and concern for them. To say "no" to suffering that is inevitable, as I have described, is futile as well as self-defeating. It is like pouring oil on what is already a raging fire. The typical initial reaction of resistance to suffering rooted in fear is dissolved when one is able to meet such suffering with compassion.

However, there remains a great deal of suffering that is not essential because it is based on causes that are not necessary and so capable of change. Meeting such suffering with indifference and apathy or saying "Yes" to suffering created by ourselves or others is clearly reflective of a failure of compassion and justice. In order to aid the understanding of how the demands of justice are unmet in failing to put an end to avoidable suffering, I need to introduce a major cause of suffering that again highlights the necessity of integrating the dialectic of the individual and collective into the process of healing—that is, oppression.

Oppression as a Major Cause of Suffering

The central argument I made in my previous book, *Embracing Disillusionment: Achieving Liberation through the Demystification of Suffering* (Gruba-McCallister, 2019), was that oppression is the principal cause of human suffering. This continues to be a central theme of this book. This focus is particularly important in light of the general neglect or denial of the significant role of oppression in causing suffering and the economic and political factors responsible for this. Critical psychology and its critique of mainstream psychology's (and health care's) exaggerated focus on the individual provides one understanding of this omission (Schraube & Osterkamp, 2013; Teo, 2015). This one-sided emphasis leads to a narrow level of analysis that restricts the causes of suffering to what is going on "inside of" individuals. These internal factors could be anything from a biological defect or chemical imbalance to a damaged self-concept or a set of dysfunctional beliefs.

A central tenet of critical psychology that corrects for this one-sidedness is the need to recognize the essential societal nature of human beings. We must situate human subjectivity and agency within the inherent social embeddedness of human beings. In other words, we must balance this individualistic focus with an appreciation for the equally important impact on the quality of life of the many different contexts in which human beings are born, develop, and live. A one-sided individualistic view of human beings obscures and even denies their societal nature and, correspondingly, the considerable impact of the environment on them. Instead it exaggerates the responsibility of individuals and the degree of control they have over their lives—essentially "blaming the victim" (Ryan, 1971) for any maladies or afflictions they experience. This skewed point of view plays an especially important political or ideological role in our current society. As such it not surprisingly exerts a profound impact on the way in which healing is both understood and practiced.

The individual and the collective, understood dialectically as interrelated and inseparable, affirms the importance of both as key elements of respecting and fostering wholeness central to healing. Moreover, the interdependence of the individual with other human beings as well as with the natural world (or physical environment) provides a crucial framework for understanding how and why oppression exerts such a significant impact on human well-being. The degree to which the various material and psychological conditions that operate outside of individuals satisfy fundamental needs and provide the support essential for well-being determines whether they are able to realize the fullest extent of their development. The extensive literature on social determinants of health (Marmot & Wilkinson, 2006; Wilkinson & Pickett, 2009) that is described in more detail in a later chapter provide a comprehensive framework from which to understand the substantial impact of one's environment.

Recognizing the role of the environment, however, does not mean that it exerts a unilateral impact on human beings to which they passively react. Critical psychology asserts that human beings play an active role in responding to the conditions under which they live. They are able to exert a certain degree of control over their lives, particularly when done in conjunction with others. This is again in keeping with their essential social nature and the key role that cooperation with others has played in human evolution. Human beings are not merely products of their environment but actively shape and give meaning to their circumstances. It is imperative that the healing process not only gives clear consideration to the influence of life conditions on people but also engages their capacity for self-determination in order to promote their liberation.

Oppression is not inevitable; nor is it the product of something inherent in human beings—contrary, for example, to the prevalent assumption of capitalism that human beings are innately selfish and competitive (both common causes of oppression). It is a form of self-created suffering produced by choices and actions that cause immeasurable harm. It is based on the dehumanization of the oppressed and, therefore, is morally condemnable. As Morton Deutsch (2006) observes, "Oppression is the experience of repeated, widespread, systemic injustice" (p. 10). For an extended examination of justice, the reader should consult my earlier book (Gruba-McCallister, 2019, Chapter Two). Oppression as a form of *systemic* injustice means that it is rooted in larger social, economic, and political factors and expresses the ways in which power is exercised—who has it and who does not. The need to address the role of power becomes clearer when looking at a fuller definition of oppression.

Prilleltensky and Gonick (1996) observe that oppression is defined both as a state and as a process and that it has both political and psychological dimensions. They define it as follows: "*...oppression entails a state of asymmetric power relations characterized by domination, subordination, and resistance, where the dominating persons or groups exercise their power by restricting access to material resources and by implanting in the subordinated persons or groups fear or self-deprecating views about themselves*" (italics in the original, p. 130). Political oppression refers to material, legal, economic, and/or social barriers to individuals' ability to exercise self-determination, the equitable distribution of resources and opportunities, and democratic participation. It is the exercise of power by oppressors to advance their interests at the expense of the oppressed.

Psychological oppression is the internalization of a negative view of self as not deserving of resources or participation in social affairs. This negative view is based in affective, behavioral, cognitive, linguistic, and cultural mechanisms that enable oppressors to enforce political domination.

Similar themes are echoed by Hardiman and Jackson (1997), who state that social oppression is an interlocking system that encompasses ideological control in addition to domination and control of social institutions and resources of society. This leads to a condition of privilege for the oppressors relative to the disenfranchisement and exploitation of the oppressed. It involves four key elements. First, oppressors are able to exercise the authority and power to define, name, and prescribe what is normal, real, and valued in society. Second, unequal treatment of the oppressed group is consciously and unconsciously institutionalized and embedded in social structures. Third, the oppressed internalize their oppression through socialization, such that they consent to their oppression by acceptance of the oppressor's ideology and social system. Fourth, the oppressor's worldview is dominant, while that of the oppressed is distorted, discounted, and eradicated. Like Prilleltensky and Gonick, Hardiman and Jackson assert both a political and psychological dimension to oppression.

This analysis of oppression makes it not only clear but imperative that engaging in the work of healing requires an examination of the workings of power and privilege. This is not merely in terms of the specific consequences it has on individuals but more broadly in terms of the unjust systems and policies that are responsible for people's suffering. Here again we can see the adverse consequences of mainstream psychology and health care's excessive focus on the individual level. This results in what Klaus Holzkamp, founder of the German School of critical psychology called the "worldless" individual (Schraube & Osterkamp, 2013). This is an utterly artificial and, even more destructive way of looking at human beings. Abstracting individuals from the material and social conditions that exert such powerful influences on them leads to problems being solely attributed to them. One way this manifests is accusing individuals of not exercising their responsibility (or power) to deal effectively with life's demands upon them. Another is paradoxically criticizing them if they do not passively defer to the authority or power of the care provider whose interventions are necessary to "fix" the problems that reside within them. In other words, they are caught in a "damned if they do, damned if they don't" trap that is designed to place the onus on the sufferer and, in doing so, obfuscate or deny the role of adverse life experiences in causing their affliction. When individuals "fail" to take the necessary actions to deal with their problems (or in other instances fail to comply with the authority of the "healer" in taking prescribed measures), they are left feeling inadequate, helpless, deficient, and ashamed. In this way, the individualistic orientation becomes another form of oppression by reproducing and reinforcing the negative psychological consequences that have already been inflicted upon the oppressed.

To summarize, a truly holistic approach for both identifying and addressing the causes of human suffering is essential for genuine healing. The "biopsychosocial" model (Engel, 1980) that has been touted by health care providers since it was first proposed claimed to provide such a comprehensive framework. However, it has sorely failed to realize this promise as the dominance of the biomedical model (and its individualistic and materialistic bias) has continued unabated (Armstrong, 1987; Ogden, 1997). It is more hype than reality. At best, this approach considers the biological, psychological, and social as separate and distinct factors that should be "considered" when assessing and treating a person presenting with an "illness," with biological causes continuing to carry the greatest weight in the case of medicine and the social receiving superficial treatment in the case of psychology (Spicer & Chamberlain, 1996; Suls & Rothman, 2004). The truly radical and now extensive body of empirical literature that continues to be amassed demonstrating the clearly interdependent relationship among all three of these dimensions of human existence and experience continues to be unappreciated and thus neglected (Kelly et al., 2007; Murphy, 1992; Schwartz, 2012). One excellent example of such interdependence is the extensive research done on social determinants of health (mentioned earlier) and the adverse health impacts of inequality (Marmot & Wilkinson, 2006).

For example, Wilkinson and Pickett (2009) describe how inequality gets "under our skin" due to the ways in which assaults to self-esteem, a persistent sense of material insecurity, and feelings of shame associated with being of a lower social status give rise to elevated states of stress that then have adverse physical and psychological consequences. Another example is the profound impact that lower childhood socioeconomic status has on the developing brain. These changes lead to life-long negative consequences in areas such as education, income, and occupation (Loued-Khenissi et al., 2022). Essentially, inequality fuels a vicious cycle in which those born into conditions of poverty and disadvantage are impaired by these conditions in ways that prevent them from ever escaping. The role of one's early environment has a profound and often lasting impact on multiple areas of functioning. The mere accident of birth for some individuals, something which they had no control over, condemns them to a life of cumulative deprivation and with it an increased risk of a vast range of forms of suffering (Barry, 2005; Rank, 2004).

In other words, at its worst the biopsychosocial approach is merely a public relations and marketing ploy that cynically purports to abandon a biomedical model. However, behind the scenes an ever-growing number of problems are "medicalized" in ways that are designed to feed the greed of a health care system and Big Pharma that puts profit over people (Aho, 2008; Boggs, 2015; Conrad & Barker, 2010). A deeper discussion of the ways in which this model serves the dominant neoliberal ideology is discussed in a later chapter. For now, it is important to expose the tired and pretentious claims made by health care providers that they provide holistic or "whole-person" care. Healing must always be two-fold. Healers must promote the optimal development of individuals (liberation) and strive—in cooperation with others—to ameliorate and, where possible, remove the environmental obstacles and harmful conditions that impair their development (emancipation). The continuing neglect and even outright refusal to embrace both of these obligations are actually a major source of suffering rather than a means of sincerely alleviating it.

In view of the centrality of individual–collective dialectic to human existence, healing requires an understanding and implementation of methods for expanding awareness and raising consciousness that are aimed at uncovering causes of suffering on *both* levels. However, the dominant one-sided focus on the individual defeats such an understanding. A case in point is the enduring and prevalent methods employed by psychologists and other mental health providers to engage individuals exclusively in an exploration of their internal world in order to alleviate their suffering. The goal is to bring to light the conflicts, defenses, and dysfunctional beliefs that give rise to their suffering and subsequently to call upon individuals to recognize their responsibility for their unhappiness and to exercise their choice and intention to bring about change. This *psychologization* approach has become so predominant that it has been extended beyond the treatment of "psychological conditions" and applied to an ever-expanding range of human ills (De Vos, 2012). Accordingly, this over-extension of psychology and psychotherapy has also led to more problems coming under the authority of what Foucault (1975/1995) called the psy disciplines. This trend is accompanied by a diversion of attention at best or a denial at worst of the clear role of social, economic, and political processes in causing suffering.

As a result, the psi disciplines are increasingly being employed as instruments of power to maintain the status quo. One advantage offered by these disciplines to those in power is that it allows them to employ what is believed to be their "scientific" expertise to actively divert attention or deny the role of social, economic, and political factors in causing suffering. Moreover, rather than employ overt, coercive, or even violent means of ensuring compliance and stifling resistance to the existing power structure, the psi disciplines provide the technology and authority to get citizens to internalize societal norms and rules and thus supervise their own conduct—a process called *governmentality* (Rose, 1998).

Radical Healing: Moving from a One-Sided, Individualistic Focus

A natural question that follows from this argument is what would an alternative way of understanding and addressing suffering look like that takes a fuller account of the role of diverse environmental factors. For one example, we can consider the work of David Small (2005), a cogent critic of the overemphasis on the individual and internal processes in psychology. One note of caution is that I believe his attempts to correct for this leads him to unnecessarily underestimate the value and appropriate role of "looking within" to promote healing. I argue that the theories and methods of traditional psychology, when integrated into a radical paradigm, can still have a place in addressing the individual as a necessary part of the dialectic inherent in healing. However, Small's work does offer a number of valuable insights about the ways in which a "social materialist" approach provides an expanded framework from which to understand the role of unjust social practices and structures in causing distress.

Similar to the distinction described above, Small distinguishes between suffering that is avoidable and unavoidable and further asserts that the focal concern of psychology (and thus healing) must be to recognize and elucidate how human beings are caused to suffer avoidable distress. For Small, that distress arises from humans being *embodied*; hence his materialistic focus. His highlighting the relevance of embodiment is a critical component of my discussion of the need for radical healing to include the role of material factors. By embodiment, Small is not referring to biogenetic factors, which receive almost exclusive attention in the dominant biomedical model. Rather, Small sees embodiment as the central means by which we experience and act upon the world and the world likewise acts upon us. Due to the immediacy of our body, the sensations that mediate our relationship with the world provide the most certain indication of what is happening to us. Also at the social level, our interactions with others occur principally by means of direct bodily contact with people. The internal world of things such as feelings and impulses—which erroneously receives priority by psychology, according to Small—is actually derived from the ways in which we represent our physical interaction with the environment, particularly through the use of language. Thus, our personhood, along with our subjective awareness of it. is due to the interaction of our body with the world in which it is embedded.

This materialistic emphasis forms the basis for how Small understands the source of suffering. Suffering is rooted in the ways in which the social (and material) environment acts upon us (see also Jacobs, 1994). The adequacy of the environment to meet essential needs and facilitate development dictates the degree to which individuals experience well-being. It might seem that physical proximity in space and time would dictate the degree of this impact, such that factors closest to us would have the greatest influence. However, Small notes that this view is mistaken and attributable to distal influences (e.g., economic systems, governmental policies) being less apparent. As noted, we do not choose the environment into which we are born, but because of the power that the material circumstances of our lives exert over time, this fact has profound consequences for many individuals. The deleterious consequences of oppression begin with material harms and subsequently lead to psychological ones. Several useful points regarding healing can be made based on this analysis by Small.

The first is highlighting a key component of another dialectical relationship that must be integrated into the process of healing mind and body. This comes from Small's appreciation for the embodied nature of human beings. Going back to the four spheres that characterize human existence, the body is a central feature of the Ümwelt. As existentialists observe, to be in the world is to both have a body and be a body. It is the only element of the physical world that has this paradoxical quality. The body is instrumental to our mode of involvement in the world. The manner in which we experience ourselves, others, and the natural world as embodied is itself a form of knowing or consciousness that must be engaged in the process of healing. Moreover, the way in which we understand and relate to our body is often an issue that must be addressed in healing. Alienation from the body is one way in which our sense of wholeness can be compromised.

Support for Small's view is provided by theory and research on the role that embodiment plays in social determinants of health. Krieger (2005) reiterates the complex interaction of biological and social in explaining how and when we die, and the degree of suffering we experience in the course of our lives. She advances an *ecosocial theory* that integrates research on the social production of disease with evolutionary and developmental biology. She spells out four constructs making up this theory. The first is embodiment, which refers to how human beings, literally, incorporate their lived experiences biologically. The second is pathways of embodiment, which pertains to how often multiple ways and levels are involved in leading to a given health outcome. The third is the cumulative interplay of exposure, susceptibility, and resistance across the course of one's life, which describes the ways in which various risk and protective factors shape the likelihood of illness and death. The fourth is accountability and agency, which speak most directly to the process of healing. Awareness and appreciation for the power of the environment on well-being must be accompanied by measures on both the individual and collective level to assess and address this power. Omission results in healing not being truly holistic.

Small's assertion that the environment into which one is born is not chosen and thus beyond his or her control serves to underline the importance of justice to healing. This is explained in my book (Gruba-McCallister, 2019, pp. 46–52) in terms of the problem of *cumulative disadvantage.* Barry (2005) argues that a true understanding of social justice requires an appreciation for the interdependence of rights, opportunities, and resources. Rights are based on the intrinsic value and dignity of the human person. In this case, justice is achieved through recognition of the right of human beings to strive for maximum well-being and to be provided with the greatest opportunity to realize their possibilities as unique individuals and members of larger communities (Gruba-McCallister, 2019, p. 82). This view of justice is an expression of the *eudaimonic* tradition (Nussbaum, 1992). In order for this right to be exercised, there first needs to be resources, which are those things that can be used by people to achieve their goals or increase their ability to do so. Additionally, opportunities or a range of possibilities need to be available to people to realize their possibilities. In the absence of resources and opportunities, rights are essentially impotent in ensuring one's chances of achieving well-being.

Social and material conditions play a significant role in both providing opportunities for individuals to fulfill their needs and exercise their choices and giving them the resources needed to do so. As both Small and Barry observe, the circumstances into which certain individuals are born have significant material inequality, with no means of social intervention to address environmental disadvantages. Barry documents research showing how factors such as poor nutrition, exposure to toxins, inadequate quality of prenatal and medical care, and parental limitations in terms of devoting time to raising and caring for growing children lead to progressively more damaging effects. He writes,

> Children start with, and grow up with, an enormous variety of different resources. On the basis of just a few facts about a child, such as its social class and its race or ethnicity, we can make a good prediction of where it will finish up in the distribution of earnings, the likelihood it will spend time in jail, and many other outcomes, good and bad. (p. 41)

This leaves little doubt that understanding and addressing the material/social environment and the manner in which it exercises either favorable or unfavorable influences on the course of development must be a part of healing.

Returning to Small's (2005) critique of the one-sided focus of psychology on the individual, he employs his materialist view to discredit the role of rationality and internal factors widely employed by mainstream psychology (e.g., motives, cognitions, and responsibility) as valid causes for human action. Describing the problem as the philosophy of "magical voluntarism," he states:

> In the world of twentieth-century therapeutic psychology, people do things because of impulses, intentions, cognitions, or conditioned reflexes of which they may or may not be aware. This inevitably means that, at least implicitly, they are *responsible* for their actions and that change can be brought about only through some kind of *decision* on their part. (italics in original, p. 6)

Small's assigning the causes of human action substantially to the environment means he believes that for the most part human beings are not in control of their conduct and the decisions they make. Like a number of postmodern thinkers (Cushman, 1990; Gergen, 1991), he regards the modern notion of an autonomous, masterful, bounded self as an illusion as it implies that power is a personal property rather than something derived from sociopolitical and economic contexts.

No doubt there is a need to correct for the current over-emphasis of such individual factors and, relatedly, for the ways in which this serves to disguise the role played by social processes, especially the workings of oppression. Also Small's assertions that insight is not sufficient to bring about change and that an over-emphasis on responsibility leads to excessive self-blame for one's problems are legitimate points to bear in mind. However, it is essential that we do not lose sight of the dialectic of the individual and societal nature of human beings. Both must be embraced in order to truly promote healing. Thus, while the modern view of the autonomous self deserves criticism, I maintain that human agency rooted in one's individuality must play some role in healing. I also believe that Small makes the error of underestimating the legitimate role that can be played by introspection and reflection. It is true that over the course of history and across diverse cultures, different ways of defining what is meant by "the self" have been advanced. And strengths and weaknesses of these diverse understandings have likewise been found when submitting them to critical examination. Bearing these things in mind, I believe that an integrative and balanced description of what is meant by "the self" is not only possible but essential to healing.

Small highlights a further pivotal issue regarding healing. That is the issue of power, which refers to the means by which the social environment works upon the individual embodied subject. Small writes:

> The person exists as an embodied being in a material environment that is structured both physically and (more important for our purposes) socially. The principal dynamic of social structure is *power*, which is transmitted through *interest*...The most powerful influences that end up impinging upon the individual tend to be those furthest from him/her, i.e., economic, political, and cultural powers, etc. These are mediated by lesser powers closer to the individual, ultimately via other individuals encountered in families, social groups, workplaces, etc. (italics in original, p. 26)

Small's inclusion of power and interest in understanding the impact of the environment is in keeping with the previous discussion of the role of oppression. It is through the exercise of power that the privileged group inflicts material and psychological harms on the oppressed group in order to derive benefit at their expense. The intrinsic political dimension of human existence is likewise a core principle of critical psychology and the work of Foucault (1975/1995). For Small, power is the means of obtaining security or advantage. As noted previously, he sees power almost exclusively as having its origins in the social environment. A necessary counterpoint to this view is provided by Prilleltensky (2008), who proposes a psychopolitical view that sees human beings as equally capable of exercising agency. Power can be exercised both in terms of engaging in oppression and as a means of resisting oppression and promoting fairness and well-being. For Prilleltensky, power is a combination of ability (rights and access to needed resources) and opportunities that combine to enable individuals to exert influence on their lives. Additionally, various properties of individuals, including cognitive, physical, emotional, and behavioral, affect their ability to exercise power.

Small states that power takes three forms: biological, coercive, and ideological. These forms of power are channeled by means of interests. Interests are determined by our embodied nature and can range from more biological necessities, such as food, sex, pleasure, to more social ones, such as attachment, affiliation, or status. Interests cannot be satisfied without power and the exercise of power is governed by the impact of the environment, which can satisfy, frustrate, impose, and mystify interests. Small also specifies how time and space can shape interests and the resultant exercise of power by noting that social influences may seem more apparent at the immediate level of family and workplace, but may actually be much greater from further removed sources. This observation fits well with Bronfenbrenner's (1979) work, which describes an ecological model in which various systems that exert an influence on individuals are arrayed in nested fashion, moving from those most immediate to those most distal. All these various systems interact with one another and evolve dynamically over time.

The second form of power, coercive, is most evident in the various forms of violence that are perpetrated by human beings on others. This violence takes many forms and occurs across a large spectrum. It is sometimes dramatic and large in scope, as in war, and at other times may seem inconsequential but still taking its toll due to its being unrelenting and inescapable. The philosopher Jean Harvey (2000, 2010) describes this second form as *civilized oppression*, which has its roots in distorted and inappropriate moral relationships. This may be take the form of expressions of disrespect, being unheard, and verbal slights that convey demeaning and discriminatory attitudes. The literature on microaggressions (Sue, 2010) is another example of less overt violence. Violence is thus not restricted to being physical but may also be emotional and psychological.

As noted in the description of governmentality above, the most pervasive form of power occurs in a more veiled form by means of control over language, meaning, and perspective. It is far more effective for those in power who wish to maintain the status quo to employ a means of control that is not obvious because this decreases the risk of individuals becoming aware of their domination and responding with resistance. Instead the aim is to first inhibit or distort the awareness of the exercise of power over those dominated in a process called *mystification* and then to instill within them an unthinking acceptance of the status quo and inhibitions that deter their resistance. This, as Small states, is ideological power. *Ideology* is another core concept in my examination of healing. In support of the need for a cultural context for therapy, Small describes the use of propaganda and other forms of mind manipulation by media, education, and marketing to justify inequality and disparities in power arising. He attribute these to capitalist ideology. While the social causes of their suffering are obfuscated, blame for individuals' failure to achieve wealth, prestige, and success is laid at their feet based on an extreme form of individualism. Mainstream psychology is again identified as playing a significant role as a tool of ideological power. The knowledge acquired by psychology is used by various ideological apparatuses to inculcate beliefs, values, and interests in individuals that make them more susceptible to manipulation and exploitation and to inhibit their ability to call the unjust status quo into question. In addition, psychology reinforces the view that human beings are principally responsible for their lives and in control of the power needed to fulfill their interests by replacing an analysis of the relations of power and interest with a focus on internal causes of distress. People's suffering becomes a private matter requiring their own efforts to resolve, rather than the consequence of unjust and adverse environmental conditions.

This has important implications for healing as not only a means of removing or alleviating human suffering but also as a means of preventing suffering and fostering optimal development stifled by the ruling ideology. This requires a correction of the over-emphasis on pathology in mainstream health care. The process of healing must expand consciousness and encourage critical examination that is not be confined to the narrow boundaries of individuals' so-called "internal world." We must no longer neglect their equally valid lived experiences of the ways in which the physical and social environment affects them and intrudes on their well-being. Analysis of a world believed to be substantially of their own making and rooted in processes located in their individual psyche is not only incomplete, but harmful. This is reflective of the exaggerated individualism that dominates our current culture. As Small asserts, insight must be coupled with what he calls *"outsight."* And that means exploration of the harmful ways in which individuals have internalized an ideology impressed upon them through the exercise of power. The principal basis upon which oppression rests is a toxic and unjust ideology.

Ideology, Hegemony, and Internalized Oppression

In view of the substantial role played by ideology in causing suffering, we need to closely examine how it is formed and subsequently internalized by human beings, what functions it serves, and the ways in which its impact is rendered invisible. While the term "ideology" has many meanings (Hamilton, 1987), an ideology can be thought of as a mental map or system of beliefs and values shared by members of a society that is used to explain and give meaning to their experience and provide answers to life's substantive questions. Jost and Amodio (2012) observe that human beings are ideological animals because they have a basic and powerful need to impose a sense of order, stability, and predictability on their experience. This enables them to exercise a certain degree of control over their lives. Jost and Amodio describe this as the epistemological function of ideology. It provides ready-made answers to important questions and problems of life and helps human beings understand themselves and others.

It would be a mistake to view ideology solely from an individual perspective, such that its inherent limitations, biases, and areas lacking awareness are seen as idiosyncratic or personal. This narrow conception implies that individuals are solely to blame for their prejudices and preconceptions. An ideology is a shared worldview imparted and enforced by various social apparatuses to ensure compliance with the extant ruling order. One vital function performed by that ideology is to justify and make normative the prevailing economic and sociopolitical interests of the powerful. It is a total, more-or-less coherent system of ideas, beliefs, attitudes, and values that is so thoroughly internalized by members of a society that they are unaware of its assumptive nature. As Augoustinos (1999) observes:

> The individual is viewed as failing to perceive reality accurately and failing to recognize his or her true self and group interests. Such approaches fail to acknowledge that reality construction is not an isolated cognitive task involving the direct and unmediated perception of the world. People are constantly and actively engaged in a complex and socially situated process of constructing reality, but they do this by using the cultural and ideological resources that are available to them...These resources are shaped by existing material and power relations and are embedded in the very nature of people's lived social relations and practices. (p. 302)

The ideology that is dominant in a society at a given time is described by the philosopher Antonio Gramsci (1971) as *hegemony.* His work provides a way of understanding how at a certain point in history one concept of reality becomes prevalent and diffused throughout society at all levels including political, economic, social, religious, and cultural. Because this worldview is so taken for granted, it is regarded by those who hold it as "common sense" or "popular wisdom." However, hegemony is actually the official version of reality upheld by the ruling class and acts in the service of maintaining their power and privilege. It justifies the existing social, political, and economic hierarchy and individuals' place within it. Thus, posing it as common sense is intended to convey that the status quo is objective, true, universal, and incapable of change. It is "the way things are" and because of this people have no choice but to accept it. This helps to elucidate how hegemony serves to stifle opposition among those who are marginalized, exploited, and oppressed and how people willingly consent to these unjust practices. If "the way things are" is accepted as fixed, natural, and inevitable, people resign themselves to their situation and conclude that their present state is as good as things can get.

This only succeeds if powerful and pervasive measures are in place to indoctrinate members of a society into internalizing a hegemonic ideology. One means of achieving this, noted earlier, is Foucault's (1975/1995) concept of governmentality. However, another explanation that is an important part of my examination of healing is the work of Erich Fromm (1941) on *social character.* As Foster (2017) notes, while Foucault's view provides a top-down description of the internalization of ideology, Fromm's description of the formation of social character provides a corresponding bottom-up view. From the start of life socialization, various cultural institutions such as family, education, and religion shape who we believe ourselves to be, our desires, and our goals in order to align these with social expectations and demands. Social character can be understood as internalized hegemony (Gruba-McCallister, 2019). Another way of understanding this process as it relates to those at the lower end of the social hierarchy is *internalized oppression* (David, 2014), which is a concept that also helps to explain how individuals consent to their own oppression and are disempowered to take actions to oppose their domination. Internalized oppression is associated with a broad range of physical and psychological harms, including greater likelihood of illness or shorter lifespan, feelings of self-hatred and self-doubt, helplessness and passivity, pessimism and fatalism, guilt, anger, and a number of mental health conditions.

Reasons for the success of the means used to inculcate an oppressive ideology whereby it becomes thoroughly internalized and blocks awareness of its impact clearly have relevance to understanding a great deal of suffering. The first reason is associated with the inherent societality of human beings and the longer period of human dependence as a percentage of their total lifespan compared to other species. In an article on the role of environmental failure/oppression in the development of psychological disorders, Jacobs (1994) uses the term "world openness" to highlight how this protracted period of dependence makes human beings especially vulnerable to the impact of their physical and social environment. This responsiveness or openness rooted in dependence means that the quality of the environment can exert a profound and, in some instances, even an irreversible impact on well-being. It is true that human beings are not infinitely malleable and that even at an early stage human beings are able to exercise some degree of agency in response to the environment. Nonetheless, much of how we come to see and act on is shaped by means of internalization of early experiences. Later, language plays a significant role in consolidating the inculcation of ideology. This hearkens back to the point made previously that human beings do not choose the conditions into which they are born. To ensure justice, it is imperative that an optimal environment be provided for all infants. Given the significance of early experience and its influence on individuals' life course, the promotion of healing must give careful attention to the substantial role played by development.

Deadly Illusions

The second point that emerges from an examination of the internalization of ideology is the significant role played by fear. This, in turn, brings to light two processes that help explain how awareness of the workings of ideology is blocked or distorted and why we find the illusions it provides so seductive and comforting. Fear is a potent tool employed by the powerful to internalize an oppressive hegemonic ideology. Though this fear takes many different forms, its most basic expression is rooted in the powerful need that human beings have to minimize uncertainty, impose order, and exercise control. One of the best expressions of this principle is the concept of *existential anxiety* (May, 1958). This anxiety is best thought of not as an emotion but rather as a central element of human experience that has its roots in awareness of our mortality. Death is the ultimate loss and our greatest fear. All other losses—large and small—that we inevitably experience throughout our lives are a constant reminder of death. As a result, when we experience these losses, we also experience a sense of apprehension and dread, feelings that are so painful that we react in ways to stifle and avoid it. Fear—as will be explained in a later chapter—engages the autonomic nervous system, constricts awareness, inhibits reflection, and creates a state of alienation in which we disavow or disown disturbing experiences.

A common way of responding to this anxiety is to engage in a variety of means of evading it—often referred to as defense mechanisms. We weave a pattern of illusions, soothing half-truths, and comforting fabrications. We engage in various forms of self-deception. No understanding of healing is possible without an appreciation for the incredible capacity of human beings to engage in self-deception. A detailed exploration of the dynamics of self-deception is provided in my earlier book (Gruba-McCallister, 2019). This includes an examination of its relationship to consciousness and the unconscious, to the biologically hard-wired fight-or-flight response to situations that pose a threat and are perceived as out of our control, and to the experience of alienation. Understanding the obstacles to well-being posed by self-deception is essential to the work of healing.

However, to focus solely on self-deception addresses only one side of the individual–collective polarity. The dynamics of self-deception as an intrapsychic process provides a necessary foundation for a social process that also manufactures illusions and operates to render ideology's influence on our thoughts, feelings, and actions invisible. This is *mystification,* a process in which human consciousness is conditioned by the material and social conditions established by prevailing power relationships. The principal means employed by mystification to achieve this is invalidating the experience of individuals (Laing, 1960, 1967), which then serves to attack their sense of reality and even their very being. In doing so, it too evokes a powerful fear that is then just as quickly alleviated by substituting one's experience with an alternative view of reality provided by hegemonic ideology. One's perceptions of reality are questioned by means of the propagation of so-called facts that are actually based on lies and distortions. This then leads to replacing one's perceptions and beliefs with plausible socially manufactured misinterpretations and ready-made "answers" that assuage one's anxieties.

The earlier discussion of the work of Small (2005) includes his contention that because suffering is principally due to environmental causes, an important but generally neglected function of psychotherapy should be *demystification.* This removes blame from individuals for their problems and correctly attributes them to external reality. Like Small, I believe the unveiling of the workings of mystification is essential to understanding how to remove avoidable causes of suffering and promote healing. One facet shared by self-deception and mystification is that both are ultimately self-defeating. This self-defeating character is a big reason for how both are so harmful but also offers an advantage when exposed to help individuals strive toward greater well-being.

The Destructive Consequences of Neoliberal Hegemony and Fascism

One consistent element of the ruling ideology that has been identified as destructive is its extreme individualism. This is just one part of the current hegemonic ideology, neoliberalism, which is an extreme form of capitalism. As I argued previously (Gruba-McCallister, 2019), the current neoliberal hegemony is the root of the vast majority of suffering experienced at both the individual and collective level. It has also proven disastrous to the environment on which the survival of not only our species but other species depends based on its clear contribution to the ever-growing specter of ecological catastrophe (Klein, 2014). The primacy that neoliberal ideology gives to individualism, combined with its elevation of selfishness, greed, and competition as ideals, creates an economic system based on corruption, rampant commodification, massive accumulation of wealth and resources in the hands of a few, and gross inequality. All of these have had widespread destructive consequences on individuals, communities, and the world (Harvey, 2007 Piketty, 2014). Another of its negative consequences is the destruction of liberal democracy, which rests on enabling individuals to meaningfully participate in decision making on matters that affect their lives (Ayers & Saad-Filho, 2015; Brown, 2006). With the concentration of wealth and power created by neoliberalism in the hands of the few, the exploitation of workers, the control of government by corporations, the ability of average individuals to exercise control and autonomy is shrinking and, in many instances, absent. Extreme inequalities and power disparities undermine values central to distributive justice, such as fairness and equity and erode respect for individual rights and dignity. The valorization of selfishness and privatized consumerism tears away at any sense of community and solidarity and instead fosters mistrust and competition.

In light of the elevation of power and wealth of corporations and oligarchs at the expense of those upon whom they prey, a growing militarism, and the manipulation of the masses based on propaganda by advertisers and the government, it is not surprising that writers such as Giroux (2008), Hedges (2008), and Teo (2021) see a clear connection between neoliberalism and a rise in fascism. For example, Giroux writes:

> Under the politics and culture of neoliberalism, despite its tensions and contradictions, society is increasingly mobilized for the production of violence against the poor, immigrants, dissenters, and others marginalized because of their age, gender, race, ethnicity, and color...at the center of neoliberalism is a new form of politics in the United States, one in which radical exclusion is the order of the day—a politics in which the primary questions are no longer about equality, justice, or freedom but instead concern the survival of the slickest in a culture marked by fear, surveillance, and economic deprivation...the question that now seems to define neoliberal "democracy" is "Who has the right to live or does not?" (p. 9)

These damaging elements of neoliberalism—such as fear of difference, dehumanization, violence toward "the Other," and authoritarianism—also highlight the close relationship between neoliberalism and fascism. As Giroux observes, the form of fascism in places like the United States will not mirror the form it took in Italy and Germany before and during World War II. However, this does not mean that it cannot occur in a liberal democracy such as the United States. Giroux describes what he calls *proto-fascism*, in which a constellation of elements characteristic of fascist ideology such as extreme authoritarianism, corporatization of civil society, utilization of fear-based propaganda, and control of the public by mass media can take different guises and forms. In his examination of fascism, Stanley (2018) points to the rise and election of Donald Trump and his followers in the United States and the increasing number of fascist governments in other places in the world as signs of the growing threat it poses. Teo's (2021) work is of particular relevance to approaching this issue from a psychological perspective based on his description of what he calls *fascist subjectivity*. This is a worldview that encompasses not merely an individual's subjective viewpoint, but also his or her relationship with others and with the larger social context. It is currently shaped by the political and economic ideas and practices of capitalism. The belief that there is not enough material wealth and other social goods to go around advanced by capitalism fosters a sense of competition and provides justification of greed and the appropriation of wealth from the weak by the powerful. This ideology readily meshes with elements of fascism described previously to form a worldview in which members of certain groups are regarded as subhuman and dispensable or what Teo calls "dieable." This accords with Giroux's observation of how neoliberalism moves from a concern with equality and justice to a concern with who is or is not worthy of life itself. The connection with the dangers posed by oppression is not difficult to see. The centrality of neoliberalism and fascism to current hegemony serves to explain a great deal of social suffering. Thus, examination of both these ideologies and their relationship is a central theme of this book.

Summary of Key Points

1. Healing must be practiced, taking into account the multiple and diverse contexts within which human beings are situated in order to be truly holistic. This can be described in terms of four spheres of relationships: with oneself, with others, with the natural world, and with a higher or transcendent order. These four spheres must all be integrated into an understanding of the different sources of human suffering and their importance for achieving well-being.

2. The relational context fundamental to healing is best described in terms of dialectical polarities in which the two sides are recognized as interrelated, mutual, and inseparable. Examples include individual–collective, wholeness–alienation, mind–body, life–death, universal-particular, and unity-multiplicity—all of which will be examined. A one-sided, rigid, and extreme stance toward these polarities leads to

heightened states of alienation, disharmony, and imbalance contrary to well-being. An open and accepting stance based on a tolerance for ambiguity is essential to promote well-being.

3. Healing must be based upon two values that are moral imperatives: compassion and justice. These two values underline how healing must address the impact of causes of suffering both within and outside the individual. They also provide a framework for understanding the two forms of suffering—inescapable and self-created—and the interdependent relationship between them.

4. Oppression is a major, and neglected, cause of human suffering. Thus, healing must take into account the ways in which the dynamics of power and privilege impact well-being. Power can be located both within human beings as agents and within the material and social environment in which they live. Power can also be exercised in ways that impair well-being and in ways that promote liberation and bears on issues such as responsibility, freedom, and agency. This highlights that a clear understanding about what individuals can and cannot control is a key issue that must be examined in the process of healing.

5. Healing must be practiced within a developmental framework. This is, in part because of the profound impact that the environment plays on the course of development, given the prolonged period of dependency of human beings and given that individuals do not choose the circumstances into which they are born. This bears on the problem of cumulative deprivation, in which the place where individuals begin life plays a significant role in the course of their life and life chances. This perspective is also pivotal to understanding healing as based on a teleological or perfectionist theory of development whose aim is maximization of fundamental human potentials (*eudaimonia*). The inseparable relationship between compassion and justice means that this process is not attainable if solely focused on an individual level. It must also strive to promote collective well-being. As Marx and Engels (2015) state in the *Communist Manifesto*, "The free development of each becomes the free development of all." Finally, a developmental perspective is needed to provide a framework for understanding the ways in which the polarities that characterize the developmental process are integrated in order for growth to occur.

6. An understanding of the role of the material and social environment in either promoting or impairing well-being (as in the case of oppression) requires an examination of the dominant ideology or hegemony that, through its considerable influence on members of society, is responsible for shaping and sustaining these environments. This is first achieved through the formation of social character, how by means of socialization and indoctrination individuals internalize prevailing social beliefs, norms, and motivations. These often operate

on an unconscious level, which makes it more difficult to discern their influence. On a collective level, ideology also shapes existing political, economic, social, and cultural systems and practices that exercise power on how individuals understand and give meaning to themselves, others, and life in general. The dominant ideology called hegemony by Gramsci (1971) is the worldview held by the ruling class and used by them to maintain the status quo and stifle resistance. It poses as objective, true, universal, and incapable of change. Hegemony is sometimes expressed as "common sense" or "the way things are."

7. The success of hegemony in securing its acceptance, maintaining the status quo, and justifying its consequences—both positive and negative—rests upon two processes that block and bias awareness, manufacture plausible illusions, and inhibit critical reflection. The first is self-deception, which operates at an individual level and is based upon the human need for stability and control. It is also linked to the fight-or-flight response elicited in situations posing a threat to one's sense of stability that exceeds one's ability to control. The second is mystification, a social process in which the cultural and ideological resources provided by hegemony employ language, images, narratives, and other means to render the ideology invisible and to manufacture illusions that veil its hypothetical and assumptive nature. Fear is the principal tool used by the powerful to engage individuals' capacity for self-deception and to make mystification effective. Radical healing, particularly understood as the raising and expansion of consciousness and the engagement of human agency, must address both self-deception and mystification.

8. The dominant worldview currently impacting not only well-being but also the conventional understandings and methods of healing is rooted in neoliberalism and fascism. Neoliberalism's espousal of exaggerated individualism, selfishness, greed, competition, privatization, and consumerism have documented adverse impacts on human beings. Also the adoption of neoliberal ideology by psychology and other health care systems put them at the service of the powerful and result in their engaging in oppression and other practices contrary to healing. The role of neoliberalism in undermining democracy; intensifying polarization based on extreme inequality and disparities of resources, opportunities, and rights; and legitimizing the subhumanization of those deemed inferior has been linked with fascist beliefs and values. Thus, the process of healing requires the unveiling of the workings of both neoliberalism and fascism, an exploration of their toxic consequences on both the individual and collective levels, and the fostering of efforts to make changes that promote liberation at the individual level and emancipation at the collective level (de-ideologization).

Chapter 2

The Why and How of Radical Healing

The Radical as Critical—Exposing Illusions

In the previous chapter I set forth a number of foundational principles that inform my exploration of the nature of healing. In this chapter I describe in greater detail what I mean by radical healing and the reasons for why healing must be radical in order to truly and fully address the range of factors that give rise suffering. This examination is organized around the two different forms of suffering and the way in which they are entwined, as described in the previous chapter. It also reiterates the need to take full account of all dimensions of human experience. Different meanings of "radical" are presented, followed by the relevance of those meanings to the nature and practice of healing. I also delve into the earliest roots of healing by discussing shamanism and indigenous healing practices. An examination of their core characteristics and the worldview they espouse demonstrates their enduring relevance to essential elements of healing.

This material serves to introduce some key points that are explored in greater detail in later chapters. It also paves the way for a discussion in the next chapter of an extremely critical element contributing to the efficacy of the healing process—the healer him/herself. The subsequent chapter advances the viewpoint that becoming and being a healer is a vocation or calling that requires those who respond to this call to assume two interdependent roles—one focused on the personal aspect of life and the other focused on the social aspect. Along with this, healers must be guided by two corresponding core values. This integration of the mystical/contemplative and prophetic roles by healers, together with their commitment to both compassion and justice, is essential to radical healing. This view, as will be seen, poses a significant challenge to the prevailing narrow understanding of healing rooted in neoliberal ideology.

The term "radical" may evoke certain negative connotations quite at odds with a subject like healing. Those connotations should thus be addressed at the outset to avoid any confusion or misconceptions. The ideas that I will be presenting are not bizarrely extreme; nor are they so unconventional as to be considered unreasonable, far-fetched, or baseless. Nonetheless, I want to make it equally clear that a number of current predominant assumptions, values, and beliefs regarding healing do indeed need to be radically challenged and ultimately abandoned. In many instances they not only fail to address significant sources of suffering impacting large numbers of individuals but also actively contribute to the suffering they profess to seek to ameliorate. In light of this, my proposed view of healing is in accord with the meaning of radical as that which is committed to a significant departure from tradition and existing institutions and practices. A revolution is necessary to abandon and replace the current neoliberal paradigm in which psychology and other healing professions are rooted. This challenge needs to begin with a rigorous and critical examination of basic assumptions and values of the current paradigm that typically are unexamined and so thought to be interconvertible. This opacity is the work of personal and societal forces that either veil these assumptions and values from scrutiny and thus present them as natural and incapable of change or that actively prohibit any critique by means of threats to those who seek to disrupt the status quo.

One approach to a radical submission of "taken for granted" or "common sense" assumptions to critical examination to root out biases and prejudices is set forth by the phenomenological method (Gruba-McCallister, 1989; Ihde, 1986). The first step in phenomenological inquiry is to engage in a rigorous form of self-examination aimed at identifying expectations, preconceptions, and biases that typically contaminate the point of view we bring to our experience. Once identified, these are then temporarily suspended or "bracketed" so that our stance toward the object of our attention is more likely to be open and receptive and alert to alternative ways of understanding. As Spinelli (2007) points out, this goal of phenomenology is an ideal one as it is impossible to recognize all biases that color and shape our experience. Inevitably, certain values and assumptions remain and exert an impact that can give rise to error and distortion. Nevertheless, the method still has value in terms of minimizing the impact of contaminating preconceptions and establishing a more open and inclusive stance. I will return to the value of this phenomenological stance when examining the importance of establishing a non-interfering and accepting attitude toward ourselves and others in the healing relationship.

Assuming a radical stance toward taken-for-granted and pervasive beliefs and values is also a central feature of Critical Theory (Held, 1980) and critical psychology (Schraube & Osterkamp, 2013; Teo, 2015). Both expand the identification of distorted, prejudicial, and value-laden elements of one's worldview beyond the personal to include the social. Critical Theory, or the Frankfurt School, began with the founding of the Institute for Social Research in 1923 and included thinkers from diverse disciplines—including philosophy, psychology, sociology, and the arts—whose interest was in integrating Marxist thought with psychoanalytic and existential theory. Adopting the term "critical," these thinkers set out an agenda to take a skeptical stance toward prevalent assumptions and statements of authority regarding how we understand ourselves, others, and the world. In line with Marxist thought, Critical Theory especially sought to uncover and expose the role that the dominant ideology of the time (i.e., capitalism) played in espousing what was posed as irrefutable truths and social practices. Because all ideologies are conditioned by specific historical, economic, and political conditions, power and privilege inevitably exert control over what is deemed desirable, normal, and healthy and, conversely, what is deemed as detrimental, deviant, and unhealthy. Moreover, such judgments are frequently used to justify inequitable and unjust social arrangements and practices from which individuals need to be emancipated.

To take one example from capitalist ideology, we can look at a prevalent way in which disparities of status and access to social benefits and resources, resulting in egregious inequities, is sanctioned. That is by employing meritocracy (Sandel, 2021)—the assertion that such differences are based on talent, effort, and achievement. This is a highly individualistic viewpoint that emphasizes personal merit, while neglecting the many additional social factors that play a substantial role in making available the opportunities and resources necessary for realizing one's possibilities and exercising one's rights. This perspective is promoted in images such as "rugged individualism" and the "self-made person" (Greene, 2008). The message conveyed is that there are winners who deserve the good things they fought for and achieved and losers who deserve their horrible lot because of laziness or some other personal defect.

From a Critical Theory perspective, rather than taking such assertions as objective statements of fact or the outcome of some fixed natural law, they would instead be seen as expressions of an underlying ideology, in this case capitalism. That ideology, in turn, would be understood as a set of beliefs, values, and practices presented as fixed and universal truths despite being the product of existing historical, economic, and political conditions. By conflating social and natural forces, capitalism inhibits any critique, disguises the ways in which the status quo benefits those who possess power and prestige at the expense of the dominated class, and thus undermine any threats to existing social structures and practices. In keeping with Marxism's assertion that it is not sufficient to merely understand reality but to change it, Critical Theory sought first to expose the many contradictions of capitalism, particularly those that resulted in self-defeating patterns and contributed to suffering. It then proceeded to deconstruct and dismantle its extreme claims in order to promote the emancipation of individuals from conditions that enslaved them.

Critical psychology shares many of the core principles of Critical Theory. It too examines and criticizes central assumptions of capitalism and the associated worldview of modernism. Core precepts of modernism such as objectivism, positivism, and instrumental reason also carry with them clear political, social, and economic consequences supporting capitalism. Thus, modernism as an ideology also provides a basis for ways in which power is exercised to oppress and exploit individuals. The neglect of the role that power plays in shaping human well-being is a particular focus of critical psychology. There is an inescapable political dimension to human life that determines the way in which privilege, opportunities, and resources are distributed in accordance with cultural rules and norms. While these power dynamics are significant factors in causing suffering, power can also be exercised in positive ways. In light of this, the goal of critical psychology is also to promote liberation. As Teo (2015) states, "Critical psychologists intend to challenge societal structures of injustice, ideologies, psychological control, and the adjustment of individuals" (p. 246).

In the previous chapter, I asserted that oppression is the single greatest cause of suffering. Its impact is widely unrecognized because the ideology responsible for much of the oppression inflicted on individuals is rendered either invisible or presented as natural and inevitable. True healing is not possible if the many destructive impacts of neoliberal ideology and fascism are neglected. This occurs when focus is instead diverted to aspects such as genetics, disordered biological factors, dysfunctional cognitions, psychological complexes, and the like (in keeping with materialistic, atomistic, individualistic assumptions). The result is highly distorted and value-laden notions of what constitutes health and dysfunction. A basic principle of healing is that one cannot treat a condition until the actual nature of that condition is first correctly identified. As the psychiatrist Gabor Maté (2022) observed regarding prevalent diseases and patterns of who are most at risk, we must look at the question "Why?" And while this may seem obvious, sadly all too often this is not the case.

A troubling and all too pervasive example of this is not only the highly questionable and unreliable application of psychiatric diagnoses to categorize individuals in distress (Newnes, 2014), but even more so the ways in which diagnoses function as political devices (Moncrieff, 2010) and a means of generating financial profit rather than providing care (Davies, 2022). Another is the widespread practice of medicalization and the commodification of health and illness (Boggs, 2015; Esposito & Perez, 2014; Jacobs & Cowen, 2010). The goal of promoting healing among those who are suffering is utterly subverted when a host of human problems that are justifiable and expected reactions to adversity and unhealthy physical and social environments are labeled as pathological, irrational, and undesirable based on political (e.g., to suppress dissent) and economic (i.e., for profit) purposes. We cannot oppose and redress oppression by neglecting or denying it.

This goes back to a point made previously. When the perspective of those who provide care is unshakably rooted in the beliefs and values ensconced in a toxic dominant ideology, significant dangers are posed that compromise genuine healing. This includes the risk of treating with disregard and even outright hostility the lived experiences of being impacted by harms perpetrated by that dominant ideology among those seeking help. This conveys a lack of respect and understanding for the perspective of those suffering, while at the same time validating a worldview that has been detrimental to them. This will understandably be felt to be at odds with their needs and concerns. Also when healers uncritically subscribe to beliefs and values embedded in the dominant ideology that cause harm to the oppressed, they are more likely to be complicit in doing even further harm to them. This danger is observed by Smith (2010) in her discussion of how to work with the poor within a social justice framework. As she notes, the decision regarding whether to address the issue of oppression is itself value based and political. Choosing not to acknowledge oppression can serve to support an unjust status quo by obscuring it and, in doing so, to collude with the internalized oppression of the poor.

Those engaged in healing who are so deeply committed to their own worldview often may not regard their aims or actions as malevolent. They often assume automatically that because they are in a "helping" profession, their intentions are noble and pure. However, no matter how well-intentioned their attempts to help may be, they will likely not only fail to help but run the risk of actually causing greater harm when they proceed uncritically. This is sometimes described as *clinical iatrogenesis*, a term first introduced by Ivan Illich (2000). Examples of this include misdiagnosis, overmedicating, performing unnecessary procedures or providing inappropriate care, pathologizing an expanding range of human problems, and neglecting social determinants of health. Being blind to oppression is a sure means of not only failing to recognize its detrimental impacts on others but perpetuating it.

The Radical as Humble, Encompassing and Dynamic

For healing to be truly radical it must be radically re-conceptualized. This means adopting a more encompassing and deeper perspective than the one usually assumed. It must be expansive in recognizing and accepting of the entire range of human experience, including those experiences that are viewed as abnormal. Healers must be open to the possibility of alternative realities, anomalous states of consciousness, and deeper truths. They must be willing to respond to an order of meanings beyond them that exert what Frankl (1968) called a demand quality, or moral imperative, beyond personal values. This requires willingness and courage on the part of healers to shake themselves free of the often comfortable confines of what is deemed established truth and customary practices. They must relinquish their facile acceptance of being impeccable experts whose knowledge and status assure them that they know "what's best" for those who seek care. Instead they must be prepared to demonstrate a measure of humility linked to the inevitable presence of *unknowing* in the healing process. Spinelli (2007) asserts that an unknowing stance is essential to therapy. This is expressed in an acceptance of the limitations of one's knowledge and a sense of curiosity. Such a stance allows for a respectful exploration of the worldview that clients have constructed to make sense of their world. It is conveyed through an attitude of radical validation of the way in which clients are engaged toward themselves, others, and the world (DuBose, 2014) and only achieved by setting aside and holding at bay one's assumptions and biases.

Similarly, Loewenthal (2015), citing the work of the philosopher Levinas, speaks of the imperative of "putting the other first" when providing care. In doing so, healers must not give in to the temptation of comfortably retreating to their theories in order to make sense of and categorize the worldview of another. There is always an element of mystery and uncertainty in the relationship between one human being and another. When confronted with this challenge to their sense of certitude and security, healers may experience anxiety. This is because their own worldview (as embodied in the theories they hold) and their very sense of self may be threatened in the face of uncertainty. Thus, the stance of unknowing can only be established and maintained if healers are able to show a tolerance for the dread that comes with this unavoidable uncertainty. This dread causes them suffering, but inability to confront and live through their own suffering is sure to impede their ability to be present to the suffering of those seeking their care. Without this, they will be unable to help others find their way of living through their suffering or using it to promote positive change.

To avoid the habitual narrowness that characterizes their perspective, healers must move from what Colin Wilson (1966) describes as a worm's eye view to a bird's eye view. There must be an expansive and embracing movement from the fragmentary to the whole, from the partial to the complete. In the previous chapter, I spoke of how it was imperative that healing take into consideration all the various facets of human beings and all the varied ways in which suffering impacts well-being. This is the essential first step. but it alone is not enough. There must likewise be recognition of the inseparable relationship between understanding and action or *praxis*, as asserted by Friere (1970) in his pedagogy of the oppressed. Reflection on the impact of sociopolitical and economic context elevates awareness of the workings of oppression in one's own life as well as the life of others. But, again, such a realization alone is insufficient. One must translate knowledge into action and move from the passive stance of the victim. A transition from being the object of oppressive practices to exercising agency and thus effecting change is required. This is particularly powerful when one joins with others who share the goal of liberation. This understanding of the dual nature of healing in which understanding must always be wedded to action is how radical healing achieves a broader and more complete approach to suffering. This will become clearer in the next chapter when the inseparable relationship between compassion and justice in healing is discussed.

Those who experience harm due to oppression and other forms of injustice surely deserve to have their suffering recognized. But sadly all too often even this modest measure so essential to healing is not offered. Instead, many times the suffering experienced by people, particularly that created by social causes, is met with indifference and sometimes harsh judgment. This response results from the prevalent bias of extreme individualism touted by neoliberalism, in which people are regarded as responsible for their troubles. Recognizing the actual causes of their distress would threaten their powerful adherence to this individualistic worldview and provoke the fear that accompanies this. And such fear functions as one of the most significant obstacles to connecting with the suffering of others.

Even when some degree of care and concern is shown to those who suffer, it often is rooted in an overly narrow perspective that fails to express genuine compassion. For example, a certain distance is maintained from those in distress that protects "helpers" from truly putting themselves in their place. This might be expressed as pity that often demeans those who suffer and may imply an attitude that their misfortune is somehow deserved. Another expression of this lack of compassion is labeling or categorizing their suffering as way to objectify it (Dass & Gorman, 1985). Finally, it is often assumed that just showing concern is both necessary and sufficient to bring about healing. However, all these fall short of what is required for radical healing. Praxis must be based on both an ability to truly "suffer with" the afflicted and a correct understanding of the degree to which underlying causes of suffering go beyond the individual and have their origin in unjust social structures and practices. Change must ultimately take into account the interdependent relationship between the individual and the social, between compassion and justice. In the absence of this, one is providing what is proverbially called the "band-aid approach."

Thus, to provide radical healing, individuals must be committed to engaging in a sincere, rigorous, and continuous process of self-examination. The goal of this self-examination, however, must not make the same mistake of confining its attention to solely personal factors that give rise to preconceptions and prejudices. Healers are no more self-contained, acontextual individuals than those they serve. Questioning dearly held assumptions and scrutinizing one's worldview is not complete if it fails to identify, expose, and undo the equally potent influences having their origin in an ideology into which one has been inculcated from birth. Once undertaken, it will soon become apparent that this process is neither simple nor straightforward. There will, of course, be encounters with the lies that we tell ourselves born out of our exquisite capacity for self-deception. However, as the process goes deeper, what becomes revealed are deeply rooted and taken-for-granted beliefs and values shaped and enforced by powerful social forces. What is ultimately exposed is a dominant worldview that is rendered invisible by means of mystification. This includes discovering the ways in which material and political conditions within society shape one's consciousness at every level.

Despite these hazards and pitfalls, there are clear benefits that healers will derive from this process. They will achieve a greater degree of understanding and clarity about the roots of suffering that will be indispensable to their work. One particularly important insight is the powerful role played by fear, particularly the fear of the loss of one's worldview and, relatedly, one's very existence, in both the processes of self-deception and mystification. A recognition of the innate need to maintain a sense of predictability and control is central to healing as it leads individuals to resist anything that seriously challenges their accustomed beliefs and dearly held values. Moreover, this need for control is utilized by the powerful to ensure the maintenance of the status quo. Fear has been and continues to be the most potent weapon used to enforce the dominant ideology and to silence dissent. This need to exert control becomes even more extreme when significantly threatened, causing human beings to cling even more desperately to their attachments and identifications. However, this strategy will prove to be self-defeating because it fails to reckon with the inevitability of change and the loss that accompanies it. The imperative to expand awareness, to cast off the entrapments of our attachments and identifications, and to ever strive to broaden our capacity for relationship with ourselves, others, the natural world, and someone/something greater than us—all of which are integral to radical healing— thus requires an astute grasp of the dynamics of fear. Liberation on a personal level necessitates the undoing or self-deception, and on a social level the unmasking of mystification.

A willingness to personally make this journey is a requisite for anyone committed to healing for two fundamental reasons. The first is that one cannot be a guide to others making the healing journey without first being on that journey themselves. Our healing and the healing of others cannot be separated. This is not to say that it is necessary or even possible for healers to satisfactorily complete this journey. The process of healing is a dynamic one that constantly unfolds over the course of one's life. Where one is on the path along which this journey unfolds is always subject to change. Moreover, there can be both progress and regress. The way is not smooth or straightforward. What is required is not that one has "made it" but rather that one is courageously and resolutely committed to the process. The second reason is that asking someone to engage in the journey of healing, with its rewards and perils, its joys and sorrows, without also showing that one has done so themselves will understandably be perceived by those seeking care as insincere and ingenuine. It is far more powerful and persuasive for healers "to show rather than to tell." Healers must model for those who are suffering the willingness to confront their own suffering and see in it the potential for a possible way forward.

One of the great ironies often sadly experienced by those who seek healing is how those who presume to be of service to them have failed to see the radical responsibility it places on them to be committed to their own healing. The healer and the one seeking healing must recognize and devote themselves to their shared obligations, expectations, and imperatives. This is in line with the assertion of Wampold and Imel (2015) that psychotherapy is a fundamentally social healing practice in which the relationship between therapist and client is pivotal. This naturally grows out of the inherent social nature of human beings in which the need for relationship is as fundamental as the need for food and shelter. Being-with is an intrinsic dimension of human existence and of healing.

The Radical as Revolutionary—A Developmental Perspective

A second way in which the radical dimension of healing needs to be understood is based on its meaning as something *revolutionary*. Radical healing is not possible in the absence of a revolutionary change in the existing paradigm that takes into account the essentially individual and societal nature of human beings. We have seen how the exaggerated individualistic lens from which human beings are viewed abstracts them from social, economic, and political forces that exert a powerful impact on their well-being. Rather than respecting the integrity and wholeness on which their well-being depends, they are dissected into parts that are erroneously seen as bearing no relationship to each other. Breaking away from this one-sided and reductionistic paradigm is revolutionary. Only then are the limitations, omissions, and distortions that have their roots in constricted and rigid worldviews held by individuals and perpetrated by an oppressive hegemonic ideology recognized and redressed. A radical approach is needed to seriously challenge the pervasive and significant influence exercised by the powerful and privileged to preserve unjust social structures and practices. By enabling and encouraging individuals to acknowledge and claim disowned and invalidated experiences essential to their humanity and subsequently to throw off their harmful impacts, radical healing fosters a greater degree of wholeness and well-being.

In view of this, one understanding of radical can be visualized as a horizontal continuum anchored by the polarity of health/wholeness on one end and illness/alienation on the other. This continuum represents the entire range of human functioning or potential. Another way to describe this continuum is as the total range of experiences that are available to all human beings. Radical healing embraces the assertion of the Roman thinker Terence: "I am a human being and nothing human is alien to me." No sharp distinctions can be drawn in terms of where one is along this continuum. The typical analytical approach cannot be used because human experiences and potentials do not represent discrete and easily distinguishable states. As beings in process, we experience a blending of health and dis-ease in every moment of life. This is a reflection of how life is inherently ambiguous. Human existence is lived out, moment by moment, within this continuum. The purpose of healing is to facilitate, model and encourage movement toward the healthy end of the continuum. This is achieved, in part, by cultivating a healthy tolerance for ambiguity, an openness to all facets of what it means to be human (including even those that are most abhorrent to us), and an ability to resolve seemingly conflictual aspects of life into a fuller and more complete (i.e., higher) state of consciousness.

Another understanding of radical can be visualized as depicting a vertical or depth dimension to healing. There are two ways in which this aspect of the revolutionary can be described. The first returns to the point previously made in the first chapter that healing must be practiced within a developmental framework. Development is understood here as consisting of distinct stages or levels hierarchically arranged. The second understanding is that attending to depth means that healing must get to the core—the essential, the necessary, and the indispensable—truths of what it means to be human.

Turning to the first point, revolution can be thought of as "our(r) evolution" or seeing healing or growth as having an overarching telos, purpose, or direction shared by all human beings. The significant body of work of Wilber (2000a) provides a valuable framework for describing development as the movement toward ever-greater degrees of wholeness, integration, and liberation. He integrates a large number of theories of development from diverse perspectives and includes the many different forms it can take, or what he calls lines of development. Employing this framework, both healers and those who are suffering can be thought of as being mutually engaged in an evolutionary process aimed at more fully realizing their potential, progressively expanding their consciousness, and optimizing their functioning. This view of development has long been part of the humanistic traditions of psychology, such as in the work of Maslow (1971) on self-actualization or Rogers (1961) on the actualizing tendency. Both of their theories premised that there is an innate tendency in all organisms to realize potentialities as fully as possible. Along the same lines, Wilber (2000b) in his treatment of different forms of development sees evolution having four forms of directionality: increasing complexity, increasing differentiation and integration, increasing organization and structuration, and increasing relative autonomy.

Contrary to the predominant, Darwinian view of evolution as governed by chance and without purpose, Wilber believes that it is a progressive process. It can be described as the unfolding of a series of stages in which each successive step in the process transcends and includes earlier stages. He describes this as a growth hierarchy. Though conceptualized as a series of successive stages, the process of growth is not linear. Individuals do not negotiate these stages in a simplistic and uniform fashion, and movement can be both progressive and regressive. Individuals can occupy different levels at different points and do not necessarily ascend to the highest level. Finally, it is important to note that this evolutionary process can be understood in spiritual terms as the expansion of consciousness and the attainment of liberation or enlightenment in the realization of unitive knowledge of the divine Ground, of which all existence is an expression (Huxley, 1944; Wilber, 2000a).

It is important here to avoid the common tendency in mainstream psychology and in the dominant neoliberal ideology in which it is embedded to see the process of striving to realize one's potential or maximizing one's growth as an individual task or process. This individualistic bias ends up encouraging a more narcissistic or self-centered perspective, even to the degree of asserting that achieving potential requires doing so in competition with or at the expense of others. This again negates the essential social nature of human beings. There is no "I" without "We." As critical psychology (Schraube & Osterkamp, 2013) asserts, societality is a species-specific mode of human life that made human evolution and existence possible. From their earliest beginnings, human beings had to be able to band together to pursue the common aim of creating conditions of life in accordance with their needs and to achieve the optimal use of the conditions in which they found themselves. A central human need that assured our evolution is the need for attachment, connection, affection. We cannot survive without others. Similarly, we must question the idea that agency is located solely within the individual and is something that is unique and private. In contrast, critical psychology integrates appreciation for the societal nature of human beings in its concept of *generalized agency*: the specifically human capacity to consciously determine the conditions under which we live *together with others*. This means coming to a shared understanding of the subjective necessity and possibility of exercising substantial influence on life circumstances. Once more we evolve in concert with others.

These views of development as having a purpose or goal are forms of what is called a *teleological* or *perfectionistic* theory, such as found in the eudaimonic tradition. This tradition sees development as aimed at maximizing the achievement of fundamental human potential and making it possible for individuals to live as perfect a life as possible (what is sometimes called flourishing). However, the essential social nature of human beings means that this evolution does not, and cannot, occur solely on an individual level. As Wilber (2000b) states, because of the relational nature of existence, there is a process of coevolution that occurs between individuals and the types of environments in which they participate. This same principle of co-evolution has been found to exist between all manners of living organisms (Thompson, 1994). I reference the requirement for this interdependence in my discussion of defining social justice in terms of flourishing (Gruba-McCallister, 2019). The interaction of rights or what Nussbaum (1992, 2003) describes as human capabilities with resources (those things external to individuals that better enable them to achieve their goals) and opportunities (channels by means of which they can pursue those goals) provide optimal conditions for them to flourish. Thus, I (2019) argue that a just society is:

> ...one whose systems, structures, and processes promote the optimal development of all its members with respect to fulfilling those potentials unique to each of them without regard for arbitrary or prejudicial differences in merit or worth, while also establishing conditions within which individuals are able to realize and express their capacity for freedom and self-determination. (p. 82)

In light of human interdependence, the process of healing can be viewed as both healers and those who are suffering mutually engaging in an evolutionary process in which they strive to grow together toward optimal well-being.

Adopting a developmental perspective thus elucidates the manner in which healing can promote radical change through a fundamental and comprehensive change in perspective or level of consciousness that transcends one's current worldview and achieves a more advanced one. This can occur along many different lines—cognitive, moral, ego, spiritual—again as outlined by the very comprehensive system developed by Wilber (2000b). Also as Wilber argues, what is available to consciousness, what is experienced, and how one sees the world and oneself is determined by developmental stage and the perspective associated with it. Each perspective that individuals assume leads them to co-create in interaction with the environment their own distinct reality. Given that a central aim of healing is to promote wholeness (i.e., a more encompassing and embracing stance in each of the four spheres of life), it must involve facilitating substantive shifts in perspective by means of the dissolution of one worldview and the adoption of a new and more encompassing one.

One can view radical healing by situating it within another example of a continuum based on the polarity of progressive versus regressive. Erich Fromm (1964, 1976) provides this by the distinction he draws between the biophilic versus necrophilic orientation and its relevance to health and dis-ease. The *biophilic* orientation seeks to preserve life, as well as promote productivity, creativity, and a greater sense of wonder and appreciation. It is essentially growth-directed, focused on being rather than having, and seeks a more expansive sense of awareness that embraces all beings in love and care. The necrophilic orientation, on the other hand, is death-affirming as manifested in its direction toward decay, stagnation, and treating living beings as things to possess and control. It is rooted in a malevolent narcissism in which individuals idolize themselves while demeaning others. Fromm sees each orientation as espousing its own morality, with the biophilic advancing the good by showing a reverence for life, striving to be constructive, and honoring the humanity of all individuals. The necrophilic, in contrast, is devoted to advancing evil by seeking to bring everyone and everything under control by virtue of its obsession with possessing and dominating. The goal is to ultimately bring about the destruction of what is possessed. Necrophilism is sadistic as it seeks complete mastery over individuals with the goal of humiliating, enslaving, and even killing them.

Because of Fromm's appreciation for the significance of social conditions in advancing or impairing well-being, he also described how each orientation is fostered by distinct societies. Biophilia is more likely in societies that are just and in which the material, psychological ,and social needs of individuals are met. There is a sense of security, people are treated as ends in themselves, and freedom is fostered by allowing individuals the ability to be active and responsible members of society. Necrophilia, in contrast, is more likely in societies that encourage egocentricity, selfishness, and greed. There is an emphasis on possessing and consumption that results in the transformation of human beings into things that are not worthy of respect and care. We can see in his description of necrophilic values key elements of neoliberalism and fascism.

Fromm sees the tension between progressive and regressive as rooted in human beings possessing freedom of choice and the burden that comes with this. The realization that one has alternatives from which to choose and the consequences associated with these alternatives bring a sense of both possibility and fear. Succumbing to fear and thus seeking to evade freedom not only stifles development but can actually lead to a retreat to earlier stages of the evolutionary process. When the direction is progressive, there is greater freedom, expanded responsibility for one's actions, and a fuller realization of human potential. When it is regressive, there is a forsaking of one's humanity and a turning back of the evolutionary process. Fromm also asserts that a simplistic linear view of development is mistaken. Steps taken can be retraced, refuge can be sought in what was left behind, and ambivalence can arise when looking to what lies ahead.

Fromm (1968) identifies a value or attitude essential to radical healing based on the cultivation of a biophilic orientation aimed at progressive development—

hope. Hope is an inner readiness and receptivity to the potential that each moment presents for new growth, with the accompanying understanding that while such growth may not be certain, it is always possible (what he calls faith). Along with this there must be courage (Tillich, 1952) that serves to avoid falling into despair and giving up hope while negotiating this uncertain process and encountering inevitable obstacles and disappointments. Fromm (1968) sums up this essential stance as follows:

> Hope and faith, being essential qualities of *life*, are by their very nature moving in the direction of transcending the *status quo*, individually and socially. It is one of the qualities of all life that it is in a constant process of change and never remains the same at any given moment. Life that stagnates tends to die; if the stagnation is complete, death has occurred. It follows that life in its moving quality tends to break out and to overcome the *status quo*. We grow either stronger or weaker, wiser or more foolish, more courageous or more cowardly. Every second is a moment of decision, for the better or the worse. (italics in original, p. 16)

The Radical as Getting to the Roots of Healing

One further etymological meaning of "radical"—"being rooted"—merits examination as it also helps to elucidate the nature of healing. This meaning is centered on getting to the core or foundation of healing: establishing what is essential. This need for radical therapy to see past the superficial and undo various forms of deception will be explored in coming chapters. However, another way to realize this meaning is by exploring the roots of the practice of healing and what this reveals about what is required to be a healer. Such insights can be gained through an examination of the earliest healers. The other way, to be explored in the next chapter, is seeing how the "rootedness" of radical healing is based on the interdependence of the two essential roles of healer—the contemplative and the prophetic—and, accordingly, on a commitment to the values of compassion and justice.

From the beginning of human history, all cultures developed ideas about the causes of human maladies and suffering, and culturally specific methods were developed for dealing with these experiences (Eliade, 1964; Struthers, Eschiti, & Patchell, 2004, von Stuckrad, 2002). These cultures also designated certain individuals, and sometimes groups, to be healers. These individuals have been called by different names: shamans, traditional healers, and folk or indigenous healers. Despite these traditions still being practiced and a growing body of literature that has been compiled on their efficacy and relevance to both indigenous and other cultures, most texts on the history and origins of psychology and psychotherapy give little or no attention to these important predecessors. More often these narratives tend instead to locate the roots of psychology in the work of early Greek philosophers. This neglect is reflective of the Western, modern, and reductionistic bias in mainstream psychology and medicine. It is also indicative of Western imperialism that led to the exploitation and systematic oppression of the colonized and destruction of their culture and traditions. This egregious form of social injustice and dismissive and demeaning attitude actually deprives us of a valuable understanding of essential elements of radical healing.

Thankfully, in recent times there has been a renewed interest in shamanism, such as in the pioneering work of Harner (1980) and the work of Winkelman (1990, 2000, 2013). Similarly, the National Center for Complementary and Alternative Medicine and the World Health Organization have supported more study on the clinical effectiveness of indigenous forms of healing and have asserted their value in helping to eliminate health care disparities among populations aligned with these perspectives (Struthers, Eschiti, & Paschell, 2004). Progress has also been made in recognizing the value of indigenous forms of healing as an alternative to Western forms of practice and the need to be open to working collaboratively with native healers when serving culturally diverse populations (Yeh, Hunter, Madan-Behel, Chiang, & Arora, 2004). One last point to bear in mind, asserted by contemporary practitioners of shamanism, is that it has evolved and, while attending to its earlier roots, continues to seek ways to be relevant and applicable to current issues and needs (Saloman & Ingerman, 2019).

Though not providing an in-depth discussion of shamanism and other indigenous perspectives on healing, I will describe key elements of the worldview commonly held by these early healers and common characteristics found among them. Walsh (1996) writes:

> Shamanism can be defined as a family of traditions whose practitioners focus on voluntarily entering altered states of consciousness in which they experience themselves or their spirits traveling to other realms at will and interacting with other entities to heal others or to help their community. (p. 96)

This practice of spirit travel while in an altered state of consciousness is what distinguishes shamans from other magicoreligious healers. These altered states of consciousness (ASC) can be induced by means of drumming, chanting, dancing, or the use of some psychoactive substance. Shamans may also prepare themselves for entering an ASC by engaging in certain rigorous practices such as fasting, water or sleep deprivation, social isolation, or painful exercise. The ASC is characterized as a "soul flight" in which shamans leave their body and travel to various spirit realms where they engage in health-promoting activities such as divination, clairvoyance, acquiring information about the problem for which others are seeking help, recovering lost souls, escorting souls of the dead, or securing protection against spirits.

The universe of shamans, according to Armstrong (2023), is based on a participatory understanding of the natural world animated by an intrinsic force or presence that imbues all things. This force or sacred energy is a transcendent mystery that defies definition. This way of understanding does not conceive of the supernatural or a belief in God in ordinary terms as distinct and distant. There is a deep sense of connection with the natural world, which is regarded as sacred and so is revered. The sacred force binds all things together as a living web of interrelated parts. This view has in recent times led to an appreciation of shamanism by advocates of deep ecology (von Stuckrad, 2002). The worldview of shamans has also been characterized as a belief in spirit entities, which may be animals, natural phenomena, deceased ancestors, or gods (Eliade, 1964). The power of the shamans is based on their ability to make contact and establish relationships with these spirits to acquire knowledge and gain assistance. This includes an individual's illness or a problem impacting the community (e.g., related to hunting or crops), serving as an ally, or restoring balance and harmony whose disruption has been the cause of difficulties. Spirits may be benevolent or malevolent. As a rule, shamans are not possessed by spirits (but may take on the form of an animal spirit) and are able to achieve what they set out to accomplish by exerting control over the actions of spirits. The universe of shamans is also multi-tiered, consisting of different levels (often three) connected by means of the *axis mundi*, or the center of the world. This is sometimes represented as the Cosmic Tree or the Sacred Mountain.

There are also common themes regarding how one is inducted into the role of shaman (Walsh, 1996). It begins when an individual receives a call, often in adolescence. In many instances those called are among the descendants of shamans who then receive their powers from the spirit allies of their ancestors. Often they are men but can also be women. The call received can be in the form of visions or by means of dreams of spirits or ancestors demanding that they become shamans. This is often accompanied by a period in which those who have been chosen experience a significant illness such as seizures; engage in wild, erratic and bizarre behavior; and display what may appear to be insanity.

However, individuals experiencing these problems are distinguished by the current shaman or the community from someone afflicted with a mental disorder. Rather they are seen as signs of that individual being called upon to become a shaman. In light of the demands made upon initiates, it is not surprising that they feel reluctant or ambivalent about the call. The ordeal through which they must pass is often experienced as a death (such as the body of the shaman being shattered and reduced to bones) and eventual rebirth. Once this crisis is past, shamans are found to be strong and healthy individuals. This passage of shamans through a significant crisis and their emergence from it transformed and in possession of spiritual power is sometimes described as the *wounded healer.* With this initial phase completed, the individual is then trained and mentored by a practicing shaman.

Winkelman (1990) conducted a study on individuals recognized as magico-religious practitioners in forty-seven societies that employed a questionnaire to assess individuals along one hundred variables. Based on this cross-cultural research, Winkelman developed what he called an etic model of the shaman, consisting of the following core characteristics:

- A dominant social role, a charismatic leader.
- A night-time community ritual.
- The use of chanting, drumming, dancing, and singing.
- An initiatory crisis involving the movement from death to rebirth.
- Shamanic training including the induction of ASC, particularly through fasting and isolation.
- An ASC experience described as a soul journey (not possession).
- ASC involving visionary experiences.
- The ability to practice divination, diagnosis, and prophecy.
- A healing process that involved soul loss and recovery.
- The belief that illness is caused by spirits, sorcerers, or the intrusion of objects or entities.
- Animal relations as a source of power, including the control of animal spirits.
- The ability of the shaman to transform into an animal.
- Malevolent acts of sorcery, including the ability to kill others.
- Assistance in acquiring animals for food or hunting magic.

In addition to this material on shamanism, literature on indigenous healing practices provides important insights into radical healing. This research shares a number of common themes with shamanism. Like shamanism, indigenous healing practices have been largely marginalized, misunderstood, and discredited. In spite of this, these practices are an integral part of indigenous cultures throughout the world. This examination of indigenous healing focuses on those forms practiced as part of Native American medicine and, as in the case of shamanism, identifies common elements of these practices. As Struthers, Eschiti, and Patchell (2004) state, Native American medicine

> ...is an ancient, intact, complex holistic healthcare system practiced by indigenous people worldwide that is profound and more deeply rooted and complex than commonly understood...[it] is based upon a spiritual rather than a materialistic or Cartesian world view and its ancient feature conveys that it is possibly the most ancient form of holistic medicine. (p. 142)

The holistic nature—akin to that seen as central to radical healing—of these practices asserts that there is interconnectedness between the biological, social, psychological, physical, and cosmic dimensions. It also sees individuals as inextricably embedded within family, group, and community networks as well as deeply connected to both the natural and spiritual worlds.

The spiritual and religious beliefs and traditions of the community play a vital role in indigenous healing, with an emphasis on the spirit world and supernatural forces. These magical and even mystical elements are in stark contrast to the dominant secular focus on biological factors in Western medicine. Within this framework that emphasizes wholeness and interconnectedness, any disruption of balance and harmony between spirit, mind, body, and emotions or between an individual and his/her network of relationships with others gives rise to illness. The goal is thus to restore balance and harmony to those who are suffering. This includes between the diverse dimensions that make up their life, in the life energy in their body, in their relations with their family and/or community, and in their connections with the natural world and the universe. A wide range of healing techniques are employed, including divination, prayer, chanting, drumming, music, singing, medicinal plants, laying on of hands, ceremonies, dance, storytelling, and counseling. Healers are keepers of wisdom who are able to channel supernatural power. Those who are healers can be chosen based on their ability or by their community. They acquire their ability by means of inheritance from ancestors, from another healer, or based on development through training and initiation.

These essential elements of shamanism and indigenous healing practices help to elucidate core elements of radical healing. These include the following key points that will be dealt with in greater depth in later chapters:

1. Healing must have a religious or spiritual emphasis that stands in contrast to the dominant secular, materialistic, reductionistic, and deterministic model in Western medicine and psychology. This is not merely a recognition of a spiritual dimension to human experience, but an understanding of the centrality of spirituality to human existence. Pierre Teilhard de Chardin, a French philosopher, astutely describes this: "We are not human beings having spiritual experiences, but spiritual beings having human experiences."

2. Following from the previous point is a holistic worldview. All of existence is an expression of a higher reality and, as such, a complex web of interdependent and mutual relationships among all elements of the cosmos. The work of healing requires that it take into account the embeddedness of the individual with family, community, the natural environment, and the spiritual realm. Illness or suffering arises from a lack of balance or harmony or the existence of disruptions within this network of relationships. Healing must involve restoring one's essential relatedness.

3. Healing practices include the cultivation of altered states of consciousness in the healer, in the person seeking care, and—at times—in members of the person's community. As a result, there is less emphasis placed on the role of talking, engagement of reason, focus on self-examination, and the cultivation of a discursive form of insight that is characteristic of

mainstream methods of healing. Instead, the healer may be more active in instigating change, evoking emotions, and encouraging the attainment of a transformative experience. The sufferer may also be engaged in some form of ceremonial practice, sometimes in conjunction with others, to achieve resolution to his or her problem.

4. The calling to become a healer is often one that comes with certain demands that exact a toll and give rise to a process in which the initiate undergoes significant duress. The result is a process of transformation in which awareness and acceptance of the "woundedness" of the healer deepens their compassion and better enables them to be of service to others. The healer also possesses a greater degree of charisma and authority by virtue of undergoing this transformative process.

Before continuing, an objection might be raised regarding the applicability of certain elements of the shamanic and indigenous traditions in view of what is considered the "advances" made by modern thought. Examples here might be beliefs in spirit entities, animal spirits, soul loss, traveling to spiritual realms, or practicing magic. Generally, these belief systems are dismissed as representative of an earlier stage of development of consciousness, described by Wilber (1980) as the magical and mystical and thus regarded as primitive or without merit. Several responses can be made to these objections and reservations. The first comes from Wilber (2000a), who takes a developmental perspective and warns against what he calls "wave absolutism" in which only those values and realities that one can be aware of at his or her level of development are given any validity. He observes:

> An integral synthesis, to be truly integral, must find a way that all of the major worldviews are basically *true* (even though partial). It is not that the higher levels are giving more accurate views, and the lower levels are giving falsity, superstition, or primitive nonsense...At the mythic level, [a spirit entity] is a phenomenological reality. It will do no good to say, "Well, we have evolved beyond that stage, and so now we know that [a spirit entity] is not real," because if that is true—and all stages are shown to be primitive and false in light of further evolution—then we will have to admit that our own views, *right now*, are also false (because future evolution will move beyond them). (italics in original, p. 111)

In other words, as Wilber asserts, knowledge derived from all developmental levels is right, but some knowledge is "more right" by virtue of our ever-evolving consciousness and expanded knowledge and awareness. Relatedly, beliefs that healing must involve spirituality, that human beings exist in a complex nexus of interdependent relationships, and that healing must seek to establish wholeness and harmony remain as true today as they were in earlier times—even if the exact ways in which these truths are understood has changed. This viewpoint has gained increasing credibility based on growing evidence for a post-material view of reality (Schwartz, 2012).

The Ongoing Relevance of Core Features of Healing

There is little discussion of the relevance of these earliest healing practices to current problems and issues in psychological or medical literature, although a greater degree of interest has been shown recently, for example, in transpersonal psychology (see Scotten, Chinen, & Battista, 1996). However, a comprehensive discussion of the essential elements of healing by Frank and Frank (1991) reveals a number of notable points of agreement with the key themes identified above. Indeed, Frank and Frank include in their work an examination of the relationship of healing to religious conversion, religiomagical healing, practices in non-industrialized nations, and shamanism. Thus, an examination of their work will be instructive.

For Frank and Frank, those who seek relief from a healer are suffering due to the loss of the worldview that provides them with meaning, security, and structure. The collapse of their assumptive world arises from challenges and threats they are unable to manage. They feel confused about themselves and unable to deal with their emotions, leading to fear that they are "going crazy." The loss of meaning may be experienced as a sense of emptiness. This results in what they describe as "demoralization"—feeling deprived of spirit, courage, and hope along with experiencing confusion, isolation, and alienation. The aims of psychotherapy are to help people feel and function better by assisting them to make changes to their worldview. This leads to restoring a sense of meaning, rekindling a sense of hope, improving their sense of control and enhancing their self-esteem, and re-integrating them into their network of relationships with others.

Frank and Frank find that all forms of psychotherapy share four effective features. This includes describing the significant role played by myth and ritual. Parallels with the essential elements of early healing practices should be noted, particularly with regard to the importance of myth and ritual. The four core features are:

1. An emotionally charged, confiding relationship with a helping person. Establishing a working alliance characterized by a sense of caring and acceptance by the healer, a shared understanding of the problem to be resolved, and agreement on the means used to resolve it.
2. A healing setting that provides safety, heightens the healer's prestige, and strengthens the sufferer's expectation of help.
3. A rationale, conceptual scheme, or myth that provides a plausible explanation for the client's symptoms and prescribes a ritual or procedure for resolving them. Myth acquires plausibility based on its relationship to

the prevalent cultural worldview and its ability to capture the imagination of and inspire the sufferer.

4. A ritual or procedure that requires the active participation of both the client and the therapist and believed by both to be the means of restoring the client's health.

The functions of myth and ritual in promoting healing are to:

1. Combat the sufferer's sense of alienation, strengthen the healing relationship through a shared belief system, and encourage mutual interest.
2. Inspire and sustain the sufferer's expectation of help by shaping expectations and building morale. This serves to relieve suffering.
3. Provide new learning experiences through the methods used and identification of the sources of one's suffering. This learning is also experiential in nature to engage emotions since intellectual insight alone is insufficient.
4. Arouse emotions to motivate those seeking help to endure the suffering needed to make necessary changes, break up old patterns and facilitate creation of new ones, demonstrate to those seeking help that they possess the capacity to deal with intense emotions that they fear, and encourage reflection on these experiences.
5. Bolster the sufferer's sense of esteem and control by providing a conceptual scheme that helps to explain problems and related distress that feel confusing and incomprehensible and render them in words that increase options and the ability to exercise control over them. Convince those seeking help that they have made progress through their own efforts.
6. Provide opportunities for practice of what has been learned.

Though the power of myth and ritual on human lives has become diminished, if not completely banished, with the rise of modernism and the subsequent "disenchantment of the world" (Eliade, 1959), Frank and Frank accurately point out that they can, and often do, continue to exercise a potent impact on one's experience and behavior. This again makes complete sense when looked at from a developmental perspective, as the mythic level of consciousness is one stage that all human beings must negotiate in order to progress to the rational stage associated with modernism. As described by Wilber (1998), the movement from one stage to the next in the process of growth is one of differentiation and integration. Differentiation is separating from the perspective and understanding of oneself and the world at an earlier stage. This is followed by integration of the new, deeper, more inclusive perspective of the subsequent stage. Differentiation is distinguished from dissociation, in which an attempt is made to disown or push away beliefs and values from earlier levels of consciousness. As Wilber (1999) warns, "...each level of consciousness and wave of existence...is, in its healthy form, an absolutely necessary and desirable element of the overall spiral, the overall spectrum of experience" (p. 129).

What this first means is that earlier understandings of reality, while no longer dominant, remain intact and available to us. Despite the rational, secular, and scientific worldview that is now more prevalent, we are still able to be attuned to and influenced by earlier worldviews such as embodied in myth and rituals. Images, metaphors, and rites are understood at a literal level from the vantage point of the mythic stage. Because we are still able to operate from that stage, mythic material may be taken literally and concretely. As will be described later, the tendency to take metaphors literally is a common feature of self-deception and brings with it a number of hazards. Nonetheless, myth and ritual may also exert a powerful influence on the thoughts and emotions of individuals that can be conducive to promoting healing, as noted by Frank and Frank. They write:

> Methods of supernatural healing highlight the close interplay between assumptive systems and emotional states and the intimate relations of both to health and illness. Healing rituals also bring out the parallels between inner disorganization and disturbed relations with one's group, and illustrate the healing power of patterned interactions of patient, healer and group within the framework of an internally consistent assumptive world. Finally, certain properties of healing rituals in nonindustrialized societies resemble naturalistic methods of psychotherapy in ways that may serve to increase our understanding of both. (pp. 87–88)

Another example of an approach to healing that sees myth and ritual as valuable means of promoting healing comes from the *transpersonal medical model*, a spiritually oriented perspective whose goal is to help those who are suffering to realize their inherent completeness and divinity (Lawlis, 2013). This model subscribes to the extensive work on mythology done by Joseph Campbell (1949, 1988) and the influence of the work of Carl Jung on his thinking. According to Campbell, myths play a significant role in how people live their lives by providing a sense of meaning and purpose. Based on his study of myths across time and place, Campbell put forth the idea of the mono-myth, noting that despite diversity there are variations on a single significant story that he called the "Hero's Journey." He believed that this commonality also spoke to a psychic unity of humankind. Such persistent themes demonstrate how beneath all visible phenomena lies an eternal transcendent source that expresses itself in life, time, suffering, and death. Thus, myth as metaphor (which literally means to "carry beyond") is intended to point to something beyond itself—that is, to something transcendent.

The Hero's Journey relates the story of persons who receive a call to embark on a quest that at first they are reluctant to respond to because of the demands and dangers involved. However, in spite of this they engage in the quest, enduring great suffering and facing dangers while receiving aid along the way. Eventually, they have an experience of an eternal source of power and wisdom and return from the quest with gifts that have the power to set society free. In looking at the key elements of the Hero's Journey, parallels to the process related to the wounded healer or the call of the shaman emerge. The relevance of this to what it means to become a radical healer will be explored in more depth in the next chapter. Additionally, the four functions of myth described by Campbell (1988) are pertinent to an ideology with an all-encompassing worldview that exerts a powerful influence on individuals' beliefs, values, and behaviors. These are:

1. Mystical/metaphysical: Referring to a transcendental reality that cannot be captured in words or images and evokes a sense of awe and gratitude in those who encounter it. Enactment through ritual can serve as a means of evoking an experience of the ultimate mystery and one's ability to participate in it.
2. Cosmological: An over-arching, comprehensive framework from which to understand life, nature, and the workings of the universe.
3. Social: A means of validating and supporting the existing social order.
4. Pedagogical/psychological: A guide to individuals as they move through various stages of life.

The transpersonal medical model advanced by Lawlis (2013) agrees with the observations of Frank and Frank (1999) that substantial value not only can be gained but applied from ancient healing practices and the need to see healing as taking into account the whole person. An important function of healing is to draw on the natural resources of individuals to promote their well-being in conjunction with locating and connecting with external resources and supports. It must also invoke the will of sufferers to believe in and commit to positive change and inspire hope and positive expectation. Lawlis points out that the decision to be healed and to embrace a plan of action in accordance with that goal is a crucial step toward transformative growth when confronted with a crisis. As such, the crisis can be understood as a valuable wake-up call that needs to be recognized both by the healer and the one seeking help.

Lawlis adds a much needed dimension for understanding the power of myth and ritual by describing through multiple examples how they do not act merely on a psychological level but also on a biological or embodied level. This assertion is based on the belief similar to that espoused by shamanism and indigenous traditions of healing that consciousness is not merely a mental phenomenon but is present at every level of existence—even down to the cellular level. Another point of agreement with these earlier forms of healing is the role that altered states of consciousness (ASC) can play in enabling those who are suffering to change their perception of their problem, acquire useful wisdom about the origin and resolution of that problem, and lead to a transformative experience. One other powerful way in which ASCs promote healing is based on the use of the meditative practices used to achieve them, which can also serve to both enhance the attunement of healers to the experiences of those suffering and cultivate an attitude of compassion.

***

In summary, this chapter has examined a number of meanings for radical healing. This involved first challenging the basic assumptions of mainstream healing, especially those values and beliefs rooted in the dominant neoliberal ideology. Many of these values and beliefs are not only contrary to the aims of healing but are actually harmful, such as extreme individualism, the commodification of health, and the fostering of extreme inequality. This process begins with healers themselves engaging in a rigorous and resolute self-examination to detect those detrimental beliefs and values that they have internalized. It then progresses to an equally rigorous and careful critique of the dominant ideology, with particular attention to the role of oppression and other forms of social injustice in creating and perpetuating suffering. Because of this self-examination, the healer is better able to gain a deeper understanding of what factors play a significant role in defining what is health and illness, who is more likely to become ill or at risk of death, and how decisions are made regarding whether and what care is provided to those who are suffering. A radical view that is deeper, more inclusive, and integrative is thus achieved.

Another understanding of radical is discussed within a developmental framework in which higher stages of growth lead to greater degrees of well-being. Development is not merely personal but must also include consideration of the deeply social and spiritual nature of human beings. The goal of development is to achieve ever-expanding degrees of flourishing or the realization of human potential at both the personal and social levels. Adopting the work of Erich Fromm (1964, 1976), human beings can negotiate the process of development, moving in either a progressive/life-promoting direction or a regressive/death-affirming direction. Managing the fear and anxiety that are inherent in human experience, as well as the way in which prevailing social conditions foster fear and insecurity, influences how individuals deal with this polarity of life vs. death.

Finally, the roots of healing are explored by examining the earliest forms of the practice of healing: shamanism and indigenous traditions. Valuable and enduring insights and values about the role of the healer and the healing process are gained from this examination. These include the interconnectedness of all the various aspects of the human person as well as between the person and his/her community, the natural world, and a spiritual dimension; the wounded healer; health as harmony and balance; the role of ASCs in promoting healing; the cultivation of hope and positive expectations in healing; and the potential power of myth and ritual as part of the healing process. These various points will be considered in greater detail in later chapters.

Chapter 3

The Call to be a Healer

A Brief Excursus into the Spiritual Foundations of Healing

In this chapter I expand on some of the ideas discussed in the previous chapter in order to further explore and explicate radical dimensions of healing. I particularly focus on two central elements of becoming and being a healer. The first is understanding healing as a vocation—more specifically, as originating in a call issued from a higher or transcendent source. This call, as previously described, is not "toll free." It is accompanied by demands and expectations that lead to those called experiencing a crisis accompanied by a sense of upheaval, distress, and suffering. Those accepting the call must be willing to engage in a rigorous and sometimes frightening process in which they experience a sense of brokenness, fragmentation, and dis-integration. These experiences give way to the realization that they must relinquish their former sense of identity and understanding of life. This can culminate in a "dying to self" that paves the way for a profound transformation. After emerging from this process, individuals may acquire certain benefits/gifts. These include special insights/abilities, a deeper capacity for compassion, and power/charisma that enable them to be of true service to others.

The second idea to be explored further, connected with the first, is that of the "wounded healer"—that is, the ability to make one's own wounds a source of healing not only for oneself but for others. By moving from a state of brokenness to wholeness, darkness to light, alienation to integration, death to life, the healer is better enabled and empowered to assist others to make a similar journey and achieve a similar life-changing transformation.

A deeper examination of these two essential elements of the vocation of healing builds on the discussion in the previous chapter of the various tasks that healers must be willing to undertake in order to be faithful to the vocation they have chosen. The goal of this process is to refine and transform as much as possible what is an essential, although not exclusive, element of healing: the personhood of the healers themselves. Similar to the reflections of Parker Palmer on what is required for those who choose the vocation of teaching, *the transformative potential of the healing process and transformation of those who seek to be healed begins in the transformed heart, mind, and spirit of the healer.* This means uncovering how our heart, mind, and spirit "...have been deformed by lust for power, by our fear of mutually accountable relationships, by our self-destructive tendency toward an alienated life" (Palmer, 1993, p. 108). It also means embracing with both courage and humility the inherently paradoxical nature of human experience and the contradictions and imperfections of being human. This is all, of course, quite daunting and may be experienced as sufficiently frightening to dissuade many from this path. However, what must be borne in mind is that what I am describing is an ideal that those who seek to serve must aspire to. It is a commitment to what is actually ongoing progress toward that ideal.

The paradoxes that must be negotiated are inherent in the process of transformation itself. This is because of where that call originates. This can best be understood through the work of the theologian Rudolf Otto (1958) regarding the source of the call: a higher or transcendent reality (what I term the Absolute). Otto describes how human beings experience amazement, stupor, wonder, and speechless astonishment when encountering the Holy or what he described as the *numinous*. What is experienced in this encounter is a sense of awe that reveals the inherently paradoxical nature of the Absolute. This is conveyed in the two meanings of awe. One is the experience as awe-some, and so is accompanied by feelings of attraction, fascination, bliss, and captivation. The other is the experience as awe-ful, accompanied by feelings of dread, horror, repulsion, and the uncanny.

It is no surprise that those receiving a call from the Absolute respond with a deep sense of ambivalence. First there is the recognition that answering the call will be arduous and painful and require sacrificing what one believes to be important, true, and valued. However, this is accompanied by the promise that undergoing the experience of purgation, purification, and the relinquishing of the attachments that make up one's ego will lead to the realization of one's essential identity with the Absolute. The attainment of this sense of wholeness, harmony, and bliss enables healers to work with others in order to bring about the same transformation.

This discussion makes clear that any understanding of healing as a vocation requires us to recognize the essentially spiritual dimension of being human. This was previously described as the sphere of existence called the Überwelt or one's relation to a transcendent order or ultimate concern (Tillich, 1957; van Deurzen, 1997, 2002). This spiritual dimension of healing forms the foundation for the later discussion of the dual roles of the wounded healer as contemplative and social critic (Nouwen, 1972) and the dual meanings of "radical" as expressed in both a personal (mystical) and social (prophetic) response to life (Fox, 1972). Likewise, in earlier works I (Gruba-McCallister, 1992, 2002, 2007, 2019; Gruba-McCallister & Levington, 1995) have argued that spirituality provides an essential framework for understanding the problem of suffering. Any serious study of the problem of suffering reveals that it is inseparably linked to religion and spirituality. Sadly, just as the role of larger social factors in suffering is generally neglected in the education and training of those in the healing professions, so too is the centrality of spirituality.

The subject of spirituality and the reasons for why it forms an essential foundation for suffering requires full discussion in a later chapter. However, given its relation to the call to be a healer, some preliminary points need to be considered here. While there are clearly elements which they share, a distinction is often made between religion and spirituality (Hartelius, Friedman, & Pappas, 2013). Religion is seen as "...a method for publicly and privately expressing a set of beliefs, values, symbols, behaviors, and practices relating to what is considered sacred" (p. 47). Thus, religion for some thinkers is embedded more in subscribing to a set of beliefs or creed, engaging in certain prescribed forms of worship or ritual, and membership in a community. In contrast, spirituality denotes the experiential and personal element of our relationship with ultimate reality or the divine and the transformative effects of this relationship (Nelson, 2009). What is shared by religion and spirituality is first the recognition that there is one ultimate reality or Absolute that transcends time and space and is ineffable in terms of conceptual and logical thought. Nonetheless, it is capable of being directly experienced and realized by human beings (Huxley, 1944). The Absolute is the Ground of all beings. All existence is a manifestation of this one ultimate Reality. This idea was found in the previous chapter's discussion of shamanism and indigenous forms of healing. Both espouse a belief in an essential oneness and interdependence that connects all beings based on their being expressions of a sacred reality or force.

According to the mystical schools of thought across religious traditions, our true identity is spiritual in nature. For example, in Quakerism this is expressed as "that of God" in all people. This does not to negate other aspects of our humanity but sees them as subsumed by and included within our spiritual nature. In accordance with this belief, all human beings have a mystical vocation of coming to know and live in accordance with their spiritual nature. Thus, our greatest longing, the most basic and powerful of all human needs, is the need for transcendence. This is the desire to experience the sense of wholeness and harmony that comes from reconnecting with the Absolute (Huxley, 1944). All other human needs can be understood as being derived from and an expression of the need for transcendence (Wilber, 1980). One way this need for transcendence can be fulfilled is by attaining direct knowledge of the Absolute. Such spiritual experiences can be achieved by means of a contemplative method, but also can occur spontaneously (Bucke, 1923). Based on this, the Absolute can also be understood as Consciousness (Wilber, 1977). Viewed within this context, the goal of healing can be described as enlightenment or the attainment of an elevated state of consciousness.

However, human beings encounter an inescapable dilemma in the process of seeking to know and affirm their true identity. This has been described as the problem of the ego (Huxley, 1944; Watts, 1951, 1961, 1966). It will be examined in greater detail in a later chapter due to the significant role it plays in suffering. In brief, the problem of the ego poses an obstacle to our need for transcendence due to a hallucination or false and distorted sense of being a separate self that is rooted in our socialization (Watts, 1951, 1966). The ego is also characterized as an illusion created by our powerful capacity for self-deception (Gruba-McCallister, 2019). This prevents our realizing or experiencing our essential unity with the Absolute and, accordingly, with our fellow human beings and the rest of creation. When taken to an extreme, we make ourselves an absolute onto ourselves—an extreme form of idolatry or narcissism.

According to mystical traditions, this resistance to recognizing our true nature and clinging to various forms of false identity is motivated by fear, selfishness, and greed. Of these, the most powerful and pervasive obstacle is fear. This fear can come from various sources, including rejection or alienation from significant others, the loss of control and sense of security provided by our worldview, and realization of the transience of the things to which we have become attached. However, as long as we refuse to surrender our ego, to "die to self," we will not come to a genuine understanding of who we really are. Instead we will experience alienation, separation, and a sense of brokenness that brings with it great suffering.

One of the best and most perceptive descriptions of the willful denial of our true self and its essential relationship with the Absolute is provided by Kierkegaard (1941) in his analysis of despair. In keeping with the focus here on healing, it is interesting that Kierkegaard described despair as a sickness, but likewise in keeping with the fundamental spiritual nature of this sickness also described it as "sin." For Kierkegaard, despair can be "cured" only by openly, willingly, and transparently seeing ourselves as essentially spiritual beings and by acknowledging that our genuine selfhood is both a gift from God and a task that God has set for us.

This discussion of the centrality of spirituality to healing highlights several key facets of responding to the call to be a healer issued from the Absolute. Otto's (1958) work on the experience of the numinous provides a framework for this. Receiving this call is accompanied by a confrontation with certain vexing paradoxes that evoke ambivalence. One paradox is that to experience a sense of wholeness that enables them to promote it in others, healers must first accept themselves as broken. This is the realization of how false notions about who they are stand in the way of achieving a deep sense of connection and relatedness with the Absolute. Another way this brokenness and lack of wholeness is recognized comes from encountering an inner emptiness that is the source of one's deepest longing. This prompts the search for what will ultimately answer that longing. Another paradox pertains to the need to assume a life-affirming stance (Fromm, 1964, 1976) that is central to healing. This is an incontrovertible belief in the value of life. This belief enables one to say "Yes" to all of the inescapable facets of life—positive and negative, joyful and tragic. This means that one must be prepared to undergo the most frightening of all experiences—a willingness "die to self" and endure the suffering that accompanies this—in order to achieve wholeness and the well-being this brings. This is the paradox of the inseparability of life and death inherent in the process of healing.

Contrary to what many might wish for, healing cannot be achieved by means of evasion of loss and the suffering it brings. Nor can it remove all suffering. Healing is not fixing. It is not making everything okay. Only through an open stance toward suffering is a deeper and more profound sense of wholeness possible, rooted in an experience of union with the Absolute. It is thus no wonder that intense ambivalence precipitated by recognition of these paradoxes is woven into the process of healing. Along with the promise of liberation that comes with responding affirmatively to the call of the Absolute—and the freedom and bliss this brings—there is also the uncertainty and dread provoked by the demands that the Absolute makes of us.

This description of what it means to be called a healer makes clear the involvement of another of the four spheres of existence. That is the Eigenwelt, or one's relationship to oneself. The importance of this relationship was a topic in the previous chapter's discussion of the need to engage in a resolute and rigorous process of ongoing self-examination in order to identify detrimental assumptions and biases. In the act of surrendering to the call of the Absolute and taking on the vocation of healer, individuals must realize that they put themselves at the disposal of not merely those who come to them to seek healing. More important, they must also place themselves at the disposal of the true source of their power and authority as healers—the Absolute. A pivotal element of healing is making oneself a channel or instrument of a higher power that then becomes the source of true healing. As a teacher and supervisor of students providing psychotherapy, I often reminded them that unlike other healing professions such as medicine, they only have themselves as the means to help clients. Their ability to be of service depends principally not on the knowledge and skills they have acquired through their education and training but on their personhood, their way of being. However, a correct understanding of their personhood must include a realization of their need to have access to a higher power to aid them in their work. This understanding of "personhood" and how it makes healing "radical" is rooted in two core roles and two core values. And it is to these that we must now turn.

The Radical as Rooted and Uprooting

Looking first at the work of Matthew Fox (1972), in keeping with the focus on spirituality he begins his explication on the meaning of "radical" with a discussion of prayer. Prayer has a number of different meanings. For example, Huxley (1944) notes petition, intercession, adoration, and contemplation. The meaning relevant to this examination of healing is prayer as contemplation. This is aligned with the methods practiced to cultivate openness to the Absolute and bring one's intentions and will in line with it. Fox describes prayer being a "response," meaning an answer to a call accompanied by a promise or a sense of conviction. It is done freely and with responsibility to see through what is being promised. When that response is radical, it is "rooted" (in accord with its etymological root) or comes from one's very core. It represents what is cherished and deeply valued by the person. This requires the capacity to assume a self-critical stance in which those called are willing to also be challenged and changed at a deep level. Finally, this deeper dimension transcends our rational and logical understanding of ourselves, others, and life itself. It is thus based on the ability to be open to the inevitable uncertainty that comes with being alive and to appreciate life as mystery.

Fox (1972) next describes two important directions of radical prayer. The first is psychological and refers to healers accepting their mystical vocation. He then outlines four areas of psychological rootedness. The first is awareness, which he describes as "...the capacity to be *wholly* where one is and be alert to the possibilities of enjoyment and wonder, awe and beauty, goodness and peace exactly where one is" (italics in original, p. 78). The contemplative stance is focused on the here and now. It brings the past and the future to bear on the present. This awareness is also committed to total honesty and unmasking and rejecting all elements of deception and illusion. The second area is freedom and letting go. Fox sees this as a process of growing in freedom to be oneself, letting ourselves be who we are (and likewise showing that same attitude toward others), and opening up to life in all of its mysteries. The third area is appreciation and savoring, which is meeting life with an attitude of thankfulness and a capacity for enjoyment. This includes living life both with a serious passion and a capacity for play and spontaneity.

Finally, and most important, a radical response that is based in contemplation makes it possible to undergo conversion or a change of heart that brings with it a fundamental change of attitude toward life itself. Fox describes conversion as a "high-water mark of one's spiritual capacity" (p. 89) or the culmination of the three previous areas of expanded awareness, freedom, and appreciation. The term *metanoia* is sometimes used to describe this transformation. It is achieved by passing through a crisis in which one experiences a heightened degree of fragmentation, conflict, and disintegration that shatters one's initial perspective and system of values. This is followed by growth that extends to the very roots of one's being.

As a result, there is a radical change in how one thinks and lives (Dabrowski, 1964, 1967; James, 1958). This includes responding to life by loving radically. This radical form of love or compassion is made possible because the boundaries of the self are extended to embrace the entirety of all existence in what is called the "unitive experience." There is a profound expansion of consciousness that enables those transformed to feel one with the suffering of all beings (even one's enemies). This bond is based in part on the realization that suffering is universal and thus a reflection of not only our shared humanity, but our connection with all living beings. This compassionate awareness has a moral dimension, such that one cannot regard the suffering of others with apathy or indifference. There is the desire and intention to not only respond compassionately to the suffering of others but to remove as much as possible the causes of their suffering (Soelle, 2001; Williams, 2008).

In Fox's discussion of the radical dimension of prayer as a psychological response, we find a description of the mystical vocation of the healer and the means by which this vocation can be fulfilled through the practice of contemplation (also described as meditation). Throughout mystical traditions, a common theme is that one of the principal fruits of contemplative practice is the cultivation of compassion, which is an essential element of healing. Because of its importance to healing, a more extended treatment of compassion will be pursued later. However, prior to this, a second element of the healer's vocation needs to be discussed, which looks beyond the personal and takes into account the essential social nature of human social beings.

Fox (1972) writes, "The way to encourage authentic mysticism is to encourage its sister, prophecy. For the radical lover moves beyond the world of the personal and the psychological" (p. 95). While compassion expresses the need to be *deeply rooted* in order to heal, accepting the call to be a prophet points to a different meaning of "rootedness." It is being committed to a radical social response to life in which the causes of injustice are identified and *uprooted*. This extends healing to the entire world and hearkens back to the assertion that oppression in its various forms constitutes the single greatest cause of human suffering. As Morton Deutsch (2006) states, "Oppression is the experience of repeated, widespread, systemic injustice" (p. 26). Radical healing is thus impossible without understanding the nature of justice. This includes a capacity for anger and moral outrage when confronted with egregious consequences of injustice. However, such anger does not negate compassion. Rather, it gives it direction and force by promoting activism for change that extends beyond individuals impacted by injustice to the social systems and practices that cause suffering. This is recognized by Fox, who writes, "I suggest that love today means before all else justice. Justice is the direction given to love" (p. 105).

The meaning of "prophet" here is different from its usual connotation of a fortune teller who warns of coming calamity. Rather, as Eagleton (2003) points out, prophets are those who speak out against the corruption, greed, and abuses of power of a social order (and the ideology upon which it is based), warn of the terrible consequences if this order goes unchanged, and cry out for reform and, if necessary, revolutionary change in order to restore justice. The prophet must be a fearless and vocal social critic and an agitator for reforming the status quo. Fox (1972) elaborates the characteristics of a true prophet. The first is personal re-rooting. In other words, justice must begin at home. Individuals must scrutinize the ways in which they engage in injustice and change these beliefs and values before being able to work for justice in the world. The second point, which we are already familiar with, is a reluctance to heed the call to be a prophet. This is evidenced, for example, in many of the stories in the Bible that describe the hesitance of those called by God to speak out against the "sins of a nation" and to stand up for the lowly and dispossessed. Those who criticize the status quo and challenge the powerful and privileged are often met with a range of reactions from indifference to ridicule to outright hostility. They may even, in some cases, pay with their lives. The hesitance one feels is another sign of a true prophet. In spite of these painful and frightening elements of being socially radical, the message of prophets (and likewise healers) is not just one of tearing down and sweeping away what is harmful and destructive. Another part of their important message speaks of hope and the promise of creating a new and fuller life. This third sign is related to the final one. That is imparting a vision that goes beyond personal transformation to create a new community based on a shared commitment to live together in accord with compassion and justice.

Radical Healing and Two Ways of Knowing and Being

Another useful discussion of the dual roles of mystic and prophet and the associated values of compassion and justice is provided by Nouwen (1972). He offers further insight into how the woundedness of the healer can become a powerful source for promoting the healing of others. What is called the *archetype* of the wounded healer has a long history extending back not only to shamans, but over 2500 years to Greek mythology, as in the example of the centaur Chiron. Chiron was noted for his knowledge and skills with medicine and other forms of healing. Carl Jung is credited with being the first person to apply this archetype to psychotherapy. This was based on his own experience of transformation and attainment of a higher state of well-being. This followed a very difficult period in his life that required him to deal with his own conflicts and emotional issues. In light of his experiences, he believed that healers are the principal instrument of healing and so must be suited to provide genuine care for others (Jung, 1933).

A number of studies have provided support for the frequency of histories involving abuse, loss, physical illness, and mental health conditions among mental health and medical professionals (Barnett, 2007; Farber et al., 2005; Rotenstein et al., 2016; Victor et al., 2022). Zerubavel and O'Dougherty Wright (2012) provide a thorough review of research on the construct of the wounded healer that includes both the potential benefits and hazards of how the struggles, painful experiences, and troubled backgrounds of psychotherapists can impact their work with clients. They assert that certain crucial factors need to be considered in discerning whether the experience of their own woundedness can be conducive to the healing process of others. These are the degree to which those with troubled backgrounds have done the necessary work to resolve those issues in a manner that promotes their growth and well-being, their ability to be open about their issues despite shame and stigma, and the ability to separate their issues and concerns from those of clients. Thus, the mere fact that individuals have been wounded does not indicate that they can translate their suffering into positive personal growth and a deeper capacity for compassion. It is what one does with their woundedness.

Nouwen also provides some valuable insights and practical guidance about how individuals' open and authentic recognition and acceptance of their suffering opens ways for them to be of service to others. Similar to Fox (1972), Nouwen identifies two ways to achieve liberation. The first is the mystical way, which is inner and personal and whose goal is to connect with the Absolute. The second is revolutionary or social and aimed at a total and radical upheaval of an existing order that inflicts widespread suffering due to oppression and other forms of injustice. These two ways are again not distinct or irreconcilable, and must be properly integrated, as Nouwen astutely observes:

> Therefore every real revolutionary is challenged to be a mystic at heart, and he who walks in the mystical way is called to unmask the illusory quality of human society. Mysticism and revolution are two aspects of the same attempt to bring about radical change. No mystic can prevent himself from becoming a social critic, since in self-reflection he will discover the roots of a sick society. Similarly, no revolutionary can avoid facing his own human condition, since in the midst of his struggle for a new world he will find that he is also fighting his own reactionary fears and false ambitions. (p. 19)

He then proceeds to spell out how these two vocations must be practiced in order to achieve radical healing. One way to engage in and integrate these two roles is to see them as two perspectives or stances that one must take in working toward the goal of healing—whether it be at the level of the individual or in reforming a sick society. More specifically, these two perspectives are ways of knowing or forms of consciousness that constitute a dialectic or polarity such that while they are each different, they are nonetheless complementary (Gruba-McCallister, 2002; Wilber, 1977).

What is meant here by "knowing" needs to be broadened. This point is made by Parker Palmer (1993), who observes that different forms of knowing are actually ways of being or, more specifically, being-in-relationship. He writes:

> The shape of our knowledge becomes the shape of our living; the relation of the knower to the known becomes the relation of the living self to the larger world. And how could it be otherwise? We have no self apart from our knowledge of the self, no world apart from our knowledge of the world. The way we interact with the world in knowing it becomes the way we interact with the world as we live in it. (p. 21)

For Palmer, epistemology or our theory of knowledge is inseparable from ethics or the values that inform how we live our lives. These ways of knowing or being, along with the form of relationship and the values that underlie them, are critical to my understanding of radical healing. Because they form a dialectic, embracing both ways of knowing and being and the ability to move fluidly between them as required by circumstance is necessary to address personal and social suffering. Acceptance of both is essential to promoting a sense of wholeness. This once again requires a tolerance for the ambiguity that is an inescapable part of the human condition. An extreme and one-sided approach to life, in which one side of polarity is emphasized to the exclusion of the other, is a central characteristic of all forms of dis-ease.

The first perspective can be described as *direct knowledge*. In this form of knowing, one does not experience a sense of separation between the knower and the known. Instead, they are seen as closely and inextricably interrelated. The goal of direct knowledge is to establish intimate and immediate contact with the reality that exists behind the language and symbols we ordinarily use to characterize or categorize something. The nature of the relationship between knower and known is mutually participatory. The scientist/philosopher Michael Polanyi (1966) describes this way of being as a personal "indwelling" of the knower with the known, such that knowledge is neither subjective nor objective but the transcendence of both. This is achieved by assuming an open, permissive, receptive, and non-interfering stance toward the known. Another dimension of this knowledge noted by Polanyi is that it is tacit. This refers to certain experiences or dimensions of reality being ineffable or beyond description. In other words, there are times when we know more than we can say.

Nouwen (1972) asserts that this form of knowledge is attained by means of contemplation or meditation. Contemplative practices are means of quieting the mind and the body, in addition to enhancing attention and concentration. Those who practice contemplation are able to become less reactive to internal and external events, dis-identify with the ever-changing content of their thoughts, and be more fully present to the here and now. With diligence and practice, they are better able to go beyond mere appearances and get to the core of the known. Directing that form of attention inward toward oneself, again combined with a non-judgmental attitude, is similar to the application of the phenomenological method described in the previous chapter. By this means, individuals are better able to identify biases and preconceptions that distort their experience and to dismantle illusions that cloud or constrict their self-awareness.

Nouwen describes the goal of contemplative practice as becoming an "articulator of inner events." In embarking on rigorous self-examination, individuals become more aware of the complexity and confusion inherent in their inner life. They also encounter many barriers to arriving at authentic self-understanding. Self-opaqueness is first the result of the powerful capacity for self-deception possessed by human beings (Gruba-McCallister, 1993, 2019). When confronted with situations that threaten our sense of security and control, we engage in a range of strategies to evade awareness of these painful experiences. However, social influences also play a powerful role in the fabrication of illusions and other forms of duplicity that contaminate self-understanding. This is due to the mystification of experience that forms the basis of much of societal indoctrination. Such falsehoods and distortions of our consciousness make up what Fromm (1941) calls *social character*—deep and unconscious beliefs and values that are the product of the dominant ideology. Mystification provides the means by which the formation of social character is both legitimated and disguised (Gruba-McCallister, 2019). Social control is best achieved by preventing individuals from becoming aware of the exercise of power over them and by having them police their own actions.

However, through disciplined and diligent practice one is able to strip away these falsehoods and distortions and achieve a more genuine grasp of reality. This awakening to what lies behind the veil of falsehoods promotes not only their own liberation, but the liberation of others. This is in line with the attitude inextricably tied to the cultivation of direct knowledge: compassion (Gruba-McCallister, 2002). The ability to transcend the separation between self and Other is based on the recognition of their shared humanity. This realization requires that the pursuit of one's own liberation be inseparable from the liberation of everyone. As Nouwen (1972) writes, "For a compassionate man nothing human is alien: no joy and no sorrow, no way of living and no way of dying" (p. 41). This means that compassion enables individuals to come to terms with suffering, their own and that of others.

The intimate and mutual way of being-with associated with direct knowing enables healers to convey sincere concern toward those who are suffering. This is done by entering with their whole being into the painful condition of another person, even at the risk of becoming hurt or wounded in the process. Radical compassion is the recognition that one cannot respond in a caring way to one's own suffering or the suffering of another if there are any reservations motivated by fear or self-interest. In perhaps the most revolutionary sense, it is the realization that in some cases this may require the ultimate sacrifice: that is, putting one's very life on the line. As Eagleton (2003) observes, martyrs are willing to give up the most precious thing they have. In other words, they are willing to sacrifice their happiness or life in order that others may thrive. What sustains healers in this weighty commitment, according to Nouwen, is faith in the value and meaning of life even in the face of despair and death, and hope rooted in a vision beyond suffering.

Though direct knowledge, as noted by Nouwen, is tacit and more intuitive, there is nonetheless some value and need at times to articulate or put words to the often difficult experiences that accompany suffering. This is because dialogue is an equally essential element of the healing process. The key is for the healer and the one suffering to understand that such use of language is not to be taken literally and so not get lost in the words. Rather, the power of language often can be found in its more metaphoric or even mythic dimensions. In such cases words are used as a way to describe what experiences are like. This is based on an appreciation that language can be used to point beyond itself (the literal meaning of metaphor) to some deeper or higher truth. As Palmer (1993) states, "Hidden inside our words, buried at their very roots, are ancient word-pictures which often tell us more than contemporary usage reveals" (p. 22). Care is taken to avoid words becoming labels and concepts that stand in the way of getting to those roots.

With these cautions in mind, seeking to articulate elements of the inner world of another can provide some degree of clarity for both healers and those they care for to better understand what they are experiencing. More important, engaging in this process can enable them to be of greater service to those seeking help at those times when they are experiencing confusion and difficulty in trying to put words to their experience. Finding a shared language for troubling and puzzling experiences fosters a stronger sense of empathy and understanding by enabling the healer to "speak to the condition" of the one suffering. When individuals are in the throes of suffering, it is particularly difficult to put their experiences into words (Gruba-McCallister, 2019). At such times, it is not unusual for their expressions to be vague or conveyed in a disguised or implicit form that serves to evade making contact with their distress. Helping individuals to experience their suffering on a visceral or non-verbal level can promote healing, but such experiences remain resistant to being openly shared. Still, when healers establish a deep connection with those in distress based on compassion, the hidden meanings embedded in these experiences can be brought to their attention by articulating or labeling them. This illustrates a key component of healing that makes the implicit explicit. The better healers are able to detect hidden meanings and uncover what is left unsaid, the better they are able guide others through the confusing morass in which they find themselves ensnared.

This description of direct thought, in particular its close association with contemplative practice, highlights the ways in which it can positively contribute to the healing process. However, direct thought also has some notable limitations and relying on it exclusively can even be detrimental. The suspension of judgment may convey a more open and accepting stance that provides a sense of safety to explore frightening and painful experiences. However, because it is based on a non-critical stance, it may be prone to take things at face value and not probe more deeply into what lies behind the obvious. As a result, it can fail to get to the core of another's experience and uncover hidden disturbing emotions and painful aspects of experience that individuals have disowned. These omissions can then lead to an incomplete understanding of what is inhibiting a sense of wholeness on the part of both the healer and those seeking help. Additionally, if healers identify too deeply with those in distress, there is the danger that they can lose themselves in their experience. As a result, they are less able to provide alternative perspectives or offer a different way of being-in-the-world. The creative use of difference or even conflict by questioning taken-for-granted assumptions or challenging rigidly held beliefs is a central element of promoting positive change.

As noted, there is a second way of knowing or being. Nouwen (1972) identifies this in what he describes as the "contemplative critic." This expresses the prophetic vocation of the healer. In this role, healers continue to show compassion for other's suffering. However, they also accept and express the moral authority to courageously speak out against not only the harmful impact of self-deception but, what is more important, the social injustices that cause suffering. This requires healers to assume a more critical and distant stance in which judgment is not suspended when trying to ascertain the causes for one's suffering. This more detached and critical perspective is a characteristic of *discursive knowing*. This form of knowledge, for example, is commonly associated with the scientific method. This is a means of acquiring knowledge designed to develop hypotheses about the object of study and then employing procedural rules to gather evidence to test these hypotheses. Discursive is analytic as it breaks down what is being studied into its component parts in an attempt to determine what is most basic about it. Various elements discovered through this process are then organized by means of abstraction and categorization. One result of this is the development of a theory used to explain the phenomenon being studied. In discursive thought, language and concepts function as a means of representing, classifying, or measuring what is being observed. They are a shorthand way of organizing data. Discursive thought is based on reason, logic, and objectivity. As such, it seeks to discover regularities, rules, or patterns that are regarded as existing "out there," independent of the observer.

It is not surprising that a good deal of discussion about what is essential to healing has been critical of discursive knowing. Among these criticisms are failing to appreciate the essential interrelatedness that underlies reality by fragmenting it into parts, reifying concepts or confusing names with the actual nature of the object of study (not recognizing the metaphoric nature of labels), and dehumanizing human beings by studying them as if they were things. These are concerns that should be taken seriously and guarded against. A particularly cogent example of this is criticism of scientism. This is a view often associated with modernism. It asserts that the scientific method, as utilized in the natural sciences, is the only valid way to study reality and establish any truth claims. When regarded as such, the scientific approach becomes dogma or an ideology that rejects all alternative means of establishing truth claims.

However, that said, it needs also to be recognized that discursive thought performs an important and necessary function. It satisfies the need that human beings have to exercise control over their experience by simplifying it and making it manageable. It does so in several ways. The first is that based upon the selective function exercised by the brain and the senses, it focuses on what is deemed most important to one's survival and screens out everything else. In addition, by categorizing experience and integrating it into an overarching theory or worldview, it enables human beings to create a stable, ordered, and predictable view of the world. The human need for control can, however, sometimes be so powerful that it is taken to an extreme. This is particularly the case when that is significantly challenged. The resulting experiences of insecurity and anxiety often give rise to significant suffering. Thus, careful consideration must be exercised as to how to give consideration to this need and to the potential benefits of discursive thought without letting it become too extreme.

There is a particularly important application of discursive thought pertinent to healing. This is when a more critical examination of the causes of suffering is needed to get beyond what may at first be superficially evident. This is especially true because those who are in the midst of experiencing pain and distress often find it difficult to take a more detached attitude toward their circumstances. The reason for this is that fear evokes a visceral response that inhibits the capacity for critical thought (Gruba-McCallister, 2019). This is the foundation upon which self-deception rests. The effects of self-deception can be profound in impairing one's ability to achieve true self-understanding or a clear understanding of a situation. Knowing this, in addition to conveying compassion toward those seeking help, healers must be able probe and question their assumptions in order to achieve a clear and complete grasp of what is contributing to their suffering. This is not just the case when the causes are merely personal. It is equally important when suffering has social causes in view of the power of ideology to obscure awareness of what is causing harm. This hearkens back to the prophetic role and the responsibility of healers to be committed to justice as well as compassion.

The ability to question, to challenge what is given, by means of discursive thought goes back to the inherent capacity of human beings to think dialectically. The dialectic is the logic of implication in which one thing always implies its opposite. This is because opposites are inseparable from and mutually define each other (Watts, 1963). Because one thing always implies its opposite, given any situation we are able to conceive that there is always at least one other possible way of understanding or responding to it. The power of dialectical thought to generate possibilities means that individuals are not bound to what is given. And this is what makes change possible. Another way to express this is understanding how the dialectic is the foundation upon which imagination rests. It enables us to think hypothetically or wonder. It allows us to act *as if* things were otherwise. The ability to conceive of alternatives to personal or social circumstances means that one can challenge them and, more important, change them.

This capacity for dialectical thought is indispensable to being able to make changes at the systemic level or performing the prophetic role of the healer. As Nouwen (1972) points out, the prophet needs to keep a certain distance from the existing social order to avoid accepting it uncritically. To be revolutionary one must recognize the necessity of discovering the roots of what makes society toxic and to then effect what may be a radical upheaval to correct these wrongs. Nouwen astutely points out that this examination must not be just focused outwardly. True revolutionaries are also willing to engage in self-reflection in order to find those same destructive roots within themselves. This is because they share the same human condition with others who are similarly adversely affected. By this means they are able to discern the causes of suffering that are avoidable and have their roots in the abuse of power, to expose the illusions that obscure awareness of these causes, and to conceive of ways that things can be otherwise. Contemplative critics are guided by a vision that sees beyond the trivial. They are willing to ask genuine and trenchant questions—whether posed to individuals or when examining the status quo—even if they are painful and upsetting. Only by getting to the core of issues at work can they carry out their commitment to discovering and fostering positive change.

The revolutionary potential of such penetrating examination is also recognized by Friere (1970) in his work on a pedagogy of liberation as integral to exposing, opposing, and undoing oppression. He discovered that the oppressed must develop *critical consciousness*. This occurs when they unveil the contradictions inherent in an oppressive ideology. Next, they must validate their experience of being oppressed, which is often denied by the system. This is followed by being willing to sit with the suffering caused by these discoveries in order to learn from them. Finally, they must give a name to what is happening to them, which then opens up a way of reframing it into a problem capable of being critiqued. This is done by means of dialogue conducted jointly by all those engaged in revolutionary action. As he (1970) writes, "To exist, humanly, is to *name* the world, to change it. Once named, the world in its turn reappears to the namers as a problem and requires of them a new naming" (italics in original, p. 88).

The illusions created by the harmful ideology that continues to enslave its victims are demythologized. The causes of suffering can be seen with fresh eyes. Once this is accomplished, it is possible to then conceive of an alternative vision of a more just world (*annunciation*). This gives way to action or *praxis,* the interweaving of reflection and action to bring about change. Though Friere describes this process as occurring on a collective level, as will be described later, this model of change can be equally applicable to healing on a personal level.

The Wounded Healer

Throughout his discussion of the healer as both contemplative and prophet, Nouwen (1972) considers how the woundedness of the healer can be a valuable resource from which to draw. He locates the sources of woundedness in the experiences of alienation, isolation, and loneliness, which are inescapable parts of human experience. While these experiences pose a threat to the wholeness that we strive to achieve, they cannot be avoided or summarily dismissed. Rather, they require us to enter fully into the affliction that comes with these experiences while understanding and accepting the accompanying risk and hurt. Within this experience of suffering, healers can find meaning and a sense of purpose that better enable them to help others do so as well. When healers open up to their woundedness, they are also better able to discern how the desire for praise and recognition, as well as fear of rejection or failure, serve to undermine a commitment to compassionately serve others.

In short, the wounds of the healer become a true source of healing for others when those wounds are recognized and acknowledged as an inescapable part of being human. This reveals a bond that unites all those who share this condition. That bond enables healers and those suffering alike to transcend the boundaries that separate them. Acceptance of being wounded likewise silences the reactivity and resistance that works to push away the discomfort and fear that accompany the tragic dimension of life. Nouwen (1972) describes how hospitality must accompany concentration when engaging in service to others. This enables healers to pay attention to others because they are not absorbed in their own needs and worries. Instead they create a welcoming space for those suffering "...based on the shared confession of our basic brokenness and on a shared hope" (p. 93).

It also makes it possible for healers and those they serve to extend a welcoming response to their distress and pain. Nouwen writes that a healer:

> ...is not a doctor whose primary task is to take away pain. Rather, he deepens the pain to a level where it can be shared. When someone comes with his loneliness to the minister, he can only expect that his loneliness will be understood and felt, so that he no longer has to run away from it but can accept it as an expression of his basic human condition. (pp. 92–93)

This resolute attention to the cause of an individual's distress also communicates another important message. Nouwen states that the main task of healers is to prevent people from suffering due to the mistaken belief that they can be free of any suffering. Rather they can offer the promise that suffering that cannot be avoided can be dealt with creatively. This is a significant insight central to healing as it is based on an often neglected distinction between suffering that is necessary due to our humanity and suffering that is created by the choices we make.

There is one other theme included by Nouwen (1972) in his examination that has significant importance not only to a task required of the wounded healer, but to the entire process of healing itself. That is the role of forgiveness and its relationship to the problem of good and evil. Forgiveness has been recognized as playing a beneficial role in healing (Sanderson & Linehan, 1999). For now I will examine the positive function played by forgiveness in terms of how it can enable healers to deal with their woundedness in a manner that promotes their wholeness. This, in turn, enables them to promote the wholeness of others.

We have seen that healing is an inherently moral endeavor based on the core values of compassion and justice. An example of this moral dimension was described in the previous chapter using the work of Erich Fromm (1964, 1976). He described it in terms of the biophilic and necrophilic orientations. This distinction is also viewed by Fromm as the polarity of good and evil. This is particularly relevant as historically the problem of suffering has been inextricably interwoven with the nature of good vs. evil, particularly when examined from a religious or spiritual perspective (Hebblethwaite, 1976). This highlights once more the religious and spiritual foundation of healing. This fundamental element of healing, as it pertains to forgiveness and its relationship to good and evil, was asserted by Carl Jung (1933) in a chapter entitled "Psychotherapists or the Clergy." His examination of this issue provides a valuable framework for the discussion here of the wounded healer. He writes:

> Healing may be called a religious problem. In the sphere of social or national relations, the state of suffering may be a civil war, and this state is to be cured by the Christian virtue of forgiveness for those who hate us. That which we try with conviction of good Christians to apply to external

situations, we must also apply to the inner state in the treatment of
neurosis. (p. 237)

The "civil war" that Jung describes is created when the conflict between good and
evil is understood as absolute and unresolvable. The point advanced by Jung is that
the relationship between good and evil is based on a fundamental law of life. He
called this *enantiodromia*, or the reversal into the opposite (an example of the
dialectic). This means that good and evil constitute a polarity in which there is an
inseparable and mutual relationship between them. The only means of ending the
"civil war" is by recognizing that what is evil can be turned to good and what
appears to be good can contribute to evil This is not to equate the two; nor is it to
deny the clear distinctions that exist between them. Rather, it is the recognition
that one cannot exist without the other. Both are fixed and inherent aspects of
reality. Seeing them as an irreconcilable dualism based on a one-sided and extreme
stance gives rise to ceaseless conflict, dissociation, and fragmentation—all of
which have disastrous consequences.

In the case of most people, this one-sidedness is due to their inability to
recognize and take ownership of their evil potentialities and proclivities. Because
evil is just as much a side of us as good, denying that side shatters our sense of
wholeness. Moreover, resisting the very worst about ourselves only serves to make
it more likely that we will succumb to it. Alan Watts (1966), who was influenced
by Jung's thinking on this question, writes, "No one can be moral—that is, no one
can harmonize contained conflicts—without coming to a working arrangement
between the angel in himself and the devil in himself, between his rose above and
his manure below" (p. 123). As he further notes, there is an element of "irreducible
rascality" that exists in all human beings, and acceptance of this in others requires
first an acceptance of it in oneself. In other words, there is virtue in healers
acknowledging their vices, frailties, and weaknesses, all of which they share with
others based on their common humanity. In doing so, they demonstrate a healthy
tolerance for ambiguity indispensable to their work. As Watts again observes,
"...the real goodness of human nature is its peculiar balance of love and selfishness,
reason and passion, spirituality and sensuality, mysticism and materialism, in
which the positive pole always has a slight edge over the negative" (p. 125).

Embracing the dialectical relationship between good and evil does not mean
that healers should ignore the destructive power of evil The dangers of evil are
very real on both an individual and collective level. Once more the values of
compassion and justice must guide how we must respond to these dangers. An
essential first step is ensuring that the workings of evil are acknowledged. Miller
(2013) criticized psychology's neglect of the subject of evil and related this to its
general disregard for the applicability of moral philosophy and theology to its
study and work. While he cautions that the label of evil not be applied globally to
wrongful actions, Miller correctly points out that certain human actions are vile
and destructive. This is because they jeopardize the very basis of human existence.
In light of this, he defines evil as follows:

Any act that destroys our trust in the reciprocity of human relationships and creates the belief that individuals need only look out for themselves...It seems that the greatest evils are perpetrated with the most deception and generally result in the greatest immediate advantage to the perpetrator." (pp. 232–233)

Another central feature of evil is noted by Erwin Staub (1989) who studied the causes of genocide. Staub states, "The essence of evil is the destruction of human beings. This includes not only killing but the creation of conditions that materially and psychologically destroy or diminish people's dignity, happiness, and capacity to fulfill basic material needs" (p. 25).

These two definitions highlight several key features of evil that need to be integrated into radical healing. The first, similar to Fromm's necrophilic orientation, is that evil is contrary to life and rooted in an extreme need to control others. Victims of acts of evil are regarded as things and so essentially stripped of their humanity. The second feature, closely related to the first, also echoes the work of Fromm as it associates evil with malignant narcissism. Perpetrators of evil display an inflated sense of self-importance and self-centeredness. Their degree of self-love is irrational and excessive, even to the point of idolizing themselves. This extreme narcissism and self-idolatry is described in spiritual literature as the problem of the ego, as noted earlier. Due to their sense of superiority, malignant narcissists are incapable of empathy for others. This contributes to their using others to meet their needs through manipulation and exploitation. This also gives rise to the destruction of trust in relationships, noted earlier by Miller (2013). However, their lack of empathy extends even toward themselves. In denying the humanity of others, they themselves become inhumane. Finally their extreme self-focus and self-concern divorces them from the natural world. Armstrong (2023) provides a cogent discussion of how this leads to a lack of reverence and respect for the natural world and its connection with today's ecological crisis.

The final feature of malignant narcissists described by Miller is how they are inclined to disguise their disregard and malevolent treatment of others in subtle and deceptive ways. One common means is by cloaking their actions in a façade of benevolence or concern. This pattern is echoed in M. Scott Peck's (1983) observation that evildoers have an extreme need to maintain a self-image of being perfect, righteous, and morally upright. To maintain this image, they vigorously resist acknowledging that they, like all human beings, are imperfect and capable of doing bad things. Thus, Peck asserts that just doing wrong is not evil. Rather it is the refusal to acknowledge their imperfection that distinguishes people who are evil. When confronted with their wrongdoing, evil individuals are quick to deny this and take offense. They cannot tolerate awareness of their evil actions because it threatens their self-image of perfection and causes them pain. As a result, they resist reflecting on their evil actions and so do not feel remorse or learn from their misdeeds. In other words, a central feature of evildoers is engaging in self-deception. They employ a variety of defenses to deny or distort their motivations and the consequences of their actions. One common form this takes is projecting their evil on others or scapegoating them. Another is to lash out at their accusers and take refuge in their presumed moral superiority. A variety of other rationalizations might be employed, including asserting that their evil behavior was based on benign or even noble motives.

This discussion of evil and the dynamics that give rise to it highlights another task for those called to be a healer in dealing with their woundedness. It is likely that the confrontation with their evil proclivities as well as with the evil they have done is the greatest source of their woundedness—as it would be for most people. Just as our natural and automatic response to pain and suffering is resistance or the effort to disown such experiences, so too is the case with our confrontation with the evil within. Jung (1933) described this process of disowning as giving rise to a part of the human psyche that he called the *shadow.* The shadow is unconscious and consists of anything that poses a threat to one's conscious self-image. These are negative experiences that cause individuals to feel discomfort, pain, or shame, as well as experiences that are not allowed or acceptable based on social norms. However, this strategy does not succeed in removing these experiences or in depriving them of the ability to continue to exert an influence on our thoughts, feelings, and actions. They persist in an autonomous form that at times can cause us to act in harmful or destructive ways contrary to our conscious intentions. In extreme cases they can even torment us. Moreover, the more we try to disown these experiences, the greater the degree of alienation we create. This not only results in feeling torn within and at odds with ourselves, but actually increases the likelihood that we will act on evil impulses or intentions.

Thus, there is a pivotal task facing healers who seek to mend their wounds, move toward wholeness, and derive from this process valuable learning that will enable them to help others do likewise. That is, they need to come to terms with what Watts (1963) calls the irreducible rascal or their dark side. Wilber (2000a) describes this as "cleaning up" or shadow work in which repressed and disowned material is brought to awareness and integrated into one's sense of self. This means admitting and accepting evil as an inherent part of themselves without regarding it as the "enemy." Inability to see that what we often believe to be the enemy is actually ourselves makes it more likely that we will regard others as evil and malevolent. One way to describe this process of coming to terms with "the enemy," noted by Nouwen (1972), is *forgiveness* that is rooted in self- compassion: "Thus the authority of compassion is the possibility of man to forgive his brother, because forgiveness is only real for him who has discovered the weakness of his friends and the sins of his enemy in his own heart and is willing to call every human being his brother" (p. 41). The ability to recognize our moral weakness, our failures, and the wrongs we have committed toward ourselves and others requires us to simultaneously suspend judgement toward ourselves and others. It requires that one be honest, humble, and resolute.

However, there is a substantial challenge involved in meeting evil with compassion or, as Jesus called upon us, to "love one's enemy." This is observed by Jung, who believed that acceptance of the shadow side of human nature verged on the impossible. Similarly, Joseph Campbell (1988), who was very influenced by the work of Jung, asserted that the most difficult thing required of human beings was to say "Yes" to that which is most abhorrent to them. Staring unblinkingly into the degree to which human conduct can be vile, destructive, and inhumane is indeed daunting. However, this pernicious cycle will never be broken as long as we try feverishly to evade or deny evil. So while healers must strive not to resist evil, they are nonetheless required to recognize it and seek to avoid its impact on them and others. Even though it is futile to eradicate the ever-present potential for evil to do harm, it is nonetheless proper to fearlessly call out and express anger toward injustices. Similarly, while healers should not pass judgment on encountering the very worst and most feared in those they help, they must also compassionately confront them with the negative impacts of evil actions directed toward them or others.

That means doing whatever is in their power to put an end to avoidable suffering on both an individual and collective level. This satisfies both the contemplative and prophetic vocations of the healer. Clearly this goal is an ideal—but nonetheless a worthy and important one toward which to aspire. As Cohen (2023) astutely points out, even those who have achieved elevated states of consciousness do not simultaneously achieve perfection. We are always a work in progress and must possess the courage and humility to struggle with our imperfections and flaws in the unfolding process of becoming. The distinction introduced here between suffering that is inescapable vs. avoidable is a central element of healing, and the different ways in which these forms of suffering must be addressed will be discussed at length in a later chapter.

Chapter 4

The Spiritual Foundation of Radical Healing

The Relevance of Spirituality

The integral relationship of spirituality to radical healing has been discussed in previous chapters. In the first chapter, spirituality was described as one of the four spheres of human existence, the Überwelt. This realm refers to human beings' relationship to a higher transcendent order that provides them with meaning, value, and purpose. The second chapter discussed the role of spirituality in the evolution of consciousness, noting that the highest state of development was achieved in the attainment of elevated states of consciousness that reveal our essential spiritual nature. Also, some form of spirituality was observed to be a pivotal feature of shamanic and indigenous practices of healing. Finally, the third chapter elaborated on the centrality of spirituality to radical healing in terms of how assuming the vocation of healer requires individuals to respond to a call from a higher power, or the Absolute. Some preliminary observations regarding spirituality were offered in order to provide a context for understanding the contemplative and prophetic dimensions of healing and their relationship to the core values of compassion and justice.

I devote this chapter to a more in-depth examination of spirituality that builds on this earlier material. The contributions of critical psychology and related schools of thought rightly provide a cogent critique of the adverse role that extreme individualism and the neglect of the substantial role of social suffering play in understanding and addressing a great deal of human suffering. As such, they are indispensable to radical healing. That said, in order to truly practice radical healing committed to compassion and justice, another element needs to be added to critical psychology. It is an area that has been equally neglected and maligned by current models of healing and by the dominant ideology in which those models are rooted. That area is spirituality or, more specifically, the teachings of the great wisdom traditions. The value of these areas has been recognized and integrated into transpersonal psychology and so I will be integrating this school of thought into my model of radical healing.

While the different dimensions of human beings all need to be taken into consideration, spirituality is the most essential. This assertion will become clearer when the nature of Spirit, as that which encompasses and integrates all the diverse facets of human existence and experience, is explicated. Recognition of the centrality of spirituality is essential to correct for the pervasive tendency to either neglect or give little thoughtful consideration to its relevance to both understanding and addressing the physical, psychological, and social sources of suffering. Indeed, in the history of thought, there is nowhere in which the problem of suffering is more thoroughly and deeply examined than by religion and spirituality (Hick, 1989, 2007; Rahula, 1974). As with critical psychology, a significant reason for the disregard of spirituality is the continuing predominance of a biomedical model of health and illness that is rooted in modern and neoliberal ideology. Likewise, a serious misunderstanding of religion and spirituality is found in fascist thought (Hedges, 2008).

A number of thinkers (Armstrong, 2023; Tart, 2010; Wilber, 1998)) have observed that we live in a largely secular age, or what the sociologist Max Weber (1993) described as "the disenchantment of the world." Significant reasons for the dismissive stance toward religion and spirituality can be found in modernity and the ascendance of science. The antagonism between science and religion/spirituality that occurred in the modern era is described by Wilber (1998) as the universe being seen as a "flatland" composed basically of matter. The preeminence assigned to matter was based upon the restriction of determining what is real to evidence gathered by means of sensory experience capable of being objectively observed and measured. The resulting image is of a cold, harsh, uncaring universe that has no purpose or meaning. Human beings are seen as fundamentally determined by physical processes and motivated to maximize pleasure and minimize pain. They are alienated from the natural world and seek to control and plunder it. Because mental phenomena or the data acquired by means of introspection cannot be acquired by objective means and quantified, they were deemed to be either unworthy of serious study or mere epiphenomena, by-products of materialistic causes. A particularly cogent example of this perspective is radical behaviorism (Skinner, 2002).

Based on this worldview, religion and spirituality are rejected as mere superstition and vestiges of a backward worldview characteristic of a prescientific era. They are dismissed as dubious attempts to make people believe that their lives have purpose. Some, like Marx, asserted that religion and spirituality serve as "opium of the people," making them passive and content in the face of injustice by the promise of happiness in the afterlife. Even with a more open attitude toward what has traditionally been understood as spirituality, it is not unusual for it to be attributed to underlying neurobiological causes (Newberg & d'Aquili, 2002)) or psychologized (Sperry, 2008), reducing spiritual experiences and practices to psychological constructs and denying their independent and distinct existence.

Spirituality has also not fared well in the current postmodern era. As Wilber (2000a) observes, there are beneficial contributions made by postmodernism. This includes its assertion of the importance of interpretation, context, and the need to privilege no particular perspective. However, postmodern thinkers have generally criticized the teachings of the wisdom traditions. This includes their rejection of any objective truth. An example of this is found in the work of Jorge

Ferrer (Ferrer & Sherman, 2008) regarding mysticism and spiritual experiences. Such experiences are asserted to occur entirely within the subjectivity of the individual and so are inherently private and have no ontological reality. These experiences may make individuals feel better, but they are not real in the same sense as objects in the external world.

There have been some half-hearted attempts to move beyond a solely materialistic view of reality and to modestly attempt to include spirituality as part of the provision of care to those who are suffering. However, we have seen that the claim of adopting a holistic approach (i.e., biopsychosocial with spiritual sometimes added) has been largely a pretense. In spite of the now voluminous body of research that demonstrates the impossibility of separating body and mind, limiting what is called "mind" to the brain, accompanied by neurobiological reductionism, continues to be ascendant. A major factor behind the persistent neglect of the role of psychological, social, and spiritual factors with respect to well-being has been financial, reflecting the influence of neoliberal hegemony. As literature on medicalization and the commodification of health (Boggs, 2015; Davies, 2022; Esposito & Perez, 2014) makes clear, immense profits by health insurers, health care corporations, and Big Pharma ensure that there are no meaningful challenges to the biomedical model. Moreover, the extreme individualism advanced by neoliberal ideology continues to situate the causes of illness and affliction within persons. Thus, just as little if any regard is given to the large body of research that demonstrates the role played by social determinants on health (Marmot & Wilkinson, 2006; Wilkinson & Pickett, 2009), so is there also a lack of any genuine acceptance of the importance of spirituality to well-being.

In assigning prominence to spirituality in the practice of radical healing, I am mindful of the need to avoid making the mistake of advancing a narrow and one-sided view of human beings. This will be made clear in my utilization of the integral perspective developed by Ken Wilber (2000a). This provides a framework in which the four fundamental dimensions of human beings are included to achieve a truly holistic perspective. However, given the neglect of spirituality, it is important to provide a definition of spirituality and explain why it is important to understanding what it means to be human. Similarly, it is necessary to explain the importance of spirituality in integrating different facets of human beings. In doing so, I am adopting the principal insights of the great mystical traditions that assert humans are spiritual beings. What this means is that spirituality must be seen more broadly, particularly as it pertains to the fundamental nature of not only human beings but existence itself. This more expanded perspective may at first seem remote from caring for those in need of healing. However, as will become apparent in this chapter, the place of human beings within the larger scheme of existence provides a framework for answering a number of questions extremely relevant to what it means to be human, what is our deepest longing, why we suffer, and how we can achieve liberation.

The Meanings of Spirituality

There have been multiple definitions and understanding of spirituality. For example, Richards (2012) discusses that despite widespread agreement spirituality is a universal human characteristic and capacity, there has also been considerable diversity in how spirituality is understood and practiced across time and religious traditions. To illustrate this, Richards compiles a detailed list of views of spirituality across multiple world religions and a range of different thinkers. As might be expected, there are some notable differences in how spirituality is defined and practiced in these examples. Western religious traditions tend to be more theistic and have a more personal understanding of the Absolute. In contrast Eastern traditions tend to regard the Absolute in more impersonal terms or associate spirituality with appreciation for nature or living in the here and now. Nonetheless, based on his comprehensive review, a number of common and central elements of spirituality can be derived. They include:

- A universal human characteristic/capacity or that which constitutes the essential nature of human beings
- A longing and search for the sacred in life, including seeking a direct and immediate experience of a transcendent reality
- A desire to find meaning, purpose, and value in life based on a relationship with or experience of a transcendent reality
- Living in a manner congruent with such meaning, purpose, and value
- Experiencing a sense of peace, connectedness, wholeness, wellness, and compassion for oneself and all other beings

One additional and valuable way of understanding spirituality is provided in the scholarly work of Ken Wilber (1977, 1980, 1996, 1998, 2000a), which is exceptional in terms of its scope and depth. It integrates material not only from diverse religious/spiritual traditions but also across multiple disciplines and over the course of human thought. Wilber's thought has been significantly influenced by what has been called the *perennial philosophy*, which he states has its origins in premodernity. It expresses the common core of the world's great spiritual traditions. Since I will also be adopting this perspective, a logical place to begin is by presenting the core tenets of the perennial philosophy described by Nelson (2009, pp. 122–123) based on the ground-breaking work of Huxley (1944):

1. The ultimate goal of life is liberation and enlightenment, achieved by means of cultivating one's spiritual life and culminating in a higher state of development and consciousness in which one experiences union with a transcendent reality. This experience is accompanied by feelings of harmony, bliss, and peace and the realization of the interdependence and interconnectedness of all beings.

2. Salvation is not found in material possessions or other forms of attachment that feeds one's sense of self-importance. Rather the path to enlightenment requires an attitude of selflessness, purity of heart, and trust toward others and the world. Contemplative practices that are aimed at relinquishing attachments, disidentifying from the ego, and shedding social programming give rise to self-surrender, a "dying to self," and union with the Absolute. This, in turn, results in compassion and an appreciation for the sacrality of oneself and all beings.
3. The Absolute that we seek and is our deepest need is timeless and beyond the world that we experience in our daily lives. It cannot be expressed in language or concepts and transcends rational thought. Nonetheless, it can be directly experienced and realized in mystical experiences.
4. The Absolute also has a personal, loving quality. It reaches out to us and invites union with it. Also, the Absolute sometimes becomes incarnated in human form to assist those who seek liberation through their teaching and example.

Another value of Wilber's (1977, 1980, 1996, 1998, 2000a) work is his addition of a developmental perspective to the perennial philosophy that helps to elucidate stages of the spiritual path. These stages are pertinent to both personal and social evolution. This developmental scheme not only enables a fuller understanding of the nature of the Absolute but also explains the essential connection between different levels of existence and of consciousness. As Wilber (2000a) asserts about the perennial philosophy,

> The evidence continues overwhelming[ly] to mount in its favor: human beings have available to them an extraordinary spectrum of consciousness, reaching from prepersonal to personal to transpersonal states...And the evidence says, in short, that there exists a richly textured rainbow of consciousness, spanning subconscious to self-conscious to super-conscious." (p. 9)

Wilber's (2000a) discussion of five common definitions of spirituality lays out this developmental dimension:

1. *Spirituality involves the highest level of any of the developmental lines.* This definition is based on the view that there are many different lines (or types) of development, such as cognitive, emotional, and moral. Based on this, spirituality involves achieving the most developed level of any of these lines. Wilber notes this is a common usage that sees spirituality as attainment of one's highest capacities and aspirations.
2. *Spirituality is the sum total of the highest levels of the developmental lines.* This is similar to the first definition, but while each of the developmental lines unfolds hierarchically (as will be explained later), the sum total of the

highest stages of these lines would not follow such a stage-like development. In this definition, every person's spiritual path would be individual and unique.

3. *Spirituality is a distinct developmental line in itself.* This represent a very important contribution made by Wilber, as the idea of spirituality developing along a series of hierarchically arranged stages is a more recent discovery. His model of spiritual development draws from approximately two dozen theorists representing both Western and Eastern perspectives.

4. *Spirituality is an attitude that one can have at whatever stage he or she is in.* This might include openness, love, compassion, or kindness.

5. *Spirituality is basically an elevated state of awareness (e.g., peak experience, enlightenment, liberation).* One key point made by Wilber that merits consideration is that how such experiences are understood and interpreted depends on the stage of spiritual development a person is at. This may also influence whether such experiences remain temporary states or are converted into enduring traits.

In the remainder of this chapter, I will expand further on these key elements of spirituality, giving particular attention to how they provide insights regarding causes of human affliction and the process of healing. As will become clear, understanding the nature of Spirit or the Absolute goes beyond locating it in one of four spheres of human existence but provides an essential framework for understanding all of them.

The Nature of Spirit or the Absolute—the Great Nest of Being

One cannot truly comprehend the nature and meaning of spirituality without a clear knowledge of the nature of Spirit or the Absolute. From the mystical perspective, there can be no question more important than what is Spirit. This is because it provides the answer to the ultimate question of what reality itself is and, accordingly, what is most essential about human beings. In other words, the first principle of the perennial philosophy is an ontological one that addresses the very nature of being. The mystics assert that the entire universe is Spirit. Given that spirit is typically understood as something insubstantial, otherworldly, invisible, and immaterial, Ken Wilber (1977, 2000a) provides a way to make sense of this assertion, drawing from diverse mystical traditions. Based on the modern worldview, the way we experience ourselves and the world around us is in terms of what is observable, material, and capable of being rendered into labels and categories. From this standpoint, there is no room for thinking of it in spiritual terms. As Wilber (1977) notes, a description of the conventional view of the universe is "...as a complex of things extended in space and succeeding one another in time" (p. 77).

However, according to the mystics, this view is illusory because it is incomplete and based on mere appearances. It is a result of a way of thinking that seeks to break down reality into its observable components and represent experience in terms of either/or categories. Because Spirit encompasses the cosmos in its entirety, any approach that seeks in any way to divide and segment it ends up leaving out something essential. Such a view is too constricted and superficial to capture reality with the depth and scope necessary to comprehend it accurately. Spirit is an expression of the essential interrelatedness of all elements that make up reality integrated into a seamless whole. In place of a reductionist view, exponents of the perennial philosophy view reality as various levels of existence ranging from matter to body to mind to soul and—ultimately to spirit. These are not merely levels of being. They are also levels of knowing or consciousness, as Reality or Spirit is likewise understood as consciousness itself.

These are truths whose evidence is derived by means of what Wilber (1998) describes as the eye of contemplation. Rather than restricting the means of securing phenomenological evidence to sensory experience and the application of logic (as in the scientific method), Wilber makes the case for a less restricted understanding of empiricism as experiential in the broadest sense. Experience can be attained by various means based on a set of injunctions or rules of which contemplation is a valid example. It is by just such means that those who attain the highest stage of development or consciousness are able to experience Reality or Spirit directly. Wilber (2000a) goes on to elaborate that these levels of being or consciousness can be regarded as basic structures of reality. What he means is that they can be seen as enduring holistic patterns of being and consciousness that form an orderly spectrum or continuum. They can also be seen as basic waves that emphasize that these levels are not rigidly separated from each other but rather shade and blend into each other.

Going back to the different definitions of spirituality described by Wilber (2000a), these different levels can be understood from a developmental perspective. In light of this, he proposes that the earlier term used to describe these levels—the Great Chain of Being—be instead the Great Nest of Being. The reason for this change is that it better captures how the different levels are interwoven and interrelated. It also highlights how, in terms of developmental progression, each successive or higher level subsumes and envelops the level that precedes it. This envisions Reality as a rich tapestry of interwoven levels in which the various elements of existence from the most basic and primary to the most advanced and elevated are harmoniously integrated within a multifaceted whole. Wilber depicts this Great Nest as a series of concentric circles moving outward, with Spirit as the highest level. While Spirit transcends as well as includes all the levels that come before, it is likewise the source or ground from which all other levels of existence are derived. In other words, Spirit is expressed and ever-present in all the other levels down to the material dimension. Matter is Spirit made visible. Thus, the common tendency to focus exclusively on the material dimension leads individuals to mistakenly take the material to be only what is real.

Additionally, the Great Nest, when understood as a representation of levels of knowing or consciousness, conveys the point that the nature of the Absolute is

Consciousness. Consciousness is thus a property of entities at all levels of existence. Again, this may seem not only counterintuitive but even nonsensical when applied to objects in addition to human beings or other animals believed to possess consciousness. However, there is growing evidence that some form of consciousness exists in what are regarded as lower forms of life. For example, Simard (2022) has done research on what she calls the "mother tree," which is the tallest tree in a forest. Her research has found that there is a web of interdependence based on communication by means of an underground fungal network that enables the mother tree to support seedlings and trade nutrients with other trees in need. Similarly, even the single-celled, brainless slime mold organism demonstrates a primitive form of intelligence by which it makes decisions and demonstrates a capacity for learning and memory (Reid & Latty, 2016).

While these findings may seem surprising, similar ideas have been found in early systems of thought. One example is the existence of a fundamental energy or force existing in all living entities, such as the Chinese principle of Qi (Jonas et al., 2012). Or the widespread belief among premodern civilizations that a sacred force or presence pervaded all of existence. including the natural world, with an essential bond between humans and all beings. The validity of this perspective can also be seen in the post-materialist perspective advanced by quantum mechanics (Wilber, 1977). As Wilber (2000a) states, the various levels that compose the Great Nest are "...*not* the product of metaphysical speculation or abstract hairsplitting philosophy. In fact, they are in almost every way the codification of *direct experiential realities*, ranging from sensory experience to mental experience to spiritual experience" (italics in original, p. 8). Thus, one can access the spiritual dimension of life in many forms from everyday experience to elevated states of consciousness because it is everywhere and always present and available.

As raised in the previous chapter, attaining direct experience of Spirit as ever-present in all of existence is based upon a particular way of knowing that has considerable relevance to promoting healing. A consistent theme found in the mystical view of the Absolute is that those who seek to know it must abandon a dualistic or either/or point of view. A dualistic mode of thought, when taken to an extreme, is a consistent feature of dis-ease. Dualism is a feature of what was described in the previous chapter as discursive knowledge. This conventional way of understanding reality is based on bifurcating and analyzing it as distinct and separate things. One of the most common forms of bifurcation is based upon conceiving knowledge in terms of the duality of subject and object. The philosopher Alfred North Whitehead (1969) was a critic of this bifurcation. This is because some salient characteristic of the object is symbolized and, as a result, one only knows part of the truth. The essential unity of the universe is lost. This is compounded when our symbols or abstractions are taken as concrete realities. Whitehead calls this the Fallacy of Misplaced Concreteness. This error is also characteristic of many forms of dis-ease in which metaphors are taken literally.

Another reason why this typical mode of knowledge fails to grasp the spiritual basis of realty is because there are a number of inescapable paradoxes characteristic of the Absolute, as will be described below. These paradoxes are instances in which a dialectical or interdependent relationship exists between what may be regarded as opposites. The application of an either/or point of view characteristic of discursive knowledge thus fails to comprehend the important truths embedded within these paradoxes. They are important not only because of the valuable insights they provide into the nature of the Absolute but also into the nature of human existence and experience.

One such paradox is observed by Wilber (2000a) in his description of each of the basic levels in the Great Nest. He describes each level as *holons* of consciousness that are organized in a nested hierarchy, or what Wilber calls a *holarchy.* Wilber borrows the term "holon" from the work of Arthur Koestler (1967). Koestler saw holons as the basic building blocks of reality, an entity that is both whole in itself and at the same time a part of some other whole. Thus, wholes and parts in the absolute sense do not exist. Rather, all elements that make up the universe have properties of both whole and part. Which side is expressed depends on where the holon is within the holarchy. A holon may express itself more as a whole relative to levels below it and more as a part relative to levels above it. This polarity of Whole and Part, sometimes also described as One versus Many, can be used to characterize the Absolute.

This polarity is exemplified in what is widely regarded as the common central feature of the mystical consciousness across time and place: the experience of oneness or unity in one's direct encounter with the Absolute. What is revealed is that all of existence, as an expression of a single Reality, is a network of interrelationships encompassed within a single integrated whole. This unity or expression of wholeness does not obliterate the diversity that is encompassed within its embrace. As noted, both whole and part exist but are harmonized within the unitive vision of the Absolute. While there is One Absolute for which there exists no contrasts or opposites, this Reality nonetheless exists in perfect communion with the vast diversity of all things in a manner that allows each of them to retain their uniqueness.

Thus, seeing the relationship between One and Many, Whole and Part as opposed to each other or incommensurate is an error. It is based on our everyday experience of being riddled with contradictions rooted in our tendency to bifurcate and categorize. All contradictions and opposites are encompassed and harmonized within the compass of the Absolute (Arber, 1957). Paradoxes that defy conventional logic are incontrovertible truths regarding the nature of the Absolute revealed experientially by means of direct knowledge. This mode of knowing rejects all dualities that try to sever Reality and categorize it into particular ideas, concepts, or viewpoints. This stance held by the mystics has been called *"non-dual."* As Wilber (1977) observes, to say not two is to imply one, but the truth of Reality is neither one nor two. This non-dual way of knowing is an important element for understanding the relationship between wholeness and healing, the need to embrace the entirety of what it means to be human without exception or preference.

Returning to Koestler (1967), Wilber relates the polarity embedded in holons to two fundamental tendencies that all beings possess, what he calls the "Janus Effect." Wholeness is the *self-assertive tendency*, as expressed in autonomy, independence, self-assertion, competition, or aggression. Partness is the *integrative tendency*, as expressed in dependence, cooperation, or submission. Each holon must maintain both its autonomy or agency as well as its relationship and communion with others in order to function optimally within the holarchy. As Wilber (1996) observes, holons can be found at every level of existence. Thus, all organisms/beings must constantly negotiate the tension that may exist between these seemingly opposed tendencies. The way in which this tension is negotiated dictates whether or not development progresses.

To explain this, Wilber expands on the work of Koestler. He states that holons have four fundamental capacities: self-preservation, self-adaptation, self-transcendence, and self-dissolution. Self-preservation, or the wholeness aspect, describes holons functioning as relatively autonomous and exercising agency. Self-adaptation is a holon's capacity to function as a part of a larger whole, or act in order to preserve community. If a holon fails to maintain both its wholeness and its partness, it will break down in what Wilber calls *self-dissolution.* Conversely, holons have a capacity for creativity or establishing novel forms in what is called *self-transcendence.* The interaction of these various tendencies, when managed in a way that seeks to harmonize them and appreciate their interdependence, contributes to development or evolution. This developmental process eventually culminates in Spirit. This description of the need to creatively negotiate existential polarities provides an important understanding of the process of radical healing. This capacity to recognize and utilize tension or conflict in a productive and life-affirming way promotes individuals' development and evolution and, ideally, can lead to the attainment of the highest state of wholeness through the realization of Spirit.

The Nature of the Absolute—Transcendent

There is another polarity pivotal to understanding the Absolute that has relevance to understanding human existence. It occupies a pre-eminent place because in many respects it encompasses all other polarities. The two sides of this polarity are, again, inseparable and mutually interdependent. This interdependence is illustrated in the following quote by Huxley (1944):

> The divine Ground of all existence is a spiritual Absolute, ineffable in terms of discursive thought, but (in certain circumstances) susceptible of being directly experienced and realized by the human being. This Absolute is the God-without-form of Hindu and Christian mystical phraseology. The last end of man, the ultimate reason for human existence, is unitive knowledge

of the divine Ground—the knowledge that can come only to those who are prepared to "die to self" and so make room, as it were, for God. (p. 21)

When Huxley describes the Divine Ground as having no form, being beyond words and incapable of being conceptualized in terms of discursive thought, he is referring to the first side of this polarity, the Absolute as Transcendent. This transcendent aspect of the Absolute speaks to its total "otherness." It is infinite, beyond time and space, and impersonal—or, some would say, supra-personal. It cannot be grasped in terms of any words, categories, concepts, descriptions, and the like. Nonetheless, terms are used to try to capture this transcendent dimension of the Absolute, such as Godhead, Void, or Emptiness. These descriptors are not meant to imply non-being because the Absolute is Pure Being, encompassing all that exists. Rather, the Absolute is devoid of all particulars, distinctions, separate things, or any other form of categorization. Positive terms are also used to describe it, such as Abundance, Plenitude, and Perfection. However, no matter what descriptors might be used, they can only approximate the transcendent nature of Spirit. An encounter with the Absolute as Transcendent evokes a sense of mystery, reverence, wonder, adoration, submission, and gratitude. Individuals having such an experience may feel that they have been taken possession of by something incredibly powerful and utterly beyond their comprehension.

Several quotes can serve to further illustrate the nature of the Absolute as Transcendent. The first comes from the Eastern wisdom tradition of Taoism:

> The Tao that can be told of
> Is not the Absolute Tao.
> The names that can be given
> Are not Absolute names.
> The names is the origin of Heaven and Earth.
> The named is the Mother of All Things. (Yutang, 1948, p. 59)

The second quote comes from the great Christian mystic Meister Eckhart:

> Some people want to see God with their eyes as they see a cow and to love him as they love their cow—they love their cow for the milk and cheese and profit it makes them. This how it is with people who love God for the sake of outward wealth or inward comfort. They do not rightly love him for their own advantage. Indeed, I tell you the truth any object you have on your mind, however good, will be a barrier between you and the inmost truth.

As the first quote states, naming or otherwise seeking to categorize Reality ends up severing or fragmenting the seamless whole, the sheer "isness," of the Absolute as Transcendent. The direct realization of the Absolute noted by Huxley, as in the mystical experience, defies all expression. This ineffability is a common element of such spiritual experiences. One is rendered speechless. Just as a thimble cannot contain all the oceans of this world, no word or concept can contain the Absolute. Looking next at the quote by Eckhart, we find that he astutely observes that attempts to reduce or confine the transcendent dimension of the Absolute into finite things frequently have their basis in individuals wanting to impose their own particular needs, wishes, and priorities on the Absolute. The God such individuals seek is one that is intended to secure them some benefit or make them feel better. The result is a false image of God (idolatry) rooted in projection. This attitude is a consequence, as Huxley asserts, of the refusal to die to self and make room for God.

How then does one best approach the Absolute given its transcendence? There are three windows on the Absolute (Wilber, 1977) that offer three ways of coming to understand the Absolute and our relationship to it. The one most associated with the transcendent nature of the Absolute is the negative or *apophatic* method in which one attempts to describe the Absolute by what it is not. In Christian theology this is called the *via negativa* or negative way. In Vedanta Hinduism it is called *"neti, neti"* which means "not this, not that." That is, each time we try to employ some term or image to describe the Absolute, we reject it until we come to the realization of the futility of any attempt at description. By abandoning all such attempts to encompass the Absolute, we can eventually attain an intimate and direct experience of it. The negative method highlights the dangers of employing language and conceptual thought in order to capture the Absolute. This is especially the case when these efforts are motivated by fear and the need to exert control and impose order on what one is experiencing. As noted by Evelyn Underhill (1915), "Because mystery is horrible to us, we have agreed for the most part to live in a world of labels; to make of them the current coin of experience, and ignore their merely symbolic character..." (p. 7).

However, is language completely destructive to our seeking to establish some connection to the Absolute? As Huxley (1944) observed, the use of language is in many respects unavoidable and indispensable when seeking to make sense of ourselves and the world around us. Through the ages language has been developed by human beings to describe their experiences, communicate them to others, and establish some degree of control over the material world. In the earlier quote by Underhill, we find an answer to this question in her observation that words can function as symbols. This then is another window on the Absolute called the analogical or *cataphatic* method. It is important because it opens a way of discussing the other side of this polarity regarding the Absolute—that is, the Absolute as Immanent.

The Nature of the Absolute—Immanent

While the analogical method recognizes the limitations of language, it nonetheless acknowledges its value when it is used symbolically or metaphorically. This is in line with the root of the word "metaphor." It comes from Greek and means "to carry beyond." That is, the names, images, or other forms of representation of the Absolute, if not taken literally, can serve a useful purpose by pointing beyond themselves to a deeper truth. Thus, the metaphoric use of language serves to make the Absolute in some way intelligible and knowable to us. It provides human beings with ways to describe what the Absolute is in terms of what it is like. The ideas or symbols used are often rooted in forms that have their basis in traditions, cultures, and myths that are familiar and even meaningful to those using them. Though they do not fully capture the Absolute, they nevertheless provide some means of making contact with the Absolute or relating to it. And out of those experiences can come profound truths that provide our lives with meaning and purpose.

This second window on the Absolute is based on one of the central principles of the perennial philosophy noted earlier. Individuals can experience the Absolute as possessing a personal and loving quality. Alan Watts (1966), recognizing the hazard of trying to confine the Absolute using linguistic conventions, nevertheless asserts the value of poetic language. Appreciating this symbolic and metaphoric aspect of language enables individuals to discover the immanent dimension of the Absolute in ways that allow them to have some access to it. As Watts asserts, the analogical method enables us to recognize the immediate experiential realm as a source of true knowledge of the Absolute. One way that this experience can be achieved is through engagement in spiritual practices designed to purge ourselves of anything that serves as an obstacle to such knowledge. Such practices allow us to see the entirety of existence as a revelation of the Absolute.

It would be an error to state that making experiential contact with the Absolute is only possible in elevated states of awareness. An argument can be made for what I call *everyday transcendence.* Based on its immanent nature, the Absolute is manifest and present in all existence. Thus, one can also essentially encounter the Absolute in any of the vast and diverse forms that it takes. Soelle (2001) makes this case, noting that it is not just the experience that matters but how one understands and deals with this experience. She writes:

> In principle, mystical experiences are no different than those promised and celebrated in many religions. Mystical experiences are neither above nor below those heightened experiences described in religious language as being made whole, liberation, the peace of God, coming home, and redemption. The difference lies only in *how* mysticism deals with these experiences. Mysticism lifts such experiences out of the abstractness of religious doctrine and frees them for feeling, experience, and certainty. (italics in original, pp. 17–18)

Another example of this is provided by Armstrong (2023) in her book *Sacred Nature*. The natural world is an expression of a universal force or the revelation of the divine. Thus, in making intimate contact with nature and recognizing one's essential relationship with it, individuals are also able to make contact with the Absolute.

This discussion serves to underline why the polarity of Transcendent and Immanent is so essential to understanding the Divine. If the Absolute were solely transcendent, it would be utterly inaccessible, incomprehensible, and unattainable. We would be incapable of establishing any sort of relationship with it. Understood as immanent, the Absolute manifests itself in a multitude of forms that make it accessible to us. In other words, all of existence is a *theophany*, or the Absolute disclosing or expressing itself in all things. Although it is infinite, the Absolute communes with all of finite existence and participates in it in a very real and intimate way. This paradoxical relationship between finite and infinite is conveyed in the *Taittiriya Upanishads*: "Creating all things, he entered into everything. Entering into all things, he became that which has shape and that which is shapeless; he became that which can be defined and that which cannot be defined...He became all things whatsoever: therefore the wise call him the Real."

The perspective of the Great Nest of Being provides another way to explain this seeming contradiction. The Absolute is present in all things, but to different degrees. As we ascend the holarchy, we find that each level represents a higher degree of being and consciousness or a fuller expression of the Absolute. Thus, everything represents the Absolute but in its own manner and degree. As Dionysus the Areopagite states, "The Good sends the rays of Whole Goodness into all existing things according to their receptive powers." The Absolute imparts itself to everything in creation. It is, in turn, received to varying degrees by all things based on the level of being they occupy. Nonetheless, no matter what level they occupy, all things are transfigured by virtue of the indwelling of the Divine. This gives all beings a sanctity that requires that they be accorded absolute respect and reverence.

What this means, of course, is that human beings are an expression of the Divine. A state of union with the Absolute exists as an ever-present reality for every person—regardless of whether that state of union is recognized and experienced by him or her. As the Quakers assert, there is "that of God, the Divine Spark, the Inner Light" in all human beings. This constitutes the true identity of all human beings and is the basis for their mystical vocation. The immanence of the Absolute will be important to the later discussion of the nature, purpose, and meaning of this mystical vocation and the ways in which it is and is not realized and appreciated. For now I will examine what is meant by Divine Incarnation in the widest sense: that is, as an expression of the immanent nature of the Absolute.

The process by which the Absolute moves from a state of oneness to multiplicity by unfolding itself into diverse finite beings has been described as *involution*. This has also been described as an act of creation. The term *kenosis*, which means "emptying oneself" or "outpouring," has been used to describe analogically how the Absolute incarnates or embodies itself in plural manifestations of separate—and thus knowable and accessible—forms. As Arber (1957) writes, "...individual things are not lost and obliterated in the unity of God but transfigured, seen as more perfectly and uniquely themselves. For, if the unity of God is truly all-inclusive and non-dual, it must include diversity and distinction as well as one-ness; otherwise the principle of diversity would stand over against God as something opposite to and outside him" (p. 141).

Using the developmental framework of the Great Nest of Being, Wilber (1980) asserts that the relation of the Absolute to the manifest universe consists of two major movements. One is evolution in which the developmental process is directed upward toward the attainment of the Absolute. The other is involution expressing the immanent nature of the Absolute, which moves from the highest level down to the lowest in the ongoing act of creation. These two movements are inseparable and can be regarded as cyclic. This means that in order for evolution to occur, higher structures must be present from the start as potential in the lower structures. Watts (1972) makes this point powerfully:

> ...if the word "evolution" means anything at all, it denotes not the building of a tower to which more or less unessential trimmings are added when the main edifice is complete, but the unfolding, the outward volution of properties contained within the structure from the beginning. What, therefore, appears latest in time upon the surface will, so far from being unessential and superficial, be properties of the most deeply ingrained and fundamental order. Evolution is "matter" turning itself inside out so as to manifest its deepest powers, the things most interior and essential to its nature. (p. 86)

As this relates to human beings, this means that the potential to attain a state of unity with and consciousness of the Absolute is always present within them based on given fact of their essential oneness with the Divine. This union can be realized by means of evolution or ascending the levels of the Great Nest.

Based on this description of the interwoven processes of involution and evolution, creation is unlike what is depicted in Genesis. It is not a one-time event that has a specific starting point in time. Rather the Absolute is always already in a constant, ongoing, dynamic process of becoming. Beginning and ending as implied in a linear, time-bound view have no meaning in this understanding. As Armstrong (2023) states, creation is not attributed to some divine power external to time and space. Instead it is seen as a dynamic force working within everything or participating harmoniously in a mysterious self-generating process.

Stories of creation are found throughout history and across diverse cultures because they seek to answer significant questions pertinent to the meaning of life and death. These stories function as myths or an analogical approach to the Absolute expressed in metaphorical or finite terms. We encountered the importance and relevance of myth (and its relationship to ritual) in an earlier chapter to the healing process. Here again we encounter their potential value and importance to the work of healing. First, they poetically describe what might otherwise defy expression by means of ordinary language. Second, they are an important means employed by human beings to make sense of their experience and to give their life meaning. Their greater significance is asserted by Armstrong (2023) as well as in the work of Joseph Campbell (1988).

Armstrong distinguishes between mythos and logos as two ways of thinking, speaking, and knowing that are complementary to each other. Both are essential to comprehending reality. Mythos is focused on providing timeless answers to life's deepest questions. Thus, it provides meaning to life by focusing on what is eternal and universal. This includes enduring issues such as life vs. death, why we suffer, and the purpose of our life. She sees a myth as an event that, in some sense, happened once but continues to happen throughout time. The essential truths of myth become reality when they are enacted and embodied in rituals and ceremonies. Logos, on the other hand, is dominant in modern society. It is pragmatic, rational, logical, and focused on establishing objective facts that help us to exercise control over our world. This distinction is similar to the one previously discussed between direct and discursive knowledge.

When viewed from the perspective of the Absolute as Transcendent, seeking a "reason" for creation makes no sense as it mistakenly adopts an anthropomorphic view. To say the Absolute has a purpose or goal that it wants to attain is meaningless because it is utterly complete and sufficient unto itself. However, certain mythic understandings of creation have value due to their providing beneficial insights into the meaning of life. One explanation for why the Absolute or the One chose to become Many is offered by Sri Aurobindo, an Indian nationalist, freedom fighter, and philosopher. He suggested that creation is an expression of bliss or delight (*ananda*) on the part of the Absolute. Alan Watts (1966) calls this the Dramatic Model, which sees creation as a playful and aimless display in which the Absolute takes a diversity of forms spontaneously and freely. It is not done out of any sense of necessity or for any purpose. The Hindu term used to describe this is *lila* which means "play." Play is done for itself, just for fun and enjoyment. In a sense, the Absolute engages in a kind of masquerade with human beings by concealing itself and revealing itself. It wears a masked face that must then be unveiled in order to attain truth and liberation. Watts (1966) writes:

> In the Vedanta philosophy, nothing exists except God. There *seem* to be other things than God, but only because he is dreaming them up and making them his disguises to play hide-and-seek with himself. The universe of seemingly separate things is therefore real only for a while, not eternally real, for it comes and goes as the Self hides and seeks itself." (italics in original, p. 16)

This illusory donning of a mask by the Absolute that hides its identity mirrors the same process in which human beings retreat into an ego that must be exposed and abandoned in order to attain their true identity.

The second significant myth that seeks to provide an understanding of the mystery of why there is something rather than nothing posits that creation is an expression of the infinite and boundless love of the Absolute. While it is true that the Absolute is suprapersonal and thus no predicates and qualities can be attributed to it, throughout time revealed religion has sought to make the Absolute accessible and knowable. The most powerful way in which this has been achieved is by means of another mystery—that of Divine Incarnation. This was touched on earlier in terms of the Absolute as Immanent by pouring itself out into all of creation. However, seeing creation as an expression of Divine Love introduces a deeper and more profound understanding of the meaning of love and how it is central to mysticism. As Underhill (1961) asserts, "The business and method of Mysticism is Love" (p. 85). Caution must be exercised here because of the many different meanings that love has. A number of them fall short when referring to the highest form it takes as an attribute of the Absolute.

The love referred to in mystical thought is *agape*. Watts (1971) describes *agape* as the free, conscious, and deliberate desire to give oneself to God in an act of absolute self-surrender. Huxley (1944), as do others such as Underhill (1915, 1961) and Palmer (1993), sees love as more than mere emotion, but as a way of knowing. He writes, "We can only love what we know, and we can never know completely what we do not love. Love is a mode of knowledge, and when the love is sufficiently disinterested and sufficiently intense, the knowledge become unitive and so takes on the quality of infallibility" (p. 81).

In other words, love is giving oneself to another entirely and unconditionally. That is what is meant by love being disinterested. It seeks no reward. It is free of any egoistic attachments, needs, or demands. It is given freely and solely for its own sake. It asks nothing and refuses nothing. As such, it seeks to attain union through total relationship and fellowship with the Other. Quaker theologian Rufus Jones (Walters, 2001) observes, "Our religion—any religion on a higher level—begins with the fact that it belongs to the essential life of God to impart Himself, to give Himself in love, in sympathy and in fellowship, and to share his life with men; and the secondary fact that we are capable of appreciating such love when we see it and of responding to it" (p. 65). This love, again, is not a one-time act but a selfless and ongoing donation of the Absolute in every facet of existence.

What the doctrine of the Incarnation reveals, as noted by Arber (1957), is the possibility of an almost human relationship between the Absolute and human beings—that of Lover and Beloved. Love as *agape* is equally essential for human beings to attain unitive knowledge of the Absolute. As stated in the mystical classic *The Cloud of Unknowing,* "By love may He be gotten and holden, but by thought never." What is revealed in the Incarnation is the highest form of love that human beings can attain in their relationship not only with other human beings but with all of existence and thus the Absolute itself. It is an ideal that is the foundation for the values of compassion and justice—both of which are fruits of a unitive experience with the Absolute. The obstacles that stand in the way of attaining such love will play a prominent role in explaining how and why human beings suffer and fall short of achieving a sense of wholeness and harmony.

Perhaps the most powerful expression of the Absolute taking on flesh or becoming incarnated are those instances in which the Absolute is asserted to have actually taken on a specific human form. In Christianity this is believed to be in the person of Jesus. However, it is also found in other faith traditions, such as an avatar (Hinduism) or a bodhisattva (Buddhism). These examples are powerful instances of the Absolute relinquishing its exalted status and accepting in utter humility the imperfections of mortal existence. In doing so, the Absolute demonstrates the highest expression of compassion by willingly submitting itself to all aspects of human life and the entire range of human emotions, including those that are painful and even abhorrent. In this regard, Arber (1957) states:

> The contribution which the finite makes to the Absolute Infinite involves the experience of changes, frustration, grief, and loss, which are the very texture of humanity, and if the Absolute was not inclusive of personal individuality there would be no incongruity and irony—no comedy, laughter, and nonsense—no fruitful diversities arising out of differences of race, sex, and age." (p. 94)

This quote by Arber offers the most powerful and profound message conveyed by those instances in which the Absolute, by taking on human form, spares itself of nothing. It partakes as fully in life's painful and tragic dimensions as its pleasant and joyful ones. We witness this in Jesus dying on the cross and in the Buddha's making the end of suffering the central focus of his teachings. It is another way in which the Incarnation reveals the unconditional love of the Absolute, extending to a willingness to be fully present and participate in even the most painful and horrific human experiences. This is especially important because it is precisely at those dark moments that human beings feel most isolated, alienated, and abandoned. Underhill (1961) eloquently makes this point:

> If God, too, is one who suffers, then suffering is not simply something bad to which one can surrender or stand up in resistance. It becomes instead a reality that has something to do with the far-near God and that fits into God's incomprehensible love. The way of suffering that is not just tolerated but freely accepted, the way of the passion, becomes therefore part of the disciple's way of life. (p. 138)

Compassion thus is not just a gift of those who have experienced a deep sense of connection with the Absolute and have thus made the "way of passion" part of their lives. It is an attribute of the Absolute itself, demonstrated in a willingness to suffer with those who are suffering. This is a powerful model for those who devote their lives to the vocation of healing.

Moreover, in taking on human form, the Absolute provides invaluable guidance to human beings about achieving liberation. Such individuals are exemplars not only of the highest degree of development of which humans are capable but models for those committed to radical healing to emulate in light of their commitment to compassion and justice. The Incarnation reveals that our ultimate goal and purpose is to realize "...that we do not have to *attain* union with God. Man does not have to climb to the infinite to become God, because, out of love, the infinite God descends to the finite and becomes man" (Watts, 1971, italics in original, p. 74). The Absolute is incarnated in each of us, but most of us are forgetful of this fact. The call to fulfill our spiritual destiny must first be heard and affirmed if it is to be realized. This is asserted by Meister Eckhart, who stated, "Our Lord says to every living soul, 'I became man for you. If you do not become God for me, you do me wrong.'" And this mystical vocation again must be wedded to a prophetic one. The end of suffering is not just an individual matter but a collective one. Love as *agape* is pivotal to anyone who seeks to put an end to injustice. Such an affirmation that liberation must not restricted to individuals but extended to bringing about a more just and compassionate world is asserted in one of the most important scriptures in Hinduism, the *Bhagavad-Gita*. Krishna, an incarnation of the Absolute, says:

> When goodness grows weak,
> When evil increases,
> I make myself a body.
> In every age I come back
> To deliver the holy,
> To destroy the sin of the sinner,
> To establish righteousness. (Prabhavanda, S. & Isherwood, 1951, p. 50)

The third window on the Absolute, the *injunctive* method, needs to be described. This is a set of instructions for how a direct experience of and union with the Absolute can be accomplished. These methods can be found throughout the mystical traditions of diverse religions and take various forms. This diversity is valuable as it provides paths that can accommodate different interests, beliefs, values, and abilities among those who choose to engage in spiritual practice. However, amid this diversity there are also common elements and stages in the process that offer valuable insights into how to promote wholeness and healing. These will be explored in greater detail in a later chapter.

The Light and Dark Side of the Absolute

One further paradox inherent in the nature of the Absolute needs to be considered because of its pertinence to understanding the forms and causes of suffering and how they must be addressed in order to promote healing. This dimension bears on the earlier discussion of the problem of good and evil. Of all the paradoxes, this one is the most challenging and complex. The problem of evil—what it is, how it came about, what are its causes, how it should be dealt with—has been the subject of long study and constant debate. That being so, my examination will be mindful of these various unsettled questions and issues, realizing that any treatment of evil and its relation to good will be incomplete. However, despite this, avoiding any examination of evil, and its inextricable relation to suffering, makes any serious examination of healing impossible. As Nieman (2002) observes in her comprehensive examination of the subject, "To abandon the attempt to comprehend evil is to abandon every basis for confronting it in thought and practice" (p. 325).

Nieman asserts that the experience of evil gives rise to the response that it is something that ought not to have happened. This is because evil poses a significant threat to the structure of the world as we understand and are able to think and act in it. It strikes at the heart of the powerful need that human beings have to make the world intelligible and upends any sense of trust. This gives rise to efforts to make meaning of such events. When evil challenges our sense of morality (e.g., due to wrongdoing), it challenges our sense of fairness and is accompanied by a demand for justice. Thus, as Nieman observes, the study of evil raises both metaphysical (why does evil exist) and ethical (why do human beings do evil) questions that are impossible to separate. As she notes, these different dimensions resulted in the distinction made between two kinds of evil. The first is natural evil, which is woven into the fabric of existence and cannot be avoided. Examples include natural disasters, illness, old age, and death. The other is moral evil, which is suffering created by the choices and actions made by human beings. These two forms of evil and suffering need to be addressed differently.

The understanding of good vs. evil that I am presenting is based on the perennial philosophy. From this perspective, the polarity between good and evil must be integrated and embraced within the Absolute. When regarding the Absolute as Transcendent, any attribution of characteristics or qualities (such as good and evil), as we have seen, is meaningless. The Absolute is a unity in which any form of duality is impossible. That said, from a mystical perspective, all of existence is a manifestation or expression of the Absolute. That being the case, the reality of the existence of good and evil must somehow be reconciled with the Absolute. However, this has been regarded as problematic in many religious traditions. For example, any understanding of the Absolute as encompassing both good and evil is particularly foreign and disquieting to monotheistic religions that regard God as all-good, all-loving, and all-powerful. This is observed by Watts (1963) who writes:

> One of the principal difficulties which the Westerner, and more especially the Christian, encounters in trying to understand polarity is...the absolute gulf which our tradition has set between good and evil. It is inconceivable that there should be any common ground, let alone common cause, between God and Satan. The conflict here is seen to be ultimately real and serious so much so that the suggestion that there is some profound, inner level at which God and Satan are at one seems to be height of blasphemy. (p. 33)

One way in which this polarity can be understood is provided in the work of the theologian Rudolph Otto (1958). Otto describes how the experience of the Absolute evokes a sense of awe and mystery. This experience is accompanied by a sense of ambivalence in which individuals are both drawn to and repelled by their encounter with the Holy. This ambivalence is based on the two sides of the experience of awe. On the one hand, there is the sense of the awe-some (*mysterium fascinans*) in which one experiences bliss, fascination, captivation, and a sense of attraction. On the other hand, there is a sense of the awe-ful (*mysterium tremendum*) accompanied by the contrasting emotions of dread, horror, terror, and repulsion. Tillich (1957) describes the same ambiguity in terms of the Absolute being both creative and destructive, capable of healing as well as destroying. Another powerful representation of these two sides of the Absolute is found in Eastern religion. An example is the Hindu god Shiva. Shiva is a deity of ambiguity and paradox who is both benevolent (creator, protector, conferring happiness and blessings) and malevolent (destroyer, terrible, frightful, fearsome).

What these examples are intended to convey is, first, that the relationship between good and evil is one that cannot exist without the other. The Absolute is able to integrate and harmonize what would appear to be conflicting opposites through an inclusive non-duality and encompassing love. Watts (1963) gives an example of this, "In Chinese thought the essential goodness of nature and human nature is precisely their good-and-bad. The two do not cancel each other out so as to make action futile: they play eternally in a certain order, and wisdom consists in the discernment of this order and acting in harmony with it" (p. 54). From this mystical perspective, good is not equated with evil. While it does not deprive evil of ontological status, it does allow for evil serving a higher good.

When we move to the Absolute as Immanent, the polarity of good and evil becomes manifest or unfolded out into creation. This is due to the infinite becoming finite in the act of abandoning or expressing itself in the act of creation. Good and evil continue to be interdependent and inseparable. This point was made earlier in terms of the importance of recognizing the potential for good and evil in all human beings. Their interrelationship is recognized by the Christian theologian Thomas Aquinas, who wrote:

> There are in the world many good things which would have no place unless there were evils. Thus there would be no patience of the righteous, if there were no ill will of the persecutors; nor would there be any place for a vindicating justice, were there no crimes; and even in the physical order there would be no generation of one thing, unless there were corruption of another. Consequently, if evil were entirely excluded from the universe by divine providence, it would be necessary to lessen the great number of good things. (cited in Watts, 1972, p. 116)

As Aquinas observes, this polarity is not restricted to human beings but can be found in all of existence. Throughout the cosmos we can find the ongoing cycle of creation and destruction. In fact, seeing existence as a dynamic process of becoming necessitates how bringing about something new requires the destruction of the old and how life and death are inescapably interwoven. Death and resurrection is, not surprisingly, a persistent theme in myth and spiritual literature.

However, the necessity of accepting both good and evil, life and death is often resisted based on the fear that accompanies this realization. This fear can take many different forms: fear of pain and suffering, fear of the unknown, fear of judgment, and fear of the power and responsibility that comes with exercising free will. This fear is a part of the very process by which the Absolute becomes immanent in the act of creation. This goes back to the idea that creation is motivated by love, as described eloquently by Watts (1972), who explains that the Absolute finds its supreme finite analogy in love. Love consists of two movements: one toward union and satisfaction and the other toward separation and frustration. These two movements also form a dialectic that parallels the dialectic between good and evil. Watts explains:

> To love there must be a union with the beloved, but also a separation. For love is a creative tension; it is like the string of a musical instrument—a single string yet pulled in opposite directions. If there is too little tension, or if there is too much so that the string breaks, it will give forth no sound. The perfection of love is like the perfect tuning of the string, for love attains its fulfillment as there is the maximum union between two beings who remain definitely separate. Unity in duality is the law of the finite. (p. 141)

The separative movement of love is experienced as evil from a limited finite perspective. And this sense of separation from the Absolute is a consistent theme in how mysticism understands the nature of evil and suffering. It can give rise to a sense of brokenness, alienation, and isolation that fosters insecurity. As Huxley (1941) points out, it can be expressed by an urge toward separateness, along with a refusal to submit oneself to a higher power rooted in an extreme form of pride. Such individuals are denying their essential identity as an expression of the Absolute and instead making a god of themselves.

At its root, suffering arises from a refusal to accept that in the finite realm good cannot exist without evil. An extreme and one-sided stance toward life is incapable of tolerating the paradoxes inherent in human existence. The experiences of evil and suffering are often met with resistance and denial, rooted in the belief that the world should comply with our preferences and purposes and resulting in a sense of outrage and unhappiness when it does not. Because there is a refusal to see reality as it is, there is a strong element of both self-deception and self-defeat connected with evil and suffering. As described in the previous chapter, this is particularly the case when individuals refuse to accept their potential for evil and disown sides of themselves that are experienced as disturbing or dissonant with their self-ideal. The inner conflict that results gives rise to various forms of suffering that afflict not only the individual but extend outward into relationships with others and with the natural world.

Our capacity to be open and accepting of such ambiguity, even when it is uncomfortable or frightening, is essential to health understood as wholeness and a sense of harmony. From the perspective of the perennial philosophy, the Absolute makes a place for evil as integral to the ongoing process of creation and evolution, and permits it as it enables human individuality and freedom. The Absolute does not oppose evil but ultimately overcomes it through nonduality and encompassing it by unconditional love. The process of growth (and thus healing) poses an inescapable paradox, as experienced in the encounter with the numinous. The paradox can promote growth and evolution toward attaining our true identity and the experience of wholeness that comes with this, or it can trigger conflict, anxiety, and fear that thwart growth and leads to greater suffering. This examination of the Absolute and how the Absolute is embodied and manifested in human beings not only affirms the centrality of spirituality to healing. It also provides an essential framework for the material to be covered in the next chapter, which will explore its application to a broader understanding of the nature of health and illness and how one attains well-being based on the application of the principles of the perennial philosophy.

Chapter 5

The Causes and Forms of Personal Suffering

Laying a Foundation

In previous chapters I advanced the core assumptions and principles required to make healing "radical" and described the qualities and values necessary for those who choose to pursue the vocation of radical healer. These ideas drew heavily from critical psychology, while also including concepts from existential psychology and philosophy and transpersonal psychology. I will continue to integrate these approaches as this chapter exams the principal concern and commitment of those who practice radical healing: that is, to provide care for those who are suffering. In line with the interdependent values of compassion and justice, this involves two obligations. The first is to demonstrate an open, accepting, and caring attitude toward those who are suffering. When the suffering is due to reasons that cannot be avoided or changed, the intent cannot be to make the suffering go away. There are times when suffering cannot be helped. Nonetheless, in those instances compassion enables healers to connect and identify with those who are suffering and, in doing so, validate their experience. This helps to ameliorate their sense of isolation and fear.

This ability to unconditionally suffer with others, and in doing so feel one with their suffering, is based on our spirituality. That is, all beings are expressions of one Reality or Absolute; all human beings are interrelated and interdependent. Because this realization is present in all of us, our capacity for compassion is innate. As Williams (2008) states, as a virtue compassion cannot be selective. In no instance can suffering be a matter of apathy, which Soelle (1975) describes as the inability to acknowledge and participate in the suffering of the oppressed. It is equally important to realize that compassion for oneself is a prerequisite for compassion for others. An indifference to our own suffering not only causes us to suffer more but inures us to the suffering of others.

The second obligation continues to require compassion but involves circumstances in which the suffering is due to causes that are avoidable and capable of being eradicated. Soelle (1975) rightly asserts that it is a categorical imperative to strive to abolish conditions under which people "...are exposed to senseless, patently unnecessary suffering, such as hunger, oppression or torture" (p. 3). Encountering this form of suffering can give rise to a sense of moral outrage and invoke the demand for justice. When it does, the role of the healer becomes prophetic (Fox, 1972) and extends beyond attending solely to showing compassion toward those who are suffering. A commitment to justice requires forthrightly and courageously speaking out against social wrongs. The harm that injustice inflicts on its victims must not only be acknowledged but must be accompanied by concrete action to end such suffering by means of systemic and structural changes.

This brief summary recapitulates a number of critical ideas from previous chapters that will be expanded upon in this chapter as I shift the focus away from healers. The focus now is on the needs, concerns, and problems experienced by those they serve. This requires providing a more complete analysis of the roots and causes of suffering, the forms that it takes, the ways in which it impacts the different facets of human beings, and the means by which it can be addressed and, where possible, eliminated. In particular, I will describe how the way in which suffering is understood and responded to can either lead to greater degrees of affliction and harm or to the attainment of a greater degree of wholeness and well-being. These processes will be situated in terms of two dimensions relevant to understanding healing described in previous chapters. The first is the continuum defined by the polarity of fragmentation/alienation versus wholeness/integration and its alignment with Fromm's (1964) biophilic vs. necrophilic orientations. The second is understanding healing from a developmental perspective, as outlined in the work of Wilber (2000a).

Further, remaining true to my radical orientation, I provide a critique of a number of current theories and practices in terms of how suffering is negatively viewed and misunderstood. This leads to inadequate and sometimes detrimental impacts on those seeking care. These misconceptions are particularly due to pervasive contradictory attitudes held in our society that impair compassion and undermine justice. On one hand, there is a generally negative view toward suffering that leads to a tendency to deny or minimize its impact on individuals and its potential to promote healing. In these situations, the cause of one's suffering is typically misattributed to factors that deflect attention away from the true source of harm, exaggerate individuals' responsibility for their unhappiness, and invalidate the experience of the sufferer. All of these prove to be not only unhelpful but harmful. On the other hand, there is also a tendency to exaggerate what is wrong with individuals whose suffering is an expected, natural, and justifiable response to adversity, trauma, and unhealthy physical and social environments. Rather than see such reactions as attempts on the part of individuals to come to terms with their circumstances and try to give meaning to them, they are instead attributed to forms of pathology. This is accompanied by assigning diagnoses to them that prove to be stigmatizing, alienating, and invalidating.

Based on the individual vs. collective dialectic inherent in the human condition, individuals possess personal agency and are capable of directing their lives and influencing their circumstances. However, care must be taken not to exaggerate their degree of agency. As Jacobs (1994) points out with the concept of "world openness," human beings also possess an extremely high degree of species-specific dependence on the influences of their social environment. This is not only a reflection of the essential societal nature of human beings but also of the higher percentage of biological immaturity to the total life span of the human species. These two facets of human beings are highlighted by critical psychology. Human beings are able to exercise a certain degree of control over their lives. However, as social beings, they are often required to exercise this control in communication and coordination with others. In addition, individuals, particularly powerful ones, are able to exercise an inordinate degree of control and influence over others. In light of this, suffering has two sources that need to be acknowledged: personal and social. For the sake of clarity, I will look at these separately; however, the relationship between them is interdependent. We must continue to view the human person as a unity within which diverse facets are integrated. It is essential that a comprehensive and balanced approach be taken to avoid a constricted and fragmented perspective that is counter to promoting wholeness.

In the previous chapter I offered an in-depth description of spirituality as set forth by the perennial philosophy. Its understanding that spirituality constitutes the most essential dimension of the human person is likewise integral to promoting radical healing. This is not to deny that biological/material and psychological factors play a role in causing human suffering. However, these factors have predominated current discourse regarding both the reasons for why people suffer and what should be done to alleviate their suffering. The neglect of spirituality is rooted in the materialistic and individualistic emphases advanced by neoliberal views. This leads to an exaggeration of the role of personal responsibility for one's well-being and the corresponding obfuscation of the prominent role played by an unjust and oppressive status quo. It advances a constricted and incomplete understanding of what it means to be human. Spirituality corrects for this by asserting the essential oneness between all human beings and all of existence as a manifestation of the Absolute. Appreciation for the true identity of human beings provides a cogent critique of viewing them in an isolated and acontextual way. It also helps to dispel narrow notions of what constitutes health and illness. Recognizing the mystical vocation of all human beings allows for a broader and deeper way of understanding the roots of suffering and the path to wholeness, while still allowing for the role of standard biological and psychological explanations.

Buddhism and the Nature of Suffering

A good place to begin the examination of the personal sources of suffering is with important insights provided by Buddhism. Of all the spiritual traditions, Buddhism stands out for its placing the problem of suffering at the very center of its concern. This is a reflection of the spiritual journey of its founder, Siddhartha Gautama. The story told is that his father, Suddhodanna, a king of the Shakya clan, sought to keep Siddhartha sheltered from the pains and sorrows of the world to prevent the prophecy that he might one day become a great religious leader and not a king like him. However, despite this plan, Siddhartha discovered the reality of suffering by being exposed to illness, old age, and death, which stripped away the illusions he grew up with. He also saw a wandering ascetic seeking spiritual enlightenment, and this inspired him to seek answers to the problem of suffering. And so he left his home, his wife, his child, and his family and pursued his own spiritual path. After trying and rejecting various methods, he is said to have sat beneath the Bodhi tree and resolved to meditate there until he achieved liberation. He eventually attained enlightenment, which gave rise to the Four Noble Truths that form the foundation of his teachings. They are centered around the nature of suffering and how it can be overcome:

- All existence is suffering (dukkha). This is due to the inherently transient nature of life as reflected in birth and death. Illness, aging, and other forms of inevitable loss.
- The origin of suffering is craving, desire, or attachment (tanha). This can be thought of as clinging or holding fast to those things to which we are attached because of the pleasure they provide us or the significance we ascribe to them. It can also be a broader desire to be free of pain and disappointment or a relentless dissatisfaction that leads us to place more importance on having rather than being. Attachment is fundamentally rooted in the powerful human need to be in control in order to make our lives stable and predictable. In Buddhism, tanha gives rise to samsara (wandering), which is an endless cycle of life and death generated by persistent reactions of attraction and denial that thwart liberation.
- The cessation of suffering is achieved by relinquishing or letting go of one's attachments. This is typically achieved by means of some form of spiritual practice in which one learns how to disengage from the pattern of reactivity to internal and external events through the cultivation of acceptance and equanimity. There is an open acceptance of the ephemeral nature of life and an embracing of its inherent insecurity. Individuals disengage their sense of identity from attachments with which they have become identified and surrender unwholesome habits of mind (ignorance, greed, anger) that are the roots of craving.
- The final Noble Truth is described as the Eightfold Path. Whereas the first three Noble Truths are concerned with accepting and understanding the nature of suffering, the fourth spells out teachings for how individuals can end suffering. They are different paths to achieve enlightenment. These paths each have relevance to the process of healing.

Together these insights of the Buddha form an excellent framework around which to provide a more detailed examination of the forms and causes of suffering and the dynamics behind them. This provides knowledge and guidance on how to promote healing based on how one understands and responds to suffering and is in keeping with the values of compassion and justice. A logical place to begin is with the three forms of suffering or dukkha identified by Buddhism. The first, called *dukkha-dukkha* or inherent suffering, are those things that naturally cause us physical pain or mental anguish (e.g., physical injury, hunger, or illness). The second called *viparinama-dukkha* is suffering that is caused by constant change and the transient nature of human life (*anicca*) and our own impermanence (anatta). As noted previously, life is a ceaseless cycle of creation and destruction that undermines constancy or permanence. The third form of suffering, *samkhara-dukkha*, has its roots in what are called five "aggregates" that interdependently give rise to false ideas and illusions regarding the nature of the world and ourselves. The most important of these is the idea of an enduring self, or what I will call the ego. The ego consists of attachments to objects and persons believed to be essential to one's well-being and happiness. Destructive motives including greed, fear, power, and selfishness are the roots of these attachments.

Examining these three causes of suffering, we can see how they can also be organized using the previous distinction made between inescapable suffering and self-created suffering. A closer examination of this distinction and the diverse causes of suffering is essential to understand more fully what is and is not capable of change and how healing can only be promoted based on this understanding. Beginning in the 18th century, a distinction began to be made between natural and moral evil by thinkers such as Rousseau. As Nieman (2002) argues, the 1775 earthquake that destroyed the city of Lisbon had a profound impact in prompting diverse thinkers to reexamine the problem of evil. This distinction was part of modernism's attempt to not blame God for so much suffering in the world and place more responsibility on human beings.

Natural evil refers to the properties and forces of the natural world that cause harm. Illness and death can be attributed to such causes as can natural disasters such as hurricanes, earthquakes, and droughts. This description is clearly in keeping with *dukkha-dukkha*. But what about *viparinama-dukkha*, which is attributed to the dynamic and ever-changing nature of existence? It can be argued that this, too, is a function of the nature of things based on the connection between suffering and loss. An example of this is what Viktor Frankl (1967) calls the tragic triad: to be human is to be fallible, finite, and mortal. It is innately human to respond to losses attributable to things not going our way, our limitations, the fragility of our existence, and death, with a range of negative emotions that give rise to physical pain and mental anguish. The implications of loss for one's very existence will be examined further in looking at the third form of suffering.

Thus, the first two forms of suffering in Buddhism and what is referred to as natural evil constitute a form of suffering that is inherent in human existence, or inescapable suffering. The most distinguishing characteristic of this form of suffering is that it is beyond our control. It does not arise from something we choose or for which we are responsible. For example, it would be an unsound argument to contend that the natural world should be differently arranged and governed to prevent natural disasters or make illness and death impossible. This is because the very processes that cause harm are the same as those that make the development and operation of the natural world possible. This lack of control due to necessity is why the term natural "evil" has been criticized. As Nieman (2002) writes, "The mistake seems to lie in accepting the eighteenth century's use of the word *evil* to refer to both acts of human cruelty and instances of human suffering" (italics in original, p. 3). Similarly, Hebblethwaite (1976) in his book distinguishes evil from suffering because evil is more commonly connected with acts of cruelty and wickedness that result in suffering.

This moves the discussion to the third form of suffering, *samkhara-dukkha* or self-created suffering. This suffering is the consequence of human agency and choices made by individuals that cause harm to themselves, others, and the natural world. This moral dimension of suffering is particularly connected with human freedom and its inextricable relationship with the problem of good vs. evil. However, it is important to understand that while free will is certainly integral to understanding how suffering can arise from choices and has its roots in human wickedness, a complete understanding of self-created suffering is complex. This point is made very well by Briere (2013), who points out that while the case can sometimes be made that the conduct of evil requires free will, in many instances the reasons are actually murkier. He writes that there is extensive psychological literature that human behavior is not always under an individual's control, such as genetics, biological factors, mental disorders, adverse childhood experiences, trauma, and socialization. An interesting alternative that he proposes also comes from Buddhism. It is the concept of *dependent origination*, which suggests that the idea of unilinear causality is too simplistic. Instead, change is caused by the mutual and interdependent interaction of multiple factors. Briere (2013) writes, "...humans (and other beings) are embedded in a complex web of reciprocating conditions, actions, and reactions, across time, such that any given behavior may be influenced by a wide variety of causes and conditions" (p. 144).

This complexity is also due to the ways in which the distinction between inescapable and self-created suffering is at times unclear and how they are often interdependent. It does not in any way negate the suffering that results from either. Nor does it minimize or negate the capacity that human beings possess for doing harm to themselves, others, or the world based on cruelty or wickedness for which they bear some responsibility. What it does require is a careful balance between the values of compassion and justice when dealing with suffering, a broad understanding of the roots of suffering, an appreciation for the powerful capacity for self-deception among human beings, and clear attention to the social causes of suffering. All of these points will be considered in what follows.

The Problem of Self-Deception

An appreciation for the close interrelationship between inescapable and self-created suffering can be gained by returning to the role of loss in suffering. We have seen that loss is a fixed element of existence. However, a close examination of the way in which human beings innately react to loss (that is, how it is in their nature) reveals how this response can subsequently give rise to suffering that they inflict on themselves and others. At work in this self-defeating pattern are the dynamics of self-deception. I have provided a detailed description and explanation of self-deception elsewhere (Gruba-McCallister, 1993, 2019). Here I will highlight some aspects of self-deception that illustrate how certain innate aspects of human beings explain why they have such a profound capacity for it and how fear provoked by loss and subsequent resistance to the suffering it causes proves to be self-defeating.

Human beings have a powerful need for control that has been evolutionarily hard-wired into them. This need is expressed in efforts to impose order and predictability on their experiences to achieve a sense of security and stability and maintain a stable worldview and sense of identity. Loss is experienced as a threat to one's survival. This view of human beings' deepest fear has been proposed by numerous thinkers. One is the cultural anthropologist Ernest Becker (1973), who believed that much of individuals' character was formed around denying their mortality and that such denial was often the source of a great deal of evil. This idea is also found extensively in existential philosophy and psychology. Yalom (1980) asserts that death is the source of a primordial sense of anxiety and thus an extremely influential determinant of human experience and behavior. He supports this assertion with ideas taken from philosophers such as Kierkegaard, Heidegger, and Tillich. He also notes that this idea has been supported by empirical research.

A notable example is research that has been done in support of Terror Management Theory (Solomon, Greenberg, & Pyszczynski, 1991), which takes up Becker's assertion that denial of death and the threat of utter annihilation that it poses is a major human motive. This leads to efforts to make sense or meaning of it that may offer individuals some degree of positive protection from anxiety. However, it also fosters the creation of fictions and belief systems (e.g., manufacturing a false sense of personal invulnerability) that are perpetrated by social and cultural institutions. Thus, the manner in which individuals respond to death anxiety can be either life-affirming and promote health or death-affirming and lead to adverse physical, psychological, and social consequences.

These innate self-protective processes have been identified at a biological level and are the product of evolution in that they serve an adaptive function. The first example of this is an automatic response found in many species called the fight-or-flight response. It is initiated by circumstances that pose a danger to the homeostatic or balanced state that organisms seek to maintain. It is a concept central to the extensive research done on the role of stress in health and illness (Selye, 1974, 1976). A threat triggers a state of hyperarousal that mobilizes various parts of the body to take actions necessary to deal with the threat. The fight-or-flight response originates from the autonomic nervous system responsible for a range of automatic functions of the body (i.e., functions that occur without our conscious awareness). The ability to respond automatically and without our conscious awareness is an evolutionary advantage as it prevents a delay in taking action in response to danger that might prove to be costly.

Selye reframed the fight-or-flight response as the *stress reaction*, which is the nonspecific response of the body to any demand made upon it. This was later refined by Lazarus and Folkman, who found that two cognitive appraisals are made of events that trigger a stress reaction—again without conscious awareness. The first is whether the situation poses an immediate threat or the possibility of future danger. The second is whether people feel they have the necessary resources to deal with the threat. Both of these appraisals hearken back to how loss is experienced as a matter of life or death. The stress reaction, according to Selye, leads to a stereotyped series of stages that he called the General Adaptation Syndrome. The first stage, or alarm reaction, occurs when a threat to homeostasis (i.e., the need to maintain stability and control) is perceived and the body is mobilized to meet the threat. The second stage, called *adaptation* or the *stage of resistance*, is the body responding to cope with the threat and restore balance. However, if these efforts fail and the danger persists, the state of heightened arousal begins to cause the body to lose the energy and resources to resist and actually begins to inflict damage on the person. This *stage of exhaustion* can lead to illness and even death.

A second example of how response to loss can be self-defeating is described by Goleman (1985) in his discussion of the processes underlying self-deception. Once again, based on the process of evolution, the human brain has developed a filtering function. It is necessary to protect the brain from being overwhelmed by the vast amount of information posed by any situation and to pay attention to and gather information vital to survival. Humans use data to organize, categorize, and construct representations to make sense of their experience and impose order upon it. Goleman calls these basic units of experience *schemas* that condense data into manageable categories. These schemas are then integrated into a more comprehensive framework called a *worldview* (Spinelli, 2014) that is made up of fundamental beliefs, values, and attitudes about ourselves and life. Our view of reality is a construction in part forged by individuals and in part shaped by social influences. However, as noted, every individual's worldview is partial and incomplete not only due to the inevitable filtering process but also because the mind protects itself from anxiety by dimming awareness to disparate data which, according to Goleman, creates blind spots or lacunae that function as defenses to avoid pain. This becomes the basis of self-deception as a compromise is struck. A sense of security is created by narrowing attention by means of various forms of psychological defenses, while at the same time creating an understanding of a situation that is inaccurate and biased in line with our need for control. Experiences are distorted to make them fit with subjective assumptions that often have their origins in socialization. Human beings identify themselves with their worldview—along with all of their limitations, biases, and misconceptions. As a result, situations that pose a threat to one's worldview are particularly terrifying and lead to efforts to maintain it, even if it means essentially lying to oneself.

This discussion highlights another theme integral to understanding suffering. It pertains to the paradoxical nature of human life. The threat posed by loss can be framed based on the polarity of wholeness vs. alienation. Heightened experiences of alienation cause us to suffer. The experience of loss is frequently associated with conflict involving this polarity that results in states of disunity, fragmentation, brokenness, and separation—all of which are elements of alienation. A loss of integrity and wholeness and a sense of estrangement are characteristic of all forms of dis-ease. The role of conflict in suffering is highlighted by Moulyn (1982), who writes:

> We have been thrown into a terrestrial existence which is rent by many blemishes, imperfections, contradictions, unresolved problems, dichotomies, and fractures. These blemishes and fractures are inherent in the human condition and they are the source of the many levels of suffering. Inasmuch as we have to accept our being thrown into the world, we also have to accept periods during which we suffer. But instead of devaluing suffering and rejecting it as something that should not befall us, we ought to make an effort to become aware of the meaning of suffering. Its value and its meaning are that it heals the blemishes and fractures in our problem-ridden existence. (p. 4)

Examples of these dichotomies and contradictions have already been noted, such as life vs. death, good vs. evil, and love vs. fear. Likewise, when describing the nature of Spirit, we saw how it embraces a series of paradoxes. Because human beings are an expression of Spirit, they embody these same paradoxes and must ceaselessly negotiate them over the course of their lives. As Underhill (1961) observes, "We are amphibious creatures: our life moves upon two levels at once— the natural and the spiritual. The key to the puzzle of man lies in the fact that he is 'the meeting point of various stages of reality'" (p. 34). Otto (1958) asserted in his description of the encounter with the numinous how it gives rise to positive and negative responses. So, too, dichotomies or paradoxes inherent in existence can provoke a range of negative feelings such as tension, ambivalence, alienation, anxiety, and even terror that are forms of inescapable suffering. However, they can also bring about positive responses such as humor, wonder, or insight (Koestler, 1964). Further, as Moulyn observes, they can also be the prelude to healing and growth. It is the way in which we negotiate these paradoxes that is pivotal to understanding whether the outcome is suffering or healing. Thus, a more detailed examination of this source of suffering is warranted.

A Developmental Perspective on Resolving Paradoxes

This can begin by returning to the work of Fromm (1947), who asserts that there is a paradox distinct to human beings. Due to their development of reason, and with it a capacity for self-awareness and imagination, humans are both part of nature and subject to its laws and at the same time set apart from and able to transcend nature. Reason presents a blessing and a curse in that it creates an insoluble dichotomy within human beings with which they must constantly come to terms. Existence is thus a problem that human beings are required to solve and from which they cannot escape. As Fromm (1947) observes, "It is one of the peculiar characteristics of the human mind that when confronted with a contradiction it cannot remain passive. It is set in motion with the aim of resolving the contradiction. All progress is due to this fact" (p. 52). This requirement of seeking to come to terms with contradictions is a dynamic process that governs human development both individually (e.g., Erikson, 1950; Wilber, 2000a) and collectively (Hegel, 2007 [1907]); Marx, 1978). Different stages of development can be seen as posing a task that involves resolving a conflict related to a polarity distinct to that stage. An example is the series of tasks framed as polarities in Erikson's (1950) eight stages of human development. Moreover, the way in which individuals understand and seek to resolve polarities is shaped by the tools and rules available to them based on the level of development that they occupy (Wilber, 2000a). For example, at the earliest stage of development a primitive state of union exists between the infant and the world that is absent of dichotomies or distinctions. However, in subsequent stages of development, human beings are inclined to adopt a more rigid, conventional, and rule-bound worldview and, as a result, assume a very narrow perspective. Individuals at these developmental stages are generally unable to demonstrate an understanding of paradox and are incapable of dealing productively with the challenge it poses.

Fromm distinguishes between two different dichotomies that share similarities with the distinction between the two forms of suffering. The first, which he calls existential dichotomies, are rooted in human existence, the most fundamental being life and death. These dichotomies cannot be eliminated or evaded. They may provoke a sense of fear that can lead individuals to try to resist or deny them, often with futile and tragic consequences. Historical dichotomies, on the other hand, are created by human beings and so are capable of being resolved or eliminated through action. An example here might be the dichotomy between rich and poor. Here we can see that the attitude that one takes toward these dichotomies, along with an understanding of the limits of control that they may present, are both pivotal to whether and how they give rise to suffering.

Understanding the different outcomes that follow from the stance and actions one takes toward inevitable conflicts embedded in these dichotomies is important, particularly if individuals are to avoid engaging in a destructive cycle of self-deception. Thus, expanding on this distinction will help to further elucidate the process of healing. A distinction provided by John Kafka (1971) between contradiction and paradox in his discussion of the value of healthy tolerance for ambiguity is instructive. In a *contradiction* the opposing elements can be easily distinguished and separated from each other by the application of reason. This is because there is no interdependent or reciprocal relationship between them. Kafka gives the example of a sign posted at an intersection that reads "Stop. Don't stop." In this case, two conflicting alternatives are clearly drawn. One can either do one or the other. Contradictions can thus be dealt with using reason and a conventional form of black-or-white logic. They may provoke the experience of ambivalence if one is torn between the two alternatives. However, this ambivalence is resolved once individuals opt for one alternative over another.

Kafka's description of contradictions is similar to Fromm's historical dichotomies. Going back to the distinction between rich and poor, there is nothing that necessitates these opposing statuses in society. It is conceivable for human beings to create a society that is governed by equity and fairness in the distribution of wealth, income, and other social goods. However, despite historical dichotomies being capable of change, it is often the case that individuals respond to these damaging contradictions with indifference, inaction, and even approval, giving rise to avoidable suffering. The suffering is a consequence of human beings choosing to maintain a harmful degree of inequality.

In contrast, a *paradox* is a polarity in which there is a dialectal and inextricable relationship between the opposing elements. Because one requires the other, there can neither be any feasible means of severing their relationship nor opting for one alternative to the exclusion of the other. An example of a paradox given by Kafka is a sign that states "Do not read this sign." In order to obey the sign, one must read it, but in reading it one simultaneously disobeys it. Another example is if one is told, "Don't think of a pink elephant." The very act of issuing this injunction makes it likely that it will be disobeyed. Paradoxes can also provoke negative emotions. In such instances, persons may feel as though they are caught on the horns of a dilemma from which they cannot escape. Paradoxes stymie rational thinking and defy ordinary logic, as the opposing elements cannot be separated into distinct categories. One common reaction to paradox, according to Kafka and others, is the experience of *uncanniness* in which our familiar and accustomed way of looking at the world is suddenly stripped away (derealization). This is accompanied by our typical way of seeing ourselves being questioned (depersonalization). Both are extremely disturbing.

This description of paradox highlights key aspects of the experience of alienation. When individuals' accustomed sense of reality is jeopardized or stripped away, they feel as though they have been thrust into a strange alternative reality. This experience of one's bottom falling out and completely losing one's bearings is an extreme situation described in existential literature as a *boundary experience* (Jaspers, 1984). Not only is one's world turned upside down, but one feels disconnected and estranged from him- or herself and, accordingly, from others, the world, and a higher reality. There is a sense of being at odds with oneself or losing control over oneself. This can sometimes be experienced as falling under the control of some external force or alien entity. Typical expressions of this are "I was not myself" or "Something came over me." This state is accompanied by extreme anxiety and even profound dread or horror.

Existential dichotomies are examples of paradox. These include polarities that constitute potentialities possessed by all human beings. For example, human beings can be both autonomous and dependent, secure and insecure, good and evil. These are possibilities that human beings are able to actualize based on choices they make. By virtue of possessing free will, human beings must negotiate realizing one or another possibility moment by moment in a constant process of becoming. This process can neither be avoided nor denied—despite these responses sometimes being used to evade anxiety that accompanies freedom. These dichotomies form the framework of the ongoing challenges necessary for human growth and development to occur. Though they defy any straightforward resolution, they are essential to what it means to be human. As Fromm (1947) states:

> Man can react to historical contradictions by annulling them through his own action; but he cannot annul existential dichotomies, although he can react to them in different ways. He can appease his mind by soothing and harmonizing ideologies. He can try to escape from his inner restlessness by ceaseless activity in pleasure or business. He can try and abrogate his freedom and turn himself into an instrument of powers outside himself, submerging himself in them. But he remains dissatisfied, anxious, and restless. There is only one solution to his problem: to face the truth, to acknowledge his fundamental aloneness and solitude in a universe indifferent to his fate and to recognize that there is no power transcending him which can solve his problem for him. Man must accept responsibility for himself and the fact that only by using his own powers can give meaning to his life. But meaning does not imply certainty; indeed, the quest for certainty blocks the search for meaning. Uncertainty is the very condition to impel man to unfold his powers. (pp. 53–54)

The Contributions of Kierkegaard

The necessity of embracing the paradoxical nature of human existence, of tolerating the ambiguity this poses, and avoiding the temptation to impose an extreme, either–or understanding on existential dichotomies is also astutely addressed by the philosopher Kierkegaard (1941) in his analysis of despair. His in-depth examination provides some profound insights into the nature of suffering as it arises in terms of human beings' relationship to themselves, others, and the Absolute. Kierkegaard believes that we are essentially spiritual creatures. For Kierkegaard spirituality is rooted in humans being radically relational both in terms of who they are and what they must become as their selfhood is a gift from God. What individuals relate to and the character of those relationships shape their identity. Kierkegaard conceives of these relationships as a synthesis of paradoxical elements that make up the human person.

Human beings are both finite and infinite, temporal and eternal, determined and free. These paradoxes, not surprisingly, all bear a similarity to the paradoxes characteristic of the Absolute, as human beings are created in God's image. Kierkegaard calls these opposing tendencies an *existential paradox* because they can never be harmonized with each other. Encountering these paradoxes leads to anxiety which Kierkegaard describes as a paradoxical experience in which one is both attracted and repulsed by the same thing (note the similarity to Otto's description of awe in response to the numinous). To be a self requires that one exercise free will. Individuals must possess both courage and vigilance in order to exercise the effort needed to hold together the opposing elements that make up the self.

Based on this understanding, despair (suffering) is examined by Kierkegaard from several lenses. One form of despair is due to an intolerance of ambiguity that leads individuals to attempt to resolve the tension between the different forms of existential paradox by imposing an either/or approach. Only one side of a polarity is asserted, while the other is negated. Nordentoft (1978) describes this: "The despairing person wishes to find unambiguousness, and his very attempt to do so is despair; but because the attempt consists in denying ambiguity, it is doomed to fail, and the result is simply an intensification of despair, i.e., doublemindedness" (p. 138).

Thus, in trying to assert one's finite tendency, an individual is trying to be someone other than who he/she truly is or engaging in doublemindedness or self-deception. The result is self-defeating as one flees from their true identity by exaggerating only one of the opposing tendencies to the exclusion of the other. Further, trying to escape from the anxiety that accompanies existential paradox ends up being a form of despair because it is denying a central element of what it means to be human. When persons attempt to achieve complete certainty and security by evading or stifling awareness of a state of despair, they relinquish their free will and responsibility to take up the ongoing task of being a person. These maneuvers are equally futile and instead lead to higher degrees of uncertainty and insecurity.

Despair is a rejection of the essential relatedness of human existence that then creates a state of alienation. One form this alienation takes is to distance oneself as much as possible from one's self by stifling awareness of one's experiences and trying to hide from oneself. This is an example of how self-deception is related to the idea of the unconscious (Gruba-McCallister, 1993). Human beings are able to create a state of self-opacity by allowing themselves to be governed by automatic or well-ingrained habitual patterns of inhibiting awareness that they can then deny having any control over. Similarly, this sense of alienation from themselves can be feigned by regarding themselves as objects rather than conscious agents and thus incapable of exercising self-awareness and insight. Finally, this passive stance is achieved by assuming an attitude in which individuals detach themselves from an overwhelming situation by not examining it from a self-critical or reflective point of view. What is assumed instead is an either–or, concrete perspective incapable of dealing with paradox. This is accompanied by a tendency to interpret the experience in literal terms. This impairment of the critical function and subsequent missing of the metaphoric significance of one's experience are both essential features of various forms of dis-ease responsible for significant suffering. One other form of alienation that can accompany despair is an exaggerated exercise of willfulness and inflation of self-importance that results in a state of estrangement from the Absolute. This will be discussed at greater length later as the *problem of the ego*.

The Self-Defeating Nature of Resistance

These various points are astutely and convincingly integrated into an important rethinking of the nature of dis-ease by Bakan (1968). He sees a significant parallel between Selye's (1974, 1976) observation that the way in which the body responds to a stressful situation can actually bring about the very destructive effects it was intended to defend against and the work of Freud (1920) on defense mechanisms. In Freud's theory, it is not the initial conflict that constitutes the core of suffering and dis-ease, but rather the defenses erected against the anxiety created by the conflict. Bakan writes, "Paradoxical as it may appear, I suggest that *'defense' is a key notion for unlocking at least some of the mystery of the disease process*" (italics in the original, p. 22). In other words, the very measures we take to make things better actually make things worse.

In the theories of both Selye and Freud, an event that disrupts the balance or homeostasis of the organism or mind triggers defenses aimed at restoring it. This disruption is accompanied by pain or suffering that signals a threat to one's existence that exceeds one's resources or ability to control. However, pain—as well as suffering—has a paradoxical character. This is observed by Bakan (1968), who writes:

> Paradox haunts just about every effort that has been made to understand the nature of pain...Among the many paradoxes associated with pain, one of the most significant is that pain seems to have both positive and negative values with respect to the continuing function of the organism and its survival. (pp. 67–68)

In terms of its positive function, pain performs an essential function by alerting the person that there is a threat to well-being that needs to be addressed and acted upon. In the absence of pain in dangerous situations, individuals would be at significant risk of even greater danger and harm. With respect to its negative character, pain is experienced as aversive and frightening, which then leads to responses aimed at decreasing or eliminating it. Moreover, there is another paradox connected to pain and suffering. In those cases in which defenses directed against them are rigid and extreme and go well beyond the actual threat posed, the pain and suffering is only made worse. This describes the essential dynamics of self-defeatism. What we resist persists.

Looking at Freud's theory, when defenses are deployed to deal with a psychic conflict, the result are symptoms that function as compromise formations. On the one hand, the symptoms may temporarily alleviate anxiety and forestall danger, but, on the other hand, they themselves are a source of distress and impairment.

What this means is that what constitutes the core of neurosis for Freud is not conflict itself but the constellation of defenses used by the individual in an ineffective attempt to deal with the conflict. This mirrors the dynamic described earlier by Selye in the General Adaptation Syndrome where the stress response intended to adapt to the threat can actually have the opposite effect.

These damaging responses are clear examples of a form of self-deception because the cause of the more substantial suffering inflicted by the defenses used to deal with the threat are misattributed to conflict or the perceived dangerous circumstances. Individuals fail to see that they are actually responsible for making their situation worse. Behind this, individuals cling to the belief that they should not be required to deal with unavoidable suffering and that they need to be in control of every aspect of their lives. They fail to see that avoiding suffering that is inevitable is not only harmful but futile. Because these beliefs are clung to as a matter of life or death even when they fail to deal with the pain and suffering, they are not abandoned. Instead they are applied even more rigidly, thereby making the situation even worse. A significant factor behind this inflexibility and seeming inability to change one's approach is based on a sense of alienation embedded in the experience. Individuals incorrectly believe that the defenses are happening outside of one's control—as if they have a will of their own. This is related to their automaticity as explained by Bakan (1968):

> Neurosis may be defined as a condition in which some regular response occurs in the individual in spite of his conscious wish that he not make that response. In obsessions, phobias, and compulsions, the classical forms of neurosis, the individual has thoughts or fears, or engages in acts in opposition to his conscious intentions, and even to his disadvantage. The responses indeed occur as though there were "some extraneous force at work." It is precisely this *automatic* occurrence, occurrence independent of the conscious ego, that marks the response as neurotic. The way in which events take place *automatically* in the organism is what Freud identified as reflecting the work of the death instinct. Now, when we read Selye describing how physiological reactions are triggered quite automatically, resulting in the injury of the organism, we are led to the opinion that automatic defense processes constitute the major factor in disease and death. Both Freud's death instinct and Selye's diseases of adaptation may be identified with those automatic mechanisms in the organism, the primitive, elementary, and instinctual mechanisms, which are phenomenologically extraneous to the conscious ego. (italics in original, p. 29)

The operations of defense, in other words, are experienced as phenomenologically alien to the person—as if they act independently of one's conscious intentions. Given that this is what the experience feels like, it is no surprise that persons use a language that accords with it. "Something has come over me. It feels as if my body has a mind of its own. I am helpless in dealing with the situation. I am not myself." Such is the language of alienation. Yet no matter how well these descriptions may seem to fit with what appears to be happening, these appearances are deceiving. And it is dangerous to be seduced by appearances. To do so is based on a failure to utilize one's ability to exercise self-reflection and examine critically what is occurring. Instead the metaphoric nature of the language being used is missed and the description is taken literally. There is no "it" or "other" at work. We are our own worst enemy. The only means of avoiding the catastrophic consequences that can follow this self-defeating spiral is to recognize the deception at work. So Bakan (1968) writes:

> How could the injuriousness associated with the mechanisms be mitigated? Clearly, the way to overcome the injuriousness of a mechanism is to change that which is ego-alien to something which is not ego-alien, to recognize that which may have the sense of being "other" (as the word 'id' so strongly suggests) is really the person himself, to overcome the automaticity of the functioning of such mechanisms that have on the *appearance of defense* so that indeed the person may be really defended instead of injured by them. (italics in original, p, 30)

In summary, there are ways in which human beings respond to unavoidable pain and suffering related to the experience of loss that have their roots in natural processes occurring outside of conscious awareness. There is a natural tendency for human beings to meet pain, fear, and other disturbing experiences with resistance. While this response has certain adaptive functions, when it becomes extreme, indiscriminate, and rigid, it leads to ever more adverse consequences. However, human beings are capable of becoming consciously aware of these adverse consequences, particularly when they are manifested in a self-defeating cycle characteristic of dis-ease. Free will and the capacity for self-reflection inseparably linked to it enable human beings to uncover harmful illusions and self-defeating beliefs and choose to change them.

Extreme, rigid, and one-sided efforts to deal with threat and loss are fueled by the most dangerous of all lies: the belief that we should be exempt from any pain and suffering. As will be seen, this lie becomes even more dangerous and destructive when fostered by pervasive and powerful social influences used to preserve the status quo. The dominant ideology on which it is based must be discovered and dismantled. Ideological forms of deception tap into and intensify the human proclivity for self-deception. These forms of deception serve a political purpose and give rise to social sources of suffering such as discrimination, exploitation, oppression, and violence.

Radical healing requires a realization that self-created suffering is the greatest source of our pain and unhappiness. Though it is clearly linked to suffering that is an extricable part of life, the good news is that it is nonetheless capable of being ameliorated and even eradicated. There are ways in which fear and other negative emotions triggered by loss can become an opportunity to transform suffering in ways that can promote personal transformation and social liberation. This requires human beings to alter mistaken beliefs and abandon illusions, particularly the insistence that life should conform to their expectations and desires and the unwillingness to accept that suffering is inherent in life.

Summary of Key Points

- The causes of human suffering and what are deemed as forms of dis-ease are rooted in essential and inescapable elements of the human condition. Buddhism describes this as the inherently transient nature of existence and the experience of loss. The existential psychologist Yalom (1980), attributes suffering in the form of existential anxiety to certain givens of existence or what he calls "ultimate concerns." These are death, freedom, isolation, and meaninglessness. Frankl (1967) describes the tragic triad of finitude, fallibility, and mortality as unavoidable sources of suffering.
- The continuum of health and dis-ease can also be seen as inherent in the human condition. This continuum represents the entire range of human functioning or potential. It encompasses the vast varieties of experience that are available to all human beings. These human experiences and potentials do not represent discrete and easily separable states. As beings in process, we experience and possess a blending of health and dis-ease each moment of life. This intermingling of health and dis-ease is but one example of how human existence is inherently ambiguous. Health and illness, as endpoints on this continuum, represent "ideal" anchor points for understanding one's place on the continuum. As such, absolute health and dis-ease do not exist in the human realm of experience. The distinction between health and dis-ease is a matter of degree.
- This understanding challenges the current biomedical ideology and disease model that categorize forms of human suffering into discrete categories that presume underlying biological or psychological bases. This includes an overemphasis on pathology and the focus on identifying what is wrong with those who are suffering. These diagnoses attribute suffering to factors such as deviance, dysfunction, abnormality, maladaptation, and the working of pathological biological, and psychological processes. In keeping with the neoliberal ideology in which the biomedical model and most psychological theories are embedded, problems are accordingly mostly situated within individuals with little to no attention given to the role of adverse environmental and social factors. These roots in neoliberal ideology account for its endurance despite an ever-growing body of evidence that points to its fallacies and the destructive impacts of its biases. Moreover, its underlying assumptions operate to serve neoliberal dictates and values by means of serving the political and economic interests of the powerful and the elite.

- There needs to be more attention given to a *salutogenic* orientation (Antonovsky, 1987) in which the focus is on what factors protect individuals from the adverse effects of threat and trauma and serve to promote well-being. This would be aligned with a *eudaimonic* philosophy, translated as "flourishing" in the sense of enabling human beings to maximize to the greatest extent possible their fundamental and unique human potentials or capabilities. Well-being would no longer be defined as the norm, but instead be based on optimal states of functioning, such as higher states of consciousness. Fostering flourishing is not solely an individual task. It also requires establishing environmental and social conditions that enable and promote the greatest degree of development of well-being possible for all human beings in the service of social justice.
- Categorizing experiences of human suffering into forms of illness creates false barriers between the well and unwell that exclude and stigmatize those who are labeled "ill." By virtue of everyone sharing the same human condition, everyone suffers from the same problems or issues. There are not many "conditions," but only one condition—the human condition. We must be guided by the maxim articulated   by the Roman philosopher Terence, "I am a human being and therefore nothing human is alien to me." Moreover, there is now substantial evidence that the reliability and validity of systems that employ categories to label and differentiate forms of human suffering, such as the DSM, are highly questionable social constructions shaped by social, economic, and political factors (Boggs, 2015; Conrad & Barker, 2010; Moncrieff, 2010). As such, they function principally to advance and serve a toxic neoliberal ideology.
- These universal problems and issues can be expressed in terms of the various polarities that are inherent in the human condition. These polarities play a significant role in how human beings define themselves. They are associated with the construction of a worldview as a basis for making sense of and giving meaning to their experience, as well as establishing a measure of control over their lives. These fundamental polarities can also be seen as core issues that human beings must negotiate over the course of their development. One way in which they can be categorized is in terms of the three central polarities characteristic of psychic life (Freud, 1920): active vs. passive, pleasure vs. pain, and subject vs. objective—along with variants on each of them. In conceptualizing disease, it is a general practice to attribute the onset of problems to what are called precipitants. These precipitants express a polarity that poses some challenge to a person's self-understanding and worldview. It is this polarity that needs to be identified as part of the healing process. The question to be examined when seeking to understand precipitants is "What is *at issue* for the person?"
- What are commonly described as symptoms are actually the means being employed by individuals to *come to terms with* what is at issue. While

symptoms cause individuals suffering and can be incapacitating, a solely pathological approach to understanding them is incomplete and harmful. Symptoms have adaptive function as they are an attempt to restore a state of balance and harmony that has been disrupted, to manage distress, and to cope with conflict. This argument is made by Sedgwick (1982), who looks at what are called symptoms from an evolutionary perspective. He asserts that symptoms are justifiable reactions to the vicissitudes of life that occur naturally, automatically, and unconsciously. An example of this is dissociation, which is a naturally occurring process as revealed in experiences such as in daydreaming, becoming absorbed in a book or movie, or in hypnotic states (Hilgard, 1986). However, it has also been found to be an automatic response to trauma and may give rise to forms of derealization and depersonalization that are intended to protect individuals from a highly threatening event. Similarly, Jacobs and Cowen (2009) make a compelling case against the presumption of the medical model that psychopathology is due to impersonal and biological processes. Feelings, thoughts, and reactions to life circumstances are rooted in human agency and reflect the influence of personal and subjective processes in which individuals seek to give meaning to their experiences. Jacobs and Cowen see symptoms as narratively comprehensible reactions to adversity. Symptoms can have a restitutive function as well, such that they are used to set a situation right and restore order and control. However, as Bakan (1968) observes, despite short-term benefits these defenses or attempted solutions are ultimately self-defeating as they result in making the situation worse and create greater suffering for the individual.

- What constitutes dis-ease is not the problem that individuals are dealing with, but how they choose to deal with the problem.. Whether that response moves individuals in the direction of health or dis-ease, wholeness or alienation is *how they respond to the problem*—the attitude or stance they assume toward what it means to be human. Extremism and rigidity are the hallmarks of dis-ease. A narrow and one-sided perspective fails to appreciate the inherently ambiguous nature of human experience. When confronted with the polarities inherent in human existence, persons with this extremist stance refuse to acknowledge the necessary relationship between the two sides of these polarities. Instead they try to separate them into iron-clad, absolutely separate categories based on either/or, black-or-white thinking. This approach to polarities actually leads to more ambiguity. When attempting to apply an either/or solution to dialectically related opposites, individuals end up "wobbling" or "dithering" between the two extremes and feeling increasingly conflicted.
- Health is promoted by openness to the inherent ambiguity of human existence and a commitment to negotiating these polarities in the ever-unfolding process of becoming. What this means is that well-being requires individuals to embrace what it means to be human and to accept

the inescapable givens of life. Conversely, dis-ease is rooted in a static, rigid, extreme approach to life's paradoxes that proves to be self-defeating. This stance is also based on self-deception or clinging to various harmful illusions and false beliefs about oneself and life. This pattern of self-deception gives rise to heightened states of alienation that undermine one's sense of wholeness.

- The ways in which individuals understand and respond to shared problems and issues that constitute the human condition is influenced by where they are developmentally. As noted, development has been conceptualized along a number of different lines (Wilber, 2000a). One of the most significant of these developmental models describes stages of ego development (Loevinger, 1976). Wilber, Engler, and Brown (1986) provide a detailed description of how different levels of development are related to different forms of dis-ease rooted in distinctive worldviews held by individuals at these stages. Situating individuals developmentally is an essential element of practicing radical healing.

Chapter 6

The Problem of Suffering:
Spiritual Foundations

The Integrative Nature of Spirit

Continuing with an analysis of the sources/causes of suffering adopting a holistic framework, it is necessary to next examine this from the perspective of the spiritual nature of human beings. This point was made in Chapter Four. It is important to recall that focusing on the spiritual dimension of human beings in no way negates the other dimensions. The interrelationship between these diverse facets is based, first, on the understanding asserted by the perennial philosophy—that what we take to be reality is Spirit or the Absolute. Employing what Wilber (2000a) describes as the Great Nest of Being, Spirit encompasses what can be thought of as the different levels of reality: soul, body, and matter. Matter is understood as the most visible form of Spirit, but any of these levels can be employed as a means of viewing human beings. However, it is only by ascending the levels of the Great Nest of Being that a complete and integrated understanding can be achieved. Additionally, the Absolute as the divine ground of all reality is expressed or immanent in all levels of the Great Nest. This serves as the basis for the true identity of human beings being spiritual and conveys their inherent mystical vocation.

From this perspective, patterns and principles that function at the lower levels, such as the biological and psychological, are to some degree mirrored at the higher levels. Thus, the description in the previous chapter of the physical and psychological processes giving rise to suffering such as alienation, attachment, extremism and rigidity, and the interrelationship between the two forms of suffering, will continue to be a part of understanding suffering from a spiritual perspective. These parallels will also be apparent when the social causes of suffering are discussed in the following chapter. That said, because of the centrality of spirituality to what it means to be human, suffering is ultimately a spiritual problem, and a failure to accept and appreciate this will thwart any genuine effort to achieve healing.

Liberation as the Realization of our Mystical Vocation

An apt place to begin this examination of the spiritual roots of suffering is to return to the problem of the ego, which was discussed earlier. This problem has occupied a central place in explaining human affliction and evil in diverse religious and wisdom traditions throughout time. From the perspective of the perennial philosophy, the principal obstacle to the ultimate goal of liberation or enlightenment is craving that gives rise to attachments, such as material possessions, power, social status. These attachments are transient and bound to disappoint us. They are fostered by illusions or fictions in which human beings stubbornly impose their expectations and demands on reality as a means of asserting their will in defiance of the demands that reality places on them. This self-centered, narcissistic orientation reveals the most powerful and destructive of all attachments—the illusions and attachments that make up individuals' ego or their sense of self and worldview. This elevating of the ego to the status of an absolute (what is called idolatry or false transcendence) expresses an urge to separate, or craving for independent existence. It represents a state of alienation from and forgetfulness of our essential oneness with the Absolute. Huxley (1944) powerfully describes this problem and its destructive consequences:

> It is because we don't know Who we are, because we are unaware that the Kingdom of Heaven is within us, that we behave in the generally silly, the often insane, and the sometimes criminal ways that are so characteristically human. We are saved, we are liberated and enlightened, by perceiving the hitherto unperceived good that is already within us, by returning to our eternal Ground and remaining where, without knowing it we have always been. (pp. 14–15)

Huxley (1944) also makes an important observation that this urge toward separateness and desire to maintain one's individual existence expresses itself at all levels of life. This accords with understanding Spirit as encompassing various levels of reality and with the need to honor the interrelationship of all the dimensions of human beings. Suffering's origin at the level of the ego is mirrored on the other levels due to their interdependence. Huxley elaborates on this point:

> If every human being were constantly and consciously in a proper relation with his divine, natural and social environments there would be only so much suffering as Creation makes inevitable. But actually most human beings are chronically in an improper relation to God, Nature and some at least of their fellows. The results of these wrong relationships are manifest on the social level as wars, revolutions, exploitation and disorder; on the natural level, as waste and exhaustion of irreplaceable resources; on the biological level, as degenerative diseases and the deterioration of racial stock; on the moral level, as overweening bumptiousness; and on the

spiritual level, as blindness to divine Reality and complete ignorance of the reason and purpose of human existence. (p. 233)

These quotes highlight key points that need to be examined in more detail. First, the principal cause of suffering is a failure to realize our true identity or spiritual nature. It is an unawareness of our essential at-one-ness with the Absolute. As Underhill (1915) writes, "Mysticism is the art of union with Reality. The mystic is a person who has attained that union in greater or lesser degree or who aims at and believes in such attainment" (p. 3). The goal is thus to regain and reclaim our mystical identity and with it a realization of our being an incarnation of the Absolute. This lack of knowledge or awareness is the cause behind a host of human ills that range from the trivial to the horrible.

Moreover, this realization is not a goal that must be strived for and attained. Rather it is remembering who we truly are and always have been. In other words, it is the recognition of how we have erroneously tried to separate ourselves from the Absolute by making ourselves our central concern and preoccupation. As asserted by mystics throughout time, our union with the Absolute is an ever-present given that is "already within us." Liberation requires our acknowledging that we are an embodiment of the Absolute as both Transcendent and Immanent. As Watts (1971) writes:

> The point is rather that Reality, God, the Eternal Now, is entirely beyond speech and understanding and attainment, but at the same time is right here. If you try to catch hold of it, you will miss it. But go straight ahead with your ordinary life, 'Walk on!,' wash your dishes, think your everyday thoughts, and you will see that you can't get away from it. (pp. 110–111)

It is true that liberation can be attained in elevated states of awareness or mystical experiences, as described in the previous chapter. However, because our union with the Absolute is a constant reality, it can also be experienced in every facet of human life, as described in the above quote by Watts. Liberation is a state of consciousness, a way of perceiving and experiencing in which there is a radical shift in our perspective on ourselves and life itself. It begins with a gnawing intimation of a sense of emptiness and incompleteness that we may at first attempt to resist or deny but persistently reasserts itself. Other manifestations of this state of longing are keen boredom and loss of meaning, chronic discontent, frenetic restlessness, a powerful sense of disappointment or even despair, and a sense of feeling divided within or alienation. Such experiences become particularly intense in those moments when a shock shatters our accustomed sense of self and view of the world—what has been previously called the boundary experience (Jaspers, 1984). In other words, a wake-up call. But it can also make its presence known in milder and more attenuated forms of emptiness, dissatisfaction, sadness, and isolation. As Underhill (1999) correctly observes, "The divine discontent, the hunger for reality, the unwillingness to be satisfied with the purely animal or the purely social level of consciousness, is the first essential stage in the development of mystical consciousness" (p. 20).

Additionally, union with the Absolute is not something that human beings need to earn or deserve. It is freely given by the Absolute, and the sole decision that must be made is whether to say "Yes. Amen." Underhill (1961) eloquently describes what it means to answer the persistent call of the Absolute and fulfill one's mystical vocation:

> To be a mystic is simply to participate here and now in that real and eternal life; in the fullest, deepest sense which is possible to man. To share, as a free and conscious agent—not a servant but a son—in the joyous travail of the Universe: its mighty onward sweep through pain and glory towards its home in God. (p. 447)

Examining the various parts of this description highlights the core elements of liberation and, as such, the elements of the highest state of well-being. Liberation is not attained by individuals asserting their will or trying to make something happen. This only gives rise to a heightened sense of the self as separate and in need of absolute control. Instead one takes the stance of surrendering to something bigger than one's self and aligning one's will with it. Another way this is expressed in mystical literature is the attainment of enlightenment by being fully open to the present, to the here and now. This is the meaning of eternity—not time without end but no time. Huxley (1944) writes, "The present moment is the only aperture through which the soul can pass out of time into eternity..." (p. 188). Similarly, Wilber (1977) observes, "In this spiritual world there are no time-divisions such as past, present, and future; for they have contracted themselves into a single moment of the present where life quivers in the truest sense" (p. 93).

Though enlightenment is achieved by surrendering to the Absolute, as Underhill correctly describes, individuals nonetheless retain their free will and agency. As is the case in any genuine relationship, there must be reciprocity. The act of surrendering is not passive or compelled. It is a choice, a decision that must be made. While the Absolute, out of perfect love, gives itself completely and without reservation to human beings, they in turn must respond in kind. Once more, Watts (1972) makes this point clearly:

> ...if we get rid of the notion of sin and free will, if we saddle God with the responsibility for good and evil alike, if, in short, we deny that the ego is God's image, we seem to be faced with two dangers. The first is that man becomes nothing more than God's puppet, and God himself becomes arbitrary, amoral and cruel as the sole author of crime, war and tyranny. The second is that such an idea would undermine the very moral impulse in man, and give him every excuse for an attitude of total irresponsibility. (p. 105)

The previous quote by Underhill also underlines that the paradoxical nature of the Absolute is fully apprehended and embraced in the experience of liberation. In her using the expressions "joyous travail" and "pain and glory," we find an affirmation of how good and evil, bliss and suffering, creation and destruction are not irreconcilable contradictions. They are essential elements of existence that are harmonized in the experience of liberation. To fulfill our longing for the Absolute, we must be willing to accept and fully experience the inherently paradoxical nature of life. That means assuming an attitude of equanimity and non-judgment to everything that comes with being human, even saying "Yes" to that which is most abhorrent and painful to us.

The Problem of the Ego

Having described the nature of our mystical vocation and how it is fulfilled, we can return to the problem of the ego as it provides a clear understanding of what stands in the way of the attainment of liberation. What gives rise to and sustains the ego is thus pivotal to understanding the roots of suffering and what hinders the promotion of radical healing. The genesis of the ego is rooted in fear that is expressed in a keen insecurity, or what Laing (1960) called ontological insecurity. Similar to existential anxiety, ontological insecurity is the apprehension that one's being is at issue. This experience undermines one's sense of being real, alive, whole, and temporally continuous. This fear has been discussed previously in terms of the impact of loss and its destabilization of one's sense of identity and worldview. Ontological insecurity can also have social sources, such as repeated invalidation of one's experience, propagandization, oppression, and violence—which will be dealt with in greater detail in the following chapter.

A primary function of the ego is to establish a sense of control, stability, and order over one's experience. It serves as a buffer against the unexpected, the unknown, or other types of profoundly disturbing experiences. As noted, this need for control is immensely powerful and is rooted in innate biological and psychological processes that served an evolutionary purpose. Another way to understand the basis of this need for control is to look at the ego as an outgrowth of human development. It develops as a means of establishing separation or boundaries between itself and others/the outside world by means of creating a distinct sense of identity. Though the ego is not present at birth, the processes that form the foundation of it are. This is illustrated in the work of the psychiatrist Harry Stack Sullivan (1953) regarding the development of what he called the self-system. From the start of life, infants as social beings respond to experiences based on how they assess them—positive or negative, pleasant or unpleasant; this process is significantly shaped by how caretakers respond to infants. In response to these experiences, infants form different parts of themselves. This process also explains the origins of the experience of alienation. While some experiences are identified with, others are disowned and make up what was previously described as the shadow. Viewed developmentally, the state of union present at birth over time gives way to a sense of distinction and separation. The experience of alienation is an inevitable part of this process.

Sullivan asserts that infants are motivated to secure feelings of approval and acceptance because these experiences are positive, while at the same time avoiding disapproval and punishment because these are painful. Positive experiences are integrated into the good-me or the person we believe ourselves to be. Painful experiences create an interpersonal form of anxiety as infants feel that the love and approval they seek is being withdrawn from them. These experiences are organized into the bad-me and are connected with feelings of regret or remorse. According to Sullivan, the good-me and the bad-me eventually are integrated into a single self-image, or what might be called the ego.

There is a third part of the self-system in which alienation plays a principal role—the not-me or the *shadow* or alter-ego. This part is formed in response to situations involving extreme anxiety, terror, and dread. These experiences severely threaten one's sense of control, order, and safety. They evoke emotions described as "uncanny" in which individuals feel unmoored from any sense of reality. It is as if they have been thrust into a state of utter confusion and estrangement from what was once familiar and predictable. To protect the self-system, these experiences are disowned and repressed. The purpose of the self-system is thus to control awareness and manage experiences by employing a range of defenses to suppress or repress threatening events, maintain a sense of security and harmony in one's relationships with others, and direct the ongoing development of the personality.

In a similar vein, Wilber (1977, 2000a) describes a model of ego development based on a series of stages or levels that individuals negotiate with the goal of moving toward an ever-more expansive, embracing, and integrated understanding of self and the world. Similar to the Buddhist idea that human beings form attachments to objects or persons they believe are essential to their well-being and happiness, the formation of the ego unfolds by means of identifying with particular objects of awareness considered essential. This creates a sense of self in contrast to the rest of the world. Thus, the creation of the ego inevitably establishes a sense of difference and separation. In asserting, "I am this, not that," a duality is created between subject and object, self and other. Where there had been unity, there is now multiplicity. When this is extended to one's view of the outside world, this process leads to the creation of the realm of *maya*, in which things are separated by time and space. The fundamental oneness and web of interrelationships that exist because all things are an expression of Absolute Reality is repressed by the imposition of distinction and boundaries. The most important of these is the self-boundary that separates self from the rest of the world. This boundary is accompanied by a threat zone that is erected to maintain a sense of security and stability by means of defenses that push experiences deemed alien out of awareness.

The ego is tightly and rigidly organized around a set of important identifications. They are held with a life-or-death attitude. In the process, these identifications assume such importance that they actually enslave us. The Italian psychiatrist Assagioli (1965) makes this point, "We are dominated by everything with which our self becomes identified" (p. 22). Contrary to the need for control being achieved by identification, our identifications actually control us. Nonetheless, we fail to appreciate this contradiction. In the face of threats to our identifications, we resist sacrificing them and cling to them all the more tightly. The tighter the control, the more fragile it becomes. This leads to a great deal of suffering among those who fail to see this contradiction. They resist exercising control over those things they can control, and futilely persist in trying to control those things they cannot control.

This self-defeating pattern, which is a core characteristic of dis-ease, is found in the most extreme state of alienation, rooted in what Sullivan called the not-self. Experiences that pose a serious threat to our identifications and, if accepted, would actually unmake our sense of self and worldview, provoke a sense of terror. These experiences are completely disowned and banished to the unconscious. The role of the ego in banishing such unwanted and undesirable experiences provides another way of understanding the formation of the *shadow*. While the substance of the ego is made up of attachments and identifications based on our illusory preferences and desires, nowhere is self-deception more apparent than in the creation of the shadow. It is forged by a stubborn rejection of the inescapable givens of the human condition—for example, the necessity of accepting the tragic triad of our finitude, fallibility, and mortality. Or resistance to submitting to the inescapable suffering of life that only results in further self-created suffering.

The formation of the shadow is another manifestation of the catastrophic consequences of a rigid and one-sided stance that sees polarities that define human beings as a duality in which one side must be affirmed and the other negated. The result once more is a self-defeating cycle in which the more we assert one side of the polarity, the more we succumb to its opposite. Wilber (1977) notes, "All opposites are mutually interdependent and inseparable non-dual, *coincidentia oppositorum,* and he who imagines otherwise does so at the price of sending reality underground" (italics in original, p. 145). Because human existence is inescapably ambiguous, wellness requires a capacity to embrace this ambiguity. Any attempt to evade this reality is doomed to fail. As Jung (1933) observed, disowning experiences and banishing them from awareness does not result in their elimination. The shadow will make its presence known in the form of projections: That which we disown is attributed to others; material that we have thrust out of awareness will be expressed, often in some metaphoric form, in what are called symptoms. As observed by Wilber (1980), a symptom is some aspect of ego that has become dissociated from consciousness and generally remains at some lower level of development. However, eventually what is disowned makes its presence known. This is because the more one tries to oppose or resist the shadow, the more powerful it becomes. What we resist persists.

Malignant Narcissism and the Major Causes of Evil

Throughout this discussion the role of self-deception and the pattern of self-defeat inextricably linked to it are again highlighted as the principal causes of suffering. The ego and the shadow are both based in lies we tell ourselves. They express a defiance of reality, in particular, the transience of existence and ultimately death. As the Buddha observed, suffering is rooted in desire and attachments that give way to inevitable disappointment because they are transient. Watts (1961) writes:

> For the ego is the role, the "act," that one's inmost self is permanent, that it is in control of the organism, and that while it "has" experiences it is not involved in them. Pain and death expose this pretense, and this is why suffering is almost always attended by a feeling of guilt, a feeling that this is all the more difficult to explain when the pretense is unconscious. Hence the obscure but powerful feeling that one *ought* not to suffer or die. (italics in original, p. 69)

There is another facet of the ego that requires mention. That is the exaggerated importance assigned to the self, as in the common expression, "inflated ego." Of all the attachments with which we identify, the most precious and powerful is the ego itself. As described later in this chapter, the most extreme manifestation of the ego's assertion of its importance, uniqueness, and autonomy is elevating itself to the status of an absolute. Fromm (1964) describes this irrational and excessive form of self-love as *malignant narcissism*. Such individuals transform themselves into idols to be worshipped before which everything and everyone is to be sacrificed. We encountered this idea in the earlier discussion of evil and the work of Peck (1983), who describes evil people as individuals who have an inordinately elevated opinion of themselves. They believe they are so perfect that they are incapable of failure and error, and thus of engaging in evil. These individuals are motivated by selfishness and greed and are unable to experience empathy for others. Instead other people are like possessions. They are transformed into things to be acquired and used in accordance with the malignant narcissist's desires and wishes. Neoliberal ideology has been critiqued for fostering malignant narcissism by encouraging extreme individualism and selfishness (Lasch, 1979). This is the most destructive manifestation of the ego. In some spiritual literature it is called demonic as such individuals historically have been capable of the most heinous forms of wrongdoing.

The role of the ego in creating suffering is astutely summarized by Watts (1972) as based in three causes: insecurity, pride, and inertia. All of these are based on self-deception. Insecurity is principally connected to the need for control and stability associated with the ego. In the face of the dynamic flux that is characteristic of human existence, the ego seeks to impose order. The experience of complexity and diversity triggers insecurity as it disturbs one's sense of stability and predictability. By narrowing one's perception and utilizing a constricted stance, potentially disturbing information is filtered out of awareness. A discursive mode of thinking is employed in which images, concepts, and language are used to reduce reality into manageable bits of information. A danger this poses is that the ego becomes fixated on or even enthralled with the symbolic and representational nature of images and words. There is a failure to see them as merely conventions used to make sense of experience. When their symbolic function is forgotten and they are taken literally, negative consequences follow. Insecurity is a manifestation of the persistent fear of the annihilation of the ego whenever its desires and attachments are ultimately subject to loss. Watts (1951) captures the self-defeating nature of insecurity:

> It must be obvious, from the start, that there is a contradiction in wanting to be perfectly secure in a universe whose very nature is momentariness and fluidity. But the contradiction lies a little deeper than the mere conflict between the *desire* for security and the *fact* of change. If I want to be secure, that is, protected from the flux of life, I am wanting to be separate from life. Yet it is this very sense of separateness which makes me feel insecure. To be secure means to isolate and fortify the "I," but it is just the feeling of being an isolated "I" which makes me feel lonely and afraid. In other words, the more security I can get, the more I shall want. (italics in original, p. 77)

The afflictions caused by pride in the form of *hubris* (that is self-idolatry) were described in the discussion of malignant narcissism above. Such exaggerated self-importance, of course, is bound to be frustrated when confronted with human limitations and the underlying realization deep within all human beings of a persistent sense of emptiness and incompleteness. This, as we shall see, gives rise to the most powerful of all needs—the need to acknowledge and commit oneself to a transcendent reality or meaning. Moreover, this sense of self-inflation is an attempt to hide an underlying vulnerability that creates suffering by responding in extreme and destructive ways to the slightest injury.

Inertia is resistance to change, the preference to always take the path of least resistance. It is the expression of an unchecked need for control that insists on maintaining order and stability. Peck (2002) sees inertia, or what he calls "laziness," as an expression of evil. He describes how this laziness is expressed in a refusal to engage in serious self-examination and the resultant need to make changes in response to the demands of reality because it is inconvenient, unpleasant, or even painful. Rather than do the work and put forth the effort necessary to advance one's spiritual development, individuals cling to their current state and make excuses for their lack of action.

The Fate of the Ego

There is one last point to consider regarding the ego. A common area of disagreement found across different spiritual traditions pertains to the fate of the ego in the attainment of enlightenment. Certain Eastern traditions, such as certain schools of Buddhism, espouse the doctrine of *anatta* or "no self," in which the ego is seen as completely illusory. This was a critique of the teaching of Hinduism regarding the existence of Atman, the individual soul or essence of the individual as a manifestation of Brahman, or the universal soul. Through deep meditation one can achieve a state of *samadhi* in which there is a realization of union between the two, accompanied by the experience of infinite being, consciousness, and bliss. For Buddhists, the notion of self is insubstantial, and concepts such as Atman are just inventions of language that have no reality. However, Western mystical traditions are more personalistic. The ego is not lost or obliterated in the experience of union with the Absolute but rather is transfigured and becomes more completely and uniquely itself.

As an example of this, Arber (1957) argues that an error that sometimes arises from the mystic's experience of illumination is the disdain and negation of the ego in which the finite is lost in the Infinite. She maintains that there is persistence of the individual. She writes: "In this communion the individual does not sacrifice his finite identity, but on the contrary he gives as well as receives. The finite self thus enters into the untold happiness of offering an element without which the whole would be the poorer" (p. 44). Watts (1961) also argues against the annihilation of the ego. The goal is not the loss or destruction of the ego, but the ability to see it for what it is and thus see through it. In other words, one needs to recognize both the value and the limitations of the ego and, in doing so, experience and understand the ego as a necessary but limited perspective from which to understand oneself and life.

The preservation and transformation of the ego can be understood from a developmental perspective. In reviewing diverse developmental theories, particularly Loevinger's (1976) theory, Wilber (1980, 2000a) outlines the various stages in which a sense of ego develops and passes through various transformations as it moves across these levels. He (1980) divides these into three chronological stages: early (ages 4 to 7), middle (ages 7 to 12), and late (ages 12 to 21). Over these stages, there is progression in the areas of cognition, emotion, motivation, and self-understanding. The acquisition of an ego is a necessary phase of human development (and evolution) and, as such, represents an important level of achievement that is accompanied, as we have seen, by certain blessings and certain curses. The negotiation of these challenges thus represents a necessary step in the process of evolving toward advanced levels of wholeness and well-being. Wilber (1980) summarizes this point, "The individual ego is a marvelously high-order unity, but compared with the Unity of the cosmos at large, it is a pitiful slice of holistic reality. Has nature labored these billions of year just to bring forth this egoic mouse?" (p. 2).

This point is likewise observed by Hick (1989), who states, "In so far as anyone, female or male, lacks the ego-development and fulfillment necessary for a voluntary self-transcendence, the prior achievement of a self-fulfilled ego may well be necessary for a true relationship to the Real. For in order to move beyond the self, one has first to *be* a self" (italics in original, p. 54). In order to transcend the ego, individuals must first acquire one. This idea is crucial for another reason, which Wilber (1996) discusses in what he calls the pre-trans fallacy. Based on an antagonistic opinion toward religion, a number of thinkers, such as Freud and other psychoanalytic theorists, denied that human beings are capable of elevated stages of consciousness. Instead they interpreted mystical experiences and other forms of enlightenment as a manifestation of regression and severe psychopathology, such as psychosis (Alexander, 1931). This was based on certain similarities, such as the loss of a sense of boundaries, a sense of unity, the presence of religious themes, or signs of hysteria (Leuba, 1925). However, when viewed developmentally, clear differences become evident. Psychosis and severe psychopathology occur at stages of development prior to the development of ego or a stable sense of self-identity; while enlightenment represents the highest stage of development in which the ego is transcended. Wulff (2000) critiques the association of genuine mystical states with psychopathology as does Jackson (2001).

One final and very insightful perspective on this issue is offered by Carl Jung (1933). It begins with once more realizing and acknowledging the importance of acceptance of oneself in one's wretchedness and imperfection. He frankly admits that this is the hardest of all tasks, one that is practically impossible to achieve. However, even though this is an ongoing process, failure to engage in it will result in a resistance to admitting to the evil in oneself. This often gives rise to seeing it in others and to creating an inner cleavage in which individuals are at war with themselves. Regarding the ego as something that is evil, shameful, or reprehensible can thus be seen as an expression of an inability to accept oneself. Rather than engage in such condemnation and guilt, individuals can only end the inner war by means of forgiveness for oneself as well as for others, as noted in an earlier chapter.

Operating from this framework, Jung asserts that when working with others to promote healing, he needed to "acknowledge the deep significance of their egoism" and "recognize in it the true will of God" (p. 237). True or radical healing necessitates allowing individuals to give full expression to their egoism even if it leads to their alienation from other people and complete isolation. He goes on to explain:

> However, wretched this state may be, it also stands him in good stead, for in this way alone can he take his own measure and learn what an invaluable treasure is the love of his fellow-beings. It is, moreover, only in this state of complete abandonment and loneliness that we experience the helpful powers of our own nature. (p. 238)

The inextricable relationship described before between good and evil enables egoism, once accepted without judgment, to give rise to its opposite, a surrendering of it that makes a higher union with others and with the Absolute possible.

The Need for Transcendence as the Master Motive

A key insight of the perennial philosophy's assertion of the essential mystic vocation and identity of all human beings has a significant bearing on explaining the spiritual sources of human suffering. It asserts that the greatest and most powerful human need or motive is spiritual in nature. *It is the need for transcendence or to rediscover and reaffirm one's true identity as a manifestation of the Absolute.* This is not some abstract notion, a mere intellectual realization, or the satisfaction of some physical urge. Because this need is rooted in spirituality, it engages the totality of human beings and is an act of the total person. It is fulfilled experientially in the realization of union with the Absolute. This is the true meaning of liberation. It is a state in which all alienation is overcome, wholeness and integrity are attained, and a deep and essential relationship with a Reality that transcends this world is experienced. *All other needs, drives, or motives are derivatives or expressions of this overarching need.* As Hick (1989) notes in describing what he calls the *soteriological character* of religion that emerged in the Axial age, this need begins with a recognition of the misery, triviality, and unsatisfactory nature of everyday life. Nevertheless, it is also founded on a cosmic optimism that affirms the ultimate goodness of the universe. This highlights the essentially ethical nature of religion that places emphasis on how one acts and not on what one believes (i.e., deeds not creed). A renunciation of the ego, paired with a commitment to compassion and justice, is required to facilitate human transformation on both an individual and collective level. This is what radical healing is all about.

Thus, an integral part of fulfilling this need is a willingness to accept without judgment the unavoidable suffering that is an inextricable part of the process. We have seen that this suffering can take many forms. In addition, it may be discovered in a passionate longing for connection with the something bigger than us and a nagging feeling of unfulfillment based on separation from true source of ultimate bliss and contentment. This intermingling of bliss and anguish is another polarity inextricably interwoven in our ordinary experience. In recognition of this, Underhill (1961) notes that in addition to the experiences of beauty and religion, suffering is a common trigger for elevated states of awareness. Based on this, she asserts that suffering can be a means of opening oneself to experiencing union with the Absolute. She writes, "Watching life, he (the mystic) sees in Pain, the complement of Love: and is inclined to call these the wings on which man's spirit can best take flight toward the Absolute" (p. 19). This observation has been borne out by others. Laski (1968) conducted a study using a questionnaire directed to individuals who reported having an ecstatic experience and based on a review of texts written by individuals who had such an experience. Common triggers she found for those experiences mirrored those noted by Underhill, including beauty (nature, art, music, poetry), religion, and negative triggers (loss, sorrow, pain).

However, the experience of suffering does not assure that one will move toward reconnecting with their essential nature and ever-present relationship with the Absolute. Rather, it has the potential of provoking a crisis that then can become a pivotal turning point in the search for transcendence. At that point, a choice must be made. One choice is to respond to the call of the Absolute and to follow this with a decisive act that enables individuals to progress on the path that leads to a higher stage of development. This choice is still accompanied initially by suffering rooted in the fear of what feels like the ultimate loss—that is, sacrificing one's sense of separate identity. But it is suffering that can then give way to bliss. The other choice—rooted in insecurity, pride, and inertia—is to persist in the illusion of the ego. This is accompanied by engaging in self-defeating strategies that resist affirming one's true identity and thus faltering or even regressing in one's development. As we will see, this leads to seeking fulfillment in symbolic substitutes of the Absolute. This is called *false transcendence* or *idolatry* and is the source of a host of forms of self-created suffering. Rather than accepting the deep spiritual longing inherent in being human and making a life-affirming choice, one shrinks back from one's highest potential in a death-affirming choice that maintains separation and so undermines wholeness and well-being (the most destructive form of self-deception) .

Tillich: Preliminary versus Ultimate Concern

Two major contributions to understanding the need for transcendence and the ways in which it can be expressed in both healthy and destructive ways are made by Tillich (1957) and Wilber (1980). Beginning with Tillich, we find in his description of faith another way in which the deep spiritual need of human beings is framed. For Tillich, faith is the state of being ultimately concerned. He describes the restlessness of the human heart, based on our awareness of an infinite to which we belong, as necessitating a commitment to an ultimate concern. The object of the ultimate concern is sacred and holy. As such, it transcends all ordinary realities and demands total surrender and that all other concerns be sacrificed. The ultimate concern unifies and gives depth and direction to all other concerns. In doing so, it integrates and unifies all facets of human beings and thus has healing power. It fulfills the deepest need and longing of human beings.

However, for Tillich faith is impossible in the absence of doubt. There is always an element of risk and doubt in committing to an ultimate concern based on the magnitude of sacrifice that must be made. An act of faith is rooted in courage that is affirmation in spite of doubt. Tillich (1957) writes:

> The risk to faith in one's ultimate concern is indeed the greatest risk man
> can run. For if it proves to be a failure, the meaning of one's life breaks
> down; one surrenders oneself, including truth and justice, to something
> which is not worth it. One has given away one's personal center without
> having a chance to regain it. (p. 17)

To succumb to fear deprives human beings of that which alone can fill their sense
of emptiness and longing and leads to despair. Tillich describes this in powerful
language:

> ...there is a place where the ultimate is present within the finite world,
> namely, the depth of the human soul. This depth is the point of contact
> between the finite and infinite. In order to go into it, man must empty
> himself of all finite contents of his ordinary life; he must surrender all
> preliminary concerns for the sake of the ultimate concern. He must go
> beyond the pieces of reality in which sacramental faith experiences the
> ultimate. He must transcend the division of existence, even the deepest and
> most universal of all divisions, that between subject and object. (p. 61)

Nonetheless, the anxiety and uncertainty that must always accompany the act
of faith, and the necessity of being willing to sacrifice all to an ultimate concern
often proves to be too much to bear. When this happens, the need for
transcendence cannot be totally be silenced but is channeled in ways that prove
destructive to one's well-being and causes suffering that could have been avoided.
Tillich describes this as committing to a *preliminary concern*. A preliminary
concern is that for which individuals are willing to sacrifice everything but that
fails to provide the total fulfillment they are seeking. Tillich (1957) calls this
idolatrous faith. It is looking for God or the Absolute in all the wrong places. It is
seeking the infinite in the finite. The forms that preliminary concerns take are
many, and all prove not only to disappoint and disillusion but to cause serious
harm.

Tillich describes one form as fanaticism based on resistance to any degree of
uncertainty. Fanatics fail to understand the symbolic and mythic expression of the
Absolute, instead taking these literally and erroneously and ascribing absolute
truth to them. These individuals succumb to authoritarian systems, religious or
political, that feed on their fear and promise to provide security in order to assure
that there is no challenge to their power and control. Tillich's description of the
dangers of fanaticism support the observations I have made previously about the
adverse consequences of extremism and its common link with dis-ease. Such
fanaticism is also characteristic of fascist ideology, which I have also identified as
a significant threat to well-being.

Another way in which committing to a preliminary concern can be understood
is to use an example found a number of times in literature. That is, selling one's
soul to the devil, as in the classic story of Faust, particularly its telling by Goethe.

As the story opens, we find that Faust is a man who has devoted his life to serious study and has mastered all knowledge available at that time. He is respected and renowned. Despite this, he feels a profound sense of discontent, disappointment, and depression because his search for the ultimate has failed. He is torn by a powerful conflict within him between his higher and lower nature. All other paths having failed him, Faust turns to magic which, as Underhill (1961) correctly observes, is the obverse of mysticism because it seeks to achieve transcendence by means of the exaltation of the ego and human will. Its goal is control, not surrender.

While practicing magic, Faust is visited by the devil, Mephistopheles, who recognizes his insatiable desire for power, fame, and glory. And so he offers him an enticing proposition. He will serve Faust and be completely at his bidding. Whatever Faust desires, Mephistopheles will give him without question. However, in exchange Faust must pay with his soul and, after his death, serve Mephistopheles. Faust agrees but asks for one provision. Since his entire life has been the frantic search for complete fulfillment and the answer to his deepest desire, this is what Mephistopheles must provide to him. Only when Faust utters the words, "Linger on, thou art most beautiful!," can Mephistopheles claim his soul. In the remainder of this classic work, we see how Faust is taken on many adventures and exploits by Mephistopheles in search of that perfect experience. Faust falls in love, has a romance with Helen of Troy, acquires riches, and is given tremendous power. All that is priceless and precious to the worldly mind is laid at his feet. But throughout it all he is unable to utter the words Mephistopheles is longing to hear.

Eventually, Faust realizes that what he is seeking is something truly transcendent and so is eventually saved. However, the tale serves to make amply clear that the seductions of preliminary concerns are considerable and that people are often willing to sell something as precious as their very soul for very little. The story of Faust is the story of all of us. Something that can be described as the Faust Syndrome can be found in all human beings. It consists of the following "symptoms":

- Boredom and a sense of emptiness
- Chronic discontent and a frantic restlessness
- Depression and despair in response to life's disappointments
- A feeling of being divided within based on an either/or attitude toward life
- An excessive sense of pride and egocentrism

In response to these experiences, human beings may choose not to heed their mystical vocation but instead be lured by the many false promises offered by the world and by those who prey upon their discontent. Hedonism, consumerism, fame, fortune, power—there are no lack of idols to ensnare and enslave us. And the greatest of these idols is ourselves, the overweening ego, so that there is no room for the Absolute in our lives. As Huxley (1944) correctly asserts:

"Our kingdom go" is the necessary corollary of "Thy kingdom come." For the more there is of self, the less there is of God. The divine eternal fullness of life can be gained only by those who have deliberately lost the partial, separative life of craving and self-interest, of egocentric thinking, feeling, wishing, and acting. (p. 96)

Wilber and the Atman Project

This quote by Huxley provides a fitting introduction to the important work done by Wilber (1980) on the need for transcendence and the destructive forms it can take. One of the significant contributions that he adds to our understanding of this need is situating it within a developmental framework. As noted earlier, human development can be described in terms of different types or lines and as unfolding as a series of progressive levels in which higher stages encompass and subsume earlier stages. Among the most important of these development lines is the evolution of human consciousness and sense of self both on a collective and individual basis. Viewed within the framework of the perennial philosophy, spirituality can also be understood as a developmental line. As Wilber (2000a) observes, descriptions of stages of spiritual development have been a fairly recent area of study. These theories can be used to elucidate steps along the mystical path and outline how the need for transcendence unfolds toward achieving a state of union with the Absolute.

Where individuals are developmentally or what stage they occupy exercises a profound impact on every aspect of their life. Thus, applying this developmental perspective is pivotal to the work of radical healing. Each developmental stage is like a world unto itself as it substantially influences one's self-understanding or worldview and provides the tools and rules one uses to negotiate life. This includes how individuals engage in their search for the Absolute. As Wilber (1980) describes, though human beings are consistently motivated by the need for transcendence, each stage prior to the attainment of final enlightenment and liberation poses constraints on how that motivation is channeled. The desire of the Absolute at these earlier stages ends up being both a conscious and unconscious compromise and substitute for the Absolute—an idea akin to the preliminary concern. Wilber writes: "The point is that each stage or level of growth seeks absolute Unity, but in ways or under constraints that necessarily prevent it and allow only for compromises: substitute unities and substitute gratifications" (p. 161).

Wilber (1980) describes the need for transcendence as the *Atman-project,* which has three different strands. The *Atman-telos* describes how each stage of growth seeks unity with the Absolute. The *Atman-restraint* describes how seeking unity at these stages is in ways or under conditions that prevent it and allow only for substitute gratifications. The Atman-project is then a compromise formation between the Atman-trend and Atman-constraint. The principle dynamic involved in the Atman-project centers on the polarity of wholeness vs. separation, which has been discussed earlier. While according to the perennial philosophy the greatest need and want of human beings is the re-discovery of their essential infinite and eternal nature, they are also terrified of real transcendence because it requires the "death" of their sense of being an isolated and separate self. In this way, the polarity of wholeness and separation is inextricably entwined with the polarity of life and death. Thus, as Wilber observes:

> ...men and women are faced with a truly fundamental dilemma: above all else, each person wants true transcendence, Atman-consciousness, and the Whole; but above all else, each person fears the loss of the separate self, the "death" of the isolated ego or subject. All a person wants is Wholeness, but all he does is fear and resist it (since that would entail the death of his separate self). Atman-telos vs. Atman-restraint. And there is the fundamental double-bind in the face of eternity, the ultimate knot in the heart of the separate self. (p. 102)

The Atman-project provides another way of elucidating the role that spirituality, under some circumstances, can be the source of different forms of suffering based on what Wilber calls symbolic substitutes. As in Tillich's discussion of preliminary concerns, Wilber states that these substitutes come in many varieties, including sex, food, money, fame, knowledge, and power. He also provides a useful way of categorizing forms these substitutes can take that parallel Kierkegaard's (1941) description of different forms of despair. One "wing" of the Atman-project is *subjective* in which rather than seeking to be one with the Absolute, individuals try to play God by means of inflating themselves and imagining themselves to be infinite and eternal. This focus on maintaining a separate self must contend with two major drives that then give rise to positive and negative sides of the Atman-project. These are the drive to perpetuate one's own existence, or Eros, and the drive to avoid anything that threatens one's existence, or Thanatos. The perpetual conflict between life and death. The dilemma posed is that while seeking to perpetuate one's existence is experienced as imperative, its ultimate fulfillment cannot be achieved without the "death" and dissolution of the sense of a separate self. Thus, individuals can manufacture and succumb to diverse symbolic substitutes that promise satisfaction of Eros but fail to deliver on that promise. Instead, the need for transcendence is perverted into the insatiable seeking out and acquiring of substitute gratifications fueled by the false belief that having all is a way of being all.

Clinging to a separate sense of self must always contend with Thanatos in the form of death and fear of death. Wilber believes that there are two forms of fear and anxiety arising from this encounter. One is so terrifying and overwhelming that extreme defenses are employed to resist or repress it. This, he believes, is the basis of many forms of mental disorder. The other is an accurate perception of a fundamental truth about human existence—what has been called existential anxiety—the inevitability of loss and death. Human beings have one of two choices in the face of death: to either deny and repress it or to transcend it. But to transcend terror of death, one must transcend the self since they come into existence together and can only disappear together.

In this respect Thanatos is not a destructive force but is actually the means to transcendence. Despite this, if individuals do not submit to Thanatos by sacrificing their self, they will instead channel the death wish or drive into *substitute sacrifices* that give rise to negative and destructive consequences. As Wilber (1980) asserts:

> ...all that is wretched in human affairs, all that marks man as the most insidious of beasts, all that brands him as a mass murderer and victimizer comes under the heading of *substitute sacrifices*. This was perfectly explained by Otto Rank's formula, which brilliantly summarizes everything we might say on the subject: "The death fear of the ego is lessened by the killing, the sacrifice of the other; through the death of the other, one buys oneself free from the penalty of dying, of being killed." (italics in original, p. 106)

This casts an important light on the act of killing. This insight, long understood symbolically in myth and ritual, is based upon the belief that less life for the victim is more life for the killer. This has been enacted in various sacred forms of sacrifice. It acknowledges an essential and fundamental truth of existence: that life lives off life. However, when the need for transcendence is perverted by the illusory desire to completely avoid death and to live forever, the denial of death becomes a powerful force that leads to terrible destruction. With the fact that the need for transcendence is the most powerful human motive comes the necessary corollary that it can be the basis for great good. However, when transformed into what Wilber calls symbolic substitutes, it can also be the motive for great evil, the most dramatic examples being murder and widescale killing as in genocide and war.

This leaves the *objective wing* of the Atman-project to be considered. Individuals who mistakenly aspire to immortality and grandiosity may seek out external props to support this illusion and alleviate their terror of death. Again these external props can be positive or negative. Positive substitute objects might include wealth, fame, or knowledge. Negative substitute objects might include criminal acts, drugs, or alcohol. In either case, the outcome is the same—a self-defeating and self-deceptive strategy that leads to disappointment and greater suffering for the individuals and for others.

When situated within a developmental framework, the Atman-project is present from the very start of the process and so is actually the thrust of evolution or ascending different stages. It gives rise to successive structures of consciousness, which then partially meet the need for transcendence while simultaneously failing to meet this need due to the creation of various substitutes for Atman. When there is a realization that these substitutes fail, they are abandoned and—as Wilber (1980) describes it—consciousness dies to that level, disidentifies with it, and transcends it. And so this process may continue to unfold until the need for transcendence is truly met in the experience of union with the Absolute—liberation and enlightenment. This perspective provides insight and guidance into what constitutes the trajectory of radical healing.

In the next chapter, the final source of suffering will be examined. That is suffering that arises from social factors. This discussion will build on the review of personal and spiritual sources of suffering. As I conclude the examination of the integrative and holistic framework necessary to correctly identify and respond to reasons for individuals' suffering, certain common patterns and themes will become evident across the three levels. This is an important contribution I hope to make to elucidating a model for radical healing that illustrates the ways in which, despite their differences, the processes that either promote wholeness or contribute to alienation share commonalities. These commonalities reflect what is basic to being human and aspire to realize what lies at the very core of healing.

Chapter 7

Social Sources of Suffering:
Ideology, Oppression, and Mystification

The societal nature of human beings must be both recognized and affirmed in order to provide a complete examination of the sources of suffering and to ensure that healing is truly radical. While the essential spiritual nature of human beings has historically received a dearth of attention by psychology and medicine, neglect and sometimes outright denial of the relevance of social factors have been even more prominent. This has not always been the case. For example, public health has a long history of being a discipline that has understood the significance of social, economic, political, and ecological factors in the prevalence of a wide range of diseases and other forms of affliction (Schneider, 2006). Its contributions to the elimination of deaths due to infectious diseases have been significant, as has its advocacy of primary prevention and the integration of social and behavioral factors in illness.

Likewise, community psychology, which emerged in the 1970s, has been critical of the overly individualistic focus of mainstream theories of psychology. In contrast, community psychology is the study of people in context, emphasizing the need to appreciate the interdependent relationship between individuals and the community. Community psychologists have critiqued reliance on individually based interventions, such as psychotherapy, to enhance well-being (Albee, 1990). Rather than intervening after the fact, community psychologists have advocated for primary prevention as a means of promoting competence and health before problems develop. They have argued for the need to work on economic and political issues in order to implement social change, framing problems in terms of different forms of diversity, and developing interventions designed to collaborate with members of the community. Finally, as described in previous chapters, critical psychology has shared in these critiques and has built upon them by means of expanding on the role that power plays in health and dis-ease, the ideological basis of the workings of power (i.e., neoliberalism), and the responsibility of psychology to promote justice and emancipation.

Despite these critiques, the dominance of neoliberal ideology has grown stronger over the years—particularly, as documented by Davies (2022), in the 1970s with the radical changes made to economic policies by Margaret Thatcher in the United Kingdom and Ronald Reagan in the United States. The work of

Friedrich von Hayek (2007) and Milton Friedman (Friedman & Friedman, 1990) became highly influential in advocating for deregulation and privatization, not interfering with the impact of market forces on shaping society, promoting consumption, and implementing radical tax cuts based on the belief that these would create wealth and maximize individual freedom to choose. These economic policies have exercised a profound impact on all aspects of life. More important, they have radically influenced how human beings are understood and treated, as will be discussed in more detail in this chapter.

This ideology has played a substantive role in how and why the fundamental social nature of human beings has not merely been neglected, but omitted from any thoughtful consideration of the role it plays in the quality of life. Neoliberalism not only shapes the ways in which human suffering is conceptualized and addressed but actually how it operates to minimize or trivialize the suffering it causes, and at times render it invisible. Similarly, it blocks awareness of the role of power in creating socioeconomic and political forces that cause a broad range of material and psychological harms, particularly on the vulnerable, excluded, marginalized, and oppressed.

In light of this, any analysis of the social sources of suffering must begin with an examination of ideology, what it is and what functions its serves. Of particular importance is how an ideology becomes so dominant that it becomes regarded as natural, inevitable, desirable, and incapable of change. The work of the Marxist philosopher Antonio Gramsci (1971) offers an important framework for understanding this process based on his idea of *hegemony*. Substantial work has since utilized Gramsci's work to analyze how the ruling class gets subordinate classes to willingly consent to their oppression. Understanding the ways in which hegemony is formed and maintained provides a powerful tool for exposing and opposing social injustice.

Following this is a description of the manner in which ideology profoundly shapes the sense of identity of individuals and their worldview. This provides insight into how this process functions to maintain ideology by thwarting awareness of it, thus undermining any effort aimed at challenging and changing it. The actual processes used to achieve this often lead individuals to unconsciously consent to and uncritically accept a toxic dominant ideology by tapping into fear and other destructive emotions. Moreover, the internalization of such an ideology is a significant source of social suffering due to the inculcation of beliefs and values that distort and damage individuals' understanding of themselves and others. This point leads to revisiting the problem of the ego discussed previously, as it helps to elucidate a number of the deleterious impacts of a harmful ideology.

The concept of hegemony provides the foundation for a discussion of the current dominant ideology, neoliberalism. A brief exploration of its historical roots follows a description of the key elements of neoliberalism. These common features allow for an examination of the critiques that have been made against neoliberalism, particularly in terms of the multiple ways in which it has been harmful to human well-being. The most significant and egregious way in which neoliberalism has exerted its negative impacts is by means of oppression, which I assert is the single greatest source of human suffering. To support this claim, I provide a comprehensive definition of oppression and its core elements, a review of the material and psychological harms it inflicts, a description of the levels on which it operates, and an elaboration of the process by which it becomes internalized. The work of the critical psychologist Thomas Teo (2021) on the close association between capitalist ideology and fascism will also be reviewed. This is necessary because identifying and undoing the workings of both must be a principal goal of radical healing.

The examination of the social sources of suffering concludes with an examination of a social process associated with hegemony that functions to mask the powerful influence of ideology and to distort or deny the suffering it inflicts. This is *mystification*. Understanding of mystification builds on the material discussed in previous chapters on the dynamics of self-deception and their role in all forms of dis-ease. It extends this work by providing a framework for understanding how pervasive and often hidden social processes are used to both provoke and quell fear and anxiety in order to manipulate human beings. Like self-deception, mystification is based on the powerful human need for stability and control. It uses this need to first trigger fear and paralyze the capacity for critical thought and then induce individuals not to question their experience. Preying on this state of vulnerability, mystification then uses extant cultural and ideological rules and resources to frame the problem and to offer ready-made answers and solutions that assure compliance and provide a false sense of security. Just as self-deception plays a prominent role in creating suffering on a personal level, mystification does likewise on a social level. In particular, the invalidation of the experience of human beings is an extreme and all too common form of violence used by the powerful to exert control and domination. In doing so, it exacts a terrible toll on the exploited and oppressed.

The Pervasive Power of Ideology

In looking at what ideology is and its functions, we need to return to a point made previously regarding the powerful human need for order, control, and meaning. This need is rooted in certain innate biological and psychological processes that were discussed in Chapter 5. The human brain is hard-wired to filter information to protect persons from being overwhelmed by the vast amount of environmental input that bombards them and to selectively attend to information important to their survival. Information is then organized and categorized into constructs or categories based on commonalities to impose order and thus create a stable worldview. These basic units of experience were described as schemas by Goleman (1985). Once these schemas are established, the need for control and stability continues and is expressed in measures taken to maintain these schemas. This is achieved by only allowing information that fits with them to be processed and screening out information that does not. These schema are then further organized into a comprehensive framework (worldview) for making sense of ourselves and the world (Spinelli, 2014). As a result of the narrowing of attention and blocking out of conflicting information, as Goleman (1985) observed, all worldviews have certain blind spots or lacunae that reflect biases, prejudices, and distortions. Nonetheless, because they serve the need for control, they are often rigidly defended.

A related biological process also described in Chapter 5 is the fight-or-flight response. It is automatically triggered by situations that pose a danger because they challenge our worldview and are experienced as beyond our control. Such situations are experienced as a threat to our survival because they disrupt homeostasis, or the state of balance that the body and mind seek to maintain. Additionally, they are experienced as posing a serious threat to one's existence because of the tendency for human beings to identify with their worldview. The fight-or-flight response has been a principal component of theory and research on stress and the various adverse physical and psychological responses that occur in response to events that are unpredictable and distressing. Thus, stress plays a significant role in understanding the development of a wide range of medical and psychological conditions.

Based on these processes, the creation of a worldview can be understood on an individual level as the capacity possessed by human beings to construct a mental map made up of categories and concepts, often rooted in language, which they believe is an accurate representation of their experience. They equate the reality they have created within to the reality that exists outside of them. Moreover, this mental map is believed to be indispensable to their well-being by providing a sense of coherence and intelligibility to their experiences and with it the feeling of control. However, because of the partial and symbolic nature of one's worldview, it is not a faithful or true representation of reality. Based on this, it is inevitably subject to challenges. Regarding one's worldview as true has been described as confusing the map with the territory, or the Fallacy of Misplaced Concreteness by the philosopher Whitehead (1969). Despite this, innate resistance to challenges of this mental map continue, even in the face of mounting contradictions. In its most extreme form, human beings adopt an increasingly rigid attitude toward these challenges and strive to maintain their worldview at all costs. When this occurs, the strategy becomes self-defeating and actually undermines the feeling of control, making stability even more fragile.

However, this is a one-sided understanding of the creation of a worldview because it situates the process solely within individuals. In doing so, it blames only them for prejudices and biases that contaminate their understanding. To correct for this, there is a need to include a social process also at work in the development of a worldview and this is where ideology comes into play. The term "ideology" has many meanings; Hamilton (1987) describes twenty-seven different elements of them across diverse literature. The meaning employed here defines ideology as the prevailing worldview present in society at a given time, shaped by existing social, historical, economic, and political factors. Human beings are born into circumstances that they do not choose. The worldview that they adopt is substantively impacted by these circumstances because they must use the cultural and ideological resources available to them. They employ language, ideas, and symbols that are shaped by the material and power relations embedded in their everyday social relations and practices. Individuals' worldviews are held in common by members of the community to which they belong. It is a comprehensive and more or less coherent system of ideas, beliefs, attitudes, and values that is so thoroughly internalized by members of society that its assumptive nature is unrecognized. Instead it is regarded as absolutely true.

This view of ideology, according to Jost (2006), has garnered research evidence in terms of its ability to predict attitudes and behavior, such as the difference between liberal vs. conservative ideology. For Jost, ideology is an interrelated set of moral and political attitudes that have cognitive, affective, and motivational components. Individuals espousing a conservative ideology, for example, believe that people are inherently unequal and thus deserve unequal resources and treatment. Conversely, those holding a liberal ideology are egalitarian, tolerate dissent, and are open to social reform. In terms of behavior, conservatives have been found to see the world as a dangerous place, accompanied by a fear of death, crime, and terrorism, They also tend to be rigid, dogmatic, and prejudiced toward groups regarded as deviant or posing a threat to them. Liberals demonstrate greater tolerance for ambiguity and openness. These findings support the relevance of ideology to understanding roots of social forms of suffering such as segregation, exclusion, and oppression. But the form that ideology takes and the worldview it espouses must be understood within broader historical, social, economic, and political circumstances (Rehmann, 2013). Its function is to uncritically reify or concretize social structures and practices in order to portray them as objective, natural, and universal. As a result, ideology is not subject to question or change.

Jost and Amodio (2012) explain the success of ideologies in achieving this function by highlighting that their existence is grounded in something inherent in human beings. They assert that human beings are ideological animals who have a basic need to decrease uncertainty, maintain a sense of order, and experience control. They base this observation on the work of Becker (1973) and terror management theory (Solomon, Greenberg, & Pyszczynski, 1991), both of which propose that the greatest anxiety of human beings is their imminent mortality. Ideologies serve to alleviate this anxiety, which is achieved by three basic functions. The first is the *epistemological function*. This provides answers to important questions asked by human beings regarding the purpose and meaning of life. Ready-made, common sense guidelines are given regarding how to deal with day-to-day social realities. The second function is *existential*. The beliefs and values imparted are not merely intellectual but are passionately held commitments rooted in powerful emotions. Jost and Amodio (2012) situate the affective underpinning of this function to parts of the brain and nervous system associated with the fight-or-flight response.

However, the existential function does not solely operate in extreme conditions. As will be discussed in greater detail later, despite being presented as coherent, rational, and absolute, all ideologies are riddled with inconsistencies and contradictions that become exposed in the extreme effort made to protect them. These contradictions open ideologies to dispute, often based upon the realization of the suffering that these create. The realization of the harms perpetrated by a dominant worldview is a potent stimulus for change. In light of this, to ensure that an ideology remains unquestioned and not subject to opposition, this suffering must be silenced and stifled by invoking the specter of an existential threat. Fear is a powerful weapon in maintaining the status quo. This is the foundation upon which mystification rests. This first blocks the exercise of any critical examination of its fundamental assumptions. Then the emotional appeal or seeming sensibility of the pragmatic guidance it provides is emphasized as a means of offering immediate benefit in stifling disquiet or anxiety.

The third function of ideology is *relational* as it provides a means of connecting with those who share it with us. This taps into the powerful need for belonging. Because one's identity is so thoroughly bound up with one's ideology, it is affirming and reassuring to experience a sense of solidarity with those who share it with us. This sense of identification with others who share our worldview is intensified under conditions in which there is a perceived threat to that group. Staub (1989) provides a powerful example of this in his study of mass killing and genocide. He finds that a common precursor to these events is what he describes as "difficult life conditions" in which shared beliefs and values are perceived as facing possible annihilation. Fear of this leads to an intensified need to maintain control and sense of purpose. One means of achieving this is by submitting to an ideology or a powerful, authoritarian leader. Another emotion provoked by uncertainty is anger. In order to deal with this anger and reassert a sense of security, those who do not share one's ideology become an outgroup that is dehumanized and subject to acts of aggression, including mass killing. Erich Fromm (1941) makes a similar observation. The radical social nature of human beings leads them to seek connection with others upon whom they depend for their very survival. When anxiety becomes intensified due to a perceived significant threat, this sense of connection can lead individuals to abandon their sense of individuality and autonomy and submerge themselves into a mass identity. Again, this can take the form of an unquestioned ideology or absolute authority. This is often accompanied by surrendering one's freedom and following the orders or dictates of authorities.

Hegemony: The Contributions of Gramsci

With this general framework for understanding ideology provided, we can turn to the important contributions made by the Italian Marxist philosopher Antonio Gramsci (1971) in his work on *hegemony*. As indicated above, both individual and social processes are at work in the creation and internalization of ideology. This is in line with critical psychology's emphasis on the social embeddedness of human subjectivity and agency. While larger social forces exercise a notable impact on the formation of a worldview, their effect is not absolute. Adopting the work of Marx and Engels (Eagleton, 2018), Gramsci regarded human beings as active, self-determining beings who were capable of shaping their own lives and history. For Marx, consciousness is a sensuous human activity, or what he called praxis. In his discussion of hegemony, Manders (2006) utilizes symbolic interactionalism and phenomenology that emphasizes the social nature of humanity and human activity, while also appreciating the uniqueness of human experience. Human beings are able to exercise agency on the world and not merely respond passively to social pressures. This understanding of the inextricable interaction between human agency and social processes and structures is important in providing clarity about how ideology serves as a substantial source of social suffering and how that suffering can be diminished and avoided by exercising one's agency.

According to Gramsci (1971), hegemony is a concept of reality held at a certain time in history that is dominant and is diffused throughout society such that it informs it at political, economic, social, cultural, religious, and moral levels. It functions as a form of "common sense" in that it is uncritically accepted and absorbed and, as such, utilized by individuals as they go about their lives. It is common in the sense that it is a kind of popular wisdom made up of beliefs, values, and attitudes that saturate society to the extent that they are widely subscribed to by its members.

Hegemony, however, is not merely a form of folk wisdom. It serves an important political function by which a dominant social group secures the loyalty and compliance of the masses in order to maintain the status quo. Hegemony portrays current power arrangements and the prevailing hierarchy as the norm. In doing so, it justifies social arrangements and practices that perpetuate inequities and oppression by presenting them as natural and thus inevitable. As such, hegemony is asserted to be the "official version of reality" and is posed as objective, veridical, and universal. The term "common sense" is understood as "the way things are," a matter that requires no justification or explanation. Based on the fixed and indisputable way that hegemony is posed, individuals are led to believe that any hope of changing it is futile and to conclude that they must resign themselves to circumstances no matter how unsatisfactory or painful they are.

The diffusion and dissemination of hegemony, as well as its enforcement, is achieved by means of an ensemble of apparatuses that organize the way individuals relate to themselves and the world. This includes institutions at every level of society. It is also described by Giroux (2008) as a form of public pedagogy in the sense that it is internalized by all members of society through cultural institutions charged with ideological control. In a sense, it is taught to everyone using language, discourse, metaphors, narratives, and moral precepts that organize the conduct of everyday life. This is a process that continues to unfold throughout the life of members of society because hegemony cannot be fixed or static. It must be constantly produced and reproduced in order to be sustained.

While hegemony is the basis of economic and political domination, it is also a ruling intellectual and cultural force. There is no area of human life that it does not touch.

Another characteristic of hegemony asserted by Gramsci (1971) is that it reflects national traits and characteristics. This reveals the role that historical factors play in the creation and formation of hegemonies at various times and in different places. This is similar to a point made by Wilhelm Reich (1969) in his discussion of the mass psychology of fascism. He observes that, particularly in a democratic society, a political program or movement will be successful only if it has some resemblance to the generally held expectations and beliefs of a broad category of citizens. There must be a certain degree of psychological preparation and receptivity to the beliefs and values purported by an ideology. Because of this, psychic repression depends on social oppression. This fits with the earlier discussion of the psychological dynamics involved in genocide and Fromm's (1941) analysis of the rise of fascism in Germany prior to World War II.

To secure consent to hegemony, it must be in accord with existing understandings that individuals have of themselves rooted in long-standing traditions, national myths, and important historical events. Manders (2006) provides a clear illustration of this in his examination of U.S. hegemony, which includes the ideals of freedom and democracy, the ethic of individualism, the value of competition, attitudes regarding authoritarianism and anti-authoritarianism, the American dream, and the cult of efficiency. These ideas resonate with U.S. citizens based on historical factors. As we will see, they continue to be a part of the neoliberal ideology.

Gramsci also asserts that hegemony is historically necessary. This goes back to the idea that human beings are ideological animals who require a worldview in order to render their experience as intelligible, coherent, meaningful, and to some degree manageable. This means that hegemony is not arbitrary. For good or evil, it is in many ways indispensable to the conduct of everyday life. However, that does not mean that hegemony is irrefutable and unassailable. Quite the contrary. It is not monolithic, fixed, or final. Rather, it is a compromise of competing views and values. It involves a dynamic equilibrium constantly negotiated between the privileged and oppressed. The sway of the ruling class, though dominant, is never absolute. Gramsci stated that at any time there are various worldviews that exist, and individuals have the possibility of making a choice between them. There is always a counter-hegemony present.

Moreover, while hegemony may be posed as universal, it always contains contradictions and inconsistencies that reflect opposing interests. This leads to the experience of conflict and ambivalence, particularly among the dominated. Efforts are exerted to disguise these contradictions and stifle ambivalence by means of mystification of events, issues, and power relations, which, if successful, get the dominated to consent to their exploitation and suffering. This is facilitated by the use of fear and anxiety by the powerful to block consciousness of the workings of hegemony. Manders (2006) points this out:

> Relying on common sense wisdom in everyday life does grave injury to a specific and centrally human characteristic: *the potentiality for critical thought*...Under the sway of common sense rationality, individuals' ability to entertain general political or social ideas in their own right, outside of their immediate, linear, instrumental context, becomes increasingly difficult, and often undesirable. The intellectual possibilities and powers of critical self and historical reflection atrophy. (italics in original, p. 90)

However, as described in a previous chapter, the experience of contradictions and ambivalence, and the suffering that inevitably comes with it, have the potential to allow for a genuine questioning of one's worldview. Though this experience may necessitate negotiating the anxiety and fear that accompany the experience of loss, it also offers the potential for emancipation. A critique of the taken-for-granted assumptions of hegemony expose not only the role that power plays in their creation and employment in various forms of injustice, but also enables individuals to take seriously their ambivalence and doubt regarding them. Disowned experiences can be reclaimed. And, most important, alternative beliefs and values that offer the possibility of emancipation and empowerment can be chosen.

Neoliberalism: The Current Hegemony

The previous discussion of ideology and hegemony makes clear the significant role played by social processes and structures in their formation and operation. This forms the basis for understanding the origins of social suffering. At birth, human beings possess a number of vital needs that due to their dependency they are unable to satisfy. As described in the earlier discussion of cumulative deprivation, it is the material and social circumstances into which they are born—shaped by powerful historical, economic, and political forces as embodied in the prevailing ideology—that determine whether and the degree to which those needs are met. Moreover, as Jost and Amodio (2012) assert, human beings' basic needs, including an ability to make sense of their experiences, cope with their mortality, and feel a sense of connection with others, are satisfied by a worldview that embodies an ideology. Thus, the ideology held by individuals exercises a profound impact on how they understand themselves and others and conduct their lives. This ideology is inculcated into human beings from the start of life initially through close immediate relationships and later by larger social apparatuses. All of these influences by virtue of being embedded within larger social systems subscribe to and enforce the ideas, beliefs, and values of the dominant ideology. The pervasiveness and power exerted by ideology is considerable, making it difficult to both discern and oppose.

While ideologies satisfy certain needs and provide a framework from which to give life structure and meaning. they likewise show clear partiality regarding whose needs are met and based on biases that advantage some while disadvantaging others. This is based on the political and economic functions performed by ideology that aim at maintaining and justifying prevailing power arrangements and distribution of rights and benefits. Thus, hegemony confers status and power for members of certain social groups while exacting certain costs and sacrifices from others. Such injustices are clearly one way in which hegemony is responsible for suffering. Similarly, ideologies are intended to enable human beings to better contend with certain powerful human emotions, principally anxiety rooted in uncertainty and fear associated with the threat of significant loss. However, as asserted by Gramsci, these same emotions are used by the powerful to exert control over those they dominate as a means of inducing them to accept the status quo. The prejudices and disparaging beliefs often found in hegemony also give rise to powerful emotions such as disgust, fear, and contempt, which valorize and advantage certain groups and stigmatize and disadvantage others. This is the basis for a number of social ills such as ostracization, exploitation, oppression, and violence, including genocide. Posing hegemony—which is actually a social invention that presents political and economic interests as objective, natural, and universal—is achieved by means of inhibiting critical thought and engaging in various forms of deception and obfuscation. This aims at stripping human beings of their agency, as well as leading them to distrust their experience—both potent forms of dehumanization.

In all of this, it is clear that the specific ideas, beliefs, values, and expectations that make up hegemony need to be scrutinized and evaluated in order to elucidate whether they espouse a life-affirming or death-affirming orientation. This has significant bearing on the well-being of the individuals who ascribe to it. With this in mind, we need to next examine the current hegemony of neoliberalism and the ways it proves to be destructive to well-being on a number of levels.

It is the general consensus of many thinkers (Davies, 2022; Giroux, 2008; Harvey, 2005; Moncrieff, 2021; Piketty, 2014) that the current hegemony is neoliberalism. While some of the foundations of neoliberalism can be traced back to both liberalism and classical capitalism, neoliberalism is a distinct ideology that redefines liberalism and adopts a more extreme, right-wing, or laissez-faire position regarding economic policy. Duggan (2003) describes five successive phases in the development of neoliberal hegemony, beginning in the 1950s and 1960s with attacks on the New Deal coalition, progressive unionism, and progressive redistributive internationalism. This was a period of Fordist and Keynesian capitalism. Fordist capitalism, with its roots in the early twentieth century, recognized that mass production meant mass consumption. Workers needed to be paid relatively high wages in order to ensure that they could buy the products they produced. There was thus an agreement between corporate capitalism and organized labor power. This laid the foundation for a consumer culture that has since grown even more virulent, in which workers were seduced by the offer of freedom and relative plenty in terms of consumption in exchange economically for accepting an increased sense of alienation and general lack of control over their work life and politically accepting a democratic system that manages but does not challenge capitalism.

Keynesian capitalism, prominent in the 1930s and 1940s, espoused state interventionism as a means of managing capitalism. As described by Davies (2022), it advanced a social democratic capitalism in which the state served as the guardian of the freedom of its citizens. It functions to protect individuals from obstacles to the good life such as poverty by means of social security, illness by means of universal health care, the harms of inequality by the redistribution of wealth, and the disadvantages of ignorance by providing universal public education. In this way it promotes the flourishing of all of its citizens. As Harvey (2005) observes, there was a crisis of capital accumulation affecting everyone related to rising unemployment and inflation. The discontent provoked was a threat to economic and political elites. At the same time, there was a significant outsourcing of production to the Global South and the growth of a "service economy" (from making things to selling things) in the Global North that was accompanied by lower wages, longer work hours, increased discontent with jobs, and growing levels of debt. It was then that neoliberalism began to gain considerable prominence, as evidenced in the policies of Ronald Reagan in the United States and Margaret Thatcher in the United Kingdom. Social democracy was judged to be a failure due to its fostering an excessive degree of dependency and entitlement, undermining personal responsibility, and inhibiting competition.

The foundation for this criticism and the posing of a neoliberal alternative was laid by the economist Friedrich von Hayek (1944) and carried forward by Milton Friedman (1990), whose television documentary series, *Free to Choose*, proved to be highly influential on political leaders and others. In it he extolled the benefits of a free market, argued for government deregulation of corporations and privatization, and pushed for radical tax cuts on the wealthy and corporations on the presumption that these policies would have beneficial economic consequences by creating wealth. All these became mainstays of neoliberalism. An element used by Friedman to make these ideas attractive, especially to democracies such as the United States and United Kingdom, was to align them with the value placed on freedom. In this case this meant preventing the tendency for states to become too powerful and dominant and thus infringe on corporations seeking to create wealth. It was also posed as providing individuals with an endless array of consumer goods from which to choose and freeing them from social constraints. However, in reality this was a form of propaganda and mystification used by the elite to increase their power and freedom while diminishing the agency of the masses.

With this history provided, the core elements of neoliberalism can be identified using the work of Thorsen (2010), Harvey (2005), and Davies (2022). These are:

- Human well-being can best be achieved by enabling individuals to utilize their entrepreneurial freedoms and skills in order to act from their rational self-interest.

- The establishment of free market and trade enables human beings to utilize their creativity in entrepreneurial pursuits and thus achieve a greater degree of individual liberty.
- The sole legitimate purpose of the state is to safeguard individual and commercial liberty and strong private property rights, and establish and protect an institutional framework that promotes free markets and free trade.
- The commodification by means of privatization and deregulation of public assets and services, including public utilities, social welfare services, public institutions (such as schools and prisons), and elements of the military.
- The establishment of markets where they do not exist is a function of the state.
- The state can employ legal structures, military, and police to ensure, by force if necessary, the proper functioning of markets.
- Leaving markets and trade free of interference allows for a greater degree of well-being and individual liberty and a more efficient allocation of resources.
- Adopting a laissez-faire policy ensures that the state does not intervene unless absolutely necessary in established markets or commodification because it is incapable of possessing the necessary knowledge to make beneficial changes or adjustments to the market.
- Corporations have a legitimate role in telling the state what to do regarding legislation and regulation to enhance profits and market expansion.
- Greed and competition perform positive functions in promoting social and common good.

The Harms of Neoliberalism: Inequality

While neoliberalism has claimed to achieve significant benefits, most of those purported have proven to be false. The multiple detrimental impacts of neoliberalism range from those on the individual level to planetary survival as reflected in the ways they have led to environmental degradation (Harvey, 2005; Joseph, 2018). Neoliberalism has been found not only to contribute to significant crises, including a host of financial ones, but also to actively benefit from these crises, as documented in Naomi Klein's (2007) work on disaster capitalism. An examination of some of the major ways in which neoliberalism has proven to be a toxic ideology offers evidence of how it is responsible for significant degrees of social suffering.

The redistribution of wealth touted as generating wealth and income across all levels of society has been substantially debunked (Piketty, 2014). Instead it has generated morally indefensible levels of inequality and driven increasing numbers of people into poverty. The weakening of the social safety net by neoliberal policies, insecure employment, stagnation of wages, unemployment, and catastrophic illness have all played a role in causing individuals to fall below the poverty level. Inequality of pretax income has risen steadily in the United States since the mid-1970s. Between 1975 and 2017 the 90:10 ratio of difference rose by 49% (Semega et al., 2020). Similarly, Davies (2022) reports that while in the late 1970s the top five percent of British households had an income four times higher than the lowest five percent, the richest fifth now have over 50 percent of all income compared to the lowest fifth. The most significant factor contributing to this disparity is changes in taxation policy. A study published in *Nature* in 2017 was the largest of its kind, based on a collaboration between social scientists from fourteen different institutions (Kohler et al., 2017). It examined factors throughout human history that contributed to economic inequality as well as current trends of inequality. The study employed a well-recognized and accepted measure of inequality called the Gini coefficient, ranging from 0 (least inequality) to 1 (most inequality). The U.S. Gini index was .81, an extreme degree of inequality. For comparison purposes, the Gini index for Patrician Rome was .59. Further, the degree of inequality in the United States exceeded that of all other industrialized nations.

Important and substantive research on the many negative impacts of inequality has been done based on social determinants of health (Davies, 2022; Marmot & Wilkinson, 2006; Wilkinson & Pickett, 2009, 2018). Social determinants are defined by the World Health Organization as the conditions in which individuals are born, grow, live, work, and age. These include neighborhood (housing, safety, transportation), access to and sufficiency of healthy food, employment, education, and health care. All of these factors are influenced by where individuals are on a social hierarchy based on income/wealth. Beginning with the classic Whitehall studies in the United Kingdom, Marmot and Wilkinson (2006) established a social gradient of health in which there exists a relationship between occupational status and morbidity and mortality. This finding has been replicated across a number of other countries. The risk of illness and death related to a range of diseases increases as occupational status decreases.

Marmot and Wilkinson proposed that stress plays a key role in this pattern. Occupations of lower status tend to have less stability, a greater degree of unexpected change, and often involve a greater degree of demand and a lower degree of control. Another factor proposed is different degrees of self-esteem based on one's occupational status. Having a lower opinion of oneself can also prove to be detrimental to one's well-being. The means by which stress gets under one's skin has been explained using the concept of embodiment (Krieger, 2005), which was discussed in Chapter 1. Human beings literally incorporate on a biological level the material and social conditions under which they grow and live.

Wilkinson and Pickett (2009, 2018) have further substantiated these findings. In their earlier work, they analyzed the relationship between inequality and well-being in twenty-three of the wealthiest developed nations. Once again a relationship was found between the degree of income inequality and a number of measures of well-being, including life expectancy, infant mortality, teenage pregnancy, obesity, drug use, imprisonment, social connection, educational attainment, and social mobility. While those occupying the lowest status in a society are most adversely affected, the degree of inequality when looked at across different societies impacts individuals at every level. In their later book, Wilkinson and Pickett focused on one outcome variable: mental distress. Their findings again confirmed the relationship between inequality and degree of mental distress, with unequal societies reporting twice the prevalence.

Wilkinson and Pickett believe that this finding is related to the societal nature of human beings based on the role that prosocial characteristics like cooperation and dependence played in early evolution. Inequality fosters a greater degree of competition and ruptures our sense of social connection and community. This leads to what they call *status anxiety* or the sense of fear, shame, and lack of esteem related to being seen as inferior or less valued than others. As Davies (2022) summarizes:

> For Wilkinson and Pickett, then, one of the worst effects of inequality is rising status anxiety, which separates, divides, and breeds fear between us. It is also associated with spending less time with our families and more time at work. It is linked with higher levels of depression, and with greater levels of consumption, as we buy more stuff in an attempt to win social approval and acceptance. (p. 318)

This research makes clear that, contrary to the dominant biomedical model that ascribes distress and dis-ease to physical causes, they are mostly the products of psychosocial factors. Realizing that egregious and avoidable levels of inequality are a form of social injustice necessitates a human rights approach to promoting well-being.

The Harms of Neoliberalism: Commodification

The mention of the use of consumption to shore up one's sense of self-esteem and worth raises another issue: the commodification of all facets of life by neoliberalism, which contributes to multiple negative health outcomes. Commodification assigns economic value to social goods, public services, and human beings that make them subject to the demands of the market—leading to dehumanization and a host of other ills. This development was observed by Marx, who placed the concept of commodity at the center of his philosophy (Rehmann, 2013), as illustrated in his view of alienation and his idea of *commodity fetishism.* Alienation operates at multiple levels, beginning with alienating the working classes from what they produce. Because they work for a wage and do not own the means of production, they can claim no ownership for what they produce. Instead they experience themselves falling under control of what they produce because it enriches the capitalist who owns the means of production. The next level is alienating the working classes from the labor process itself. They function solely as a means for capitalists to acquire greater wealth. Work is not experienced as fulfilling a basic human need to create and fulfill one's potential but just a means of earning wages that provide no intrinsic satisfaction. Commodity fetishism describes how all facets of life become commodified, including how people relate to themselves, others, and the world.

These ideas were subsequently taken up by critical theorists such as Horkheimer and Adorno (1995/1944), who recognized that culture was as much of a determinant of society as politics and economics. Culture profoundly shapes the understanding of individuals about what it means to be human based on a shared ideology. This again satisfies the human need for control and illustrates that the most important function of culture is to buffer individuals from awareness of their mortality (Solomon, Greenberg, & Pyszczynski, 1991) by means of a set of shared fictions sustained by social consensus. Ideology instills the belief that life has meaning and so enables human beings to face the inevitability of death with greater equanimity. Horkheimer and Adorno proposed the idea of the *culture industry*. This is based on the observation that the growth of mass media and the entertainment industry provided a new means of social control and ideological indoctrination. With the expansion of advertising and its permeating every aspect of life, individuals are manipulated to divert their attention away from the problems created by the status quo and induce them to believe that their needs and fears can be dealt with by buying products and engaging in other forms of consumption. This has led to the observation that neoliberalism has created a *consumer culture.*

As noted by Davies (2022), the work of another member of the Frankfurt School, Erich Fromm (1941, 1947, 1955, 1960, 1976), provided a prescient warning and important foundation for understanding the creation and impact of consumer culture. This is illustrated in his concept of *social character*, which can be understood as the process by which hegemony is internalized. For Fromm, beyond the role of biology and early childhood experiences, society exerts the greatest impact on shaping individuals' identity and way of looking at the world. Because of the powerful influence exerted by life-long socialization and the pervasive nature of ideology, social character includes deep and often unconscious beliefs and motivations rooted in notions of personal identity enforced by the status quo. It also includes desires instilled by the ruling order. Though we may believe ourselves to be responsible for who we are and the choices we make, the powerful messages and dictates from society play a prominent role in who we have become.

Fromm asserts that in order to survive, any society must mold the character of its members so that they want to do what they have to do. Fear, anxiety, and preying upon human vulnerability associated with their dependence on others are all employed to instill social character. These emotions help to ensure not only a high degree of compliance but also that beliefs and values are adopted unthinkingly and performed automatically. Fromm (1960) provides a detailed description of the process:

...most of what people have in their conscious minds is fiction and delusion; this is the case not so much because people would be *incapable* of seeing the truth as because of the function of society. Most of human history...is characterized by the fact that a small majority has ruled over and exploited the majority of its fellows. In order to do so, the minority has usually used force; but force is not enough. Eventually, the majority has had to accept its exploitation voluntarily—and this is only possible if its mind has been filled with all sorts of lies and fiction, justifying and explaining its acceptance of the minority's rule. However, this is not the only reason for the fact that most of what people have in their awareness about themselves, others, society, etc., is fiction. In its historical development each society becomes caught in its own need to survive in the particular form in which it has developed, and it usually accomplishes this survival by ignoring the wider human aims which are common to all men. This contradiction between the social and the universal aim leads also to the fabrication (on a social scale) of all sorts of fictions and illusions which have the function to deny and to rationalize the dichotomy between the goals of humanity and those of a given society. (italics in original, pp. 97–98)

This social conditioning is highly effective because as social beings humans do not want to become isolated and alienated from their social group. Two means are used to inculcate a conceptual system that governs what can be experienced and how experience is understood and acted on. The first is language. Fromm writes, "Language, by its words, its grammar, its syntax, by the whole spirit which is frozen in it, determines how we experience, and which experiences penetrate to our awareness" (p. 101). We have seen before the power of language to shape and maintain one's worldview. The second way in which experience is filtered is by means of the incorporation of an Aristotelean logic that frames issues in either/or terms. This gives rise to extreme, black-or-white thinking ill-suited to dealing with life's inevitable ambiguity. Instead, experience is forced into iron-clad, socially enforced categories based on a fear of being confronted with information that contradicts the internalized ideology.

Early on, Fromm (1976) sounded the alarm on the destructive impact of capitalism on social character (Davies, 2022; Foster, 2017). In particular, he focused on how consumerism and materialism corrupted beliefs and values in ways detrimental to well-being in order to further the goals of capitalism. He described this as the instilling of a *having mode of living* in which greed for money, fame, and power become the ruling passions of life. The most urgent need is to acquire private property, to buy products, and to consume things because this is the only means of achieving security and maintaining self-esteem. This extends to the ego itself, as Fromm (1976) wrote, "Our ego is the most important object of our property feeling, for it comprises many things: our body, our name, our social status, our possessions (including our knowledge), the image we have of ourselves and the image we want others to have of us" (p. 71).

Though society exercises considerable influence on social character, human beings are not passive or blank slates. In line with Marx, Fromm believes that human beings have an inherent species being rooted in their material bodies such that they are social and communal and have certain powers and capacities that they seek to realize productively and creatively (Eagleton, 2011). Based on this, when a social order neglects or suppresses these basic needs beyond a certain point, one outcome can be individuals seeking to make efforts to change the social order. Another more detrimental outcome is what Fromm described as *socially patterned defects* in which the conflict is channeled into certain forms of disorder (Foster, 2017). As Lasch (1979) observes, "Every age develops its own peculiar forms of pathology, which expresses in exaggerated form its underlying character structure" (pp. 87–88).

An illustration of this taken from Fromm (1955): It is what he calls the *marketing orientation* by which human beings experience themselves as a thing to be employed successfully on the market, as a commodity. Their sense of self is not derived from being active, loving, or creative but is based on their socioeconomic role. Their value hinges on whether they are successful and can sell themselves favorably to others. This creates a deep sense of alienation. One's worth is determined by how one is regarded by others, what one's status is, and how much and what one possesses. The driving need to exchange becomes detached from its rational function as a mere means for economic purposes and instead becomes an all-consuming end in itself reaching into all spheres of life.

A similar pattern has been put forward by Foucault (1975/1995) and Rose (1998), rooted in Foucault's concept of *governmentality*. This is the process through which governments produce citizens that are optimally suited to their policies and purposes. Foster (2017) contrasts social character as a bottom-up analysis based on its focus on the lived experience of individuals and their affective life with governmentality as a top-down analysis focused on policies and rationality. Particularly, in non-totalitarian governments such as liberal democracies, Foucault and Rose assert that out of a supposed respect for autonomy and freedom, non-coercive methods are employed to secure compliance with the reigning ideology. Under the cover of objectivity and neutrality, individuals internalize rationalized schemes for understanding themselves and others that guide how they pursue their goals (what is called *"regimes of the person"*). They also internalize technologies utilized for governing themselves and shaping their conduct in ways that comply with the dictates of the dominant ideology. Of note, both Foucault and Rose point out the prominent role that psy-disciplines, such as psychology, play in this process.

Rose (1998) argues that neoliberalism creates an *enterprise culture* in which citizens are inducted into a role of entrepreneurs of themselves. As such, they are engaged in the process of becoming whole and striving to be the persons they want to be by seeking to maximize their own powers, happiness, and quality of life. This is achieved by means of consumption in which they seemingly freely choose from a world of goods provided by the market in order to achieve success and happiness. Problems are regarded as solely private matters and so conveniently abstracted from the impact of a toxic ideology. Individuals must align their attitudes, values, and behaviors to fit market demands. Failure to do so is defined as a form of deviance and the sole cause of personal misfortune. Even health is not a personal right but a commodity. The pursuit of corporate profit at all levels is the driving force of society.

The adverse consequences of consumer culture have been extensively studied by Kasser and his associates (Davies, 2022; Kasser, Ryan, Couchman, & Sheldon, 2004) in what they call the *materialistic value orientation* (MVO). This orientation consists of belief in the importance of pursuing affluence and financial success, having the right kinds of possessions, and defining one's social status based on wealth and things one has acquired. This research finds that a powerful means used to cultivate MVO is fear and insecurity. Advertising and other forms of propaganda are used to create worries and doubts about one's self-worth and safety. The message is how consumption can compensate for these feelings. Another significant means of stilling discomfort is based on social learning in which individuals are exposed early in life to materialistic models and values. Individuals are conditioned to engage in social comparison with others to determine their self-worth. Companies invest millions of dollars annually in advertising to essentially "brand" children (Schor, 2004).

Despite the promises made by advertising, individuals with high levels of MVO have been found to experience multiple adverse effects. They report lower levels of life satisfaction; higher levels of physical symptoms of distress, depression, and other mental health problems; greater drug use; and lower self-esteem. They are more possessive and less generous. High MVO is correlated with narcissism along with less empathy for others, a tendency to be manipulative in their relationships in order to get ahead, a higher degree of aggression and interpersonal conflict, and feelings of social isolation. High MVO also has broader social and ecological consequences based on a greater proclivity to antisocial behavior and lower levels of social interest.

Commodification is closely associated with another negative feature of neoliberal ideology, the extreme individualism that it espouses. This has been touched on in terms of the emphasis it places on competition. Not only does this fuel selfishness and greed and higher levels of narcissism, but it also defines what constitutes individual well-being in ways that are consistent with the goals of capitalist economy and the market (Davies, 2022; Esposito & Perez, 2014). Being competitive, industrious, and ambitious in order to ensure a high degree of productivity and being happy in one's work are used as the means of judging one's wellness irrespective of any adverse effects this has on the person or on society at large. As Davies (2022) correctly argues, poor work performance has become a key characteristic of mental disorder, often necessitating medical intervention.

Hyper-individualism serves neoliberal hegemony in other ways that prove harmful. As described earlier, the medicalization of individuals' problems, accompanied by their politicization, is a form of mystification in which the actual impact of unjust social structures and arrangements on well-being are obscured by instead locating the problem solely within the individual. Individualism is upheld as a moral virtue, requiring people to assume sole responsibility for their choices and actions and their consequences. This is the pattern of blaming the victim that was observed before. If individuals are poor, unemployed, or suffer from some malady, their misfortune and suffering are due to their own fault and inadequacy. This not only renders the impact of external factors invisible, but it also stifles any protests or opposition to the status quo. In a competitive world, there must be winners and losers. This creates a persistent fear of failure which, if it occurs, leads to a sense of demoralization and hopelessness. An extreme form of meritocracy is asserted in which winners deserve their success and losers deserve their horrible lot, when in actuality the system stacks the deck in favor of some and not others (Sandel, 2021).

The assertion in neoliberal ideology that the market governs all facets of the economy as a natural, self-regulating entity that is independent of human intervention poses a paradox in terms of its simultaneous assertion of the importance of the individual. On the one hand, the power ascribed to the market shifts attention away from the actual material and social conditions created by human beings as a cause of suffering by portraying its operation as based on impersonal and absolute rules called market rationality. In doing so, it strips individuals of any agency. However, at the same time it holds individuals responsible for their suffering due to their failure to conform to the demands of the market. This view of the market is one of the principal myths advanced by neoliberalism. It is a form of *reification*, or taking a metaphor literally. It conflates the social with the natural. The market is a construct fabricated by thinkers endorsing neoliberal hegemony to advance the imperative of consumerism and to disguise the ways in which this myth is used to oppress the subaltern class to the advantage of the elite.

As Davies (2022), Esposito and Perez (2014), and Boggs (2015) all correctly observe, commodification makes all forms of human suffering a market opportunity for increased consumption and profit, principally by means of the privatization of health and social services. For example, Moncrieff (2021) and Davies (2022) document how the public health system in the United Kingdom has been steadily dismantled by providing care in a capitalistic manner. This leads to negative consequences for access, affordability, and quality of care. It has driven up benefit claims while at the same time trying to reduce them. Similarly, it has created less secure forms of employment while transforming "services" to the unemployed as an opportunity for private entities to benefit financially. Both Moncrieff and Davies have particularly critiqued psychiatry's role in advancing neoliberal ideology by medicalizing an ever-growing number of human problems that actually have their roots in predictable and understandable responses to adverse social and ecological conditions and trauma. This is clearly reflected in the ever-increasing number of diagnoses established by a panel of psychiatrists, the majority of whom have financial ties to the pharmaceutical industry.

What this has meant is a soaring number of individuals diagnosed with a so-called biologically based condition being prescribed an equally growing number of drugs to treat said condition—and soaring profits for physicians and pharmaceutical companies. Boggs (2015) likewise provides an extensive critique of how the health care industry has derived immense profits from the medicalization of problems such as obesity, addictions, shyness, and grief. Playing again on fear and insecurity, the health care industry (as well as other corporations offering products intended to bring people happiness and satisfaction) tap into the desire for a quick and easy fix. The problem, of course, is that these promises prove to be false.

Authors such as Moncrieff and Davies make a powerful case that the presumed underlying biological factors responsible for individuals' suffering are unproven. Accordingly, so too are medications and many of the other interventions employed to treat said conditions. Davies (2022) details the significant work done by Harrow (2007) and Whitaker (2011, 2019) that not only documents the lack of efficacy of psychiatric medications but also their frequently adverse effects. A pivotal point made by Davies (2022) is how neoliberalism and commodification have led to a highly detrimental understanding of the causes and nature of suffering. Davies (2022) writes, "As suffering is transformed into market opportunity, it is stripped of its deeper meaning and purposefulness. It is no longer seen as a crucial call to active change, or as the organism's protest against harmful or traumatic conditions, or as anything potentially transformative or instructive" (p. 225). This is, first of all, a form of self-created suffering based on a toxic ideology. However, it is also a form of self-created suffering due to its creating conditions under which individuals respond to their suffering in a way that only serves to increase it. The principal means by which these consequences occur is through the mystification of suffering (Gruba-McCallister, 2019). It is only by means of demystification that true healing can be achieved.

Finally, the dangers of neoliberal ideology's focus on selfishness, greed, competition, and consumption can be critiqued in terms of its detrimental impact on the spiritual nature and needs of human beings. The work of the German liberation theologian Dorothy Soelle (2001) provides an explanation of how this is so. Like Fromm (1976), she sees the emphasis on having rather than being as corrupting human beings as well as having a seriously detrimental impact on the environment. What she describes as *cult marketing* causes people to feel coerced to produce more, consume more, and accumulate more. However, it fails to satisfy their deepest longing or bring them true happiness. Buying is promoted as a religious act enacted in temples of consumption fueled by the false belief, "I consume, therefore I am." Rather than promote their liberation, consumer culture—greedy for more and more things and enthralled with the possibility of many options to choose from—creates a kind of addicted personality in which individuals become enslaved to their possessions.

As in Tillich's (1957) distinction between a preliminary and ultimate concern, obsession with consumption leads people to believe that their deep sense of emptiness can be filled by material things, which become idols for which they are willing to sacrifice everything. However, as Soelle (2001) observes, "Without mysticism, the image of the human being deteriorates into that of a consuming and producing machine that neither needs nor is capable of God" (p. 44). It is ultimately only the Absolute that is the answer to our emptiness (Gruba-McCallister, 2007). Losing ourselves in something external or material is not the path to freedom. A mercantile or market view cheapens one's relationship with the Absolute to an economic one of seller and buyer. Individuals see loving God as a transaction in which God owes wealth and happiness to those who have, in turn, rendered a service to him/her. As asserted by the perennial philosophy, only becoming empty and free of the ego is the means of attaining true liberation.

The Fatal Relationship Between Fascism and Capitalism

Throughout the discussion of the role of neoliberal ideology in creating suffering, a common thread has been how ideology leads to dehumanization based upon the abuse of power and privilege. This point is made by Friere (1970), who describes the ways in which oppression not only deprives its victims of humanity but also is made possible by denying the suffering it inflicts upon its victims. Turning human beings into things renders them incapable of experiencing the multiple material and psychological harms caused by oppression and thus absolves their oppressors of responsibility for the violence they commit or for feeling any empathy for the victims. Further, as Friere makes clear, in the process the oppressors themselves become dehumanized. Both the denial of the essential dignity and worth of those being oppressed and of their suffering are core elements of a death-affirming ideology, such as neoliberalism. However, these dangerous elements are also fixed features of another death-affirming ideology that has been linked with capitalism, fascism. Exploring elements of fascist ideology and the ways in which it shapes the subjectivity of individuals provides powerful validation of the significant role of oppression in causing suffering.

It has been the observation of a number of thinkers that there has been a troubling rise of fascism across the world, including in the United States, Poland, India, Myanmar, and Italy (Applebaum, 2021; Farooq, 2019; Stanley, 2020; Teo, 2020). Notable examples are Donald Trump in the United States. and Nirenda Modi in India (Farooq, 2019). Given the devastating and far-ranging consequences of fascism in Italy and particularly Germany in the 1930s and 1940s, concern for its re-emergence is clearly merited. As Teo (2021) observes, because fascism as an ideology and as a form of subjectivity is conditioned by historical and psychosocial conditions, the current form of fascism bears both similarities to and differences with earlier forms. Nonetheless, in agreement with the previously noted authors raising alarm about its rise, he makes a convincing argument that *fascist subjectivity* actually exists and can be seen in the current social circumstances. I will be using his work to describe the relationship between the extreme form of capitalism found in neoliberalism and fascism and the ways in which this creates conditions leading to oppression.

Teo distinguishes between political fascism and fascist subjectivity (FS) while recognizing their relationship. Political fascism is expressed in laws and policies, economic system, institutions, and broad beliefs and values held by individuals. Common elements of fascism include the following: ultranationalism, authoritarianism, xenophobia, us-versus-them mentality, racism, patriarchy, suppression of opposition, demagoguery, paranoia, violence, and militarism often leading to war. Early work on the psychosocial dimension of fascism included research on the authoritarian personality (Adorno et al., 1950), Fromm's concept of social character described earlier, and Reich's (1969) writings. A theory of subjectivity is not restricted to a first-person standpoint but must also include its essential relationship with inter-subjectivity and socio-subjectivity. All these facets are influenced by historically constituted theories, values, and practices. Based on this, Teo states:

> ...one can connect FS to the rise of existential and political crisis such as increasing income inequality, rising individual debt levels in many advanced countries, global warming, environmental destruction, voluntary and forced migration, and the pandemic, laying the groundwork for the receptibility of fascist ideas and practices. (p. 329)

Fascist subjectivity, both historically and currently, is seen by Teo as based on capitalist political–economic ideas, combined with racism and/or subhumanism. Others (Applebaum, 2021; Farooq, 2019; Klein, 2017; Stanley, 2020; Staub, 1989) have observed the impact that economic upheaval and the heightening of fear and insecurity it brings have on fomenting fascism. Such upheavals are common features of a capitalist economy. Teo explains that FS is based on a view of reality focused on the sources of wealth (having, producing, and distributing more than needed for bare survival); the production and distribution of resources, goods, and services; and the connection of these with power within a society. Teo describes neoliberal capitalism as "...an economic system based on exploitation, theft, and the immense accumulation of means, assets, and affluence in a few private hands" (pp. 332–333). It has created significant inequality and disparities in the distribution of wealth, as we have seen. This is combined with a belief fostered by various ideological apparatuses that there is not enough of these sources of wealth and material/social goods to go around. The experiences of inequality and scarcity together raise questions about who should have more wealth and benefits and why this should be so. This sets up an us-versus-them dynamic and leads to the construction of an Other who is regarded as inferior and one's enemy.

Neoliberal ideology values competition and hyper-individualism that fosters the belief that those who have wealth, social goods, and power have earned and deserve them and those who do not are losers who likewise deserve their misfortune. Losers should not and cannot participate in wealth, social goods, and power because of their laziness, weakness, and other undesirable characteristics. Thus, FS combines capitalist ideology with racism and subhumanism in the construction of the other. Based on racism, the excluded and oppressed are members of a despised outgroup (e.g., racialized minorities, immigrants, the poor, LGBTQ+ individuals). Teo sees subhumanism as more malleable than racism. It is used more widely to dehumanize certain individuals, including children, the elderly, the sick, and people with disabilities who can be humiliated and are regarded as disposable because they fail to contribute to the economy. Both racism and subhumanism are employed to justify the exclusion and deprivation experienced by those so designated and the disgust, fear, hatred, and contempt directed toward them. Moreover, those individuals identifying with the in-group who see the rich getting richer and experience inequality are encouraged to direct their anger and sense of unfairness toward the Other. This serves to block any criticism toward the neoliberal ideology actually responsible for inequality.

The most extreme consequence of racism and subhumanism in FS is the way in which violence, death, and even extermination of its targets are justified. Teo states that an essential element of fascist activity is *necropolitics*, a concept taken from Mbembe (2003). It refers to how a modern sovereign power can decide who can live, who can die, and who can be terrorized. In terms of FS, necropolitics is evidenced in attitudes about who is regarded as killable and dieable. Dieability is a more passive notion, based on a kind of Social Darwinism, such that the death of the weak, the vulnerable, and the inferior is seen as an unavoidable natural consequence. Thus, it is morally acceptable to do nothing to assist them. Killability, on the other hand, is directly targeting members of an outgroup for violence and extermination as they are regarded as dangers to and enemies of the dominant social order. Such dehumanization giving rise to extreme moral evil, as displayed in mass killing and genocide, has been observed by Staub (1989). These observations by Teo employ a range of concepts that are all exemplified in oppression.

Oppression: The Most Significant Cause of Human Suffering

It is fitting that this chapter concludes with an examination of oppression because it integrates the material regarding the social causes of suffering and provides an over-arching framework for it. The philosopher Ann Cudd (2006) in her extensive examination of oppression lists four types of theories of oppression. The first is psychological and sees oppression as an internal state of mind or feeling. This provides a needed recognition of the lived experience of oppression that by itself is individualistic and neglects the role of broader factors.. The second type of theory focuses on the role of inequality in oppression. This theory is based on a distributive view of justice that is concerned with whether the distribution of rights, resources, benefits, and burdens in a society are fair or equitable. In any society there is a certain degree of inequality, but in the case of oppression inequality is due to exploitation in which the material welfare of one group is attained through the deprivation of another group. Additionally, this inequality is achieved through coercion, and the magnitude of exclusion is morally indictable. Examples include denying basic rights and dignity to certain individuals or disparities in education, employment, and health care.

The third theory is related to the second's distributive view of justice and defines oppression as the imposition of unfair limitations on members of a certain group. The form ,such limitations take pertain to the types and range of resources and opportunities that individuals have access to. In oppression, this is impacted by where individuals are on a social hierarchy such that the privileged are afforded more choices and options while those lower on the hierarchy experience infringements and limitations that often result in cumulative deprivation. The fourth theory sees the essential element of oppression as systematic dehumanization of those considered of inferior status. This theory accords more with a procedural view of justice that focuses on the basic structure of society and the various systems, procedures, and processes that govern individuals. A just society is one in which like cases are treated similarly, procedures are fair and impartial as well as transparent, and the fairness of a decision is one in which those who are impacted or influenced by it participate in the process to the greatest extent possible (i.e., democratic). The philosopher Iris Marion Young (1990) makes this point powerfully and eloquently:

> Social justice entails democracy. Persons should be involved in collective discussion and decision making in settings that depend on their commitment, action, and obedience to rules…When such institutions privilege some groups over others, actual democracy requires group representation for the disadvantaged. Not only do just procedures require group representation in order to ensure that oppressed or disadvantaged groups have a voice, but such representation is also the best means to promote just outcomes of the deliberative process. (p. 191)

Within these four theories of oppression is a debate regarding two views of oppression. Nancy Fraser (1997) classifies these views of oppression as those that call for redistribution and those that call for recognition. The redistribution view adopts the distributive view of justice and so places its emphasis on the role played by the economic structure of society and the need to achieve a more equitable distribution of material resources as well as legal rights. It highlights the importance of the material forces at work in oppression. In contrast, the recognition view adopts a more procedural view of justice in which members of society are assigned an inferior social status and denied equality. The rights of individuals to engage in participatory decision making and to exercise the fundamental freedoms that enable them to express their agency and realize their capabilities go unrecognized. Young (1990) correctly observes that these two views are not necessarily opposed but interdependent.

Based on her review of diverse theories of oppression, Cudd (2006) states that a definition of oppression requires that four conditions be met. The first is the *harm condition* in which the harm caused is due to institutional practices. The second is the *social group condition* in which oppression is directed toward certain individuals based on their group membership by individuals who are members of a different social group. The third is the *privilege condition,* stating that members of the oppressing group benefit from the institutional practices. The fourth is the *coercion condition,* in which the harm caused is due to the exercise of coercion and abuse of power. This definition provides a valuable framework for understanding the origin of a broad range of forms of social suffering.

One other way of categorizing and describing the forms of oppression is provided by Iris Marion Young (1990). She describes the five faces of oppression, noting that it is more than just tyranny; it is actually embedded in everyday practices based on the operation of unconscious assumptions and reactions of often well-meaning people. This point is echoed by the philosopher Jean Harvey (2000, 2010) in her concept of *civilized oppression.* Harvey sees the workings of oppression in distorted and inappropriate moral relationships that occur in subtle ways found in everyday relations. Examples include implicit assumptions about who can take the initiative in relationships, who is more likely to be exposed to expressions of hostility and disrespect, and who has easier access to social goods. These examples reveal how individuals can hold what is often an unconscious hierarchy regarding who occupies a superior vs. subordinate position. Another example of this is the extensive literature on microaggressions (Sue, 2010), in which denigrating and damaging messages are expressed in a casual manner toward members of marginalized groups rooted in unconscious prejudices. The five faces described by Young are:

- Exploitation: the steady transfer of the results of labor from one social group to benefit another.
- Marginalization: members of a social group expelled from useful participation in various parts of social life and as a result subjected to material deprivation and even extermination.
- Powerlessness: group members take orders from others and exercise little if any control over their lives. As a consequence, they are unable to develop skills or autonomy. Professionals often exercise this form of oppression.
- Cultural imperialism: a dominant group's experience and culture assume universal status and are established as the norm for other groups.
- Violence: actions motivated by dehumanization and the "othering" of victims.

Cudd provides two ways of understanding the harms caused by oppression. The first category consists of material harms based on various forms of violence and deprivation or denial of the material resources necessary to a decent life. This can be linked to a *capabilities approach* to social justice (Nussbaum, 2006; Sen, 1999). Capabilities refer to what human beings are able to be and to do, practical opportunities that individuals freely pursue in order to achieve happiness and well-being. Nussbaum (2006) connects this approach to the Aristotelean view of flourishing or the maximum achievement of fundamental human potentials. For Nussbaum, capabilities express something essential about what it means to be truly human. She provides of list of these, including examples such as bodily health; senses, imagination, and thought; emotions; affiliation; and control over one's environment. When individuals are deprived of realizing these capabilities, their life is lacking in humanness. Similar to Maslow's (1971) hierarchy of needs, it is logical that individuals' most basic material needs be granted primacy in examining the adverse effects of oppression. This goes back to the earlier discussion of the extended dependency of the human species and the significant impact of inadequacies within environmental conditions on the development and life course of individuals.

The most obvious material force involved in oppression is violence, with the starkest form being physically harming individuals through the application of force. Violence can be either random or systematic. It does not merely damage its target but also those who witness it due to vicarious trauma. When looked at from a temporal framework, acts of violence in the past that continue into the present create additional harm due to fear of the threat of future violence. This makes victims anxious and constantly vigilant about any sign of impending violence. Persistent violence causes terror and trauma. Structural forms of violence can be accepted or tolerated by extant power structures within a society so that it has little or no consequences for the perpetrators, and victims experience themselves of having no recourse to justice. Whatever the form violence takes, from harassment and intimidation to killing, it stigmatizes its victims and marks them as inferior. Cudd (2006) observers, "Fundamentally, systematic violence is oppressive because it alters the sense of the possible of its victims, victims who are not only the direct objects of violence but also those who share group membership with them. Systematic violence circumscribes their choices to their own detriment and for the benefit of others" (p. 116).

A second material force in oppression is economic. Social institutions and practices economically disadvantage and harm members of certain social groups initially through deprivation. Poverty is a glaring example of this. Often, forces beyond individuals' control cause them to be poor and lack what is necessary to secure a decent level of living by impairing their ability to either produce or consume goods and services. Another example is economic inequality related to membership in a lower status social group. Exploitation, as noted earlier by Young, is a social process in which the privileged accumulate resources, wealth, status, and power at the expense of subordinate groups. The most extreme form of exploitation is enslavement, which also involves some form of violence. Exploitation, as described in the work of Karl Marx (1978) operates fundamentally by means of the class system established by the dominant economic institutions and policies in a society. These define the key elements of what work is, who does what kind of work, who works for whom, how one is compensated for work, and how the value of what one produces is distributed. An oppressive economic system is rigged, such that the haves benefit at the expense of the have-nots and social institutions and processes function to ensure that the hierarchy remains unchallenged and unchanged.

Another form of harm inflicted by oppression is psychological, which Cudd (2006) describes: "Psychological oppression occurs when one is oppressed through one's mental states, emotionally or by manipulation of one's belief states, so that one is psychologically stressed, reduced in one's self-image, or otherwise psychologically harmed" (p. 24). These psychological harms often have a material basis, as noted by Prilleltensky and Gonick (1996), who see oppression as based in asymmetric power relations. Oppressors use domination, manipulation, and control to restrict access to material resources, which leads to the oppressed feeling diminished, undeserving, and inferior. This is often accompanied by the use of an ideology that validates the power differential to implant fear and a self-deprecating view in the oppressed. These alterations in how the oppressed see themselves, the ways in which their identity is corrupted and injured, constitute the psychological harms of oppression.

Moran (2015) makes a compelling case that the concept of identity as a significant social, political, and everyday concept is shaped by the cultural–political economy of capitalist society. She uses what she describes as a cultural realist framework. Identity is often understood within an essentialist framework to refer to the core quality of persons that is unique and enduring and differentiates them from others. It is related to self-esteem and self-knowledge. However, the ways in which individuals understand themselves is substantively influenced by the social, political, economic, and historical contexts in which they are embedded. Returning to Moran's argument regarding the contemporary understanding of identity, she describes how the *social logic of capitalism* impacts how individuals living in this system understand themselves and others. Certain ideas associated with the capitalist way of life are reproduced in routine practices. Moreover, culture in the form of language, ideas, values, beliefs, and discourses functions as a form of material production and conveys what constitutes human nature, exploitation, and freedom in ways that are not necessarily explicitly articulated or defended. Moran writes:

> People who live in a society organised according to a capitalist logic will come to think and behave in a way that legitimates this logic and ensuing structure—not always and inevitably, but *habitually*, as they reinforce and reproduce this logic in their everyday actions. It is entirely possible that people may not believe or rationally accept capitalism's promises but

instead may resent living in and under capitalism, yet continue to perpetuate this social logic in their ordinary lives. (italics in original, p. 77)

Moran notes the damaging impacts of neoliberalism on individuals' identity, such as the intensification of consumerism through the manufacture of new needs and wants and the tendency to identify oneself with one's possessions. She also notes that capitalism must not be understood in mere economic terms, but as a sociocultural belief system that creates inequities in social power and the distribution of social goods, as reflected in distinctions in social class. However, she also notes that in light of human agency, the idea of identity can be used in ways both to conform to capitalism as well as to explicitly challenge it—again recognizing the inherent contradictions that exist within any ideology.

Returning to the psychological harms associated with oppression, these include the following:

- A sense of worthlessness, inferiority, and low self-esteem due to the internalization of degrading images and attributes.
- Feelings of surplus powerlessness, which refer to feelings of personal impotence beyond what would be expected with respect to actual limitations placed by the social context (Lerner, 1986).
- Learned helplessness (Seligman, 1975), passivity, apathy, and over-dependency.
- A sense of pessimism and fatalism that often leads to depression.
- Humiliation, degradation, and feelings of shame related to defamation, harassment, social distancing, marginalization, and violence.
- Feelings of guilt and blame for the oppressive conditions that impact them.
- Anger that is often suppressed, directed at oneself or at other members of one's social group.
- Experiences of alienation in which one feels estranged from or in conflict with oneself, disconnected from others, or socially isolated.
- Experiences of objectification in which individuals feel stripped of their humanity, such as their ability to exercise freedom or influence their lives.
- Development of disorders related to trauma.

In discussing the psychological harms of oppression, Cudd (2006) notes that an indirect psychological force operates in the form of *internalized oppression*. This refers to harms caused by members of oppressed groups to themselves because of their internalization of social beliefs and desires that then impact their choices and ways of dealing with their oppression. Understanding the impact of internalizing the oppressor sheds light on how and why individuals consent to and participate in their own oppression—the most dangerous and insidious danger it poses. A detailed treatment of this is provided in the book *Internalized Oppression: The Psychology of Marginalized Groups* (David & Derthick, 2014).

Internalized oppression is the outcome of various processes that have been described earlier beginning, with the oppressed accepting their inferior status. This leads to feelings of self-contempt, self-doubt, helplessness, and passivity. Oppression's most destructive form is shaking individuals' ability to trust their own experience as this strikes at the very heart of what is necessary to establish a sense of identity and worldview. David and Derthick write, "...the more oppressed an individual is, the more denial the individual has about his or her own reality as an oppressed person, effectively fragmenting the individual's experience of him- or herself and the world" (p. 9). If people cannot trust their own perceptions, thoughts, and feelings, they will be unable to trust those of others. This tears at the very fabric upon which human relationships depend. In the most extreme case, one's sense of what is real is undermined and can give way to madness.

We have seen how human vulnerability and dependence lead to a powerful attunement to the material and social environment. If individuals receive the consistent message that they are inferior and worthless, these negative stereotypes become unconscious and operate at an automatic level. Their origins from attributions made by others are obscured, and they take on the status of indisputable facts. Once the oppressed believe they are inferior, helpless, untrustworthy, and disposable, they begin to act in ways consistent with these beliefs, giving way to a pernicious self-defeating cycle. This can be expressed in depression, addiction, domestic abuse and other forms of interpersonal violence, and suicide.

Friere (1970) provides some additional insights into the impacts of internalized oppression. He describes how the oppressed experience an inner duality or conflict. By internalizing the oppressor, they adopt their standards, prescriptions, and guidelines. In other words, internalized oppression is also the internalization of hegemony. The oppressor is upheld as the model of humanity and, as a result, the oppressed always see themselves as falling short of humanity and so assume a negative identity. They incorrectly see society as good and just and thus their failures and unhappiness as deserved because they are lazy, irresponsible, and ungrateful. This is accompanied by a fatalistic attitude that leads them to feel incapable of changing their circumstances or to resign their state to God's will. Once more this becomes a self-defeating pattern.

A second consequences of internalized oppression is that the oppressed fear their freedom. Because they see themselves as weak and inferior, they have no trust in their agency and capacity to make choices or guide their lives. On one hand, they are afraid that they will make their lives worse or that in challenging authority they will experience damaging retaliation. This undermines their ability to join with others who share their experience of oppression and mount resistance. Instead they submit to authorities and let them make decisions for them.

The third and final facet of internalized oppression, according to Friere, has its basis in the paternalistic attitude that oppressors adopt toward the subordinate group. This is an integral part of the strategy used to get the oppressed to consent to their domination and place their trust in those who exercise control over them. Domination is portrayed as in the best interests of the oppressed. The powerful adopt a mask of beneficence. The oppressed develop an irresistible attraction to and respect for their "powerful protector." In cases when this attraction becomes particularly powerful, oppressed people are more likely to relate to others like them in a negative and devaluing manner. In what is called *horizontal violence*, they can even act out violently toward them. This helps to explain the paradox of individuals who have been victims of oppression at some point engaging in the oppression of others that they regard as inferior and whom they subsequently dehumanize.

This chapter has described the personal, spiritual, and social sources of suffering and the various dynamics involved in them. The next chapter includes a comprehensive and integrated method of assessment that provides a truly holistic understanding of human beings based on these different sources.

Chapter 8

An Integral Framework of Assessment for Radical Healing

The Foundational Work of Ken Wilber

The goal of radical healing as the promotion of wholeness has been a consistent key theme of this book. This is in line with the roots of the term "healing" having its origins in becoming whole, well, or sound. Likewise, the word holy has the same etymological meanings of wholeness, health, and completeness. This supports the assertion that healing needs to recognize that the fundamental nature of human beings is spiritual. The corollary of both of these points is that well-being is impaired or damaged by experiences of separation, isolation, alienation, and disintegration. Suffering follows encounters with loss and the threat of one's annihilation, the experience of being broken, or the shattering of the web of interdependent relationships, leading to a sense of alienation. While spirituality has been advanced as the core of what it means to be human, it is necessary to remember it encompasses and does not negate the other essential dimensions of our humanity: biological, psychological, and social. These central facets of human existence were described in Chapter 1 as four spheres of human existence set forth by existential thought (van Deurzen, 1997, 2002). These spheres include the fundamental relationships human beings have with themselves, with others, with the physical world, and with the Absolute.

We have seen how the current dominant worldview minimizes or actually negates aspects of human beings and the complex interdependent relationship between them. This constricted perspective is responsible for creating considerable suffering. Each of these four realms not only reveals something distinct about what it means to be human but is indispensable to promoting wholeness. Moreover, separation, disharmony, or fragmentation in any one of them will of necessity be reflected in the others. Thus, consideration must be given to the ways in which they interact with each other in order to fully assess the degree of individuals' well-being. This includes considering the relationship between mind and body and the embeddedness of the individual within multiple environmental contexts.

Based on this, a truly integral approach to assessment is essential in order to take into account the diverse but interdependent factors that affect where individuals occupy the continuum between health and dis-ease, wholeness and fragmentation. A valuable contribution to just such an integral approach was made by Ken Wilber (2000a, 2000b), who devised a comprehensive scheme that honors and incorporates the full spectrum of not only the diverse aspects of human beings but also the pluralistic approaches that can be used to understand them. Key elements of this approach include multiple factors and different systems that can be used to describe human beings. It provides a trans-disciplinary understanding of human beings, explanations of growth that can be applied to a broad range of lines of development, and a theory that embraces the full spectrum of consciousness. Wilber calls this the "all quadrants, all levels" (AQAL) model and it forms the basis for the assessment approach presented in this chapter.

This full spectrum view is represented as a quadrant organized around two fundamental dimensions of existence (Individual vs. Collective and Interior vs. Exterior). Combining these two dimensions provides a framework for describing and understanding a person based on these polarities. One benefit of the AQAL system is that it corrects for the one-sided, narrow, and incomplete conceptualizations that result when one or more of these quadrants are omitted. For example, psychology tends to be very focused on the interior individual quadrant in its theories and research and, as a result, collective factors impacting the well-being of clients are either minimized or omitted. Similarly, biologically based psychiatry tends to focus on the exterior individual quadrant with its exclusive emphasis on physiological factors in diagnosing and treating mental disorders. Other benefits of this model are the recognition of the interconnection that exists between these different dimensions and allowing for diverse but equally valid forms of knowledge for understanding persons.

The quadrants can be depicted as follows:

Table 1. All-Quadrants. All Levels (AQAL) Model

Interior/Individual	Exterior/Individual
Subjective Quadrant: "I"	Objective Quadrant: "It"
Consciousness/Intention	Behavior/Organism
Interior/Collective	Exterior/Collective
Intersubjective Quadrant: "We"	Interobjective Quadrant: "Its"
Cultural Factors	Social Factors

The quadrants are organized around two core dialectical dimensions of human existence that have been discussed previously. The first is subject–object, the polarity around which human experience or knowledge is organized, represented as the relation of knower to known. With respect to the quadrants, this polarity is conceptualized in terms of the perspective taken toward the focus of study, with subjective being interior or from the inside and objective being exterior or from the outside. The other dimension that has been central to my argument for radical healing is the individual and collective. That is, recognition that human beings (and other existing things) cannot be understood in terms of isolation or separation because of the interdependent network of relationships that make up existence.

In addition, to this quadrant framework, Wilber (2000a) includes other components that he drew from his extensive exploration of diverse theories and disciplines and synthesized into a comprehensive model or metatheory for the study of human beings. Development consists of multiple lines along which human beings can be assessed. Wilber (2000a) also recognized the long tradition in psychology of developing various measures or tests intended to describe things such as personality, traits, and types. These have been employed to discover certain consistencies or characteristic ways that human beings see themselves and act in the world. One example might be introverted vs. extraverted, as proposed by Jung (1933). The centrality of consciousness as a pivotal facet of not only human beings but existence itself was discussed in the chapter on spirituality. The final component of the AQAL system that completes the picture is attending to different states of consciousness, including both ordinary and altered states. Consciousness itself is viewed by Wilber as a spectrum of different states that human beings can occupy from one moment to the next. This idea was discussed in Chapter 4.

Putting all these components together makes holistic assessment possible. A valuable example of such an assessment tool was developed by Marquis (2008) in what he calls the *Integral Intake*. Taking an integrated approach, this assessment employs a range of different theories that can be utilized to understand and provide treatment for the diverse problem(s) for which individuals seek help. The Integral Intake also adopts what is called an idiographic approach to assessment. That is, rather than comparing data collected to standardized norms based on others, it uses individuals as their own reference point. The goal is to understand individuals uniquely and in their own right. Marquis' work forms the foundation for discussions in this chapter. Marquis provides a detailed and comprehensive treatment of the various elements of the Integral Intake in his book. This includes an explication of its foundation in the work of Wilber, the various elements that make it up, how it can be used in clinical practice, and research that supports its utility and validity. Readers are thus referred to his book for an in-depth discussion of these topics. Thus, rather than repeat this material, in this chapter I will describe in broad terms the various elements of this methodology and how they can be utilized as an essential part of radical healing.

Based on my discussion of the personal, spiritual, and social sources of suffering, I devote my attention to how this material can be used to build on the work by Marquis (2008). For example, Marquis notes how the Integral Intake corrects for the over-emphasis on the individual in traditional assessment, with little attention given to the environments in which individuals function. He also observes the general neglect of the importance of religion and spirituality to individuals' well-being. The inclusion of these issues in the Integral Intake is clearly laudable. That said, I believe that an even fuller appreciation and inclusion of these two factors is needed in view of the argument I have made regarding their importance to promoting optimal functioning. Thus, I will describe how these areas can be more completely integrated into the assessment process. Moreover, I advance a number of ideas regarding the different ways in which suffering has personal, spiritual, and social sources and how these function interdependently. In view of this, I will also discuss how these points can be integrated into the Integral Intake, allowing for fuller and deeper information relevant to understanding those seeking care.

Elements of the Integral Intake:
The Individual/Intentional Quadrant

This section focuses on the upper two quadrants that examine human beings from an individual perspective. I begin by outlining what aspects of human beings these quadrants are devoted to describing and the corresponding types of data collected using the Integral Intake. I then expand on this material, as noted above, to achieve a fuller appreciation for their relevance to holistic assessment. This includes not only a discussion of the interrelationships of these two quadrants but also, where indicated, with the two lower quadrants.

The upper left quadrant is called "Intentional" to convey its focus on inward experiences of individuals (perceptions, thoughts, feelings, etc.). This is in keeping with the importance of assuming a phenomenological stance in order to fully appreciate a person's worldview. The language used to describe this quadrant is "I" talk, or a first-person/introspective stance. This quadrant has been the focus of psychology, and the types of data gathered to assess this quadrant include self-image, intentions, motives, beliefs, emotions, and states of consciousness. Questions are directed at establishing the problems or concerns for which individuals seek help (e.g., presenting complaints), circumstances that tend to trigger these problems (e.g., precipitants), the history of these problems, persons' mental and emotional state, personal history, significant memories, life satisfaction, and the degree of control that persons feel they have over their life.

The upper right quadrant is called "Behavioral" because it captures the exterior of individuals, those aspects that can be seen or measured. This quadrant is typically the focus of a medical approach. The language used to describe the person includes "it" talk, a third-person or extrospective stance. Biological aspects of the individual are typically included here as well. As generally practiced, the focus of assessment again is on the problems or issues presented by individuals, the difference being that an objective stance is taken toward the data collected. Problems are described in terms that are observable, concrete, and measurable. Examples include habitual patterns of behavior, medical history and treatment, diet and exercise, sleep, and alcohol and drug use.

Returning to the Intentional quadrant, issues noted as pertinent to personal sources of suffering, such as the necessity of negotiating the inherent dialectics of human existence and the problem of the ego, provide additional depth and detail when assessing "presenting complaints" or "symptoms." However, the dominant tendency is to frame complaints or symptoms as a form of pathology, dysfunction, or abnormality, which neglects any meaning or significance they have. This poses a number of problems. It tends to emphasize what is wrong, deficient, or defective about persons, while giving little attention to their assets, strengths, and means of support. Such a bias results in a truncated and incomplete understanding of human beings and underestimates human potential (Maslow, 1971). By setting our standards too low, we may find pathology where it does not exist or even create pathology (i.e., clinical iatrogenesis, or the social construction of illness). The limitations and hazards of this perspective are assessed by Antonovsky (1987) in his critique of how the prevalent pathogenic approach is concerned with what and how one becomes ill. In its place he offers what he calls a *salutogenic* approach that explores factors that promote health.

Additionally, the very definition of what constitutes pathology is based on the biased values and norms of the dominant ideology of neoliberalism. What claims to be objectively descriptive and value-free is in actuality prescriptive as it portrays health as conforming with a harmful status quo. This emphasis on pathology tends to situate problems within individuals in ways that blame the victim by neglecting the prominent role played by larger external factors. It can also intensify a sense of alienation by implying that individuals suffering from such problems are different from so called "normal" people.

In contrast, I argue that the problems that afflict human beings are universal or inherent in the human condition. This assumption must guide any understanding of symptoms. One way to conceptualize the issues that give rise to problems is by associating them with what Spinelli (2014) calls *existential tensions,* or polarities intrinsic to human existence. Symptoms need to be understood by utilizing polarities that have been explored in previous chapters, such as Alienation–Integration, Life–Death, Good–Evil, Independent–Dependent, Eternal–Temporal, and Infinite–Finite. This approach returns to the distinction made by Fromm (1947) that existential dichotomies are fixed elements of human existence and thus incapable of being fixed or eliminated. They must be confronted and accepted rather than denied or resisted. In contrast, historical dichotomies are created by human beings and can be impacted. Oppression is based upon many examples of this contradiction, as in the case of rich versus poor, superior versus inferior, or powerful versus powerless. The meaning of symptoms can be framed based on what type of dichotomy they are a response to and whether that response is effective in coming to terms with that dichotomy or exacerbating it.

Similarly, the pivotal distinction that has been made between inevitable vs. self-created suffering must be included in any consideration of assessing symptoms. These two forms of suffering relate to these different polarities. Those conflicts that are an unavoidable fact of life give rise to suffering beyond our control and so is not capable of being avoided or eliminated. In contrast, choices made by human beings involving polarities capable of being ameliorated or eliminated constitute an avoidable form of suffering. An important part of the assessment process is determining which forms of suffering symptoms are represented and keeping this important distinction in mind. This provides critical insights both with respect to what underlying issues are involved and whether the way in which persons deal with their symptoms actually exacerbate their suffering.

This distinction between these two forms of suffering and how they are related reveals how symptoms are based on self-defeating cycles and on self-deception. This is reflected in the commonly observed pattern among those seeking healing in which they engage in various forms of coping or defense that fail to resolve the problem and end up making their situation worse. It is their resistance to the exigencies of the human condition that cause them the greatest affliction. Elucidating these self-deceptive and self-defeating patterns is thus key to assessing and describing symptoms.

Even though inevitable suffering is an unavoidable and necessary part of what it means to be human, individuals are inclined to meet it with denial or resistance. This initial response to threats or trauma is deeply engrained within the human body and mind and thus happens automatically or unconsciously, as explained previously by the work of Selye (1974, 1976) on the stress reaction and by Bakan's (1968) discussion of defense. If this inclination is incapable of becoming identified and suspended, healing would prove to be impossible. However, the inhibition or blocking of sincere reflection on the ways individuals perpetrate harm on themselves (as well as others) induced by fear, anxiety, and other powerful emotions can be recognized and reversed. The manner in which ambiguity is negotiated is central to whether individuals move in the direction of greater alienation or integration. As observed by Bakan, the key to understanding the dis-ease process is not the experience of conflict that occurs in encountering these paradoxes. Rather, it is responding to these conflicts in a non-reflective or automatic manner. From this perspective, symptoms can be seen as attempts to come to terms with what is experienced as being at issue in an extreme, rigid, and one-sided manner.

When resolution cannot be achieved, resistance to inevitable suffering amounts to a powerful form of self-deception in which individuals not only attempt to deny their humanity, but also the givens of human existence. This response inevitably proves to be self-defeating and creates even greater suffering—suffering that is chosen and so is capable of being eradicated. As

Kierkegaard (1941) observed, the attempt of human beings to try to be other than who they are is the most ridiculous (and destructive) of all transformations. Similarly, as Franz Kafka observed, "In the struggle between yourself and the world, side with the world." Refusing to accept the reality of what it means to be human creates the vicious cycle present in all forms of dis-ease.

What symptoms metaphorically express is both the means employed by individuals to come to terms with the existential issue confronting them and at the same time ways they seek to evade that issue. As a result, the experience of alienation and the disturbing emotions associated with it are intensified. This means that another important part of the assessment of the Intentional quadrant is to understand the underlying and seemingly contradictory meanings being conveyed by symptoms through metaphor, myth, and allegory. The work of Kleinman (1988) on illness narratives provides a highly useful example of this. It also highlights the connection between mind and body (the upper right quadrant) and the significant role played by collective factors (as considered in the lower two quadrants) in shaping the experience and expression of meaning through symptoms.

Kleinman provides some useful distinctions in his analysis. Illness, which he sees as the focus of the individuals' personal narrative, is how sick persons, family members, or the wider social network perceive, live with, or respond to the symptoms of disease—that is, the lived experience of the bodily processes attached to the disease and how the person evaluates or appraises these experiences. These narratives are always shaped by both the unique life experiences of individuals and cultural factors. Disease is created and defined by those who practice health care using theories of disorder in general biological terms. Sickness is a generic understanding across a population of disease based on larger political, economic, and social issues. Given these different understandings, it is not surprising that symptoms can have many meanings that come together as a way of explaining what has happened to the person, what can be done about it, and what it holds for his or her future.

Symptoms are based on an explanatory model used by individuals when their worldview has been disrupted and sense of control and order has been challenged. The illness narrative (or the way in which individuals describe their symptoms) can be understood as a story they construct and tell, and that significant others re-tell, to give meaning and coherence to their experiences. It employs a plot line, core metaphors, and rhetorical devices that embed private meanings but are also shaped by social context, current ideology, and historical and cultural factors. This view of symptoms as a narrative by Kleinman offers another useful framework for deciphering what is being conveyed by symptoms and the factors involved in this process.

There is one other perspective on assessment of the Intentional quadrant and of symptoms needed to maintain a holistic framework. Using a spiritual perspective, symptoms can be understood based on Kierkegaard's (1941) analysis of despair. He sees despair as based on differing degrees of self-deception, accompanied by self-defeating consequences. His analysis is another way to look at the problem of the ego using a Christian perspective but bears similarities to the Buddhist view. The ego continues to be an expression of attachments rooted in the desire to oppose the inevitable transience of human existence and the impermanence of one's accustomed identity. Kierkegaard sees this as the dialectic between finite and infinite that must be negotiated by human beings. The powerful need for control is rooted by Kierkegaard in the exercise of will and the need for human beings to submit their will to God in order to achieve authenticity. One expression of this willfulness is the way in which persons define themselves by means of identifications so deeply embedded that they are experienced as intrinsic to who they are—so much so that their loss threatens individuals with annihilation. As a result, they cling to them even more desperately. At the same time, these identifications constrict their self-understanding and view of the world. In doing so, individuals actually undermine any sense of control and instead become dominated by their identifications, as noted by Assagioli (1965).

Kierkegaard agrees that the most powerful of all attachments is the ego itself. This is idolatry in which we make a god of ourselves, a malignant form of narcissism—for Kierkegaard the most extreme form of despair. As Fromm (1964) observes, "The fight against idolatry...is at the same time a fight against narcissism. In idolatry one partial faculty of man is absolutized and made into an idol. Man then worships himself in alienated form" (p. 89). Tillich (1957) would see the ego as the most dangerous form of preliminary concern that stands in the way of establishing a connection with the Absolute or ultimate concern.

This framework provides a helpful addition to the Integral Intake as it allows for the integration of a psychological and spiritual perspective in understanding the nature of the problem(s) posed by individuals and the meanings of their symptoms. From this standpoint, the meaning of symptoms and the pattern(s) in which they are expressed disclose how individuals experience alienation on the deepest level. That is, a sense of alienation in terms of their essential identity with the Absolute. Aspects of themselves experienced as at odds with or threatening the idolatrous image they have constructed of themselves are disowned (the Shadow). Nevertheless, this disowned material manifests itself in indirect and disguised forms in symptoms. A deep sense of conflict is expressed based on an inability to find ways to integrate the core polarities associated with the Absolute, such as infinite/finite, eternal/temporal, freedom/necessity, and good/evil. Examples of failures to resolve polarities are described in Kierkegaard's (1941) analysis of despair and can shed light on assessing the Intentional quadrant.

The framework of insecurity, pride, and inertia as the principal causes of evil action can also be used to explain the dynamics behind symptoms. As reflected in the formation of the ego as an idol, the need for transcendence is channeled in ways that provide limited gratification and ultimately prove disappointing. This view of symptoms fits with Wilber's (1980) discussion of the Atman Project. For example, the inflation of self may be manifested in the pursuit of wealth, possessions, power, and fame. Alternatively, fear of the death of the ego can be expressed in substitute sacrifices that, in extreme forms, can give rise to destructive consequences, including killing or even war. These substitute gratifications and sacrifices also reveal how broader sociocultural factors such as neoliberal or fascist ideology exert an influence in how symptoms are experienced and expressed. The most dangerous expression of the inflation of ego is malignant narcissism, which has been discussed earlier and represents an extreme case of alienation, isolation, divisiveness, and self-deception.

Elements of the Integral Intake:
The Individual/Behavioral Quadrant

Turning next to the upper right or behavioral quadrant, attention is given to objective and observable factors responsible for dis-ease. Based on the *Ũmwelt* as one of the four fundamental dimensions of human existence, human beings must be understood not only as inextricably related to the natural world but as biological, embodied beings. Though there is a clear overemphasis on the causal role of biological factors on human behavior and various forms of dis-ease rooted in neoliberal hegemony, the material dimension cannot be neglected. Thus, any assessment must take the possible role of the behavioral quadrant seriously. However, as was the case with the intentional quadrant, adopting a narrow understanding of it will fail to provide a truly holistic assessment. Additional detail and depth can be achieved based on the relation of the material realm of human existence with the personal, spiritual, and social sources of suffering.

One way of expanding understanding of material factors is by examining them in terms of *embodiment*, which can refer to the biological incorporation of experiences; the subjective feelings, emotions, and sensations of the felt body; and attitudes, perceptions, and beliefs regarding one's body. Using the integral perspective of Wilber, Silow (2010) examines embodiment from a developmental perspective. She notes that bodily experience is the foundation of the formation of a sense of identity at the early stages of development, beginning in the womb with the emergence of movement and perceptions associated with it. As development progresses, human beings are able to assume the role of others and develop a theory of mind. This leads to a movement away from direct experience and to experiences becoming increasingly translated into cognitive and abstract terms. This fosters a more dualistic view in which mind and body are regarded as separate and distinct. As Silow, Wilber, Tart (2010) and others have argued persuasively, dualism poses numerous problems and obstacles to achieving well-being. For example, the experience of trauma can lead individuals to disconnect from embodied experience, with negative consequences.

Moreover, a large body of empirical data exists that conclusively establishes the close relationship between mind and body. This includes research involving meditation (MacDonald, Walsh, & Shapiro, 2013), hypnosis (Wickramasekera, 2013), biofeedback (Moss, 1999b), and psychoneuroimmunology (Kiecolt-Glaser, 2009), among others. This extensive body of research has made it clear that the traditional biomedical model of health and illness is inadequate based on its failure to take into account the inextricable relationship between mind and body. Anyone adopting a radical approach to healing must be versed in this literature both in terms of understanding the etiology and meaning of symptoms and in providing truly holistic care. The adverse impact on a sense of integrity or wholeness by disharmony or imbalance between mind and body, experiences of dissociation, or being dis-embodied, should thus be an area of assessment in the investigation of symptoms.

The work of David Small (2005), discussed in Chapter 1, provides an example of the importance of *embodiment* in understanding the materialistic basis of suffering. Small not only makes a case for how the body needs to be given consideration in assessment, but integrates the ways in which the relationship between body and mind, body and ideology, and body and the physical and social environment are involved. Small believes the body is the central channel through which we experience and act on the world. Based on this, Small challenges a focus on consciousness and rationality (e.g., cognitions, motives, intentions) as the basis for behavior. His perspective helps to illustrate the ways in which the physical and social environment impacts the embodiment of human beings. Rather than restrict assessment to the intentions, thoughts, beliefs and decisions of individuals, Small uses embodiment to illustrate how the dynamics of power and the actions of the environment contribute to suffering. Thus, Small's critique highlights how neoliberal ideology and the dynamics of oppression, often mediated by means of language, must be integrated into an assessment. This includes the ways in which harmful distortions and misconceptions regarding the experience of embodiment, the connection between mind and body, and the source of one's motivations need to be considered in assessment.

A similar critique is offered by Teo (2015) in looking at the work of Klaus Holzkamp (Schraube & Osterkamp, 2013) in critical psychology. Teo acknowledges the valuable contribution made by Holzkamp in making the conduct of everyday life central to the psychological study of human beings. This provides an understanding of both human subjectivity and the social embeddedness of human beings. Holzkamp adopted a phenomenological approach in order to give due attention to the role of subjectivity. However, in doing so, Teo believes that he privileged consciousness as an explanation of human action. Holzkamp believed that in their interactions with others, individuals engage in what he called reason discourses. This means that individuals in dialogue with each other provide subjective reasons for actions. In the absence of such subjective reasons, Holzkamp believed that actions do not exist.

Teo observes that this privileging of consciousness is based on a Western and European bias. To correct this, he believes that social epistemologies in which the body is central to mediating between individuals and society be included as well. This is because human beings live through their bodies as much as through their minds. Embodiment does not have recourse to reasons in explaining actions. Instead it may involve an unconscious process and a different way of knowing. As examples, Teo cites the concept of *habitus* by Bourdieu (1984/1979) and performativity by Butler (1989, 1993).

This critique of Teo offers another useful framework for examining the ways in which mind and body, and the two upper quadrants, can be combined to show how individuals understand themselves and others. The distinction between mind and body can be expressed in the two different ways of knowing, discursive vs. direct, discussed in Chapter 4. Bodily knowledge is more direct and immediate. It is not based on abstractions, concepts, or language and thus is non-reflective and unconscious. As noted, the role of mind comes to the fore during that stage of development in which the capacity of language and abstraction occurs—the basis for discursive thought. This distinction is also sometimes expressed as emotion vs. reason. Neither form of thought is superior to the other. However, they can conflict with each other and may be used in ways that are not appropriate to the situation or that distort experience. Utilizing these different ways of knowing is thus another way of conceptualizing patterns of functioning and elucidating factors contributing to dis-ease.

Two other important perspectives regarding the relationship between mind and body need to be considered. The first is the role of spirituality as based on the perennial philosophy. Spirit represents the highest level of the Great Nest of Being and, as such, encompasses and transcends the material (body) and psychological (mind) realms—the highest level of integration. With developments in areas of study such as quantum mechanics, there has been the emergence of what is described as a *post-material paradigm* in which phenomena traditionally associated with spirituality have been supported by often innovative scientific research (Tart, 2010). Areas of study include psi phenomena (precognition, telepathy, clairvoyance, and psychokinesis) as well as spiritual healing and survival after death. Substantial data reveal that conventional linear forms of cause and effect relations are unable to account for such phenomena. Rather consciousness can interact and actually influence material events, and human intentions can impact the outcome of tangible physical events. The principle of non-locality or action-at-a-distance demonstrates that events are connected independent of time and space. These discoveries pose a significant challenge to the continued adherence to a materialistic view of the universe and require consideration of non-physical concepts such as energy or spirit. In light of the prominence assigned to spirituality in radical healing, there needs to be an open attitude regarding inclusion of the post-material paradigm in assessing human beings.

The second perspective on the relationship between mind and body is advanced by Wilber (2000a) from his integral perspective. The mind does not interact merely with the body but also with culture and the environment. All four quadrants must be included as they mutually interact and co-evolve. Thus, we need to next discuss the lower two quadrants of Culture/Worldview and Society/Environment.

Elements of the Integral Intake:
The Interobjective/Environmental Quadrant

In the discussion of the social sources of suffering in the previous chapter, the groundwork was laid for understanding how the collective quadrants are inextricably connected to the individual quadrants in many forms of dis-ease. Prilleltensky (2012), in his article on wellness as fairness, provides an excellent framework for describing the relevance of the two collective quadrants and their interrelationship with the individual quadrants. He states "...well-being is a positive state of affairs, brought about by the simultaneous and balanced satisfaction of diverse objective and subjective needs of individuals, relationships, organizations, and communities" (p. 2). Positive is defined based on the many ways in which individuals and distinct cultures define thriving. In light of the four distinct levels he specifies above, simultaneous and balanced satisfaction means that needs of individuals and the systems in which they exist must develop concurrently and in equilibrium. Lack in any component of well-being can impact satisfaction in other parts. Prilleltensky's distinction between objective and subjective needs accords with this distinction is employed by the quadrants. Objective needs are material and physical ones needed to survive and thrive, while subjective refers to emotional and psychological nurturance required for flourishing. Assessment of these two types of needs can be useful in delineating how collective factors can either promote or impair the well-being of individuals. This is illustrated by the model Prilleltensky (2012) provided for analyzing and assessing well-being along the levels of individual, relationships, organizations, and community, using both objective and subjective indicators.

The adverse effects of the larger systems and the physical environment (Social/Environment quadrant) exerted from conception and over the entire life span have been well established based on social determinants of health (Marmot & Wilkinson, 2006); the role of inequality (Wilkinson & Pickett, 2009, 2019); the negative physical and psychological consequences of poverty (Rank, 2004; Smith, 2010); cumulative deprivation (Holz et al., 2023; McGowan & Szyf, 2010); and health care disparities (Chandran & Schulman, 2022). This body of research supports Cudd's (2006) observation that the initial impact of oppression is material harm. Elements of one's physical and social environment have direct and often devastating and long-term consequences on the body (such as the immune system, the nervous system, brain development, and even on a genetic level). This is in keeping with the ecosocial theory (Krieger, 2005) described in Chapter 1. This theory has compiled research from evolutionary and developmental biology to establish how embodiment actually leads human beings to biologically incorporate their lived experiences. Such adverse factors may include abuse, neglect, inadequate nutrition, lack of access to needed medical or psychological care, environmental toxins, homelessness or substandard housing, and crime. These are all areas of assessment that can be observed objectively and integrated in understanding individuals' suffering. However, due to the prevalent individualistic bias, these broad external factors are generally neglected as playing a role in dis-ease, which perpetuates socially unjust practice. This is especially egregious in light of the observation made by Barry (2005) and Rawls (1971) that the mere accident of one's birth gives rise to deep inequalities that exert a profound impact on his or her development and life chances.

From a social justice perspective, these harms can be understood based on distributive justice. This refers to the equitable distribution of resources, collective goods, and life opportunities that enable human beings to exercise certain fundamental or natural rights and meet needs necessary for well-being. A degree of equity must be achieved that encourages the optimal development of the capacities of all members of a society. Equity is established to enable all individuals to freely establish goals in the pursuit of well-being. The lower right quadrant requires consideration of the systems that are responsible for a broad range of detrimental consequences. Critical race theory (Ray, 2022) provides a useful example of the need to take into account structural factors in its explanation of the causes and consequences of racism. A focus on discriminatory attitudes and behavior rather than on the structures responsible for the causes and consequences of racism makes the same error of over-individualizing the cause of oppression.

Similar to the concept of hegemony, (Gramsci, 1971) processes that sustained structural racism is experienced as common, routine, ordinary, and just the way things are. This is reflective of an underlying ideology that is embodied in policies and practices that privilege some while oppressing others. These cause harm through the control exercised by legitimate social organizations, including educational, legal, economic, and health care that provide differential access to resources and opportunities. The material and psychological harms related to poverty, racism, patriarchy, heterosexism, and other forms of discrimination, exclusion, and exploitation stem from a dominant ideology that is embodied in the systems and institutions of a society and conducted in their policies and practices. Examining the structural and systemic bases of suffering relates to the second view of justice. This is procedural justice, which refers to fair, transparent, respectful, and democratic processes in which all members of society are empowered and able to exercise agency and autonomy.

One further explanatory concept is needed to complete this analysis: the role of stress. Research and theories examining how and why racism, poverty, and other forms of injustice cause physical and psychological harm have utilized the work on stress that was described in Chapter 5. Stress is the link between psychosocial factors and a broad range of negative outcomes. It is the way in which inequality gets under the skin. Research on social determinants of health, inequality, the damaging impact of consumer culture, and deprivation and denigration associated with poverty have all assigned a significant role to stress. As Rose and Hatzenbuehler (2009) conclude, "In this framework, people's bodies (including their brains, minds and emotions) contain the cumulative impact of their material existence and its meaning, primarily as an outcome of unequal levels of stress and its biological impact" (p. 463).

In summary, when assessing individuals based on the Social/Environment quadrant, the following areas should be examined:

- The role of deprivation, discrimination, exclusion, and inability to meet material and psychological needs give rise to chronic stress. This is often manifested as cumulative deprivation and disadvantage and leads to serious and enduring negative consequences. Early development has long-term effects on education, occupation, social function, and risk of physical and psychological disorders.
- Individuals who have been exposed to oppression and social injustice are at greater risk of adverse early life experiences (AELEs), defined as social interchanges experienced by fetuses, infants, children, or adolescents that are stressful, threatening, hurtful, or traumatic. They include abuse, neglect, diverse types of family dysfunction, violence or experience of violence, and bullying. Consequences include social, emotional, and cognitive impairment; greater risk of adoption of unhealthy behaviors; increased risk of disease, disability, and social problems; and early death.
- Economic insecurity is based on the inability to have sufficient money for food, shelter, clothing, housing, medical care, and other necessities. This is often connected with employment insecurity and exacerbated by elevated levels of debt (Davies, 2022). It has been found to be associated with numerous negative outcomes including neonatal risk, child maltreatment, domestic violence, depression, and suicidal ideation. Related to the adverse impact of fascist ideology, economic insecurity also has been found to be associated with racial anxiety and right-wing populism (Rebechi & Rohde, 2023; Teo, 2021).
- A poor education increases risks to well-being in a wide range of ways and through multiple pathways. These include brain development, health literacy, development of health-promoting behaviors, self-esteem and self-efficacy, feeling of belongingness, and employment/income.
- An often neglected social determinant of health is food insecurity, a condition in which the availability of or the ability to acquire nutritionally adequate and safe foods is limited and uncertain. Another factor that gives rise to food insecurity and nutritional deficiency is lack of access to affordable and healthy food, or what is called a "food desert." Both psychologists and physicians tend to lack awareness and knowledge regarding the connection between nutrition and both physical and mental conditions. Food insecurity/diet has been found to be related to many prevalent chronic diseases including cardiovascular disease, type 2 diabetes, and cancer. Food insecurity is also related to being overweight and obesity. Psychological issues and conditions related to food insecurity

and nutrition include anxiety, frustration, feelings of powerlessness, poor academic performance, and depression.

- Housing can impact the well-being of individuals in a number of ways. These include structural features of the housing (e.g., mold, allergens, toxins, pest infestation); location (safety, crime, access to green spaces and recreation); and availability of support and community networks based on location. Housing instability may be reflected in the frequency with which individuals move, sleep in a car or shelter, live with friends or other family, and homelessness. Poor housing quality and instability increase the risk of upper respiratory problems, neurological disorders and cognitive deficits, and accidents and injuries. Psychological correlates include anxiety, depression, and behavioral problems in children.

- Social isolation has been found to be associated with risks to physical and psychological health and increased risk of mortality (Umberson & Donnely, 2023). It has been an area of particular concern for older adults, but recent research has recognized that a developmental perspective is needed to understand who is at risk for social isolation and why.

- Lack of access to healthcare at all levels increases the risk of illness and death.

Elements of Integral Intake:
The Intersubjective/Cultural Quadrant

Turning to the Interior-Collective Quadrant requires assessment of culture (the way in which the dominant ideology is inculcated and maintained) and worldview (what is subjectively shared by a group of individuals based on the dominant ideology). That means assessing the central beliefs, values, attitudes, and practices espoused and enforced upon individuals and the ways they contribute to forms of injustice and their adverse consequences. In order do so, we need to consider the core elements of fascism and neoliberalism that compose current hegemony and how they play a significant role in oppression and other forms of injustice. Early study of fascism occurred during the 1930s, prior to World War II. It was influenced by psychoanalysis and Marxism and focused on personality and culture. The most important was the study of the authoritarian personality (Adorno et al, 1950), which developed various measures and scales to assess it. Certain traits were proposed to be associated with higher levels of authoritarianism and a greater proclivity toward prejudice. These included a rigid adherence to conventional beliefs and values, moralism, a submissive attitude toward authorities, an aggressive attitude toward those seen as violating conventional values, intolerance for ambiguity and a tendency to engage in either/or thinking, cynicism and hostility, and to regard the world as a dangerous place (Duckitt, 2009). Subsequent critiques of the measurements of authoritarianism and the theory used to explain it led to these ideas being neglected for further study.

In the 1980s there was a resurgence of interest when Altemeyer (1981, 1988, 1996) developed and did extensive research to validate the Right-Wing Authoritarian Scale (RWA). The RWA identified what he describes as three co-varying traits: authoritarian submission, authoritarian aggression, and conventionalism. In subsequent research, Altemeyer found that scores on the RWA were correlated with conformity with established authority, prejudice toward a range of stigmatized groups, less opposition toward harming members of such groups, dichotomous and rigid thinking, close-mindedness, intolerance for ambiguity, and fundamentalist religiosity. Possible biological and psychosocial factors responsible for right-wing authoritarianism can be found in his work.

Altemeyer's finding that high scores on the RWA were related in fundamentalist religiosity relate to another area of current research on White Christian Nationalism (WCN) and similar ideologies that indicate a growing movement toward fascism. Fundamentalist forms of religiosity, such as WCN, have been found to have characteristics similar to those connected with authoritarianism, such as dogmatism, literalism, submission to authority, patriarchy, anti-science attitudes, and racism as well as prejudice toward those regarded as violating conventional norms and values (Stewart, 2019). Armaly, Buckley, and Enders (2022) found, following the attack on the U.S. Capitol on January 6, 2021, that beliefs making up WCN are related to support for political violence when associated with three factors: perceived victimhood, reinforcing racial and religious identities, and support for conspiratorial information. Stewart's (2019) detailed examination of WCN also elucidates its clear association with values and beliefs associated with neoliberalism.

This body of literature was expanded upon by Thomas Teo (2021) in his essay of fascist subjectivity. Additionally, he draws a clear relationship between this particular form of subjectivity and capitalism, which makes his analysis particularly pertinent to the argument made in this book. An explanation of the concept of *subjectivity* used in critical psychology is pertinent based on its supporting how the four quadrants must be integrated in understanding the impact of oppression and injustice. Teo (2023) states that subjectivity refers to the wholeness of first-person somato-psychological life and consists of the entanglement or inseparable interrelationship of three elements: socio-subjectivity, inter-subjectivity, and intra-subjectivity. Socio-subjectivity involves the historical, cultural, and societal dimensions of subjectivity that individual subjects incorporate and transform. The interaction is not solely determined by the societal but also is not autonomously chosen by individuals, highlighting the dialectic between the individual and the collective. Human experience and action cannot be explained based on internal dynamics in the absence of societal, historical, and cultural realities. Individuals stitch themselves into societal conditions while integrating these conditions into intersubjective or relational and intrasubjective (e.g., thoughts and feelings) contents and processes. Subjectivity is unique, embedded in concrete everyday life, constituted through materialities and discourse, comprises both actuality and potentiality, and exists in concrete forms.

One such concrete form is *fascist subjectivity* (FS). Teo (2021) distinguishes it from fascist politics, which is expressed in laws and policies, institutions, the economy, and mass/individual behavior. Teo recognizes the contributions of the work on authoritarianism and Fromm's (1941) concept of social character, but feels these are insufficient to explain FS. He asserts that FS is a socio-relational phenomenon and writes:

> Currently, one can connect FS to the rise of existential and political crisis such as increasing income inequality, rising individual debt levels in many advanced countries, global warming, environmental destruction, voluntary and forced migration, and the pandemic, laying the groundwork for the receptibility of fascist ideas and practices. These are the conditions for the possibility that liberal Western democracies will see an increasing acceptance of FS, but they are not the content of FS...it is suggested that capitalist political-economic ideas and practices, combined with racism and/or *subhumanism*...are at the core of FS. (italics in original, p. 329)

As described in the previous chapter, Teo links FS to current global crises related to spiraling inequality and growing levels of debt, the global ecological crisis, and the disproportionate accumulation of wealth, resources, and power in the hands of the few—all of which can be traced to neoliberal hegemony.

As Stanley (2020) observes, fascism is the politics of us versus them—a polarity that is also advanced by neoliberalism, based on a shared hyper-individualistic worldview that valorizes competition, selfishness, greed, self-enhancement, and an exaggerated emphasis on responsibility. The adverse impact of these values is persuasively argued by Davies (2022) in his indictment of modern capitalism. He demonstrates how this ideology elevates the values of self-reliance, independence, ambition, and self-responsibility and frames individual well-being as compliant with these values. Behaviors and emotions that might negatively impact the economy are labeled as pathology, requiring corrective action. Both fascism and neoliberalism assert a natural and inevitable hierarchy in societies supported by the existence of an inborn drive among human beings toward asserting dominance, an idea maintained in social dominance theory (Sidanius & Pratto, 1999). The existence of this hierarchy serves to deny any form of equality across diverse individuals. This gives way to the categorization of individuals, based on group membership, into superior versus inferior, winners versus losers, and deserving versus undeserving. This is described by Teo (2021) as the process of the construction of the close and distant Other, which is central to understanding discrimination, exploitation, oppression, colonization, and the general dehumanization of target groups.

Together, fascism and neoliberalism combine economic practices and systems with racism and subhumanism in order to essentially justify inequality and oppression. They often employ a misuse of science and biological explanations, an appeal to what is portrayed as common sense (hegemony), conspiratorial ideas, and extant forms of prejudice to solidify acceptance of their beliefs and values. Sidanius and Pratto (1999) call these *legitimizing myths,* which, as described below, constitute a form of mystification. An example of one such myth is *meritocracy,* which is linked with *Social Darwinism* (Stanley, 2020). Social Darwinism was developed by thinkers such as Herbert Spenser and Francis Galton. It is a misrepresentation of Darwin's thinking applied to social evolution in which so-called "survival of the fittest" was interpreted as the reason for social inequalities. Those who are strong and members of a naturally superior group or race are seen as having earned and deserved their success in contrast to weak and poor, who are naturally inferior. As Stanley writes:

> Fascist movements share with social Darwinism the idea that life is a competition for power, according to which the division of society's resources should be left up to pure free market competition. Fascist movements share its ideals of hard work, private enterprise, and self-sufficiency. To live a life worthy of value, for the social Darwinist, is to have risen above others by struggle and merit, to have survived a fierce competition for resources. Those who do not compete successfully do not deserve the goods and resources of society. (p. 177)

Along similar lines, Teo (2021) observes that individuals who are disabled, old, and sick and thus do not contribute to the economy can be regarded as dispensable or dieable. If they fail in the struggle of life, their loss can be justified. In contrast, racism and subhumanism are used to categorize individuals in stigmatized or exploited groups, who are then regarded with contempt and hatred. They are underserving, lazy, inferior, and possible threats. Their lives are seen as worthless and so they are subject, if necessary, to direct killing and even extermination.

Several other elements of fascism described by Stanley (2020) help to complete an understanding of how it contributes to both individual and collective suffering. Fascist ideology subscribes to a mythic glorious past that has been lost due to some form of humiliation. This past is typically patriarchal and again is premised on the existence of a special ingroup deserving of past glory losing its status, in contrast to despised outgroups. Loyalty to the dominant group is accompanied by a sense of aggrieved victimhood at the presumed unjust loss of its elevated status. The function of education and other major social institutions is to ensure belief and pride in the mythic past and to stifle any dissent or disagreement. Thus, there is an anti-intellectual sentiment and a stifling of free speech. The imposition of order and compliance is framed as imperative to maintain law and order, to which members of inferior groups are perceived as significant threats. The primary tool for sustaining fascist ideology is propaganda— which employs a wide range of methods to distort, obfuscate, confuse, and deny reality, such as language, myth, metaphor, control of mass media, perpetration of conspiracy theories, and appeal to powerful emotions (particularly insecurity, fear, and hatred). A major outcome of the extensive use of propaganda is the creation of a state of unreality that breeds suspicion, undermines bonds of trust and mutual respect, and eventually leads individuals to question their own experience. Stanley states, "Regular and repeated obvious lying is part of the process by which fascist politics destroys the information space" (p. 57).

While the negative consequences of hegemonic ideology are expressed at an individual level, attention to the Cultural/Worldview quadrant enables assessment of how these consequences occur based on the inculcation of a damaging ideology across all members of society. The impact of this process is particularly damaging for members of stigmatized or outgroups. Special attention needs to be given to not pathologize the experiences and problems presented by members of those groups given their being particularly subject to discrimination, degradation, and dehumanization. This mistake is based on an exaggerated individualism. The range of negative material and psychological harms due to oppression and internalized oppression was described in the previous chapter. This is not to say that oppression does not have adverse consequences for members of privileged groups. As Friere (1970) observes, in the act of dehumanizing others, the oppressor also become dehumanized. Goodman (2001) describes five negative impacts on the privileged. The first is constriction and distortion of consciousness based on indoctrination and propaganda that shields them from awareness of their privilege. Moral costs, such as guilt and shame, come with realization of complicity. There can be blindness to their own history, culture, and traditions based on an ethnocentric attitude of superiority. And finally there are material and physical costs related to the negative impacts of oppression on society in general, including lower levels of trust, instability, and higher rates of crime and violence.

In addition to the impact of the relationship between neoliberalism and fascism, the culture of consumption and related ideas that foster competition, narcissism, and preoccupation with status is another example of how hegemony creates and shapes the various forms of distress, impairment, and suffering on a large scale. Assessment of problems presented by individuals needs to take this into consideration. Research on materialistic value orientation (MVO; Kasser & Kanner, 2004) found it related to insecurity, lower feelings of self-worth, lower life satisfaction, and a host of physical and psychological problems. From an early age, billions of dollars in advertising are devoted to "brand" children and transform them into consumers. The same advertising promotes the use of upward social comparisons by which individuals are encouraged to evaluate themselves based on people of higher status. Research (Fiske, 2011) finds that this leads people to feel worse about themselves and see the purchasing of more and more commodities as a way of alleviating this. The encouragement of self-focus and narcissism has had a highly detrimental impact on a sense of community. Putnam (2000) describes this as a decrease in *social capital*, which is the value and benefits of being part of a social network that fosters trust, cooperation, and reciprocal sharing of information.

The Role of Mystification

The role of self-deception in producing and sustaining suffering on an individual level is made possible by and paralleled on the collective level by *mystification.* Understanding of this process is necessary in order to assess individuals in terms of the Intersubjective/Cultural Quadrant. The subject of mystification, the role it plays in keeping individuals unaware of and questioning the causes of their suffering and their experience of suffering itself, is dealt with at length in my previous book (Gruba-McCallister, 2019). Several key points will be noted here as they elucidate how mystification promotes the inculcation and maintenance of hegemony and is fundamental to the method of propaganda. The process of mystification rests upon self-deception, which is most likely to occur when individuals' worldview is threatened, giving way to a heightened sense of alienation and intensification of anxiety and dread associated with fear of mortality. The use of fear is a potent weapon used in propaganda. As observed by Furedi (2005):

> The term "politics of fear" contains the implication that politicians self-consciously manipulate people's anxieties in order to realize their objectives. There is little doubt that they do regard fear as an important resource for gaining a hearing for their message. Scare tactics can sometimes work to undermine opponents and to gain the acquiescence of the electorate. However, as we shall see, the politics of fear is not simply about the manipulation of public opinion. It exists as a force in its own right. Nevertheless, the political elites, public figures, sections of the media and campaigners are directly culpable for using fear to promote their agenda. (p. 123)

This same fear paralyzes the capacity for critical analysis and self-reflection, just as is the case in self-deception, and so facilitates a passive and conforming response to the hegemonic illusions perpetrated by propaganda.

The assessment and undoing of both self-deception and mystification are core elements of radical healing. As I (Gruba-McCallister, 2019) stated:

> Mystification is a *social process* that utilizes ideology to manipulate the thoughts, feelings and behaviors of individuals to define what is real, what is not, what events mean, and what is possible or not possible for human beings to do. The primary aim of mystification is a political one, the maintenance of hegemony. Mystification shares with self-deception the aim of alleviating the distress, fear and sense of disintegration triggered by disturbing experiences that challenge one's sense of identity and worldview. (p. 257)

Important insights into the process and consequences of mystification are provided in the work of R. D. Laing (1967), who observes that the experiences of individuals are apodictically evident and beyond question. What Laing (1963) calls *ontological security* or being present in the world as real, alive, whole, and temporally continuous rests on this self-validating nature of experience. However, human beings are able to act on their own or others' experience either by confirming, validating, or supporting it or by denying, undermining, or invalidating it. Laing (1967) describes mystification as a transpersonal defense and explains, "We act on our experience at the behest of the others, just as we learn how to behave in compliance with them. We are taught what to experience and what not to experience, as we are taught what movements to make and what sounds to emit" (p. 37). This helps to explain how mystification is instrumental to propaganda and can render hegemony invisible while assuring unthinking compliance with it.

Raising awareness of the impact of mystification and propaganda requires increasing consciousness regarding the various means they employ. Alan Watts (1966), similar to Fromm's concept of social character, asserts that the ego is a social creation or a "hoax" that individuals are tricked into believing by their own consent. He elaborates, "This whole *illusion* has its history in ways of thinking—in the images, models, myths, and *language systems* which we have used for thousands of years to make sense of the world. These have had an effect on our perceptions which seems to be strictly *hypnotic*" (italics in the original, p. 51). The use of language to confuse, obfuscate, manipulate, and deceive in the advancement of power and perpetuation of oppression is frequently observed. This manipulation is achieved both in terms of employing the metaphoric nature of language to misdirect and conceal and by taking advantage of individuals' understanding language more concretely (sometimes referred to as *reification*) due to the suspension of critical thought caused by anxiety or fear. For example, Joseph (2018) points out:

> Overall, political language by its very nature imposes an associative mental framework that, if reinforced properly, can narrow one's thoughts about social issues. Through this process, people lose focus on other possible factors or viewpoints. Political language also exploits our innate tendency to be superficial, shortsighted, and fragmented...Language, therefore, beyond being our main tool to learn and communicate, can also function as a tool for social control by strategically imposing or restricting ideas, values, and biases through associative influence. (p. 34)

An example of this is the characterization of members of stigmatized and oppressed groups as less than human or with derogatory epithets. This increases the likelihood that they are deemed unworthy of living (Grossman, 1995) or, as Teo (2021) describes, "dieable."

Lakoff (2002, 2004) provides another key element that plays a substantive role in the ideological use of language in his concepts of framing and metaphor. He describes frames as mental structures that shape the way in which we see the world. These frames constitute what is regarded as common sense. They are part of what he calls the cognitive unconscious. People may become aware of them indirectly through the language they use to describe their experiences. These points fit well with the taken-for-granted nature of hegemony. In advertising and propaganda, framing is employed typically to influence on an unconscious level how individuals guide their behaviors, formulate their goals, and act in accordance with hegemonic values in conducting their lives. Lakoff describes the ways in which much of the language we use in everyday life is derived from market rationality and commodification. For example, he provides an extensive treatment about how morality under neoliberalism is associated with metaphors connected with financial transactions. A few examples help to illustrate this: people talk of profiting from experience, the costs of an unwise decision, owing someone who has done something good for them, retribution as paying someone back, or canceling a debt by doing a good deed. Lakoff believes that an understanding of the system of moral concepts that characterizes a society is important because political perspectives of considerable consequence are derived from them. This is because these moral metaphors provide answers to two critical questions that guide how society is structured and governed: what is a good person and what is a good society. For neoliberalism, the market is an essential part of the answer to those questions and so, not surprisingly, plays a significant role in shaping persons' consciousness and organizing society.

The role of the mystification of the actual suffering created by the neoliberal and fascist elements of dominant ideology requires particular attention because of the powerful obstacle it poses to healing. A recognition that one is suffering and a willingness to explore the roots of that suffering is the foundation of change. To understand how and why awareness of suffering is stifled, we need to recognize the powerful message conveyed by the dominant ideology that suffering is inherently evil and so without value or meaning and that it is capable of being either avoided or eliminated. The work of Davies (2022) has been previously cited based on his cogent argument that modern capitalism is responsible for a highly medicalized, marketized, and politicized means of dealing with suffering. The medicalization of suffering individualizes it while denying its socioeconomic and political causes and promotion of neoliberal commodification. This is because people are led to believe that they can essentially "buy" their way out of suffering.

In my previous book (Gruba-McCallister, 2019), I describe this unhealthy view of suffering as *the happiness imperative*. The pursuit of happiness is enshrined as a fundamental right in the Declaration of Independence and the view that everyone wants to be happy is regarded as self-evident and irrefutably true. However, the concept of happiness is actually quite complex and at times slippery. Its meaning is not merely personal but substantially shaped by social, economic, political, historical, and cultural context. For example, the author of the

Declaration, Thomas Jefferson, was very influenced by the philosophy of John Locke, whose ideas contributed to capitalism. Locke argued that the desire for happiness is the highest human motive and instilled as a natural law in human beings by God. He utilized a utilitarian view of happiness. The morality of an action is based on its outcome. Happiness is the pursuit of pleasure, property, or self-interest. A critical feature of this view that persists today under neoliberal ideology is its extreme individualism. This is further expressed in Locke's contention that government should not interfere with individuals' pursuit of happiness.

This emphasis on happiness and the privileging of positive emotions can also be seen in the growing popularity of positive psychology. Starting with an article in 2000, Seligman and Csikszentmihalyi called for a revolutionary shift in the field of psychology that would make individual flourishing the focus of research and practice. Since that time, positive psychology has become a growing movement. This includes extensive studies investigating and measuring happiness that have actually shaped public policy. It has also developed a range of interventions designed to cultivate optimism and foster positive emotions and thinking, all with an eye to improving the quality of one's life. However, positive psychology has been critiqued for its endorsement of neoliberal beliefs and values (De La Fabián & Stetcher, 2017). For example, it again over-emphasizes individuals in the tendency to examine and measure happiness based on subjective reports and emphasizing their responsibility for their happiness. Values promoting happiness are seen as private choices that people are free to make as long as they do not infringe on others' happiness. Methods to promote happiness are likewise individually based. Self-improvement is achieved mostly through individual effort, the cultivation of a cheerful and positive outlook, and attaining states of optimal performance. The extreme emphasis placed on happiness leads to a corollary assumption that negative emotions are unhealthy and destructive. This was described by Ehrenreich (2009) as the "tyranny of positivity," in which there is a pressure on people to always think positively in the face of illness, loss, and even social injustice.

The cultural imperative to be happy is critiqued by Ahmed (2010), who sees happiness as a promise used to manipulate individuals' consciousness, align it with the dominant ideology, and direct them to make certain choices in life while avoiding others. The correct choices are those that line up with and support the values and beliefs of the powerful and privileged. True happiness is attainable only by conforming with what has been mandated by neoliberalism as morally valuable. As a result, individuals' happiness becomes conditioned upon making others happy—people who are considered authorities whose prescriptions and directives must be obeyed. Ahmed also describes *happiness scripts* that play an integral role in governance of the subordinated and marginalized. These scripts are used to justify oppression and refute the role it plays in causing unhappiness. Those who fail to make correct choices and live their lives in accord with the mandates of the status quo have placed themselves in their subjugated and unfortunate position. Their suffering is an inevitable and justified consequence of their failure. This framing of their suffering simultaneously undermines any resistance they might mount against their oppressors.

In summary, the two lower quadrants of integral assessment provide a much needed framework for ensuring that the significant collective factors responsible for human suffering are taken into account. They also provide both objective and subjective data as part of this assessment by locating the causes of suffering both within large social systems and processes as well as within individuals. Finally, the intricate interrelationships between the multiplicity of factors that together define human beings are fully accounted for by incorporating all four of the quadrants.

*****

As noted, Wilber's (2000a, 2000b) AQAL system and Marquis' (2008) Integral Intake both include consideration of the importance of taking into consideration different stages of development and states of consciousness. These elements will be dealt with in the next chapter.

Chapter 9

From Crisis to Transformation: Creating a Counter-Hegemony

Against Therapy?

In the previous chapter, I provided a method to conduct an integrative and comprehensive assessment of different factors contributing to a person's suffering. My intent, in line with my consistent emphasis on the need to make our approach to individuals truly holistic, was to correct the neglect of the role of social and spiritual factors in current healing practices. This neglect is essentially based on a combined neoliberal and fascist ideology that dominates our understanding of ourselves and our world. And this neglect is neither accidental nor inconsequential. It is intended to blind individuals to adverse forces that substantively exercise a negative impact on their well-being and, in doing so, ensure that the role of this ideology is rendered invisible and so unassailable. This process succeeds because it utilizes fear associated with the loss of one's accustomed worldview and self-understanding. In doing so, it taps into individuals' natural proclivity to engage in self-deception and immobilizes their capacity for critical reflection. Elucidating the dynamics of self-deception is one of psychology's significant contributions to understanding the healing process. Self-deception and the cycle of self-defeat that it creates are central features of all forms of dis-ease. As will be discussed later, the identification and dismantling of the harmful illusions this creates is an integral part of radical healing. This is in line with the meaning of "radical" as being "rooted in." Healing requires a steadfast commitment to be rooted in truth and the essential facts of what it means to be human.

Psychology and other healing professions have fallen short of their commitment to promoting well-being by narrowing their scope to the individual level, to what is going on "inside" of people. The issue is seen as what is wrong with individuals and how they ultimately bear responsibility for their maladies. This is because the healing professions are not only deeply rooted in the dominant ideology but sadly function to protect and serve that ideology by neglecting the actual role of sociocultural, political, and economic factors. From this broader perspective, the manufacture of illusions is not simply personal or a manifestation of internal "defense mechanisms." It stems from a hegemonic ideology and what it portrays as "common sense"—the way things are and always will be. This leads to a form of mass self-deception achieved by means of mystification. Material and social conditions shape consciousness in often subtle and covert ways that obfuscate and veil the workings of hegemony. Ready-made answers and soothing solutions are widely disseminated to quell anxiety and silence insecurity. This also leads to the mystification of suffering actually caused by that ideology. This state of apathy and numbness leads individuals to assume a passive and even fatalistic stance toward the conditions that inflict harm on them and so consent to their oppression.

In light of how wedded psychology is to a toxic ideology, one can raise the question of whether psychotherapy and other forms of healing can claim to be effective and of positive benefit. This has been a critique made by a number of individuals, including critical psychologists. The strongest objection comes from those who espouse what is called an *abolitionist* position that argues the practice of psychotherapy should essentially be abandoned. A full examination of this debate is beyond the scope of this book. However, some of its key criticisms merit discussion as they bear on the question of whether a radical approach to healing offers a viable and desirable alternative. One of the most vocal and controversial of those espousing the abolitionist position is Masson (1988). There are two parts to his critique. The first comes from an extensive body of empirical research regarding the efficacy of psychotherapy. One consistent finding is that the most important factor in the success of therapy is the relationship between the therapist and the client (Wampold & Imel, 2015), attesting to the centrality of human societality. (The importance of the healing relationship in radical healing will be discussed in the next chapter.) However, some, like Epstein (1995), assert that "...there is not one credible study conforming to the basic rules of objective proof that testifies to the effectiveness of any psychotherapeutic treatment" (p. 1). Support used for this claim is research that certain factors typically assumed to be important, such as the training and experience of the therapist, the type of therapy, and the length (Dawes, 1994; Feltham, 1999; Moloney, 2013; Watters & Ofshe, 1999) have no impact on positive outcome. Dawes (1994) argues that factors unrelated to psychotherapy can account for improvement. One example he gives is the "regression effect" in which individuals enter therapy in a heightened state of distress that over time decreases or regresses to less extreme states of distress.

The quality of outcome research has often been targeted for criticism in terms of scientific rigor, the use of a control group, selection of participants, the role of spontaneous remission, and the inadequacy of outcome measures (Dawes, 1994; Moloney, 2013; Watters & Ofshe, 1999). Attempts have been made to fashion research based on the gold standard of the randomized control trial (RCT), which is the random assignment of similar cases with similar problems to experimental and control groups. Nonetheless, these studies have also come under criticism, including not controlling for the power of the placebo effect, bias in the construction of treatment and control groups, and the use of diagnostic categories without validity (Coles & Mannion, 2017; Epstein, 1995). Another common example of research examining the efficacy of different forms of psychotherapy for different types of conditions consists of a meta-analysis of a number of studies. Some of these report evidence of positive outcomes of psychotherapy. For example, Elliot and colleagues (2021) analyzed ninety-one studies conducted between 2009 and 2018 on the efficacy of humanistic–experiential (HEP) therapies. They found significant pre–post client change, large gains compared to clients who received no therapy, and statistical and clinical equivalence in effectiveness compared to other types of therapy. On the other hand, Leichsenring and colleagues (2022) did a meta-analysis of 122 studies including over 650,000 patients with a variety of disorders and treatment methods. They found that most effect sizes for target symptoms were small so that the impact of treatment was limited. Also risk of bias in the studies included was high. Thus, the picture is inconsistent and, in some ways, confusing.

From a critical psychological perspective, the critique focuses on the utilization of experimental and statistical methods that need to be submitted to serious scrutiny. These methods subscribe to the current commitment of traditional psychology to the values and assumptions of a positivistic, objective, and atomistic natural science paradigm. As Coles and Mannion (2017) observe, mainstream psychology's claims to science are used to justify its entitlement to status and power. However, it utilizes simplistic models of science that generate data that often have little meaning and relevance to subjects being studied. The focus on individualism is also apparent in the empirical research conducted by psychologists. As argued by Holzkamp (Schraube & Osterkamp, 2013), the experimental situation examines persons from the outside, or objectively, in isolation and acontexually. This is an artificial situation that neglects the essential interconnectedness between human beings and the contexts in which they are embedded.

An example of this is the atomistic or highly narrow understanding of the role of the placebo effect in healing. This is often seen as a sort of "error" effect that interferes with research establishing a causal relationship between the treatment employed and expected positive outcome. This is not only an overly simplistic but a mistaken understanding. An extensive treatment of the role of placebo in psychotherapy is provided by Wampold and Imel (2015), and the findings are complex and sometimes conflicting. Nonetheless, as they observe, the Contextual Model they propose, in which psychotherapy is understood as a socially situated healing practice, highlights how the interrelationship between the therapist and the client is essential to understanding the efficacy of the placebo effect. The role of common factors such as the quality of the therapy relationship, empathy, positive regard, sensitivity to the client's worldview, and expectation regarding outcome (placebo) cannot be examined and understood as operating independently; they are interdependent. For example, Wampold and Imel report that a meta-analysis of whether the expectations of clients are predictive of psychotherapy outcomes is influenced by the establishment of a therapeutic alliance between the therapist and client and adoption of an approach to the problem that is compatible with the client's worldview and accepted by the client. This analysis is in keeping with the previously cited key elements of psychotherapy put forward by Frank and Frank (1991).

Critical psychology, as noted, has its roots in Critical Theory, which took aim not only at capitalism but also at the excesses of modernism associated with it, including materialism, rationalism, and positivism. The scientific method patterned on the natural sciences was declared to be the sole means of establishing truth claims. In doing so it became an ideology called *scientism*. As Wilber (1998) argues, there is a need for epistemological pluralism to attain complete knowledge of the Great Nest of Being. Science is just one of several other valid modes of knowing. He describes science as the eye of flesh that consists of sensory knowledge. In addition, the eye of mind, or rational knowledge, and eye of contemplation, based on mysticism, need to be included. Critical Theory and critical psychology both reject natural science as appropriate to the study of human beings and identify the inappropriate political use of natural science to understand significant causes of suffering. It leads to the conflation of social and natural processes that fails to appreciate the role played by historical, economic, and political contexts. The belief that one's stance is objective and value free is likewise a fallacy as our understanding of all phenomena is based on interpretation that is inextricably bound up in multiple contexts. Treating the social world as natural reifies it and transforms it into something static and unchangeable. Such reification creates a socially manufactured illusion that the status quo is natural and inevitable and so incapable of change. The transformation of nature and human beings into simply a means to an end leads to subjugation of nature and treatment of men and women as mere objects to be used and exploited.

Coles and Mannion (2017) argue that critical clinical psychology must contrast itself with mainstream clinical psychology by critically reflecting on itself and openly acknowledging that it is value-based and unable to separate itself from issues of power. A central value of critical clinical psychology is engaging in a critique of existing power structures and relations in society that fail to promote equality and justice. Adopting the mantle of being objective and value free enables psychology to veil how it subscribes to the values and assumptions of an unjust status quo and thus engages in oppressive practices (Prilleltensky, 1997). In contrast, the subjectivity and agency of human beings must be recovered and reflected in the theories and methods used to study them. Coles and Mannion write:

> The focus on RCTs is an example of professionals, including clinical psychologists, being too narrow in what constitutes knowledge, and such knowledge has not been subjected to adequate scrutiny...An unquestioning approach to professional expertise and scientific evidence often marginalizes other forms of knowledge. This has occurred significantly in mental health services where lived experience is not given

any or limited tokenistic credit or status (Beresford, 2013; Wallcraft, 2013). This is unfortunate as lived experience is often rich in detail of people's lives in comparison to the abstract and sterile data of quantitative research papers. (p. 561)

The case made against the hazards of scientism brings us to the second critique raised by Masson (1988) and other abolitionists who argue against therapy. That is, the ways in which the current practice of psychotherapy and psychiatry are socially sanctioned forms of abuse. This is a subject that has been discussed in previous chapters. We have seen that numerous authors have spoken out against the ways in which psychology and psychiatry have been corrupted by power and exercise it to enforce societal norms and values. Those deemed to be "deviant" regarding those norms and values are silenced, marginalized, pathologized, and institutionalized. Masson (1988) describes how this has been the case with women, while others have provided cogent documentation of abuses toward other marginalized and oppressed groups (Fox, Prilleltensky, & Austin, 2009). Diagnoses that frequently reflect the bias of the dominant ideology are used to veil the workings of abuse, trauma, and oppression and to justify social control and regulation of individuals' lives. Given this, it is clearly correct to condemn the misuse and abuse of knowledge and power in practices such as psychotherapy and its victimization of individuals in the service of maintaining an unjust status quo.

Reform Therapy

However, does this critique make a clear case for the abolition of therapy? Critical psychology provides a well-thought-out argument regarding the limitations and biases of an overly scientistic approach to assessing the efficacy of psychotherapy. Reliance on a method patterned after the natural sciences places too much emphasis on those aspects of healing that can be rendered in objective, material, and measurable terms. The result is what Wilber (2000a) describes as a *flatland* perspective of the universe as solely material and energy—a perspective that falls far short of the integrative and holistic view necessary for radical healing. It omits essential aspects of human beings—their subjectivity, agency, spirituality, and essential interrelatedness with the world. Moreover, this highly materialistic, individualistic, and constricted view of human beings is certainly not inconsequential in political and economic terms. Quite the contrary. It is firmly rooted in a neoliberal and fascist ideology. This same ideology is likewise the ultimate cause of the different harms condemned by those arguing for the abolition of therapy. Just as critical psychology rejects the limitations and problematic biases of the empirical method that is subscribed to by mainstream psychology, it is also a vocal critic of how its paradigm for understanding suffering and healing is rooted in neoliberal ideology. That said, arguing against what is a tool used as an instrument of oppression in the service of this death-affirming ideology ultimately does nothing to put an end to it and establish a radically new one.

A central goal of critical psychology and psychiatry is condemning the political misuse and abuse of power by psychology and psychiatry. Instead it asserts its responsibility for promoting liberation through the establishment of more just and meaningful ways of living. As Prilleltensky (1999) asserts:

> In our inseparable roles as critical psychologist and critical citizens, we are concerned with the lack of social justice and how psychology masks social injustice, we are perturbed by the lack of caring and compassion for the disadvantaged and by psychology's indifference to them, and we are disturbed by the deterioration of the quality of life of millions of people and by psychology's apathy toward them. (p. 100)

Thus, critical psychology correctly identifies a significant form of social suffering that is rooted in human choices and actions that are capable (and in need) of being altered. But putting an end to that suffering will not be achieved by simply abandoning a means (i.e., psychotherapy) by which it is sometimes perpetrated on individuals. That is true even if the current form in which psychotherapy is practiced is worthy of critique. The true target for change must be the toxic ideology in whose service it is employed. That is what radical healing is intended to do. and critical psychology plays an indispensable role in this project.

As Coles and Mannion (2017) and other critical psychologists maintain, the task that must be undertaken is to uncover, interrogate, and deconstruct the workings of the unquestioned and taken-for-granted authority of hegemony in light of how it permeates all aspects of life. This is achieved by adopting a sincere and resolute attitude of self-reflection that submits to scrutiny any and all assumptions, beliefs, and values that guide the thought and actions of the healer and those they serve. It means recognizing the ever-present issue of power, its potential for abuse, and the ways in which its workings are obscured and barred from reflection. This process requires being thoroughly faithful to one's lived experience as well as that of others. It must be guided by compassion and a commitment to justice as the core values essential to well-being. Our gaze must be freed from excessive self-absorption and a narrow focus on the individual in order to achieve fuller appreciation of the impact of the multiple contexts in which we and others are embedded. Questions must move from "What is wrong with me?" to "What is wrong with the world and not with me?" "What are the natural consequences of living life in the face of countless losses, injuries, and traumas rooted in injustice?" "How is my suffering a form of my trying to adapt as best as possible to these experiences rather than a manifestation of some manufactured disorder?"

While understanding the answer to these questions is an important first step, simply saying "No" to injustice is not enough. Yes, radical healing must uncover and dispel one's indoctrination in a toxic ideology, but it must also work to overthrow that ideology. Just as insight alone is insufficient to lead to change in individual psychotherapy, understanding that one has been impacted by injustice is not enough to achieve justice. This discovery must lead to constructive action, or praxis. It must be directed to achieving emancipation both individually and collectively. Teo (2015) speaks to this ethical–political practice, "Critical psychologists do not accept the present structures of society as unchangeable realities. An understanding of the world, of society, and of subcultures allows for change, and the truth of this idea cannot be decided in neutral reflection, but in personal thought and activism" (p. 249).

Further, that does not mean that healing can abolish all suffering. This is another major counterpoint to the abolition position. The attainment of greater justice and the elimination of healing practiced solely for purposes of profit will, no doubt, lead to some decrease in the number of people in need of psychotherapy. However, there will always be suffering inherent in the human condition—inescapable suffering—and thus a need for a compassionate response to those who are afflicted. This recalls the discussion of the earliest examples of healing in the shamanic and indigenous traditions, as well as the teaching of the Buddha and other great spiritual teachers. All of them recognize that there are sources of suffering that cannot be avoided and removed. Such experiences of suffering call upon human beings to provide compassionate care for themselves and their fellow human beings. The theologian John Hick (1989) describes this as the *soteriological function* of religion that emerged during the Axial Age, a time when human beings experienced a notable growth in self-awareness. This led them to become more attuned to human evil and weakness, ever-present insecurity, and the magnitude of suffering in the world. Despite this keener awareness of life's worries and woes, the great wisdom traditions that developed during this era espoused a cosmic optimism—the belief that human beings could move from this state of alienation to a radically better one through liberation.

The great teachers offered valuable guidance about how to make this transition and, in doing so, imparted a strong practical and ethical dimension to religion. There was instruction regarding how to live a good life. A core teaching in these traditions through time was that individuals needed to conduct themselves in accordance with the moral precept that it is evil to cause others to suffer and good to be compassionate toward themselves and others in order to alleviate suffering. It elevated the values of compassion and justice that are central to radical healing. This soteriological function and a belief that suffering can have a redemptive or liberative value must be the basis of radical healing, and so it is to this point that we next turn.

When Things Fall Apart, the Work Starts

In my previous book (Gruba-McCallister, 2019), I describe how the experience of disillusionment generally serves as the starting point of the journey of healing. There are many different thinkers and perspectives that have observed that disillusionment is an inevitable part of life. Typically, it follows an event or experience that suddenly and severely shatters our accustomed ways of seeing ourselves and the world. The initial response to this experience is intense suffering including extreme anxiety, profound insecurity, a disturbing sense of alienation, and even terror. This is because the half-truths, distorted perceptions, and mistaken beliefs behind those illusions have been cast into serious question. These illusions enabled persons to ascribe meaning to their experiences, maintain a sense of stability, and exercise a certain degree of control. However, because they function as a barrier to seeing themselves and the world as they truly are, in time they are exposed as false and need to be abandoned. However, resistance to the necessity of such change is very powerful, and the temptation, once the initial shock has passed, is to try and restore things to the way they were. Waking up is hard to do, given the powerful internal and external forces fueled by fear that press individuals to resist change. Recognizing and negotiating this intense ambivalence is a central task involved in the process of healing.

Illusions are not merely the product of self-deception but are created through mystification exercised by means of social control and internalization of hegemony. Thus, both the personal and social forces at work in instilling illusions must be recognized and dealt with for radical healing to be possible. Looking from a personal perspective, Frank and Frank (1991) describe how the experience of disillusionment is the precursor to individuals seeking psychotherapy. It follows a stressful event posing a serious challenge to their assumptive world, which was used to give life meaning and provide a sense of control. The blow to an individual's worldview creates a state of demoralization, accompanied by feeling disheartened, bewildered, uncertain, isolated, and alienated. However, it also can be a teachable moment that motivates self-examination and reveals inaccurate and unrealistic assumptions in need of change. Psychotherapy can help people face what they fear and encourage them to make modifications to their assumptive world that better enable them to live a fulfilling life. A key point made by the authors is that *the experience of disillusionment, and the suffering that accompanies it is a necessary stimulus to the possibility of productive change.*

What interferes with this process is the proclivity of human beings to hold fast to the illusion that life should be free of difficulties, safe, secure, and pain free. We have seen how this illusion is rooted in biological, psychological, and spiritual processes. People have an exquisite capacity for opacity, evasion, and denial. The ego has been described as the most powerful of these illusions. The three causes of evil associated with the ego—insecurity, pride, and inertia—provide valuable insights into how human beings invest considerable effort into maintaining illusions. They explain why anything threatening the ego with annihilation is experienced with extreme terror.

On the other hand, the argument has been made by theorists such as Maslow (1971) and Rogers (1961) that human beings also have a basic motive to strive for health and maximally realize their potentials. This is sometimes described as *authenticity.* or a state of wholeness and harmony in which human beings accept themselves and the world as they actually are, act in accordance with their beliefs and values, and resist conformity to social norms. Authenticity, as such, is an ideal. It can be aspired to but never fully realized because human beings live out existence as a process (Gruba-McCallister & Levington, 1994). As Bugenthal and Sapienza (1992) state, "To be whole is, in our view, not so much a condition to be attained and then held throughout one's life span as it is a direction in which to move, a perspective and value system to guide one's choices" (p. 279). Loss, disappointment, and falling short of that ideal are an inevitable part of that process. This gives rise to moments of crisis or disillusionment accompanied by inevitable suffering. The issue is not whether we will suffer but what stance we take toward that suffering and what we do with it (Frankl, 1959). We can retreat or we can progress.

The decision to aspire toward greater wholeness entails the recognition that transformative change requires a crisis and acceptance of the suffering that accompanies it. That does not mean that such a change is guaranteed, but it is clearly a possibility worth pursuing. Three steps must be taken in order for a crisis to be a translated into an opportunity for positive growth. These are *naming, claiming, and reframing*, and each of these will be described in more detail later. To begin that process, a particular framework must be assumed from which to understand the nature and purpose of suffering. Though the disruption and uprooting of individuals' worldview and ego makes the process painful and arduous, that does not mean that it is inherently worthless or bad. Certainly this stance is often taken toward this situation. However, it soon becomes clear that this stance leads to resistance and to a self-defeating cycle that causes further suffering. In other words, suffering because one is suffering, or self-created suffering, is by far the greatest source of suffering (Gruba-McCallister & Levington, 1995). This is based on what may be the most damaging of all illusions: that one's life should be free of any and all suffering. Moreover, the mystification of suffering rooted in a corrupted image of human beings perpetrated by neoliberal ideology fuels such resistance in ways intended to defend and maintain an oppressive status quo (Gruba-McCallister, 2019).

Undoing self-deception *and* mystification are essential for healing to occur. Assuming an open and non-judgmental stance toward unavoidable suffering enables individuals to see crisis as a catalyst to positive growth. This allows for the adoption of a compassionate attitude toward themselves. They are not suffering because they are bad or have something wrong. Likewise, they need not see suffering as something intolerable and, as a result, push it out of awareness. Instead, they can willingly bear it based on the belief that it is an essential ingredient to transformation. There are also cases when the crisis is due to recognition of social causes of suffering that are avoidable because they are based on choices and actions taken by individuals. At those times, righteous anger is to be expected and can help to motivate opposition. Yet even here care must be exercised not to respond to that suffering in ways that cause greater suffering. Along with a commitment to justice, there can still be compassion that enables individuals not to blame themselves for their suffering and connect to the suffering of others subjected to that same injustice. This can lead to constructive action taken both individually and collectively.

Developmental and Spiritual Elements of Healing

This framework for understanding suffering must be placed within a developmental framework. As noted in the previous chapter, a developmental perspective is a necessary component of integral assessment. This is because it provides a useful system for describing the course of human growth as the unfolding of distinct stages moving toward greater degrees of wholeness. A full discussion of such developmental systems is again beyond the scope of this book. However, several examples relevant to the role of suffering in development will be provided. These theories can be explored further for useful guidelines pertinent to promoting radical healing.

The first comes from the Polish psychiatrist Dabrowski (1964, 1967), who proposed a Theory of Positive Disintegration. According to this theory, development is conceptualized as a series of stages or levels through which human beings move in order to achieve progressively higher levels of functioning and well-being. However, in order to move from one stage to the next, there needs to be a disintegration or breakdown of habitual forms of thinking, feeling, and coping at one's current level of development. This collapse for a time destroys one's sense of meaning and purpose of life and brings anxiety, uncertainty, and suffering. However, what can also emerge from this experience is moving to a higher developmental level and restoration of a sense of unity and meaning. Dabrowski (1967) writes: "In relation to suffering one does not adopt an exclusively negative attitude, but begins to accept it as something that has meaning, as essential for cultural development, and as a necessary element of one's psychic enrichment" (p. 139). An example of an extensive body of theory and research that supports this perspective is in the area of post-traumatic growth (Calhoun & Tedeschi, 1999).

A rich, complex, and multi-faceted body of theory and research on development has been advanced by Wilber (1980, 1996). In the AQAL system described previously, knowing where individuals are along various lines of development provides important information about them, the types of psychological conditions they are likely to have, and what methods are best suited to treat those conditions. This is because a person's worldview and self-understanding are profoundly shaped by where he or she is developmentally. Each stage of development provides individuals with rules for living that they use to make sense of the world in as healthy a way as possible and tools for how to deal with life. Knowing where individuals are developmentally enables the healer to understand the perspective from which they experience themselves, others, and life.

As described previously, Wilber sees development as a series of stages that unfold in an invariant sequence such that each successive stage transcends and includes the previous stages. Over the course of development, worldviews become increasingly complex, dynamic, and all-embracing. With each stage, individuals become more integrated, flexible, tolerant of ambiguity and diversity, and self-reflective. Movement from one stage to another involves two actions that describe how individuals process experiences based on their fit with their current worldview. Translation is making sense of life using the tools and rules of one's current stage of development. However, looking again at a situation in which one's worldview is significantly challenged, attempting to utilize one's accustomed perspective fails. Transformation is then employed in which individuals must change rules and add tools that pave the way to move to the next stage. Individuals progress from lower to higher stages by gradually disidentifying with the worldview associated with their current stage, identifying with elements of the next stage of development, and finally integrating facets of the previous stage with the perspective of the next higher stage. This is akin to the dialectical process described by the philosopher Hegel of thesis–antithesis–synthesis, the dialectic of growth.

Though laid out in an ascending linear sequence, higher stages of development should not be regarded as inherently superior to or better than lower stages. While it is true that ascending the hierarchy does enable individuals to achieve progressively higher degrees of complexity and flexibility and to appreciate more of the "big picture," we need to be mindful, as Wilber (1999) states, that "...each level of consciousness and wave of existence...is, in its healthy form, an absolutely necessary and desirable element of the overall spiral, the overall spectrum of consciousness" (p. 129). Important tasks and functions have to be successfully achieved at each stage in order to form the foundation for subsequent stages. All human beings must negotiate the earliest stages of development as part of their evolution, and at any given time human beings can occupy places along the entire developmental continuum on any dimension. Thus, the feasibility of creating a world in which everyone occupies the highest levels is highly questionable. Instead, Wilber advocates that the health of the entire continuum of individuals is best achieved by promoting the greatest degree of health at each level. The most urgent work is not to focus on moving those at the higher levels forward but rather "...how to feed the starving millions at the most basic waves; how to house the homeless millions at the simplest of levels; how to bring healthcare to the millions who do not possess it" (Wilber, 1999, p. 130).

Wilber's work also provides valuable recognition of the importance of spirituality, such as the role of spiritual practices and experiences, to the developmental process. This includes providing a description of spirituality as an essential line of development in itself. Both his and Dabrowski's recognition of how crisis can be a catalyst that leads to levels of development beyond a conventional understanding of oneself and the world is a theme picked up by transpersonal theories of psychology (Fahlberg, Wolfer, & Fahlberg, 1992). This transpersonal perspective has opened up consideration of the use of contemplative practices in order to promote higher levels of development and the ways in which intense spiritual experiences, similar to those described in Chapter 6 as characteristic of the mystical path, can also precipitate a crisis that offers the potential for growth. The frequency of such experiences is more common than is generally recognized (Laski, 1968; Wulff, 2000). Sadly, they are often misunderstood not only by the individuals having the experience but also by significant others and mental health professionals. This misunderstanding can have tragic consequences. One is that the transformative potential of the experience goes unrecognized and so unrealized. The other is that such experiences may be incorrectly labeled as a form of pathology. This is what Wilber calls the pre-trans fallacy. Thus, another significant and much needed body of theory and research on radical healing is how to correctly assess and respond to these types of intense experiences, conceptualized as distinguishing between spiritual emergence and spiritual emergency (Grof & Grof, 1989; Johnson & Friedman, 2008).

The belief that suffering has the potential to stimulate movement toward a greater degree of wholeness and wellness has also been espoused by a number of religious and spiritual thinkers throughout time (Gruba-McCallister, 1992). This belief is a type of theodicy, a system of religious thought intended to address why individuals do evil and how the existence of so much suffering can be reconciled with an all-powerful and all-loving God. One example of this is what is called the *Irenaean theodicy* developed by Irenaeus, the Bishop of Lyons, in 177 BCE. The theologian Schilling (1977) describes it as follows:

> According to Irenaeus, God created human beings imperfect with the intention of bringing them finally, through a process of moral development, to the perfection that will fulfill his purpose for them. In this view, the fall of Adam was an occurrence in the childhood of the human species...The good and evil that we find mixed in our world provide the environment needed for the growth toward maturity that God intends. (p. 149)

As espoused in the previous developmental theories, this is a *teleological* theodicy. The goal of the evolutionary process is individuals moving toward increasing levels of wholeness, or what Hick (2007) calls "soul-making." This provides a spiritual context for understanding the necessity of suffering.

For the process of seeking to improve and grow to unfold, human beings need to possess the ability to exercise choice as moral agents. That is, endowed with free will, they must be able to make choices between good and evil. This, of course, means at times they will make choices that lead to suffering for themselves and others. It is likewise in our nature to recognize our shared nature with others and, based on this, to experience a fellow-feeling when witnessing their suffering. As Hick (1989) asserts, our capacity to experience suffering is actually the basis for our developing the ability to demonstrate love, compassion, kindness, and forgiveness. Suffering is necessary in order to make compassion possible. A pivotal choice embedded in the process of healing is negotiated in terms of two dialectical polarities described previously—moving toward greater alienation versus greater wholeness or assuming a life-affirming versus a death-affirming stance.

A Case of Mass Disillusionment

The importance of critical psychology in radical healing has been described as critiquing the role of ideology in contributing to dis-ease versus well-being; raising consciousness regarding the role of injustice, particularly for the marginalized and oppressed; working collaboratively with others to discern the impact of political attitudes and engagements on their lives; and striving to promote equality and fairness. Various forms of crises can function as a prelude to these actions. A very powerful but generally neglected opportunity to uncover illusions manufactured and disseminated by neoliberalism and fascism are those occasions when they have a significant and wide-scale impact. An author whose work has provided a highly well-researched and penetrating analysis of such events is social activist Naomi Klein (2007, 2014, 2017, 2023). Based on this, I will be using her work to describe how certain traumatic events can lead to the experience of disillusionment on a mass scale, how these events expose the role of neoliberalism and fascism, the negative impacts of these events, and how these events can provide an opportunity for consciousness raising and positive collective action. This lends support to the urgent need to abandon the current paradigm that is detrimental to the genuine goals of healing and the need for a radical paradigm shift. This will be illustrated by examining the impacts of the global Covid pandemic and evidence of the persistent failure of the existing paradigm to address these impacts.

In one of her earliest books, *The Shock Doctrine: The Rise of Disaster Capitalism*, Klein (2007) introduces some of her most important ideas that continue to be a part of her later writings. She details how neoliberal free market policies have increasingly become institutionalized across the globe, often with many significant negative consequences, following crises or disasters—both natural and man-made. She (2017) states, "The term 'shock doctrine' describes the quite brutal tactic of systematically using the public's disorientation following a collective shock—wars, coups, terrorist attacks, market crashes, or natural disasters—to push through radical pro-corporate measures, often called 'shock therapy'" (p. 2). She also describes this as "disaster capitalism" and notes that it was first used in the service of neoliberalism in the early 1970s in Latin America and has since spread to many other places in response to a number of different disasters. The potential to respond to such disasters or crises in ways that bring out the best in people and encourages them to extend help and care is stifled and instead the powerful elite capitalize on the vulnerability of the many impacted to maximize their own advantage and wealth. What is at work is the dominant death-affirming ideology that regards people and the earth itself as worthless and disposable.

Moreover, the elevation of fear and destabilization, along with a sense of disorientation and confusion that is precipitated by these crises, creates an atmosphere in which individuals question their experiences. One problematic consequence of this is the fostering of conspiracy thinking. Again, Klein (2023) explains:

> A state if shock is what happens to us—individually or as a society—when we experience a sudden and unprecedented event for which we do not have an adequate explanation. At its essence, a shock is the gap between event and existing narratives to explain that event. Being creatures of narrative, humans tend to be uncomfortable with meaning vacuums— which is why opportunistic players, the people I have termed 'disaster capitalists,' have been able to rush into the gap with their preexisting wish lists and simplistic stories of good and evil. The stories themselves may be cartoonishly wrong...But at least those stories exist—and that alone is enough to make them better than the nothingness of the gap. (pp. 7–8)

This description provides valuable and relevant insights into the complexities and potential pitfalls involved in the process of dealing with disillusionment, particularly when it impacts a large number of individuals. Klein correctly observes that human beings have a powerful need to make their experience coherent and intelligible. She labels the experience of having one's worldview turned upside down as "vertigo," borrowing the term from Alfred Hitchcock. This is particularly apt as it expresses the experience of disillusionment as being unseated from a state of stability and security or "losing one's footing." This echoes descriptions that can be found among existential thinkers such as Kierkegaard and Sartre. She also cites the work of the Mexican philosopher Emilio Uranga, who coined the term "zosobra" to describe a state of feeling torn and cast between opposites that is accompanied by anxiety and a sense of gravity and despair. This creates a sense of both vulnerability and desperation in which the discomfort of being unanchored and confronting a void leads to a powerful desire to restore some degree of meaning and control over life.

Such situations allow for a clearer view of how ideology and mystification are employed in both seemingly benevolent and clearly malicious ways in order to seize on individuals' vulnerability. This is achieved by marshalling extant social policies and systems to maintain control by reinforcing social character and by misleading people in ways that are advantageous to the ruling elite. The very harmful illusions that the crisis threatens to expose must be shored up and restored in order to thwart awareness and, with it, resistance and change. A variety of means are used to achieve this, and understanding these processes is essential for practicing radical therapy with individuals who have experienced disillusionment.

Maintaining hegemony and internalized oppression are of the highest priority to the powerful when the opportunity for waking up is presented to individuals.

Large sums of money are invested in public relations firms and advertising for this purpose. Mass media has been transformed into the principal channel for the dissemination of propaganda in order to manufacture consent (Herman & Chomsky, 2002). Think tanks are established to devise means of manipulating individuals' beliefs, values, and behaviors using language, myth, and metaphor. Governments employ spin doctors to disguise the ways in which they act at the behest of the powerful and wealthy. Chomsky (1999) writes, "The corporate news media, the PR industry, the academic ideologues, and the intellectual culture writ large play the central role of providing the 'necessary illusions' to make this unpalatable situation appear rational, benevolent, and necessary if not necessarily desirable" (p. 14). There is often a proliferation of conspiracy theories at times of societal upheaval and following catastrophic events (Kendzior, 2022; Shermer, 2022) that also function as forms of mystification.

Shermer (2022) defines a conspiracy as "…two or more people, or group, plotting or acting in secret to gain an advantage or harm others immorally or illegally" (p. 23). He goes on to describe a number of different types of conspiracy theories and gives a detailed explanation of the range of different psychological processes that contribute to the formation and endurance of conspiracy theories. For example, he cites research done at Chapman University that found that individuals more prone to subscribing to conspiracies tend to be more pessimistic about the near future, more fearful of the government, less trusting of other people in their lives, and more likely to take actions in response to their fear, such as purchasing guns. In accordance with the observation made in earlier chapters, these individuals also have a lower tolerance for ambiguity and tend toward political extremism. Whether the shock is an uncontrolled natural event or caused by human actors, there is an intention on the part of bad actors subscribing to neoliberal or fascist beliefs and values to cover up their plot or scheme and to benefit from the shock. This implies that there is actually a recognition among the powerful that a crisis can be an occasion of the unveiling of injustice and with this awareness resistance.

One particular distinction between types of conspiracy theories described by Shermer (2022) is particularly relevant to this discussion. The first is what he calls *tribal conspiracism,* in which loyalty to one's group takes precedence over the immediate truth or falsity of a specific conspiracy theory. This form is characteristic of fascism as it fosters divisiveness, conflict, and hostility among what is believed to be competing groups. Propaganda and the human proclivity toward tribalism play an important role in this form of conspiracy. The use of propaganda is to employ misinformation and deceit in ways that appeal to emotions rather than ideas. Reason and education are devalued such that doubt is cast on whether truth can be established or even exists. The heightening of emotions, such as fear and anger, inhibits the capacity for critical reflection. And perhaps most important, as described astutely by Laing (1967), individuals are led to mistrust their own experiences by those in authority by means of mystification. This is often done behind the mask of benevolence. This includes manipulation by means of language, the way in which a situation is framed, and posing paradoxes that ensnare individuals in a web of confusion. Implicit in all these machinations is the threat of punishment for non-conformity. When the whole notion of reality is undermined and nothing is trusted, succumbing to ready-made explanations for and solutions to life's questions becomes seductive—even when, on the face of them, they seem highly improbable or even ridiculous.

The most pernicious form of tribal conspiracism witnessed throughout history is the ways in which it has been used in egregious abuses of power such as enslavement, colonization, and mass killing. As Staub (1989) explains in his analysis of historical instances of genocide, a common precursor is "difficult life circumstances" in which a crisis or catastrophe threatening the worldview of a group of individuals provokes fear of their annihilation. Their loss of sense of control and stability lead them to seek a way to restore this. One way to do so is by submitting to a movement, ideology, or powerful leader that promises to give them the direction and guidance they feel they are missing. Shermer (2022) describes the working of motivated reasoning in which the value judgment and confidence in our beliefs are enhanced. This is because our propensity for tribalism leads us to form coalitions with the like-minded individuals of our group who provide support for them. Contrarily, an us-versus-them mentality is created in which one's group is seen as right and morally superior and those who hold different beliefs and values are dismissed and demonized.

As Klein (2023) and Shermer (2022) point out, not all conspiracies are false. Shermer calls this constructive conspiracism. Important truths can be found in examining these conspiracies, such as Klein's (2007, 2014) documentation of instances of disaster capitalism and the complicity of corporations in the climate crisis. Nonetheless, caution must be used when trying to delve into what might lie behind any conspiracy theory, given the frequency with which they are truly vehicles for mystification in defense of a hegemony. In her book, Kendzior (2022) makes the case that the United States has increasing become a culture of conspiracy based on increasing corruption, a greater frequency of crises, and the growing threat of a climate disaster. She warns that an unquestioned faith in the broken social institutions is as dangerous as belief in false narratives disseminated by means of propaganda. This is because government officials refuse to enforce any accountability for real conspiracies. She writes:

> Conspiracies are woven into the landscape of American life. They are how Americans reckon with hypocrisy and betrayal, how they feel around the edges of subjects they are not supposed to touch, how they navigate the twilight zone between principles and practice. Conspiracies structure American politics, but they are not called conspiracies when they are wrapped in the flag or stamped with bureaucracy or printed piecemeal in papers. They are called plans or policies or "just the way things are." When the agendas of elite actors get pushed underground and you have to dig for

them—that is when those agendas are called conspiracies, and facts are called theories, and you are called insane for noticing. (pp. 203–204)

Her warning feels particularly cogent and relevant in light of the explosion of conspiracies that occurred during and following the Covid-19 pandemic.

The COVID-19 Pandemic: An Opportunity Missed?

A recent example that powerfully illustrates mass disillusionment is the Covid-19 pandemic beginning in March 2019. It was a catastrophic event that touched virtually every aspect of our lives. As Klein (2017) correctly observes, the pandemic was a particularly difficult event because it imposed conditions that make individuals most vulnerable to states of shock: prolonged stress and isolation. A review of studies published on its impacts reflects just how far-reaching and enduring they were and continue to be. This, of course, includes the large number of deaths caused, the impact on those who lost loved ones, the increased number of individuals reporting adverse mental health consequences, and those afflicted with symptoms of what has been described as "long covid." A recent systematic review and meta-analysis (Lopez-Leon et al., 2021) of studies including almost 48,000 patients that investigated long-term health effects of Covid-19 found an estimated fifty-five long-term effects. The five most common symptoms were fatigue (58%), headache (44%), attention disorder (27%), hair loss (25%), and dyspnea (24%). The authors discuss the vast resources needed to provide care for these individuals, which currently are lacking. Extensive literature documents substantial economic impacts, changes to the workplace and employment, negative effects on agriculture and food supply chains, interference with access to pharmaceuticals and health care, shifts in educational systems and practices, and adverse consequences for the environment. Moreover, variants on covid continue to impact the health of individuals, and the pandemic revealed the likelihood of similar cases happening in the future.

The magnitude of the catastrophe caused by the pandemic establishes it as a pivotal historical event that exposed much of what is broken, unfair, and unjust in our world today due to failures and dangers posed by neoliberal ideology. This is evidenced in the large number of deaths of and the disproportionate adverse impact on the marginalized and oppressed, the costly failures of for-profit health care systems, the large number of corporations and wealthy individuals who significantly profited from the disaster, and government's responding to the crisis by expanding the privatization of human services. So-called "essential workers" were not those occupying higher status positions but generally low-paid individuals who were expected to stay at their jobs at the risk of illness or death in order to ensure the comfort of their exploiters. Similarly, health care workers were often not provided with necessary resources and protection, which led them to unnecessarily place their safety and lives on the line to care for the sick. As the negative impact on the economy grew, many lost their jobs and experienced employment insecurity while the profits of their companies soared. Trillions were spent to bail out the market and multinational corporations, but little money was provided by governments to strengthen the already fragile infrastructure necessary to take care of its citizens or to strengthen social safety nets. These inexcusable failures are a reflection of many years of neoliberal and colonial policies that diverted incredible wealth to the ten percent, created increasingly condemnable levels of inequality, and strangled resources necessary to create healthy communities. It was an example of disaster capitalism of staggering proportions.

Another important insight provided by Klein (2023) is that the pandemic dramatically exposed how the extreme individualism promoted by neoliberalism proved to be disastrous in dealing with the pandemic. Covid presented what she called "the shock of entanglement" in that we were faced with a situation that required us to realize and more fully appreciate our essential social nature and our interdependency with each other and with our environment. The overemphasis on individualism had created a society that valued placing self-interest above concern for others and competition over cooperation. This could be seen in the ways in which personal greed and power fueled actions advantageous to the few to the detriment of many (a key feature of oppression). However, it also tore away at the already delicate fabric of trust and mutual care that the circumstances posed by the pandemic required. Rather than foster responses in which people recognized and responded in a caring manner to a common plight that faced them, the powerful and the elite more often undermined collective action, stoked conflict and fragmentation, and over-emphasized personal responsibility for dealing with the challenges posed. It is little surprise then that both during the pandemic and even in the aftermath we find people at odds with one another regarding whether personal "rights" or shared concern for others should be given priority in dealing with a disaster.

It is clear that the pandemic constitutes a valuable teachable moment regarding the imperative to challenge neoliberal and fascist ideology and establish a counter-hegemony founded on compassion and justice. This is not only true for society at large but for those who take seriously their responsibility to provide radical healing founded on this new paradigm. Sadly, there are clear indications that this is an opportunity lost at present. To illustrate, I will examine how the American Psychological Association has assessed the impact of the pandemic on people in the United States and their proposed solutions. The first report for 2020 (American Psychological Association, 2020) stated that the pandemic was having a profound impact and posed a serious mental health crisis for Americans that would have long-term health and social consequences for years. Seventy-eight percent of respondents reported that the pandemic was a significant source of stress, and 67% reported experiencing increased stress. An adverse impact on behavior was reported by 49% of the sample, which included increased tension in the body, getting angry more easily, experiencing mood swings, and yelling at loved ones. Respondents also reported being worried about the long-term well-being of the nation in terms of its future and feeling that the country was at its lowest point in its history. Sources of stress—including health care, mass shooting, and climate change—reported previously continued to be noted and were seen as compounding the stress caused by the pandemic. The report concluded with what was described as "actionable advice" from a panel of experts for members of the specific groups that composed the sample: Gen Z students, parents with children, workers, and members of discriminated groups (people of color).

An article (American Psychological Association, 2021) published one year later described the findings of a previous survey that showed the predicted negative impact on physical health was coming to fruition. The key findings were that 61% of adults reported undesired weight changes since the start of the pandemic, 67% reported sleeping more or less, 47% indicated that they delayed or canceled health care services, and 48% experienced an increased level of stress. Additionally, essential workers were more than twice as likely to receive care from a mental health professional, Black Americans were most likely to report feelings of concern about the future, and Gen Z adults (46%) were the most likely to say that their mental health had worsened. The report went on to discuss how these various changes were likely to lead to more severe health consequences and provided brief advice about how to identify unhealthy habits and make behavior changes. However, there was no exploration of how larger social, economic, and political factors were likely responsible for the disproportionate adverse impact on essential workers, Black Americans, and Gen Z adults—a glaring and very telling omission.

The third report (American Psychological Association, 2023) documented how individuals were continuing to grapple with what was described as "psychological impacts of collective trauma." Continuing impact of the pandemic related to the large number of deaths and the changes in the workplace, school systems, and culture at large were reflected in the findings. For those aged 35 to 44, there was an increase in chronic health conditions from 48% in 2019 to 58% in 2023. The same age group reported an increase in "mental illness" from 31% to 45%, although the highest rate of 50% was reported in the age group of 18 to 34. Nearly a quarter of adults rated their stress between 8 and 10 on a scale where 10 means a great deal of stress, up from 19% in 2019 before the pandemic. Of particular note is what respondents indicated were the most significant causes of stress. Stress was due to increased financial strain on their household (46%), money as cause of fights in their family (58%), and feeling consumed by worries regarding money (58%)—all substantially higher than reported in 2019. Once more the role of stress was extended to other factors, including global conflict, racism and racial injustice, inflation, and climate-related disasters, but without any further discussion.

These reports clearly support the adverse impact of the pandemic on various indicators of well-being. However, the sole explanation for the range of adverse consequences on well-being was trauma-related stress. This is made explicitly clear in the repeated references to the long-term impact of stress on various physiological systems of the body and associated emotional and psychological effects, the negative consequences of lacking or ineffective coping skills, and the need for individuals to better understand stress and develop sound stress management skills. A serious and damaging error was made in failing to accurately identify the more significant factors responsible for the high levels of stress reported. By employing a highly individualistic framework, the APA perpetuated mainstream psychology's harmful denial of the political uses of its theory and practice and veiled the far more potent role played by neoliberal ideology in causing the substantial suffering reported in the survey. Neoliberalism has led to a growing disparity in wealth and income, expanding and crippling levels of debt, low wages, an undermining of social programs, and insecure employment. Given this, it is no surprise that issues of financial strain and anxiety and conflict regarding money were the most significant stressors reported.

The highly individualistic paradigm employed continues to perpetuate the bias of neoliberalism that essentially blames individuals for their affliction while also making them responsible for resolving their problems. The explicit use of the language of "mental illness" aligns the APA's analysis with a biomedical model, as does describing how physical health was harmed by individuals' inability to cope in healthy ways with the stress of the pandemic. The so-called solutions proposed were identifying and changing unhealthy habits. Similarly, the 2023 report blamed respondents by noting individual factors that interfered with effective coping, such as reluctance to talk about stress with others, overestimating one's level of well-being, and downplaying the impact of stress. All of these "deficiencies" actually reflect how individuals subscribe to damaging values associated with neoliberalism.

An utter neglect of how the physical and mental health problems were not the result of personal failure but predictable and justifiable responses to unhealthy material and social environments is also exposed in the "actionable advice" offered in the 2020 report. Some examples illustrate this. For "How to support students": Create a space for students to talk about the things that are bothering them, even if those things are not related to school or schoolwork. For "How to support Gen Z": Create traditions for Gen Z that celebrate milestones in new ways. They can be the generation that reinvents society by creating new celebrations and traditions that are meaningful. For "How People of Color can build resilience": It's to be expected that people feel stressed, angry, outraged, frustrated or a host of other feelings because of systemic problems. Acknowledge those feelings and do what you can to take care of yourself as you continue to cope and manage in today's reality. These utterly trite and tone-deaf recommendations are akin to those noted by Davies (2022) in his discussion of programs designed to silence worker discontent or decrease unemployment to avoid government aid. Emphasis is placed on personal motivation, change, and responsibility. He states that they are a form of *phony empowerment* "...found in the trite aphorisms of the self-help industry where popular psychologists ascribe to us almost magical abilities to alter circumstances despite the harsh realities constraining us" (p. 151).

A consistent finding of research on social determinants and inequality is that stress plays a *mediating role* in producing the adverse consequences of higher rates of morbidity and mortality. The experience of inequality—such as feelings of shame, anger, and inferiority—and the imbalance between demand and control for those occupying a lower status in society demonstrate that mental distress is determined by psychosocial factors. Stress is a link in this process whereby inequality gets under the skin or embodied, but it is *not* the ultimate determinant. By attributing causality to stress, the APA is not only practicing bad science but also engaging in mystification. Mainstream psychology and psychiatry both are complicit in using their power to negate the experience of individuals regarding the causes of their suffering. This is accomplished by creating plausible misinterpretations about why certain things happen to them that veil the impact of oppression and legitimize and protect the status quo. A range of strategies are used, many of which are evidence of attributing suffering to stress. These include portraying suffering as due to impersonal and natural causes that are not subject to moral condemnation; focusing attention on individual responsibility to address the problem; and peddling market-based solutions that foster consumption of products and services of the healthcare industry. Further, this secures the consent of the oppressed, which stifles both awareness of their exploitation and abuse and subsequent resistance to unjust practices.

Clearly, this is not how lessons taught to us by the pandemic need to be addressed. Radical healing can utilize methods employed in mainstream psychotherapy that have been found to be responsive to and respectful of individuals' experience and foster positive growth. However, the focus must extend beyond personal causes of suffering and, most important, unveil the social causes so that true emancipation can be achieved. This will be considered next.

The Need for a Life-Affirming Counter-Hegemony

For healing to be radical and committed as much to justice as compassion, it must aim to uproot not only the damaging impacts of a toxic ideology but the ideology itself. Change must be achieved at both the personal and social level. Patching up the wounds inflicted on individuals by oppression and then releasing them back into the very same conditions that inflicted those wounds is not only futile but immoral. The current paradigm that dominates systems of care must be discarded and replaced, which naturally raises the question of what the alternative paradigm—and related ideology—should be. What does it mean to be *anti-capitalist*? I believe that the alternative toward which those committed to radical healing must aspire is a socialist and truly democratic society. Thus, this chapter concludes with a discussion of this much needed counter-hegemony. There are a number of thinkers and writers who have argued for this counter-hegemony, but I will restrict my examination to the work of Erik Olin Wright (2019), an eminent sociologist and radical Marxist who wrote extensively on this subject.

Echoing the critique made in this book, Wright asserts that capitalism can be opposed based both on class interests and moral values, noting that clarity on values is essential for thinking about the desirable alternatives to capitalism. Three core values are central to the critique: equality/fairness, democracy/freedom, and community/solidarity—all which should be familiar to the reader. The goal is to establish a society that promotes human flourishing which Wright (2019) defines as a life "...in which a person's capacities and talents have developed in ways that enable them to pursue their life goals, so that in some general sense they have been able to realize their potentials and purposes" (p. 11). Gross inequity deprives individuals of the material and social means for flourishing. Democracy and freedom share the value of self-determination such that all people have equal access to the necessary means to participate in a meaningful way in decisions that affect their lives. Inequalities in wealth lead to disparities in power and control over decision making, along with the existence of a lack of control related to exploitation in the labor market. Finally, a communitarian view of the good society emphasizes the positive role that social bonds, cooperation, and reciprocity play in well-being. The greed and fear fostered by competitive markets corrode community. Competitive individualism and privatized consumerism undermine the collective agency and solidarity that is needed to mount a serious challenge to capitalism.

The alternative to capitalism set forth by Wright is what he calls socialism as economic democracy, or a power-centered concept of socialism, in which power is organized within economic structures, especially in terms of the allocation and use of economic resources. Power is the capacity to do things in the world or to produce effects and takes three forms: economic, state, and social. Economic and state power have been described previously. Social power is exercised by means of getting people to do things by persuading them, an idea central to democracy. This form of socialism rests firmly on the three values noted above that are central to the goal of promoting flourishing.

Wright describes central building blocks for this counter-hegemony, some of which I note in order to give substance to what this counter-hegemony would look like. One is providing to every legal resident an unconditional basic income that is sufficient to live above the poverty line without any work requirement or other conditions. The cooperative market economy established would take different forms, including the areas of work, consumption, credit, and housing. An example that can already be found is a worker cooperative in which workers own the firm and production is overseen through democratic processes. Unlike capitalist firms, these cooperatives foster solidarity, equality, dignity of work, and community development. Accompanying this would be the democratization of capitalist firms. Banking would be established as a public utility. There would be greater state provision of goods and services, among these health care, childcare, eldercare, public amenities for community events and processes, physical infrastructure, and public utilities. Finally, there would be the establishment of a knowledge commons, in which there would be a residual role for private intellectual property rights and limited patents. General scientific and technical knowledge and information would be more widely shared.

Wright describes a strategic vision of how conditions can gradually be created that erode the dominance of capitalism. This vision integrates dismantling and taming capitalism from above and resisting and escaping capitalism from below. His intent is to recognize the substantive power possessed by neoliberal hegemony and the complexities involved in bringing about change. At the same time, he describes balancing this with a recognition of its contradictions and weaknesses and sound strategies for neutralizing its harms and transcending its structures. As Wright (2019) correctly observes, "Collective actors are critical for emancipatory social transformation" and "Identities are especially critical in forging solidarity within a collective actor; interests are central to shaping the objectives of collective action; values are important for connecting diverse identities and interests within common meanings" (pp. 124–125). In these assertions we find themes that have been described as central to radical healing, making clear the parallels that exist between individual and collective liberation. Based on the work of Wright and others who advocate for socialism, it is clear that the assertion once made by former English prime minister Margaret Thatcher, "There is no alternative," is false. Instead, liberation from exploitation, oppression, and violence—and from the host of physical and psychological harms these cause—is possible and worth realizing. The final chapter will thus examine the ways in which radical healing can advance both individual and collective emancipation.

Chapter 10

Making Healing Radical:
No Wellness Without Justice

Advancing Psychopolitical Validity

In the previous chapter, I laid out in broad terms the nature and goals of the practice of radical healing as advancing both individual and collective liberation through the integration of compassion and justice. Having focused mostly on the "why" for radical therapy, in this chapter I move attention to the "how." More specifically, I present how radical healing can be practiced by describing its essential elements and illustrating how the process of naming, claiming, reframing, and taking aim at the personal, spiritual, and social sources of suffering promotes wholeness. This discussion integrates concepts and methods taken from humanistic/existential, transpersonal, and critical theoretical perspectives in addition to important recent work based on the critical pedagogy, liberation psychology, and decolonization and indigenous approaches to healing. A repeated theme found in literature advocating for critical approaches to therapy and counseling is that these practices do not necessarily have to be abandoned in light of the inadequacies and damaging impacts of the current mainstream paradigm. Ample examples of these problems have been laid out in previous chapters that are linked to the roots of this paradigm in neoliberalism and fascism. For example, Prilleltensky, Prilleltensky, and Voorhees (2008) utilize the concept of psychopolitical validity that requires actions by psychologists be informed by a knowledge of oppression and the role of power dynamics at the personal, interpersonal, and structural levels. Based on this, therapists must break free of their restricted focus at the individual level and effect change that impacts social sources of suffering, working collaboratively with clients as well as members of communities and policy makers.

Prilleltensky (2003) asserts that promoting liberation requires engagement at both the political and psychological level. He urges this to be implemented in two ways. The first is how research is conducted, which he calls *epistemic psychopolitical validity*. The second, *transformational psychopolitical validity*, is pertinent to the discussion here as it relates to practice. This begins with the personal work that healers must do and then proceeds to their work with others. They must especially develop a stronger understanding of the role of injustice in impairing wellness. This understanding must then be translated into transformative action that can include activism, community action, and efforts to change adverse social policies. Questions suggested by Prilleltensky (2003) regarding how to determine psychopolitical validity provide additional useful information about how to practice radical healing. These include:

- Do interventions promote psychopolitical validity?
- Do they educate individuals on the best strategic actions to overcome oppression?
- Do they serve to empower individuals to take action to oppose political inequalities and social injustices at the personal, interpersonal, communal, and structural levels?
- Do they promote solidarity and strategic alliances and coalitions with groups that face similar issues?
- Do they account for the subjectivity/agency and psychological limitations of the agents of change?

In light of the description of holistic assessment in the previous chapter, radical healing must move past a focus on personal sources of suffering. That means that unveiling and elucidating the inextricable relationship between personal sources and social sources is a central task. This includes identifying and undoing the detrimental impact of mystification. These dynamics are just as insidious and powerful as the workings of self-deception. There are two prongs to this exploration. The first is to raise consciousness of individuals regarding the harmful impact of hegemony in examples such as social determinants of health, inequality, oppression, consumer culture, and the social construction of illness. The second is to explore what Engels called false consciousness and Fromm (1941) called social character in order to expose how the internalization of hegemony impairs wellness. This provides the foundation for helping individuals break free of this socialization and then adopt a healthier counter-hegemony. That counter-hegemony must be founded on a sincere commitment to the values of equality/fairness, democracy/freedom, and community/solidarity. Throughout this process, the essential spiritual nature of human beings must not be neglected. Spiritual issues are invariably entwined with personal and social sources of suffering.

It is important to recall here the discussion in Chapter 3 about how transformation of the healer must precede their seeking to promote positive transformation in others. It is pivotal that the personhood of healers reflects a deep commitment to compassion and justice, embracing what it means to be human as fully as possible and a willingness to place themselves at the disposal of others. This point is central for understanding the significant role that relationship plays in healing and is supported by research on the impact of relationship on positive outcomes in therapy (Wampold & Imel, 2015). Understanding that wellness is impossible if injustice is unaddressed means that radical healing must critically examine theories and methods to evaluate the degree to which they have been corrupted by adverse elements of neoliberal hegemony. Examples are antagonistic class relations, glorification of greed, and rampant commodification. They should likewise be scrutinized for elements of fascist ideology such as authoritarianism, meritocracy, and dehumanization of the other. This provides the knowledge that makes it possible to assist clients to engage in the same process of critical examination. The typical acontextual labels and value-laden constructs employed to describe and categorize the problems of clients must also be abandoned. Distress should instead be reframed in terms of the impact of power dynamics and the consequences of living in the face of trauma, inequality, and oppression. Causes are located not within individuals but instead within systems that clients must interact with. Increasing the political literacy of clients enables them to keep in check any potentially harmful effects of practices that are intended to help them. They can then translate this awareness into a greater sense of empowerment to bring about change in themselves as well as in systems that act upon them. Thus, some of the knowledge and skills typically regarded as essential to those who are change agents continue to have utility in radical healing. Nonetheless, they must be freed of contamination by a toxic ideology and supplemented with additional knowledge and skills pertinent to addressing suffering at all levels.

Relationship: Embracing and Living Out Our Societal Nature

With this in mind, we turn to the first essential component of healing—relationship. The centrality of relationship is not surprising given the point consistently made regarding the essential societal nature of human beings. This is asserted by Wampold and Imel (2015), who believe that the ability of human beings to collaborate in order to attain shared goals and intentions enables them to achieve greater health through social means. This places relationship as the bedrock of psychotherapy effectiveness. An early theorist recognized as laying the groundwork for the centrality of relationship to therapy was Rogers (1961). Tudor and Worrall (2006) examine Person-Centered Therapy's (PCT) understanding of therapeutic relations in terms of the person of the therapist, the person of the client, and the process of therapeutic relating. The fundamental values, beliefs, and way of being of the therapist are key factors in healing. These include a belief in the capacity of persons to heal through self-reflection, a valuing of the "otherness of others," a trust in others and their exercise of free will, acceptance of individuals' ability and right to choose and their capacity to reason, and a love for what is described as "the ambiguity of therapy." Tudor and Worrall indicate that there is less literature on the person of the client and, though the logic of PCT is to focus on the client in the process of relating, there is again comparatively little literature written from the client's perspective.

PCT endorses an intersubjective view of the therapeutic encounter. When two persons come together, they create a shared field that is mutually constructed.

Tudor and Worrall describe this as co-creative relating, which sees reality as being actively constructed by both the therapist and client. This creates a sense of "we-ness" such that the relating is more powerful than the therapist or the client alone. This experience of interdependence and cooperation establishes a sense of shared responsibility. Finally, the focus in this relationship is on the here-and-now development of the client. All these principles allow for the therapeutic relationship to be seen as a practice of dialogue.

One final important contribution of Rogers relevant to radical healing is his assertion of core conditions of the process of effective therapy, ideas that have since been widely adopted. These conditions are understood as an integral whole in which none can is separable from the others. The first is the precondition of psychological contact, in which each person makes a perceived or subceived difference to the experience of the other. They are meaningfully present to each other both verbally and nonverbally. The second is congruence in which therapists convey a sense of being real, genuine, and transparent. They are faithful to their experience and thus able to convey it to clients. The third is unconditional positive regard, which is the suspension of judgment and the adoption of a non-directional, respectful attitude toward the other. It is the expression of caring or love. Finally, there is empathy, which is perceiving from the internal frame of reference of another with accuracy in terms of both emotions and meanings. A number of these ideas will be found in the subsequent discussion of the importance of relationship.

Understanding of relationship, however, must again be removed from an over-individualized perspective. Slife and Wiggins (2009) make this point in their proposal of radical relationality. Within the traditional individualist perspective, relationships are understood non-relationally due to the primacy assigned to the goals of individuals and their actively seeking to achieve those goals within relationships. Participants in relationships are conceived of as self-contained and as incorporating relationships within themselves. In place of this view, Slife and Wiggins advance that human beings are relational at their core, just as reality itself must be understood as an intricate complex of relationships. This is in keeping with the previous discussion of Mitwelt and Heidegger's (1962) assertion that being-with is an inherent given of the human condition. Humans have a powerful need to belong, and rejection is the greatest of all fears and anxieties. Thus, clients must be understood relationally across the multiple contexts of human existence, including interpersonal, temporal, situational, and moral. The here-and-now relationship of the therapist with clients provides valuable insights regarding important patterns of how clients are engaged in other relationships in their lives. This provides a channel for examining and challenging those relationships that are not healthy.

One other point made by Slife and Wiggins (2009) is central to understanding the role of relationship in healing. Relationship requires both sameness and difference, the participants being both similar to and in contrast with each other. This speaks to one side of the essential dialectical nature of relationship in terms of the "otherness" of both the healer and the one seeking healing. Their uniqueness and distinction is inescapable and is neither reducible nor capturable. This idea is found in the philosophical dialogue of Martin Buber (1971), which has been highly influential in terms of his contrasting the I–Thou versus the I–It relationship. The I–Thou relationship is a mutual, open, and authentic encounter of two beings whose uniqueness is recognized and honored. In contrast, in the I–It relationship one confronts the Other as an object to be used based on one's interests or needs. Buber believed that individuals oscillate between these two ways of relating. They express two ways of being, knowing, and willing.

Buber saw the I–Thou relationship as a means of promoting healing through meeting. This idea was expanded on by Friedman (2008) in what he described as *dialogical therapy*. The uniqueness of each person in the relationship must be confronted and embraced. It allows a certain distance between the participants as well as the recognition of their interrelationship. Thus, in dialogical therapy what is essential is not what goes on within individuals but *between* them. This direct contact between two unique human beings gives rise to the sphere of the between. Our sense of ourselves only comes in our meeting with others. This mutuality places limits on the responsibility of the healer as clients must be called to bring their inner being to unity so that they are able to respond to the address of the healer in the encounter. Friedman views empathy in a strict and narrow sense of the term. He sees empathy as trying to enter into the perspective of the other while leaving oneself aside, while identification is trying to tune into the other through focusing on oneself. In the I–Thou relationship, imagining how the other is perceiving, thinking, feeling, and willing is how the healer includes the other in genuine dialogue. One imagines the real by experiencing the other side of the relationship without ceasing to see through one's own eyes. Thus, while there can be mutual trust, contact, and concern, mutual inclusion is not possible.

Friedman sees confirmation as fundamental to human development and well-being, whereas disconfirmation impairs human beings' basic need for trust and leads to dis-ease. Confirmation is a state of interrelatedness between two independent and unique beings. The healer must be willing and open to receiving whatever the client might offer in order to restore a sense of existential trust. This starts with accepting others for who they are; but one needs to also strive for and against others as they engage in realizing some potentialities and not others. In other words, dialogue transcends polarities such as self versus other or individual versus collective. The unavoidable "otherness" of the healer in this understanding of relationship is a necessary element of radical healing and will be expanded on later in this chapter. While healers may seek to be open, non-judgmental, and non-intrusive, they must also be committed to truth and able to genuinely express what may be a contrary perspective to that of others. The experience of difference— even in terms of disagreement and dissent—is not only inevitable, but ultimately desirable. It is a necessary element of what it means to be in relationship.

Before examining such difference further, I will explore several other perspectives on dialogue, particularly as they shed light on facilitating the process of naming the actual source of one's suffering. In order to correctly name what is causing one suffering, a person must face up to the fear that elicits resistance, immobilizes critical thought, and distorts and denies undesirable facts. Both intrapersonal and social processes aimed at obfuscating, contorting, and denying lived experiences must be identified and undone. As I have illustrated, this process is daunting and fraught with pitfalls. In light of this, embarking on this project on one's own is highly unlikely to be successful. One of the best illustrations of this can be found in the extensive literature across traditions that describe in remarkable detail how the mystical path toward the attainment of enlightenment involves many complications and dangers that thwart one's progress (Underhill, 1961). For that reason, seekers must either be guided by a teacher who has attained enlightenment and so has experience regarding how the process must be negotiated or as a part of a community of other seekers. Working through disillusionment, the suffering that usually precipitates it, and the suffering that attends it, is best done in commune with others. This is particularly so when this experience exposes a shared social source. Hence, the value of dialogue.

The work of the physicist David Bohm (2004) on dialogue is instructive. It is useful to note that Bohm stated that his greatest influence in developing his ideas regarding dialogue was Jiddu Krishnamurti. Krishnamurti was an Indian philosopher and spiritual teacher who exerted a significant influence on a number of notable thinkers. He taught extensively on meditation as a means of bringing order to thought, achieving insight into the nature of consciousness and thus reality itself, and bringing an end to the confusion, sorrow, and misery that afflict human beings. Reflecting this influence, Bohm discusses the cognitive and emotional processes at work, mostly at an unconscious level, in forming beliefs, attitudes, and values and then rigidly maintaining them. In a sense, thought creates the thinker and operates at a tacit level that cannot be described. This infringes on the freedom that individuals can exercise on themselves and on their lives. Dialogue is a means of collectively observing thought as a process and how this process affects us and other people. Here one can see parallels of dialogue with contemplative and meditative practices in mystical traditions. The goal is not to solve a problem but to create a culture in which participants seek to understand themselves and their hidden motives and intention, and free themselves from the need to be secure and identified with their worldview.

The basic purpose of dialogue is to talk with others while suspending personal opinions. Individuals act as if they were displaying them for themselves and others in the group, while not resisting them or trying to convince or persuade others. Instead a relaxed, non-judgmental, curious stance helps to see things more clearly and in a new light. This is done in the spirit of goodwill and friendship rather than competition or hostility. Participants hold many different points of view in suspension, while maintaining a primary interest in creating a common meaning that emerges when individuals think together. In a sense, truth emerges spontaneously when participants adopt an open stance toward what is disclosed in the light of consciousness (Heidegger, 1962). Bohm's description also bears many similarities to the phenomenological method described in an earlier chapter

(Spinelli, 2007). By exploring crises and problems by means of this collective thought process, individuals can realize how thoughts relate to ultimate reality and achieve a creative culture that fosters creativity and advances human well-being.

Perhaps the most important thinker regarding the use of dialogue to promote liberation from oppression is the Brazilian philosopher and educator Paolo Friere (1970), who advanced critical pedagogy. Friere grew up in the northeast of Brazil in a middle class family that was thrown into poverty during the Depression. In 1961 he initiated a literacy program in Brazil where he worked with millions of people denied an education based on neoliberal policies. It was through this program that Friere put his ideas to work and developed his theory of critical pedagogy. After the military coup, he was imprisoned and subsequently expelled from Brazil. He went on to work for five years in Chile and eventually returned to Brazil.

Friere saw dialogue as co-intentional education and as a means for individuals to reflect on the world and subsequently act upon it to achieve liberation from oppression. Dialogue requires a horizontal relationship of mutual trust such that all participants are regarded as equals and their essential humanity is honored. For Friere, dialogue requires faith in human beings' ability to use their power to create and recreate in their vocation to become more fully human. It also requires hope that the world can be transformed through revolutionary action that is led by the oppressed themselves. The starting point for co-intentional or problem-solving education is the here-and-now experience of individuals in their everyday lives. The role of what is described as the animator is to help participants question their day-to-day experiences and suffering in order to see these not as inescapable givens but manufactured by larger social forces. This is done by helping participants to pose problems and questions and move from fatalism to the realm of the possible. By demythologizing reality, individuals attain critical consciousness and are able to expose the ideological foundations on which oppression rests. Dialogue affirms and respects the subjectivity and agency of participants, enabling them to meet and work cooperatively and reclaim their power. As will be discussed later, understanding their current circumstances moves them next to conceive how things can be different and more just.

The essence of dialogue is the word. Friere (1970) observes that the very act of *naming* is a form of praxis in which the causes of oppression are critically recognized, and through this insight the world is transformed. He writes, "To exist, humanly, is to *name* the world, to change it. Once named, the world in its turn reappears to the namers as a problem and requires of them a new *naming*. Human beings are not built in silence, but in word, in work, in action reflection" (p. 88, italics in original). The oppressed are often silenced and deprived of the ability to name the world. However, speaking to their experience reverses the forces of dehumanization and lets them bring what has been hidden out in the open. Once what is obstructing their vision is removed, a new word that more truly captures their experience can be spoken. The naming of a problem enables individuals to achieve some distance from it and so reflect upon it. This reflection does not merely deepen understanding; it also allows for the consideration of alternatives: new names. Friere (1970) writes:

> Finally, true dialogue cannot exist unless the dialoguers engage in critical thinking—thinking which discerns an indivisible solidarity between the world and the people and admits of no dichotomy between them— thinking which perceives reality as process, as transformation, rather than as a static entity—thinking which does not separate itself from action, but constantly immerses itself in temporality without fear of the risks involved. (p. 92)

Klein (2023) echoes the importance of naming as a pivotal first step in coming to a correct understanding of the role of neoliberal policies in many human afflictions. A better world is something that must first be imagined before it can be created. This means stripping away distortions and deceptions manufactured by hegemony to legitimize the status quo and undermine resistance. She writes:

> This starts with naming...the systems that have carved out the Shadow Lands, deemed them erasable, disposable: capitalism, imperialism, white supremacy, patriarchy. It requires teaching those words, and their true meanings, to the people in our lives, so that the next time someone tells them that their suffering and burdens are all the fault of child-stealing globalists, or job-stealing immigrants, or well-meaning teachers, or the Jews or the Chinese or the drag queens at the library, they will know better. And they will be able to fight better. (p. 327)

Achieving change requires people to free themselves from how extreme individualism fosters what Friere calls *antidialogical action* that pits individuals against one another, reduces them to objects to be used or manipulated, and encourages an attitude of domination and conquest. As Klein observes, universalism opposes fascism.

In their work on psychologies of liberation with indigenous and colonized groups, Watkins and Shulman (2008) assign dialogue a central role, recognizing the work of Friere and others. Dialogue is regarded as the principal means by which critical consciousness is cultivated and attained. As social beings, we are best able to reach for truth communally and cooperatively. However, as Watkins and Shulman observe, the capacity for dialogue is something that must be cultivated, and radical healing must be a central means by which dialogue is both cultivated and practiced. As Bohm (2004) and Friedman (2008) assert, relationship must be understood dialectically in terms of similarity and difference, individual and collective. The unique and different needs, beliefs, and desires of each person must be allowed to be expressed and listened to with attention and respect. At the same time, an essential bond that unites individuals must also be affirmed based on a shared humanity. This inherent interrelatedness has been described as having a basis in spirituality or what Watkins and Shulman describe as a "divine spark" in each being. Their description of the healing powers of dialogue provide a fitting conclusion to this section:

> Dialogical capacities that are necessary for restoring a sacred manner of relation between people are multiple: the allowing of self and other to freely arise and be given the chance for expression; to allow the other to exist autonomously from myself; to patiently wait for relation to occur in an open horizon; to move toward difference not with denial or rejection but with vulnerability, curiosity, and a clear sense that it is in the encounter with otherness and multiplicity of perspectives that deeper and more complex meanings can emerge. It also requires the psychic ability to de-center and to try on the perspective and feelings of the other. It necessitates our ability to take a third-person perspective on the self, so that one can reflect on how one's actions and attitudes have affected the other and the situation of which we are a part. (pp. 176–177)

Negotiating the Dialectics of Becoming: Claiming Suffering

While naming is an important first step in the process of radical healing, it alone will not guarantee movement toward liberation. The power of self-deception and various forms of mystification to oppose individuals awakening to the true sources of their suffering is considerable. It is common for individuals who have experienced disillusionment to see this situation as dangerous, intolerable, and thus without value. Powerful messages rooted in neoliberal ideology are aimed at mystifying the true reasons for one's suffering as well as encouraging individuals to do everything in their power to either avoid or obliterate the experience of suffering that comes with naming its source (Gruba-McCallister, 2019). Earlier discussed examples of this stifling of waking up include the valorization of happiness as the goal of life, the promotion of consumption as a means of finding pleasure and meaning, and the widespread marketing of "cures" and "quick fixes" for every malady. As a consequence, the realization that some form of injustice is responsible for one's suffering is not only squelched but may instead be labeled as a form of sickness or immorality in need of correction.

What this means for those practicing radical healing is that individuals seeking care may have serious misconceptions and mistaken expectations regarding the reasons for their suffering that can distort their understanding about what healing actually involves. Even though a loss has been experienced that cannot be made right, individuals may nevertheless harbor the false hope that "things can go back to the way they were." Despite there being an initial awareness of the true cause of their suffering (achieved by means of naming), this insight may be fragile and easily lost. The desire to shove suffering away and resist change will end up putting people right back into the very circumstances that cause them harm. In contrast, it is imperative for healers to firmly believe in the potential for disillusionment to be a prelude to positive transformation and in the redemptive value of suffering. This sets the stage for the experience of dissent and even conflict in the healing relationship. The desires of clients and the hope offered by healers that things can be otherwise are often at odds.

However, as the previous discussion of dialogue made clear, this is an essential feature of relationship as dialogue. It is rooted in true mutuality, respect, and interdependence between two human beings with their own values, beliefs, and agency. The open exploration of obstacles that inevitably arise are necessary for true dialogue. Healing must be devoted to a process of development that is inescapably rooted in negotiating the dialectics of becoming. This involves what was previously described as existential dichotomies that are a fixed element of human existence (Fromm, 1947). Polarities must be navigated in radical healing that enable individuals to move from naming to claiming suffering. These include two ways of knowing and willing, an active versus passive stance, non-reflective versus reflective consciousness, and a life-affirming versus death-affirming orientation.

The ability of radical healers to negotiate these polarities rests on their tolerating the ambiguity inherent in being human and finding in that ambiguity the opportunity for creativity and growth. As a result, they must be on guard both in themselves and toward others for the adoption of an extreme, either/or approach that not only fails to embrace ambiguity but leads to the self-defeating cycles inherent in all forms of dis-ease. By embodying ambiguity in their way of being with clients, healers can foster the experience of a kind of creative tension in clients that destabilizes their desire for stability and order and seeks to undo their resistance to abandoning rigid patterns. Radical healing is based on the realization that waking up requires shaking up. As asserted in liberation theology, healers must comfort the afflicted and afflict the comfortable because they understand that compassion and justice are inseparable. However, unlike the destructive forms of loss and trauma experienced by clients, the challenges posed by healers are tempered with compassion and a commitment to resolutely accompany clients through what at times is an arduous process.

Examining the polarities embedded in the process of becoming serves to elucidate the process of radical healing. The distinction between two ways of knowing, direct and discursive (Wilber, 1977), described earlier is a polarity that plays an integral role in healing. The relevance of these two forms of knowing is captured in this quote by Frankl (1968):

> The therapeutic relationship develops in a polar filed of tension in which poles are represented by the extremes of *human closeness* on the one hand and *scientific detachment* on the other. Therefore, the therapist must beware lest he be beguiled into falling prey to the extreme of considering only one of these. This means that the therapist must neither be guided by mere sympathy, by his desire to help his patient, nor conversely repress

his human interest in the other human being by dealing with him merely in terms of technique. (p. 144)

The distinction between closeness and detachment is related to a polarity around which consciousness itself is organized. Each results in very different ways in which we experience ourselves and others. The existential philosopher Sartre (1953) describes these two forms in his perceptive analysis of self-deception. The first is what he calls *prereflective, or nonthetic consciousness.* In this state persons are deeply absorbed in and focused on the object of their awareness. This absorption is so strong that for the moment they lose consciousness of themselves and instead are immersed in the object of their awareness. This can be experienced as a powerful feeling of identification with the other. This form of consciousness can also be described as direct knowledge in which there is no sense of separation between knower and known. They are experienced as intimately and necessarily interrelated. This immediate contact with the other means that direct knowing is free of concepts, symbols, and language. Polanyi (1966) describes it as *tacit knowing* in the sense that we know more than we can say. It is also sometimes described as an embodied way of knowing (Silow, 2010).

In contrast, human beings have the capacity to turn consciousness back on themselves and thus make themselves the object of awareness. Sartre (1953) describes this as *reflective or thetic consciousness* that allows for an examination and evaluation of our actions and experiences and an ability to deliberate on a course of action and make choices. This is connected to discursive thought, whose emphasis is on reason, analysis, manipulating or exerting control, and striving toward a goal. Discursive thought is based on categorizing, organizing, and labeling experience, using symbolization (most commonly language). Discursive thought establishes a sense of separation between knower and known.

Similar distinctions between these two ways of knowing have been made by others. Heidegger (von Eckartsberg & Valle, 1981) described the *calculative mode* of thought as rational, intrusive, dominating, and objectifying. The *meditative mode*, also referred to as "thankful thinking," is respectful, open, loving, and non-interfering. This polarity can also be seen in the earlier discussion of Buber's (1971) distinction between I–Thou (direct) and I–It (discursive). Looking from a spiritual perspective, Thomas Merton (1951) discusses the close and necessary relationship between faith and reason in the mystical process. He observes that there are two characteristics of mature spirituality. The first is *discernment*, which is the ability to recognize the expression of the Absolute in all reality by means of the cultivation of an intuitive (direct) perception or faith. The second is *detachment*, in which individuals realize and critically examine the illusion of trying to find the Absolute in the limited and transient material realm by means of reason (discursive).

A point made clear in all of these examples is that neither of these two forms of consciousness, or ways of knowing, is superior or better than the other. They constitute a polarity that must be constantly lived out moment by moment and are each suited to understanding certain situations and enabling persons to respond to them in a healthy manner. All of the above thinkers likewise caution regarding the dangers of dealing with this polarity in a one-sided manner or employing either of these two stances in a fixed and inflexible way. For example, Sartre (1953) sees this as the basis of self-deception. Another example is Kierkegaard's (1941) discussion of various forms of despair based on an inability to negotiate polarities inherent in human existence. This insight is especially pertinent to healing as it is just these patterns that must be identified and processed because of the role they play in suffering. Failure to embrace the fundamental ambiguity of existence only serves to compound one's suffering. Growth and movement toward wholeness are only possible through the ongoing negotiation of these polarities.

Based on the centrality of relationship and Frankl's (1968) observation, it is how healers *are* with those who seek care and the way in which they use *the power* of relationship that facilitates growth. Healers must be able to move back and forth fluidly between closeness and detachment, contemplation and action, intuition and reason. In doing so, they are able to convey the understanding and acceptance necessary to allow for self-examination. But that alone is not enough to enable those seeking care to question and uncover the true causes of their suffering. Nor is it enough to help them find the courage to abandon a worldview that lacks compassion and justice for themselves and others. Examples of these complementary roles of healers are provided by Spinelli (2014) and Dubose (2014) in their description of the therapy process.

Initially therapists take the stance of being-with clients in which they convey an open, curious, and non-judgmental perspective aimed at allowing for a mutual exploration and description of troubling patterns within their worldview. Therapists employ other-focused listening in order to capture the immediate experience of clients and allow their worldview to occupy the therapy space without being challenged or analyzed. Dubose (2014) describes this as being-for, or the radical validation of how clients are in the world that gets at the root of who they are. The shared human condition of the therapist and client is what enables coming to a shared understanding. No value is placed on one way of being-in-the-world over another. This is experienced by clients as answering one of their deepest needs, which is to matter to someone else simply based on who they are. Care is taken not to impose any judgment or expectation on the other so that he or she feels free to explore his or her way of being-in-the-world.

However, as the process of exploration unfolds, the "otherness" of the healer enters increasingly into the relation as a person who possesses a distinct sense of agency and worldview. To validate the experience of another is to convey acceptance and communicate that each person alone is an expert on his or her experience. It is not, on the other hand, meant to convey that the healer necessarily agrees with the interpretation or meaning given to those experiences. These are an expression of the unique subjectivity of the other. The attitude of healers must convey that there are always alternative ways of understanding experience and thus of choosing and acting in accordance with such understanding. As Spinelli

(2014) notes, entering into the second phase of therapy, therapists stand-beside clients and are able to increasingly assert their otherness based on the establishment of a relationship of safety and trust.

An inevitable and necessary facet of this process is that in the mutual exploration of clients' experiences there occurs the realization that healers may not share the same values and beliefs. Healing is essentially based on the healer's steadfast adherence to the values of compassion and justice. Often in the course of their work, they find that clients engage life in ways contrary to these values and, as a consequence, suffer. Even if healers strive not to impose their values on clients by asserting that they are better and truer, nonetheless the recognition by clients that they are experiencing an alternative way of being in the relationship is an instrumental part of what makes change possible. The healer's way of being-with others expresses the powerful message that things can be otherwise, that there are alternative ways of being that may be more life affirming and more just.

The stimulus for clients questioning their dearly held assumptions begins with the experience of disillusionment, and this can be the prelude to healing. Encouraging a more in-depth exploration of the upheaval of their worldview and the emotions it evokes can build upon this awakening. Reassurance can be offered about the expected distress and fear that accompany being shaken up, along with the belief of the healer that this can offer the opportunity of choosing a more life-affirming response. The discovery of alternative and expanded ways of being may occur simply through the discovery of certain inconsistencies, contradictions, and tensions in the unfolding detailed exploration of the client's worldview. In addition, the intentional ways in which healers negotiate the dialectic of closeness and detachment can promote questioning and eventually a deconstruction of unhealthy patterns of thinking, feeling, and behaving.

By utilizing direct thought, healers are able to convey a deep sense of respect and connection with clients; at the same time, maintaining this stance restricts healers' focus to what is obvious or apparent in what is being communicated. As a result, deeper meaning behind those communications will be missed. Moreover, the non-reflective stance of clients that contributes to their suffering goes unchallenged. Examples of this are described by Frankl (1968). He labels them as the problems of excessive attention and intention in his discussion of paradoxical intention. Paradoxical intention is sometimes described as a technique in which a therapist prescribes the symptom. Excessive attention can lead to anticipatory anxiety, in which individuals withdraw from feared situations because they expect the fear to recur. Excessive intention is found in obsessive–compulsive conditions in which individuals fight against their symptoms and, in doing so, only strengthen them. Both of these are examples of failing to claim one's problems due to resistance to experiencing the suffering that accompanies them (self-created suffering).

To break free of these destructive patterns, individuals must make use of the human capacity for self-detachment and so gain distance from their suffering. Frankl sees paradoxical intention as a means of achieving this distance. Clients are encouraged to stop fighting against their problems and instead bring to mind as fully as possible what is most terrifying and embarrassing to them. This approach will be discussed in more detail in the next section on the power of paradox to foster change. Frankl describes the movement from direct to discursive thought as de-reflection, where individuals are able to step back from their typical absorption in the outside world or preoccupation with internal processes, accompanied by a kind of self-forgetfulness. This shift enables them to ridicule their symptoms rather than running away from or fighting them. Detachment is also the basis for the human capacity for humor. Individuals cannot laugh at a situation if they are too close to it. The capacity for self-reflection is also what enables human beings to assume a hypothetical viewpoint or an attitude of wonder. Rather than bound by the immediate, they are able to imagine how things can be different and act as if things were otherwise. These are all expressions of dialectical thought.

This attitude of wonder and invitation to engage in speculative thought is an important way for healers to interact with clients in what is described by Dubose (2014) as *being-otherwise*. It offers clients possibilities of exploring ways of being beyond those that are familiar and comfortable. As individuals in the healing process achieve more distance from their rigid ways of being, healers can detect understandings and insights they may have achieved that are latent or implicit in their behavior and communication. Once more, clients are unaware of these meanings because they are locked into a non-reflective mode of consciousness. Healers need to be attuned to how people often know more than they can say.

By means of questioning, healers can make the implicit explicit by articulating or enacting what is being repressed or disowned. Such indirect forms of communication (Ramsland, 1989) are powerful channels by which healers are able hold a mirror before clients and show rather than tell them what is being disclosed in their language or behavior. Metaphors that are taken literally by clients and so using them is revealed to be a kind of poetry through which significant insights are symbolically conveyed. Stereotypical patterns in which individuals are ensnared, but which they have disowned, can be suggested to them rather than using direct confrontation. There are drawbacks to clients restricting their understanding of problems to a more detached and intellectual level. When individuals are engaged in activities, they often miss a great deal of how they are engaged because it is hidden in the flow. Creating a disturbance in that mode of engagement draws individuals' attention away from the detached perspective and enables them to have a direct and visceral encounter with their actual experience.

The most important dialectic that must be negotiated in the process of healing is inescapable versus self-created suffering. This is a subject I discuss at length in my previous book (Gruba-McCallister, 2019), given that it is the most substantive issue requiring attention in providing radical therapy. Truly understanding the nature of these two forms of suffering and the ways in which they are related is essential to ensure human well-being. The nature and cause of both forms of suffering must be correctly understood in order to distinguish between them. This enables individuals to see how each requires a very different way of responding and managing. There are several challenges involved in this. The first is the sometimes complex ways in which these two forms of suffering are intertwined. While they are distinct, they nonetheless frequently interact with each other in ways that make it difficult to distinguish what form individuals are experiencing. As a result, when individuals reflect on their experience and seek to discern the basis of their suffering, they often encounter confusion. Further, obstacles to this process are often posed by harmful messages conveyed by neoliberal hegemony that inhibit healing.

Additionally, as asserted in an earlier chapter, the greatest source of self-created suffering comes from meeting inescapable suffering with resistance. This is due to the widespread illusion that one should be free of all suffering and that suffering is inherently evil and without any merit. The reasons for this are based, in part, in physical, psychological, and spiritual processes inherent in being human. However, of more particular interest to this discussion is that there are powerful ideological processes at work specifically devoted to confusing, obfuscating, and denying the significant role of injustice in causing suffering. These points make the undoing of self-deception and mystification and the correct discernment of the two forms of suffering imperatives of radical healing.

A brief summary of how mystification operates is needed here. The first and most common form is portraying self-created suffering as inescapable suffering. This is an extension of hegemony being portrayed as a given truth that is fixed, universal, and unchangeable. Based on this, oppression stemming from existent human decisions and actions is instead attributed to blind and impersonal forces. Thus, the ruling elite are not to blame or protect from sanction and opposition. Instead, individuals are expected to passively resign themselves to poverty, war, sickness, and other afflictions that have an ideological basis. Another variation on this deception is blaming victims for social sources of suffering by attributing this suffering to their inferiority, complicity, or responsibility. This is a natural extension of extreme individualism and is accompanied by minimizing, trivializing, or denying the material and psychological costs of oppression. The most extreme form of this is outright denial, in which the suffering caused by injustice is rendered invisible and so non-existent. As Byrne (2002) notes, social exclusion theory is a multidimensional process used to shut out marginalized groups from social, economic, political, and cultural systems of mainstream society. Moreover, these groups are largely silenced, which then allows dominant discourses to explain their plight.

The sociologist Stanley Cohen (2001) describes different forms of denial that can be seen as part of this process. The first is literal denial, in which disturbing facts and information are outright denied. An example is the sanitizing or censoring of information provided to individuals by mainstream media. The second is interpretive denial, in which a fact is not denied but given a meaning that is rooted in the dominant ideological frame. For example, poor individuals being portrayed as lazy and welfare cheats. Denial of voice is the silencing of anyone who might present damaging or unwanted information, as witnessed in the persecution of truth-telling journalists. Denial of public record is the government exercising the power to define the "official" version of an event, as in human-made disasters being reframed as "acts of God." Finally, denial can be practiced through the use of euphemisms, metaphors, or other language to interpret them based on the dominant ideology, such as calling the killing of civilians "collateral damage." Mass media and the culture industry play a substantial role in denying, minimizing, and trivializing suffering.

This denial, combined with the valorization of happiness and positive states of mind as the goals of life and means to success by neoliberalism, contribute to the loss of one's ability to acknowledge and participate in one's own suffering or the suffering of others. As Soelle (1975) warns, the consequence is not only the loss of feeling or apathy but also dehumanization. in which any compassion or commitment to justice is stifled. Chapman (2013) expands on this problem by examining how resistance to the natural feelings of distress, uncertainty, and guilt that are evoked by realizing one's complicity in oppression is rooted in mystification. This leads to a devaluing of compassion and justice, as he notes:

> Acknowledging complicity in oppression provokes uncertainty, painful feelings, and a destabilization of identity. However difficult such experiences are, they are essential to politicized ethicality and accountability. I advocate that people journey with pain, uncertainty, and identity destabilization when implicating themselves in oppression, to cultivate a 'troubled consciousness'…Implicating oneself in oppression requires measuring oneself by one's impact on oppressed peoples. This causes uncertainty and pain, and destabilizes one's sense of oneself as coherently moral. (p. 182)

Chapman attributes mystification of these feeling to a discursive force he describes as *compulsory sound-mindedness*. This pathologizes and stigmatizes any experiences that depart from contentment and the mandate of liberal individualism that one be reasonable. Neoliberalism labels those who do not behave rationally and objectively as deficient and disordered. He explains:

> …such experiences, which are normatively psychologized and framed as useless, immobilizing, and best avoided. This obscures their part in ethical and political journeys. For my purposes, unreason includes: unhappy emotional experiences including anxiety and guilt; not-knowing or uncertainty; an unmoored sense of self, particularly when questioning one's morality; and a sense of self that incorporates others' presence. (p. 185)

Individuals who perpetrate oppression on others, even if not intentionally, are as a result steered away from experiences that are politically and ethically important by negating their accountability. The result is that the potential for these painful experiences to give way to personal transformation and developing a deeper commitment to compassion and justice is lost.

In order to give thoughtful consideration to the social sources of suffering, radical healers must be conscious of these various obstacles to identifying what form of suffering is being experienced by those seeking care and how easily these causes can be denied, misinterpreted, or confused. As Chapman (2013) states, this includes those who engage in oppressive practices as well as those who are victims of oppression (which can be the same person). Such preparation begins with healers seeking clarity regarding their own experiences, particularly in light of the observation of Chapman that one's complicity in oppressive practices is often avoided. This ends up increasing the likelihood of one doing further harm to its victims. Healers must also develop the knowledge and skills necessary to guide others through the often complicated process of discerning the various sources of their suffering and their interrelationships; finding a means of enabling them to be fully present to their suffering by undoing self-deception and mystification; and having named and claimed their suffering, next seeing it in a new light. This then truly sets the stage for personal and collective liberation.

Engaging in practices that enable them to foster both an openness to their experiences, particularly painful ones, and the discipline to examine them self-critically better enables healers to guide others in the same practices. This is achieved both by example and by how they utilize the relationship to persuade and guide others in the journey toward wholeness. This integration of observation and analysis or *resolute perception* is described by Hanna and Puhakka (1991) as a common factor in successful therapy. They state, "*Resolute perception* is defined as the steady and deliberate observation of or attending to something that is intimidating, painful, or stultifying with therapeutic intent" (p. 599). It combines openness to experiencing what truly is with a readiness to honestly examine it, evaluate it, and, if necessary, change it to promote well-being. It is intended to counteract the human proclivity to ignore the obvious by employing selective attention, denial, or avoidance. Methods that healers can use to encourage and facilitate resolute perception include confrontation, paradoxical injunctions, reframing, role playing, and the use of metaphor (some of these will be examined further in the next section).

Hanna and Puhakka describe the principles underlying this method. One comes from Husserl's (1982) concept of intentionality, which states that consciousness is always of something. This is implicit whenever a healer seeks to make clients more conscious of their suffering by encouraging them to describe it in order to bring it more sharply into focus. Resolute perception is also rooted in Heidegger's (1962) ideas regarding resoluteness as being ready for anxiety and a means of promoting authenticity. This resolve relates not merely to consciousness, but also to the exercise of will. Individuals must make the choice to confront their problems and actively come to grips with them. While recognizing that the therapeutic relationship continues to play a significant role in healing, Hanna and Puhakka see the utilization of the technique of resolute perception as a necessary addition. In line with the previous work by Frank and Frank (1991) on persuasion and healing, the influence of therapists on clients is an important facet of healing. Hanna and Puhakka state:

> However, all the genuineness, warmth, empathy, and influence in the world is ultimately useless if the client does not in some way face up to his or her thoughts, feelings, behaviors, and problems. This is why psychotherapy occasionally fails even in the presence of a genuine and empathic therapist. Relationship factors alone are not sufficient for change. (p. 603)

Resolute perception can thus be a valuable skill to encourage individuals to take the process of healing seriously and work toward mastery or resolution of issues causing suffering. It can be seen as an expression of courage, which is described by Tillich (1952) as affirming life in the face of anxiety, pain, and terror.

The relevance of human spirituality to this process is revealed by examining another central polarity that must be negotiated in healing. That is the polarity between active and passive volition (Gruba-McCallister, 2002, 2019). This polarity parallels the distinction between discursive and direct thought and between reflective and prereflective consciousness. In active volition individuals exert effort and apply themselves in the pursuit of achieving some goal or completing a task. Its aims are control, manipulation, and mastery. It is based on a reflective and evaluative stance that sees objects or others as a means to meeting needs. Active volition is rooted in functions over which we have voluntary control. In terms of the two forms of suffering, active volition is the appropriate response to addressing those forms of suffering that have their origins in choices and actions taken by human beings (self-created suffering).

In contrast, passive volition is a form of control in which we willingly surrender ourselves to a process and permit it to happen. Individuals assume an attitude of "letting be" in which they grant consent to a process and whatever may unfold. Passive volition is open, receptive, and non-evaluative. In a state of passive volition, individuals experience themselves as completely absorbed in someone or something else and so experience a temporary loss of awareness of self (prereflective or direct knowing). It is involved in performing functions that are not under our voluntary control, such as vital body functions like breathing, heartbeat, digestion. Other examples of such experiences are being deeply moved by some work of art, becoming absorbed in some pleasurable activity, performing some physical feat smoothly and effortlessly, and falling in love.

In terms of negotiating the process of naming and then claiming suffering, passive volition plays an important role that highlights its value to healers and those they serve. As noted, meeting inescapable suffering with resistance is one of the most significant causes of self-created suffering. This same resistance is also a powerful obstacle to people's ability to identify and deconstruct the ideological biases that distort and obfuscate the experience of suffering and prevent it from being correctly named or seen for what it is. Meeting suffering with acceptance does not mean that the pain and the injustice that causes it is denied. It also does not mean that one assumes a helpless attitude. Rather it enables one to listen to what is being conveyed by that suffering and, in doing so, achieve greater clarity about how to respond to it in a transformative manner.

Traditionally, one of the most effective means for individuals to cultivate the capacity for demonstrating passive volition is learning relaxation techniques or practicing meditation or some other spiritual exercise. The integration of mindfulness in anti-oppression pedagogy, psychotherapy, and actions aimed at social change has been a topic of growing scholarship and increasing practical applications. One example is a collection of contributions examining mindfulness in promoting personal and social change (Loizzo, Brandon, Wolf, & Neale, 2023). Similarly, Berila (2016) provides a comprehensive description of how mindfulness or contemplative education promotes anti-oppressive pedagogy and can empower students to create social change. Some of her points echo those described here. She cites the work of Barbezat and Bush (2014) regarding the goals of contemplative education, which include:

- Building focus and attention, mainly through meditation and similar techniques.
- Incorporating contemplation and introspection into the content of courses so that students discover the material in themselves and deepen their understanding.
- Developing compassion, connection with others, and a deeper sense of the moral and spiritual aspect of education.
- Being able to inquire into the nature of their minds, personal meaning, creativity, and insight.

Contemplative methods are a practical form of education that helps to develop emotional intelligence. Individuals are able to be fully present to and reflect on their inner experience by means of non-judgmental acceptance. Through the process of discernment, mindfulness enables people to disidentify from the content of their mind and recognize that they are bigger than their thoughts. Berila describes this as "the Witness," or the ability to observe what is happening without being absorbed in it. These capabilities are especially useful when individuals experience disillusionment because of the challenges that occur when their worldview has been challenged. This dissonance triggers an uncomfortable uncertainty that may lead them to change some ideas in order to make them more consistent with existing assumptions, to seek more information to support those assumptions, or to minimize conflict. By cultivating discernment, this discomfort can be embraced and reflected upon in a more intentional and less reactive manner. Individuals can hold contradictions with compassion and sit with discomfort. Painful uncertainty and fear of the unknown can be reframed as a teachable moment. Berila's model for moving through dissonance provides helpful guidelines for how to move from naming and claiming suffering to reframing. It involves the following:

- Be present to your experience.
- Embody your experience by turning inward and feeling whatever is in the moment.
- Witness by observing what you are experiencing without it consuming you.
- Accept whatever you are experiencing without judgment, aversion, or attraction.
- Reflect on your responses and consider how they are shaped by social programming, power, privilege, and implicit values.
- Engage by deciding how you want to respond and act accordingly.

The Power of Paradox: Reframing

The subject of paradox has occupied a prominent place throughout various points in this examination of the nature of radical healing. One, noted in the earlier discussion of Frankl's (1968) idea of paradoxical intention and the concept of resolute perception, is the role of paradox in promoting the healing process. Another is the role of paradox in the developmental process, in which particular polarities must be negotiated at different stages of development. There is also the growing capacity for tolerance of ambiguity as one ascends these stages. The discussion of self-deception described how the inability to either comprehend or accept paradox leads to a heightened state of alienation that impairs wholeness. This is particularly the case when individuals adopt a rigid, dualistic, and extreme stance that fails to recognize the necessary interdependent relationship between polarities inherent in human existence. This serves to explain the self-defeating pattern embedded in self-deception.

Finally, the fundamental nature of human beings has been asserted to be rooted in existential paradoxes that must be embraced and ceaselessly negotiated in order to live authentically. While this process is typically understood in psychological terms, as the chapter on spirituality makes clear, this understanding of human beings is essentially an expression of their spirituality. The nature of the Absolute, as it has been revealed by means of mystical insight, consists of a number of central polarities, including transcendent and immanent, eternal and temporal, infinite and finite, life and death, good and evil. Human beings, by virtue of being an expression of the Absolute, embody these same paradoxes. They define various facets of what it means to be human. However, awareness of the centrality of these paradoxes is often obscured or even lost when one's mystical vocation is stifled. This can be seen in examples of false transcendence, in which one's identity is narrowed to ephemeral identifications and attachments. This is the enduring problem of the ego. Despite self-transcendence being the most powerful motive, as elucidated in Tillich's (1957) distinction between preliminary and ultimate concerns and Wilber's (1980) discussion of the Atman Project, both personal and social forces can thwart rediscovering our identity with the Absolute. This is a very potent source of suffering that has devastating consequences on both the individual and collective level. The attainment of liberation is not possible without taking into thoughtful consideration how to connect individuals with this powerful motive and enable them to channel it in ways that promote wholeness, harmony, and health.

Healers must appreciate and utilize all of these forms of paradox in order to promote a reframing of suffering—no matter what its source may be. A proper understanding of the nature of these paradoxes and their relevance to our humanity provide a means of decreasing a sense of alienation and the accompanying experience of dehumanization. This requires healers to align themselves with the power of the Absolute and serve as its channel in their relationship with those seeking care. That means exemplifying and embodying the paradoxes inherent to the Absolute with openness and acceptance in their relationships with others. The healing relationship is not merely an encounter with the healer but with the Absolute itself. An example of this is found in the discussion of the role of the otherness of healers in promoting change. It described the need to express two seemingly opposite attitudes of closeness and detachment that may be experienced by clients as dissonant and conflictual. There needs to be a willingness to both comfort and afflict, to understand and challenge, to agree and disagree with the other with the intent to bring them back to an authentic encounter with what it means to be human. This mirrors the ambivalence described by Otto (1958) in the experience of the Holy expressing the two sides of awe: awesome and the awful. This is also the paradox that can sometimes be expressed in the call to compassion and justice as equal values pivotal to healing.

What this exemplifies is that paradox has the potential to create dissonance and conflict while, at the same time, providing a means for reconciling this conflict in a transformative way. These two facets are illustrative of the very nature of paradox in which seeming opposites are actually inseparably linked. It also acknowledges how the experience of crisis—which, as has been argued, is a necessary prelude to the opportunity to attain greater wholeness—must provoke ambivalence. Individuals feel the temptation to retreat to the seeming comfort of what has been lost and, at the same time, feel drawn to possibilities revealed by that loss. This lays out the fundamental framework healers must appreciate and acknowledge when working with those who find themselves torn between what feels like an irresolvable conflict. The desire to retreat from the suffering and act as if nothing has changed must be acknowledged. However, this acknowledgement cannot convey acceptance that this is the only, or for that matter, the most desirable choice facing clients. The ability of healers to remain squarely within this whirlpool of conflicting emotions and torn desires conveys a powerful message to clients that they can do likewise. Part of what makes this possible is knowing that they do not have to engage in this process on their own. The other part of what makes it possible is the ability of healers to help clients who have named and claimed their suffering, to reframe it as something of value, and a means to achieve greater wholeness.

One example of this is when individuals are ensnared in fixed, black-or-white patterns of processing their experience, characteristic of discursive thought. Using this approach, they soon find that situations involving paradox defy an either-or solution. The more they try to impose ironclad categories on their experience, the more they find themselves confused and caught up in a vicious circle. This rigid, over-reflective stance can be immobilized by intensifying conflict or posing a paradox that then can open up an alternative way of knowing and with it new insights or perspectives on the problem. Posing a paradox is the basis of the Zen method of the *koan*, an unanswerable question ("What is the sound of one hand clapping?) or absurd statement ("If you meet Buddha on the road, kill him!"), posed by a teacher to raise intense doubt in students. A koan stymies their reliance on dichotomous thinking and instead enables them to achieve insight into the non-dual nature of Reality. Literature in Zen Buddhism contains a number of stories in which the shock provided by a koan leads to a flash of insight by cutting through the pitfalls of reliance on discursive thought. This then becomes the means for achieving liberation.

The internalization of hegemony is often maintained by means of forms of mystification that rely on discursive thought. This includes the ways in which the manipulation of language and metaphor understood literally is used to narrow or distort individuals' awareness of social issues or foster destructive distortions. An example of this comes from the work of the cognitive psychologist George Lakoff (2002, 2004). He proposed the idea of *frames* rooted in a dominant ideology. These consist of certain forms of language and metaphors that function at a predominantly unconscious level, making them difficult to detect and uproot. Similar to legitimizing myths, these frames shape how people give meaning to their experience, which then shapes their values and guides their behavior accordingly. Lakoff believes that the symbolic meaning system espoused by neoliberalism is used to maintain existing power relations. It is thus important to unveil these frames and challenge them in order to achieve personal and social change.

Like the use of the koan, the posing of paradox can break through the barrage of rationalizations and self-serving explanations provided by neoliberal ideology that are calculated to confuse or deceive. The suspension of discursive thought enables individuals to return to connecting with and trusting their actual lived experience and, in doing so, come to realize their victimization by a toxic ideology. This sets the stage for *reframing*, in which a truer, more complete, and wider perspective can be brought forward that embraces what feel like contradictions. By thinking outside of the box, individuals can translate their newly discovered insights into meaningful action. They thus reclaim their agency and freedom by means of forming a counter-hegemonic understanding of their situation. This is similar to Friere's (1961) concept of *annunciation*, or creation of an alternative to prevailing oppressive conditions. Friere asserts that the oppressed must see injustice not as something fixed and unresolvable but as a limit situation that can be transformed. Thus, the naming and claiming that occurs in consciousness-raising moves from awareness of the causes of one's oppression to conceiving a society based on justice and liberatory action.

In addition, a paradoxical strategy can also be used to disrupt patterns among individuals who have fallen into processing their experience in an uncritical and non-reflective manner because they are stuck in a pattern based on direct thought. As a result, their capacity for critical thought is impaired, giving rise to automaticity and blind conformity to the dominant ideology. This is particularly likely when they experience a threat to their sense of self and worldview accompanied by fear. We have seen how fear is a potent weapon used by the powerful to maintain the status quo. Facing this fear while not being immobilized by it is a fundamental quandary that must be resolved in order to achieve liberation.

Watts (1961) likens the process of indoctrination to what occurs in hypnosis, in which there is a suspension of the critical function and a tendency for individuals to process their experience literally (Spiegel & Spiegel, 1978). This *trance logic* interprets literally statements such as hypnotic suggestions because under hypnosis individuals are operating at a prereflective level of consciousness. Thus, the purpose of liberation is to free individuals from social programming in which they mistake social conventions and institutions for reality. Watts observes that language and metaphors function as powerful means used in propaganda and indoctrination. This is because the loss of the critical function leads individuals to accept information at face level and so fail to see how these unquestioned beliefs and values condition their worldview. The greatest of all social artifacts is the ego—attachments and identifications with roots in what Fromm (1941) called social character or internalized hegemony. The ego is the greatest obstacle to coming to a realization of our true nature, but the loss of ego is also the greatest of all fears.

However, Watts notes that the posing of paradox in psychotherapy can unveil the contradictions and confusion embedded in the dominant ideology, along with their hidden metaphysical assumptions. This realization allows for a deconstructing of the ego as essentially a social artifact. This awakening promotes a playful attitude in which imagination is given free rein. Individuals can adopt an "as if" attitude that generates openness and creativity. Posing a paradox can also lead to recovering the ability to adopt a reflective stance and actively critique assumptions that restrict freedom and stifle growth. In this process, individuals come to the realization that they do not have to destroy the ego but rather see through it. They recognize that the ego is not based on complete lies but rather on half-truths involved in taking culture-bound metaphors literally. Freeing themselves from a culturally induced trance is the means to true liberation.

A significant example of a harmful metaphor prevalent in neoliberalism is the *myth of the market* (Gruba-McCallister, 2019). Similar to hegemony being posed as veridical, objective, and fixed, neoliberal ideology portrays the market as a natural, self-regulating entity that actually exists in the outside world. It operates by fixed and immutable laws independent of human beings. These rules and regularities are called *market rationality,* which also implies a market morality. For example, there is the belief that the merit and soundness of all human actions is determined based on their compliance with the demands of the market, such that it operates as a kind of absolute. This view of the market is intended to make clear that human beings are incapable of either challenging it or controlling it. It is also used to justify the harmful impacts of the market, such as commodification, unemployment, and inequality of power and opportunity. Suffering inflicted by the market is portrayed as impersonal and implacable. As a result, it is minimized, trivialized, and privatized. At the same time, attention is deflected from the true social, economic, and political causes of oppression and inequality.

This understanding of the market again highlights the dangers of taking a metaphor literally due to the suppression of critical thought. This portrayal of the market conflates the social and the natural. It is manufactured by neoliberal ideology to justify the validity of the market and stifle opposition. Assigning the market the status of an actual objective entity operating by fixed physical laws commits the Fallacy of Misplaced Concreteness. *There is not a natural force or entity called the market.* The market actually is a construct fabricated by thinkers who advance capitalist theory. Using the pretense of natural science to reify the market is nothing more than a ploy to disguise how this myth is used to oppress individuals in ways that are advantageous to the powerful elite.

The process of reframing thus requires a clear grasp of and appreciation for a dialectical stance toward life. As such, it recognizes the distinction between contradiction and paradox described in an earlier chapter. In the case of contradiction, the opposing elements posed by a situation can be clearly distinguished from each other, such that affirming one side of a polarity provides a means of resolving a conflict. For example, when confronted with the experience of being oppressed due to being dehumanized by others, individuals can realistically demand that such dehumanization be stopped because it is morally condemnable and capable of being changed. The alternatives confronting individuals in this case are clear, and individuals can challenge their circumstances by asserting the demands of compassion and justice. This situation can also be seen as an example of what Fromm (1947) called a historical dichotomy that is capable of being resolved because it is based on the exercise of choice. Thus, in pursuit of liberation, it is important that what might be posed and understood by the oppressed as an existential dichotomy inherent in the human condition is reframed instead as a historical dichotomy.

In contrast, a paradox has been defined as a polarity in which the opposing elements cannot be distinguished from each other because of the interdependent relationship between them. It represents what has philosophically been defined as a dialectical relationship in which opposites mutually define and are necessary to each other. A number of examples of such paradoxes have been described previously. One is the interrelationship between mind and body. Both define what it means to be human and inextricably interact with each other. Thus, individuals are incapable of disentwining the way they interact. Embedded in these paradoxes are the most profound conflicts that beset individuals. This is because the one-sided solutions often applied to them are self-defeating. However, just as a historical dichotomy may be portrayed as an existential dichotomy and result in injustice so, too, can existential dichotomies be portrayed as a historical dichotomy—with disastrous consequences on a personal, spiritual, and social level. Both are examples of mystification used to defend the status quo. When this occurs, a necessary step to promote liberation is reframing. This can be done by using paradox to elevate the consciousness of individuals regarding the necessity of accepting and living with that paradox.

This is discussed by Spiegel and Spiegel (1978) is their examination of the therapeutic uses of hypnosis. They describe this method as *restructuring,* or the dialectical resolution of conflicts responsible for suffering. They provide a philosophical background for their argument on the use of restructuring based on the work of Hegel, Kierkegaard, and Heidegger. All of these thinkers see human beings as involved in a constant process of seeking to reconcile opposing dimensions of being human that are inescapable. They argue persuasively that the overall aim of employing the dialectical strategy in healing is to promote wholeness through integration and synthesis rather than analysis and dissecting that lead to alienation. They write:

> The "sick" individual in a psychiatric sense, or the "unhappy consciousness" in the Hegelian sense, may be seen as one who despairs of transcending the paradoxes which confuse his selfhood. He decides that he is at one or another of the extremes, although he is actually unaware of consciously having made any such decision. (pp. 205-206)

This self-defeating stance must be identified and challenged in order to promote personal and social liberation by means of restructuring or reframing. In contrast:

> ...a relatively healthy person is one who has successfully integrated such conflicts, and who can therefore act on the basis of the inevitable conflicting elements that make up the human self...This is the "essence" of the dialectic. To the extent that people recognize and integrate these opposites, they master their lives. (p. 206)

Extending Praxis to the Community and Beyond: Taking Aim

This discussion of the role of paradox in radical healing highlights how dehumanization in any form is the primary cause of suffering. It is only through the reversal of this process that true compassion and justice can be realized. The fundamental task of reframing is to move from insight into the causes of dehumanization to action to restore the humanity of all people. By imagining a counter-hegemony, individuals are able to conceive of a society firmly grounded in compassion and justice. Clarity regarding how things can be different is the foundation on which understanding can then pave the way for transformative action or praxis. Any ideology that denies human subjectivity and agency—as both neoliberalism and fascism clearly do—must be abolished in order to enable human beings to flourish. This is why any restricted understanding of human beings that fails to take into account physical, psychological, social, and spiritual sources of suffering is bound to fail to provide the basis for true healing. Moreover, radical healing seeks not merely to transform individuals, but society itself.

A major contribution to this broader understanding comes from critical psychology. It recognizes how neoliberalism's exaggeration of individualism creates a shallow and fragile sense of narcissism while at the same time portraying extant social conditions as posing demands to which individuals must passively adapt. This gives rise to *restrictive agency*, in which persons are compelled to adapt to prevailing power relations and are able to exercise freedom only within limits imposed by authorities. Under these conditions, expressing one's agency exposes people to the risk of coming into conflict with powerful others. They are led to believe that they must accept oppression to secure some measure of immediate advantage. This realization also exposes their complicity with the status quo and reinforces a sense of dependency that only deepens their suffering.

Individuals mistakenly believe that they must engage in competition because they are able to gain advantage only at the expense of others. This *guilt discourse* makes them feel selfish and immoral; it leads people to assume excessive accountability for their actions while diverting attention from the actual role played by ideology. This description shows how neoliberalism ties individuals into knots so that they are damned no matter what they do. What may seem paradoxical is actually the experience of being confounded by the vexing contradictions embedded in a destructive ideology. Unless this ploy used to get individuals to consent to their oppression is unveiled and reframed, efforts at liberation will be foiled.

By expanding agency and subjectivity to include other human beings, critical psychology restores the interdependent relationship between individual and society. This is a dialectical reframe that enables individuals to cooperatively strive for justice. It asserts the possibility that human beings can jointly determine the life conditions to which they are subjected and engage with others in critical reflection. This capacity for transcendence enables them to productively come to terms with the conflicts and contradictions posed by neoliberalism. Critical psychology calls this *generalized agency.* It recognizes that every human being desires to engage in a self-determined life and that pursuit of their interests sometimes will unavoidably contribute to the oppression of others. The conditions under which persons live can only be realized on a supra-individual level—that is, only together with others coming to a shared understanding of their common situation.

Utilizing *reason discourse*, human beings can engage in dialogue with one another and, in doing so, work together to utilize the ability to transcend the immediate situation. They recognize how they sometimes unwittingly violate other individuals' subjectivity without judging themselves. Instead, they come to a deeper social awareness that puts the degree of their responsibility into proper perspective and increases their understanding of the role played by ideological forces. By means of *metasubjectivity*, human beings appreciate their condition from the broadest perspective. It includes all those involved in a situation recognizing that their own particular viewpoint is not privileged or advantaged. Collectively, individuals grasp how they are commonly, though differently, impacted by ideological forces. This leads to shared responsibility for overcoming restrictive conditions.

Transpersonal psychology also makes an invaluable contribution to providing a much needed expanded understanding of human beings necessary for radical healing aimed at social change.. This is accomplished through its inclusion of spirituality as an essential facet of human beings, its recognition of elevated states of awareness and higher stages of human development, and its integration of the enduring insights of the perennial philosophy. These have been long been foundations of healing, as was noted in the earlier discussion of shamanism and indigenous practices. The extreme materialism perpetrated by neoliberalism has led to a neglect and denigration of human spirituality, with many negative consequences. The mystical insight regarding the oneness of all beings is the ultimate basis for compassion and justice and provides the most powerful affirmation of the essential interdependency among human beings and the inviolable worth of all persons. However, neoliberalism denies this truth through an exaggerated individualism and encouragement of divisiveness.

This truly holistic vision makes clear that radical healing must not stop at the individual level, as this only supports the damaging limitations of neoliberalism. With regard to providing care for those who are oppressed, this means collaborating with them based on a radically egalitarian relationship in order to promote justice for all. There must be collective reflection on the impact of power and social context on well-being. This means the facilitation of "outsight" with regard to the ways that social determinants of health, inequality, disempowerment, and violence exert detrimental impacts on individuals' lives. Radical healing must engage in practices designed to cultivate critical consciousness. Work must be aimed at agreeing on a viable counter-hegemony rooted in the values of equality/fairness, democracy/freedom, and community/solidarity. Realizing this counter-hegemony provides the foundation for meaningful social action.

Prilleltensky and colleagues (2007) describe how justice-based interventions need to be proactive and community-based. Examples include participative action research, joining in class action suits, community organizing, prevention, and influencing public policy. Interventions are aimed at dysfunction in the systems with which individuals interact, such as schools, health care, and social services. They write:

> Although community members are subject to negative societal influences, they need not be passive recipients of toxic messages. They can become agents of change to transform the conditions that perpetuate their own suffering or the suffering of others...By engaging in a public act of defiance, they are likely to help themselves and others who may be subject to similar negative influences...We recommend that counseling agencies offer clients opportunities to work with others on socially related maladies such as addictions, violence, discrimination, and eating disorders. (pp. 34–35)

This expanded focus means that the training of healers must be radically revised to provide knowledge and skills pertinent to identifying and uprooting neoliberal biases that limit understanding of all the sources of suffering.

Inspired by the work of Martin-Baró (1996), there has been a growth in literature on psychologies of liberation (Watkins & Shulman, 2008) aimed at working with victims of war, racism, violence, poverty, and colonization. These approaches require healers to relinquish their role as expert and instead engage in practices patterned on critical pedagogy (Friere, 1961) that involve learning through a communal process. Truth is democratized and healing is achieved by means of transformation through critical consciousness and sociopolitical action. Comas-Diaz (2007) describes ethno-political psychology, whose goal is to foster decolonization by increasing critical awareness of colonized mentality, including its cognitive distortions and corruption of identity. Practitioners collaborate with people of color to bear witness to their suffering and offer various means of transforming it into individual and collective action to achieve racial and ethnic justice. Healers seek to integrate non-Western traditions and healing practices into their work, to reconnect individuals with their cultural roots and spiritual practices, and to restore the voices of those subjected to political repression and violence.

Social action requires healers to expand their knowledge and skills in this area as well as come to a deeper appreciation of how their existing knowledge and skills can be fruitfully integrated with effecting change to systems. As noted in the previous chapter, this includes becoming more firmly grounded in socialism as a counter-hegemony that promotes human flourishing (Eagleton, 2018; Wright, 2019). In addition, they must be better acquainted with writings on principles of social change (Smucker, 2017). Finally, they must find ways to better collaborate with others who share their devotion to compassion and justice. Only then will true emancipation be more than a dream and instead become the highest priority not only for you or for me, but for all.

References

Adorno, T. W., Frenkel-Brunswik, E., Levinson, D. J., & Sanford, R. N. (1950). *The authoritarian personality*. Harper & Row.

Ahmed, S. (2010). *The promise of happiness*. Duke University Press.

Aho, K. (2008). Medicalizing mental health: A phenomenological alternative. *Journal of Medical Humanities, 29,* 243–259.

Albee, G. W. (1990). The futility of psychotherapy. *Journal of Mind and Behavior, 11,* 369–374.

Alexander, F. (1931). Buddhist training as artificial catatonia. *Psychoanalytic Review, 18,* 129–145.

Altemeyer, B. (1981). *Right-wing authoritarianism*. University of Manitoba Press.

Altemeyer, B. (1988). *Enemies of freedom: Understanding right-wing authoritarianism.* Jossey-Bass.

Altemeyer, B. (1996). *The authoritarian specter*. Harvard University Press.

American Psychological Association (2020). Stress in America 2020: A national mental health crisis. https://www.apa.org/news/press/releases/stress/2020/sia-mental-health-crisis.pdf

American Psychological Association (2021). Stress in America: One year later, a new wave of pandemic health concerns. https://www.apa.org/news/press/ releases/stress/ 2021/sia-pandemic-report.pdf

American Psychological Association (2023). Stress in America 2023: A nation recovering from collective trauma. https://www.apa.org/news/press/releases/stress/2023/ collective-trauma-recovery

Antonovsky, A. (1987). *Unraveling the mystery of health*. Jossey-Bass.

Applebaum, A. (2021). *Twilight of democracy: The seductive lure of authoritarianism.* Anchor Books.

Arber, A. (1957). *The manifold and the one*. John Murray.

Armaly, M. T., Buckley, D. T., & Enders, A. M. (2022). Christian nationalism and political violence: Victimhood, racial identity, conspiracy, and support for Capitol attacks. *Political Behavior, 44,* 937–960.

Armstrong, D. (1987). Theoretical tensions in biopsychosocial medicine. *Social Science & Medicine, 25,* 1213–1218.

Armstrong, K. (2023). *Sacred nature: Restoring our ancient bond with the natural world.* Anchor Books.

Assagioli, R. (1965). *Psychosynthesis: A manual of principles and techniques*. The Viking Press.

Augoustinos, M. (1999). Ideology, false consciousness and psychology. *Theory & Psychology, 9* (3), 295–312.

Ayers, A. J., & Saad-Filho, A. (2015). Democracy against neoliberalism: Paradoxes, limitations, transcendence. *Critical Sociology, 41*(4–5), 597–618.

Bakan, D. (1968). *Disease, pain, and sacrifice: Toward a psychology of suffering*. Beacon Press.

Barbezat, D., & Bush, M. (2014). *Contemplative practices in higher education: Powerful methods to transform teaching and learning*. Jossey-Bass.

Barnett, M. (2007). What brings you here? An exploration of the unconscious motivations of those who choose to train and work as psychotherapists and counselors. *Psychodynamic Practice, 13*, 257–274.

Barry B. (2005). *Why social justice matters*. Polity Press.

Becker, E. (1973). *The denial of death*. Simon & Schuster.

Berila, B. (2016). *Integrating mindfulness into anti-oppression pedagogy*. Routledge.

Boggs, C. (2015). The medicalized society. *Critical Sociology, 4*(3), 517–535.

Bohm, D. (2004). *On dialogue* (2nd Ed.). Routledge.

Bourdieu, P. (1984). *Distinction: A social critique of the judgement of taste*. Routledge & Kegan Paul. (Original work published 1979)

Briere, J. (2013). When people do bad things: Evil, suffering, and dependent origination. In A. C. Bohart, B. S. Held, E. Mendelowitz, & K. J. Schneider (Eds.), *Humanity's dark side: Evil, destructive experience, and psychotherapy* (pp. 141–156). American Psychological Association.

Bronfenbrenner, U. (1979). *The ecology of human development: Experiments by nature and design*. Harvard University Press.

Brown, W. (2006). American nightmare: Neoliberalism, neoconservatism, and de-democratization. *Political Theory, 34*(6), 690–714.

Buber, M. (1971). *I and thou* (W. Kaufman, Trans.). Touchstone.

Bucke, R. M. (1923). *Cosmic consciousness: A study in the evolution of the human mind*. Viking Penguin.

Bugenthal, J., & Sapienza, B. (1992). The 3 R's for humanism: Remembering, reconciling, revisiting. *Humanistic Psychologist, 20*, 273-284.

Butler, J. (1989). *Gender trouble: Feminism and the subversion of identity*. Routledge .

Butler, J. (1993). *Bodies that matter: On the discursive limits of "sex."* Routledge.

Byrne, D. (2002). *Social exclusion.* Open University Press.

Calhoun, L. G., & Tedeschi, R. G. (1999). *Facilitating posttraumatic growth: A clinician's guide*. Lawrence Erlbaum.

Campbell, J. (1949). *The hero of a thousand faces* (2nd Ed.). Princeton University Press.

Campbell, J. (1988). *The power of myth with Bill Moyers* (Betty Sue Flowers, Ed.). Doubleday.

Chandran, M., & Schulman, K. A. (2022). Racial disparities in healthcare and health. *Health Services Research, 57*(2), 218–222.

Chapman, C. (2013). Cultivating troubled consciousness: Compulsory sound-mindedness and complicity in oppression. *Health, Culture and Society, 5*(1), 182–198.

Chomsky, N. (1999). *Profit over people: Neoliberalism and global order*. Seven Stories Press.

Cohen, A. (2023). *When shadow meets the bodhisattva: The challenging transformation of a modern guru*. Inner Traditions.

Cohen, S. (2001). *States of denial: Knowing about atrocities and suffering*. Polity Press.

Coles, S., & Mannion, A. (2017). Critical clinical psychology. In B. Gough (Ed.), *The Palgrave handbook of critical social psychology* (pp. 557–578). Palgrave Macmillan.

Comas-Diaz, I. (2007). Ethno-political psychology: Healing and transformation. In E. Aldarando (Ed.), *Advancing social justice through clinical practice* (pp. 91–118). Lawrence Erlbaum.

Conrad, P., & Barker, K. K. (2010). The social construction of illness: Key insights and policy implications. *Journal of Health and Social Behavior, 51*(5), 67–79.

Cudd, A. (2006). *Analyzing oppression*. Oxford University Press.

Cushman, P. (1990). Why the self is empty: Toward a historically situated psychology. *American Psychologist, 45*(5), 599–611.

Dabrowski, K. (1964). *Positive disintegration*. Little, Brown.

Dabrowski, K. (1967). *Personality shaping through positive disintegration*. Little, Brown.

Dass, R., & Gorman, R. (1985). *How can I help?: Stories and reflections on service*. Alfred A. Knopf.

David, E. J. R. (Ed.). (2014). *Internalized oppression: The psychology of marginalized groups*. Springer Publishing Company.

David, E. J. R., & Derthick, A. E. (2014). What is internalized oppression, and so what? In E. J. R. David (Ed.), *Internalized oppression: The psychology of marginalized groups* (pp. 1–30). Springer Publishing Company.

Davies, J. (2022). *Sedated: How modern capitalism created our mental health crisis*. Atlantic Books.

Dawes, R. M. (1994). *House of cards: Psychology and psychotherapy built on myth*. Free Press.

De La Fabián, R., & Stetcher, A. (2017). Positive psychology's promise of happiness: A new form of human capital in contemporary neoliberal governmentality. *Theory & Psychology, 27*(5), 600–621.

De Vos, J. (2012). *Psychologisation in times of globalisation*. Routledge.

Deutsch, M. (2006). A framework for thinking about oppression and its change. *Social Justice Research, 19*(1), 7-41.

DuBose, T. (2014). Engaged understanding for lived meaning. *Journal of Contemporary Psychotherapy, 45*, 25–35.

Duckitt, J. (2009). Authoritarianism and dogmatism. In Mark R. Leary & Rick H. Hoyle (Eds.), *Handbook of individual differences in social behavior* (pp. 298–317). Guilford Press.

Duggan, L. (2003). *The twilight of equality? Neoliberalism, cultural politics and the attack on democracy*. Beacon Press.

Eagleton, T. (2003). *After theory*. Basic Books.

Eagleton, T. (2018). *Why Marx was right* (2nd Ed.). Yale University Press.

Ehrenreich, B. (2009). *Smile or die: How positive thinking fooled America and the world*. Granta Books.

Eliade, M. (1959). *The sacred & the profane: The nature of religion*. (W. R. Trask, Trans.). Harcourt, Brace, Jovanovich.

Eliade, M. (1964). *Shamanism: Archaic techniques of ecstasy* (W. R. Trask, Trans.). Princeton University Press.

Elliot, R., Watson, J., Timulak, L., & Sharbanee, J. (2021). Research on humanistic-experiential psychotherapies: Updated review. In Michael Barkham, Wolfgang Lutz, & Louis Castonguay (Eds.), *Bergin and Garfield's handbook of psychotherapy and behavior change* (pp. 421–468). John Wiley & Sons.

Engel, G. (1980). The biopsychosocial model. *American Journal of Psychiatry, 187*, 535–540.

Epstein, W. (1995). *The illusion of psychotherapy*. Routledge.

Erickson, E. (1950). *Childhood and society*. Norton.

Esposito, L., & Perez, F. M. (2014). Neoliberalism and the commodification of mental health. *Humanity & Society, 38*(4), 414-442.

Fahlberg, L. L., Wolfer, J., & Fahlberg, L A. (1992). Personal crisis: Growth or pathology? *American Journal of Health Promotion, 7*(1), 45–52.

Farber, B. A., Manevich, I., Metzger, J., & Saypool, E. (2005). Choosing psychotherapy as a career: Why did we cross that road? *Journal of Clinical Psychology/In session, 61*, 1009–1031.

Farooq, M. U. (2019). The rise of fascist tendencies in the world: Causes and implications. *Journal of Historical Studies, 5*(1), 11–32.

Feltham, C. (1999). Controversies in psychotherapy and counselling. In Colin Feltham (Ed.), *Controversies in psychotherapy and counselling* (pp. 1–5). Sage.

Ferrer, J. N., & Sherman, J. H. (Eds.). (2008). *The participatory turn: Spirituality, mysticism, religious studies.* State University of New York Press.

Fiske, S. (2011). *Envy up, scorn down: How status divides us.* Russel Sage Foundation.

Foster, R. (2017). Social character: Erich Fromm and the ideological glue of neoliberalism. *Critical Horizons, 18*(1), 1–18.

Foucault, M. (1999). *Discipline and punishment: The birth of the prison* (A. Sheridan, Trans.). Vintage/Random House. (Original work published in 1975)

Fox, D., Prilleltensky, I., & Austin, S. (2009). *Critical psychology: An introduction* (2nd Ed.). Sage.

Fox, M. (1972). *On becoming a musical, mystical bear: Spirituality American style.* Paulist Press.

Frank, J. D., & Frank, J. B. (1991). *Persuasion and healing: A comparative study of psychotherapy* (3rd Ed.). The Johns Hopkins University Press.

Frankl, V. E. (1967). *Psychotherapy and existentialism: Selected papers on logotherapy.* Simon and Schuster.

Fraser, N. (1997). *Justice interruptus: Critical reflections on the "postsocialist" condition.* Routledge.

Freud, S. (1920). *A general introduction to psychoanalysis.* Washington Square Press.

Friedman, M. (2008). Buber and dialogical therapy: Healing through meeting. *The Humanistic Psychologist, 36,* 298–315.

Friedman, M., & Friedman, R. (1990). *Free to choose: A personal statement.* Houghton Mifflin.

Friere, P. (1970). *Pedagogy of the oppressed.* Herder and Herder.

Fromm, E. (1941). *Escape from freedom.* Henry Holt.

Fromm, E. (1947). *Man for himself: An inquiry into the psychology of ethics.* Holt, Rinehart, & Winston.

Fromm, E. (1955). *The sane society.* Fawcett Publications, Inc.

Fromm, E. (1960). Psychoanalysis and Zen Buddhism. In D. T. Suzuki, E. Fromm, & R. DeMartino, *Zen Buddhism and psychoanalysis* (pp. 77-141). Grove Press.

Fromm, E. (1964). *The heart of man: Its genius for good and evil.* Harper & Row.

Fromm, E. (1968). *The revolution of hope: Toward a humanized technology.* Bantam.

Fromm, E. (1976). *To have or to be?* Harper & Row.

Furedi, F. (2005). *Politics of fear.* Continuum.

Gergen, K. J. (1991). *The saturated self: Dilemmas of identity in contemporary life.* Basic Books.

Giroux, H. A. (2008). *Against the terror of neoliberalism: Politics beyond the age of greed.* Paradigm Publishers.

Goleman, D. (1985). *Vital lies, simple truths: The psychology of self-deception.* Simon and Schuster.

Goodman, D. J. (2001). *Promoting diversity and social justice: Educating people from privileged groups.* Sage.

Gramsci, A. (1971). *Selections from the prison notebooks* (Q. Hoare & G. Nowell Smith, Trans.). International Publishers.

Greene, T. W. (2008). Three ideologies of individualism: Toward assimilating a theory of individualisms and their consequences. *Critical Sociology, 34*(1), 117–137.

Grof, S., & Grof, C. (Eds.). (1989). *Spiritual emergency: When personal transformation becomes a crisis*. Penguin Putnam.

Grossman, D. (1995). *On killing: The psychological cost of learning to kill in war and society*. Little, Brown & Company.

Gruba-McCallister, F. P. (1989). Phenomenological orientation to the interview. In R. J. Craig (Ed.), *Clinical and diagnostic interviewing* (pp. 19-31). Jason Aronson.

Gruba-McCallister, F. (1992). Becoming self through suffering: The Irenaean theodicy and advanced development. *Advanced Development, 4*, 49–58.

Gruba-McCallister, F. P. (1993). The imp of the reverse: A phenomenology of the unconscious. *Journal of Religion and Health, 32*(2), 107–120.

Gruba-McCallister, F. P. (2002). Education through compassion: The cultivation of the prophetic contemplative. In J. Mills (Ed.), *A pedagogy of becoming* (pp. 73–92). Rodopi Press.

Gruba-McCallister, F. P. (2007). Narcissism and the empty self: To have or to be. *The Journal of Individual Psychology, 63*(2), 182–192.

Gruba-McCallister, F. P. (2019). *Embracing disillusionment: Achieving liberation through the demystification of suffering*. University Professors Press.

Gruba-McCallister, F., & Levington, C. (1994). Authenticity as open existence. *Advanced Development, 6*, 1–10.

Gruba-McCallister, F. P., & Levington, C. (1995). Suffering and transcendence in human experience. *Review of Existential Psychology and Psychiatry, 22*, 99–115.

Hamilton, M. B. (1987). The elements of the concept of ideology. *Political Studies, 35*, 18–38.

Hanna, F. J., & Puhakka, K. (1991). When psychotherapy works: Pinpointing an element of change. *Psychotherapy, 28*(4), 598–607.

Hardiman, R., & Jackson, B. W. (1997) Conceptual foundations for social justice courses. In Maureen Adams, Lee Anne Bell, & Pat Griffin (Eds.), *Teaching for diversity and social justice* (pp. 16–29). Routledge.

Harner, M. (1980). *The way of the shaman: A guide to power and healing*. Harper & Row.

Harrow, M. (2007). Factors involved in outcome and recovery in schizophrenia patients not on antipsychotic medications. *Journal of Nervous and Mental Diseases, 195*, 406–414.

Hartelius, G., Friedman, H. L., & Pappas, J. D. (2013). The calling to a spiritual psychology: Should transpersonal psychology convert? In H. L. Friedman & G. Hartelius (Eds.), *The Wiley-Blackwell handbook of transpersonal psychology* (pp. 44–61). John Wiley & Sons.

Harvey, D. (2007). *A brief history of neoliberalism*. Oxford University Press.

Harvey, J. (2000). Social privilege and moral subordination. *Journal of Social Philosophy, 31*(2), 177–188,

Harvey, J. (2010). Victims, resistance, and civilized oppression. *Journal of Social Philosophy, 41*(1), 13–27.

Hebblethwaite, B. (1976). *Evil, suffering and religion*. Hawthorne Books, Inc.

Hedges, C. (2008). *American fascists: The Christian Right and the war on America*. Free Press.

Hegel, G. W. F. (2007). *Philosophy of mind* (M. Inwood, Trans.). Oxford University Press. (Original work published 1907)

Held, D. (1980). *Introduction to critical theory: Horkheimer to Habermas*. University of California Press.

Heidegger, M. (1962). *Being and time* (J. Macquarrie & E. Robinson, Trans.). Harper and Row.

Herman, E. S., & Chomsky, N. (2002). *Manufacturing consent: The political economy of the mass media*. Pantheon.

Hick, J. (1989). *An interpretation of religion: Human responses to the transcendent*. Yale University Press.

Hick, J. (2007). *Evil and the God of love*. Palgrave MacMillan.

Hilgard, E. R. (1986). *Divided consciousness: Multiple controls in human thought and action*. Wiley.

Holz, N. E., Berhe, O., Sacu, S., Schwarz, E., Tesarz, J., Heim, C. M., & Tost, H. (2023). Early social adversity, altered brain functional connectivity, and mental health. *Biological Psychiatry, 93*, 430–441.

Horkheimer, M., & Adorno, T. (1995). *Dialectic of enlightenment* (J. Cumming, Trans.). Herder & Herder. (Original work published in 1944)

Husserl, E. (1982). *Ideas pertaining to a pure phenomenology and to a phenomenological philosophy*: First book. Martinus Nijoff. (Original work published 1913)

Huxley, A. (1944). *The perennial philosophy*. Harper.

Ihde, D. (1986). *Experimental phenomenology: An introduction*. State University of New York.

Illich, I. (2000). *Limits to medicine: Medical nemesis, the expropriation of health*. Marion Boyars Publisher, Ltd.

Jackson, M. (2001). Psychotic and spiritual experience: A case study comparison. In I. Clarke (Ed.), *Psychosis and spirituality: Exploring the new frontier* (pp. 165–190). Whurr Publishers.

Jacobs, D. H. (1994). Environmental failure-oppression is the only cause of psychopathology. *Journal of Mind and Behavior, 15*(1–2), 1–18.

Jacobs, D. H., & Cohen, D. (2009). Does "psychological dysfunction" mean anything? A critical essay on pathology versus agency. *Journal of Humanistic Psychology, 50*(3), 312–334.

James, W. (1958). *The varieties of religious experience*. New American Library.

Jaspers, K. (1984). *General psychopathology* (J. Hoenig & M. Hamilton, Trans.). University of Chicago Press.

Johnson, C. V., & Friedman, H. L. (2008). Enlightened or delusional? Differentiating religious, spiritual, and transpersonal experiences from psychopathology. *Journal of Humanistic Psychology, 48*(4), 505–527.

Jonas, W. B., Fritts, M. Christopher, G. Jonas, M., & Jonas, S. (2012). Spirituality, science, and the human body. In L. J. Miller (Ed.), *The Oxford handbook of psychology and spirituality* (pp. 361–378). Oxford University Press.

Joseph, P. (2018). *The new human rights movement: Reinventing the economy to end oppression*. BenBella Books, Inc.

Jost, J. T. (2006). The end of the end of ideology. *American Psychologist, 61*(7), 651-670.

Jost, J. T., & Amodio, D. M. (2012). Political ideology as motivated social cognition: Behavioral and neuroscientific evidence. *Motivation and Emotion, 36*, 55–64.

Jung, C. G. (1933). *Modern man in search of a soul* (W. S. Dell & C. F. Baynes, Trans.). Harcourt Brace Jovanovich.

Kafka, J. S. (1971). Ambiguity and individuation: A critique and reformulation of double-bind theory. *Archives of General Psychiatry, 25*, 232–239.

Kasser, T., & Kanner, A. D. (Eds.). (2004). *Psychology and consumer culture: The struggle for a good life in a materialistic world*. American Psychological Association.

Kasser, T., Ryan, R. M., Couchman, C. E., & Sheldon, K. M. (2004). Materialistic values: Their causes and consequences. In T. Kasser & A. D. Kanner (Eds.), *Psychology and consumer culture: The struggle for a good life in a materialistic world* (pp. 11–28). American Psychological Association.

Kelly, E. F., Kelly, E. W., Crabtree, A., Glaud, A., Grosso, M., & Greyson, B. (2007). *Irreducible mind: Toward a psychology for the 21st century*. Rowman & Littlefield.

Kendzior, S. (2022). *They knew: How a culture of conspiracy keeps America complacent*. Flatiron Press.

Kiecolt-Glaser, J. K. (2009). Psychoneuroimmunology: Psychology's gateway to a biomedical future. *Perspectives in Psychological Science, 4*(4), 367–369.

Kierkegaard, S. (1941). *The sickness unto death* (W. Kaufman, Trans.). Princeton University Press.

Klein, N. (2007). *The shock doctrine: The rise of disaster capitalism*. Picador.

Klein, N. (2014). *This changes everything: Capitalism vs. the climate*. Simon & Schuster.

Klein, N. (2017). *Saying no is not enough: Resisting Trump's shock politics and winning the world we need*. Haymarket Books.

Klein, N. (2023). *Doppelganger: A trip into the mirror world*. Farrar, Straus and Giroux.

Kleinman, A. (1988). *The illness narratives: Suffering, healing and the human condition*. Basic Books.

Kohler, et al. (2017). Greater post-Neolithic wealth disparities in Eurasia than in North America and Mesoamerica. *Nature, 551*, 619–622.

Krieger, N. (2005). (Ed.). *Embodying inequality: Epidemiologic perspectives*. Baywood Publishing Company, Inc.

Koestler, A. (1964). *The act of creation: A study of the conscious and the unconscious in science and art*. Dell.

Koestler, A. (1967). *The ghost in the machine*. Henry Regnery.

Laing, R. D. (1960). *The divided self*. Penguin Books.

Laing, R. D. (1967). *The politics of experience*. Pantheon Books.

Lakoff, G. (2002). *Moral politics: How liberals and conservatives think* (2nd Ed.). The University of Chicago Press.

Lakoff, G. (2004). *Don't think of an elephant*. Chelsea Green Publishing.

Lasch, C. (1979). *The culture of narcissism: American life in an age of diminishing expectations*. Warner Books Inc.

Laski, M. (1968). *Ecstasy: A study of some secular and religious experiences*. Greenwood Press.

Lawlis, G. F. (2013). Modern miracles from ancient medicine: Transpersonal medicine approaches. In H. L. Friedman & G. Hartelius (Eds.), *The Wiley-Blackwell handbook of transpersonal psychology* (pp. 640–651). John Wiley & Sons.

Leichsenring, F., Steinert, C., Rabung, S., Ioannidis, J. P. A. (2022). The effectiveness of psychotherapies and pharmacotherapies for mental disorders in adults: An umbrella review and meta-analytic evaluation of recent meta-analyses. *World Psychiatry, 21*, 133–145.

Lerner, M. (1986). *Surplus powerlessness*. The Institute for Labor and Mental Health.

Leuba, J. H. (1925). *The psychology of religious mysticism*. Harcourt Brace.

Loevinger, J. (1976). *Ego development: Conceptions and theories*. Jossey-Bass.

Loewenthal, D. (Ed.). (2015). *Critical psychotherapy, psychoanalysis and counselling: Implications for practice*. Palgrave Macmillan.

Loizzo, J., Brandon, F., Wolf, E. J., & Neale, M. (Eds.) (2023). *Advances in contemplative psychotherapy: Accelerating personal and social transformation*. (2nd ed.). Routledge.

Lopez-Leon, S., Wegman-Ostrosky, T., Perelman, C., et al. (2021).More than 50 long-term effects of COVID-19: A systematic review and meta-analysis. *Scientific Reports, 11*:16144. https://doi.org/10.1038/s41598-021-95565-8

MacDonald, D. A., Walsh, R., & Shapiro, S. L. (2013). Meditation: Empirical research and future directions. In H. L. Friedman & G. Hartelius (Eds.), *The Wiley-Blackwell handbook of transpersonal psychology* (pp. 433–458). John Wiley & Sons.

Manders, D. W. (2006). *The hegemony of common sense: Wisdom and mystification in everyday life.* Peter Lang Publishing Inc.

Marmot, M., & Wilkinson, R. G. (Eds.). (2006). *Social determinants of health* (2nd Ed.). Oxford University Press.

Marquis, A. (2008). *The integral intake: A guide to comprehensive idiographic assessment in integral psychotherapy.* Routledge.

Martin-Baró, I. (1996). *Writings for a liberation psychology* (A. Aron & S. Corne, Eds.). Harvard University Press.

Marx, K. (1978). *The Marx and Engels reader.* Norton.

Marx, K., & Engels, F. (2015). *The communist manifesto* (G. S. Jones, Trans.). Penguin Books.

Maslow, A. H. (1971). *The farther reaches of human nature.* Viking Press.

Masson, J. M. (1988). *Against therapy: Emotional tyranny and the myth of psychological healing.* Atheneum.

Maté, G. (2022). *The myth of normal: Trauma, illness & healing in a toxic culture.* Penguin Books.

May, R. (1958). Contributions of existential psychotherapy. In R. May, E. Angel, & H. E. Ellenberger (Eds.), *Existence* (pp. 37–91). Jason Aronson.

Mbembe, A. (2003). Necropolitics. *Public Culture, 15*(1), 11-40.

McGowan, P. O., & Szyf, M. (2010). The epigenetics of social adversity early in life: Implications for mental health outcomes. *Neurobiology of Disease, 39*, 66–72.

Merton, T. (1951). *The ascent to truth.* Harcourt Brace Jovanovich.

Miller, R. B. (2013). Deny no evil, ignore no evil, reframe no evil: Psychology's moral agenda. In A. C. Bohart, B. S. Held, E. Mendelowitz, & K. J. Schneider (Eds.), *Humanity's dark side: Evil, destructive experience, and psychotherapy* (pp. 213–236). American Psychological Association.

Moloney, P. (2013). *The therapy industry: The irresistible rise of the talking cure, and why it doesn't work.* Pluto Press.

Moncrieff, J. (2010). Psychiatric diagnosis as a political device. *Social Theory & Health, 8,* 370-382.

Moncrieff, J. (2021). The political economy of the mental health system: A Marxist analysis. *Conceptual Analysis, 6*, 1–11.

Moran, M. (2015). *Identity and capitalism.* Sage.

Moss, D. (Ed.) (1999a). *Humanistic and transpersonal psychology: A historical and biographical sourcebook.* Greenwood Press.

Moss, D. (1999b). Biofeedback, mind–body medicine, and the higher limits of human nature. In Donald Moss (Ed.), *Humanistic and transpersonal psychology: A historical and biographical sourcebook* (pp. 145–161). Greenwood Press.

Moulyn, A. (1982). *The meaning of suffering: An interpretation of human existence from the viewpoint of time.* Greenwood Press.

Murphy, M. (1992). *The future of the body: Explorations into the further evolution of human nature.* Jeremy P. Tarcher, Inc.

Nelson, J. M. (2009). *Psychology, religion, and spirituality.* Springer.

Newberg, A. B., & d'Aquili, E. (2002). *Why God won't go away: Brain science and the biology of belief*. Ballantine.
Newnes, C. (2014). The Diagnostic and Statistical Manual: A history of critiques of psychiatric classification systems. In E. Speed, J. Moncrieff, & M. Rapley (Eds.), *Demedicalizing misery II: Society, politics and the mental health industry* (pp.190–209). Palgrave Macmillan.
Nieman, S. (2002). *Evil in modern thought: An alternative history of philosophy*. Princeton University Press.
Nordentoft, K. (1978). *Kierkegaard's psychology* (B. Kirmmse, Trans.). Duquesne University Press.
Nouwen, H. J. M. (1972). *The wounded healer: Ministry in contemporary society*. Image Books.
Nussbaum, M. C. (1992). Human functioning and social justice: In defense of Aristotelian essentialism. *Political Theory, 20*(2), 202–246.
Nussbaum, M. C. (2003). Capabilities as fundamental entitlements: Sen and social justice. *Feminist Economics, 9*(2–3), 33–59.
Nussbaum, M. C. (2006). *Frontiers of justice: Disability, nationality, species membership*. The Belknap Press of Harvard University Press.
Ogden, J. (1997). The rhetoric and reality of psychosocial theories: A challenge to biomedicine. *Journal of Health Psychology, 2*, 21–29.
Otto, R. (1958). *The idea of the holy* (2nd Ed.) (J. W. Harvey, Trans.). Oxford University Press.
Palmer, P. J. (1993). *To know as we are known: Education as a spiritual journey*. HarperSanFrancisco.
Peck, M. S. (1983). *People of the lie: The hope for healing human evil*. Simon and Schuster.
Peck, M. S. (2002). *The road less traveled: A new psychology of love, traditional values, and spiritual growth*. Simon and Schuster.
Piketty, T. (2014). *Capital in the twenty-first century* (A. Goldhammer, Trans.). Belknap Press of Harvard University.
Polanyi, M. (1966). *The tacit dimension*. Doubleday.
Prabhavanda, S., & Isherwood, C. (Trans.) (1951). *Bhavagad-Gita*. New American Library.
Prilleltensky, I. (1997). Values, assumptions, and practices: Assessing the moral implications of psychological discourse and action. *American Psychologist, 52*(5), 517-535.
Prilleltensky, I. (1999). Critical psychology foundations for the promotion of mental health. *Annual Review of Critical Psychology, 1*, 95–112.
Prilleltensky, I. (2003). Understanding and overcoming oppression: Towards psychopolitical validity. *American Journal of Community Psychology, 31*, 195–202.
Prilleltensky, I. (2008). The role of power in wellness, oppression, and liberation: The promise of psychopolitical validity. *Journal of Community Psychology, 36*(2), 116–136.
Prilleltensky, I. (2012). Wellness as fairness. *American Journal of Community Psychology, 49*, 1–12.
Prilleltensky, I., Dokecki, P., Frieden, G., & Wang, V. O. (2007). Counseling for wellness and justice: Foundations and ethical dilemmas. In E. Aldarando (Ed.), *Advancing social justice through clinical practice* (pp. 19–42). Lawrence Erlbaum.
Prilleltensky, I., & Gonick, L. (1996). Politics change, oppression remains: On the psychology and politics of oppression. *Political Psychology, 17*, 127–147.
Prilleltensky, I., Prilleltensky, O., & Voorhees, C. (2008). Psychopolitical validity in the helping professions: Applications to research, interventions, case conceptualization,

and therapy. In C. I Cohen & S. B. Timimi (Eds.), *Liberatory psychiatry: Towards a new psychiatry* (pp. 105–130). Cambridge University Press.

Putnam, R. (2000). *Bowling alone: The collapse and revival of American community*. Simon and Schuster

Rahula, W. (1974). *What the Buddha taught.* Grove Press.

Ramsland, K. (1989). *Engaging the immediate: Applying Kierkegaard's theory of indirect communication to the practice of psychotherapy.* Associated University Press.

Rank, M. R. (2004). *One nation, underprivileged: Why American poverty affects us all.* Oxford University Press.

Rawls, J. (1971). *A theory of justice.* The Belknap Press of Harvard University Press.

Ray, V. (2022). *On critical race theory: Why it matters and why you should care.* Random House.

Rebechi, A., & Rohde, N. (2023). Economic insecurity, racial anxiety, and right-wing populism. *Review of Income and Wealth, 69*(3), 701–724.

Rehmann, J. (2013). *Theories of ideology: The powers of alienation and subjection.* Haymarket Books.

Reich, W. (1969). *The mass psychology of fascism* (V. R. Carfagno, Trans.). WRM Press.

Reid, C. R., & Latty, T. (2016). Collective behaviour and swarm intelligence in slime moulds. *FEMA Microbiology Reviews, 40*(6), 798–806.

Richards, P. S. (2012). Honoring religious diversity and universal spirituality in psychotherapy. In L. J. Miller (Ed.), *The Oxford handbook of psychology and spirituality* (pp. 237–254). Oxford University Press.

Rogers, C. R. (1961). *On becoming a person.* Houghton Mifflin.

Rose, N. (1998). *Inventing our selves: Psychology, power, and personhood.* Cambridge University Press.

Rose, S. M., & Hatzenbuehler, S. (2009). Embodying social class: The link between poverty, income equality, and health. *International Social Work, 52*(4), 459–471.

Rotenstein, L. S., Ramos, M. A., Torre, M., Segal, J. B., Peluso, M. J., Guille, C., Sen, S., & Mata, D. A. (2016). Prevalence of depression, depressive symptoms, and suicidal ideation among medical students: A systematic review and meta-analysis. *JAMA, 316*(21), 2214–2236.

Ryan, W. (1971). *Blaming the victim.* Pantheon Books.

Salomon, J-R., & Ingerman, S. (2019). *Soul matters: Modern science confirming ancient wisdom: Healing at the interface of spirit and matter.* Balboa Press.

Sandel, M. J. (2021). *Tyranny of merit: Can we find the common good?* Picador Press.

Sanderson, C., & Linehan, M. L. (1999). Acceptance and forgiveness. In William R. Miller (Ed.), *Integrating spirituality into treatment: Resources for practitioners* (pp. 199–216). American Psychological Association.

Sartre, J. P. (1953). *Being and nothingness* (H. Barnes, Trans.). Washington Square Press.

Schor, J. B. (2004). *Born to buy: The commercialization and the new consumer culture.* Scribner.

Schraube, E., & Osterkamp, U. (2013). *Psychology from the standpoint of the subject: Selected writings of Klaus Holzkamp.* Palgrave Macmillan.

Schneider, M. (2006). *Introduction to public health* (2nd Ed.). Jones and Bartlett.

Schwartz, G. (2012). Consciousness, spirituality, and postmaterialist science: An empirical and experiential approach. In Lisa J. Miller (Ed.), *The Oxford handbook of psychology and spirituality* (pp. 584–597). Oxford University Press.

Schilling, S. P. (1977). *God and human anguish.* Abingdon.

Scotten, B. W., Chinen, A. B., & Battista, J. R. (Eds.). (1996). *Textbook of transpersonal psychiatry and psychology.* Basic Books.

Sedgwick, P. (1982). *Psycho politics.* Harper & Row.

Seligman, M. E. P. (1975). *Helplessness: On depression, development, and death.* W. H. Freeman.

Seligman, M. E., & Csikszentmihalyi, M. (2000). Positive psychology: An introduction. *American Psychologist, 55*(1), 5-14.

Selye, H. (1974). *Stress without distress.* New American Library.

Selye, H. (1976). *The stress of life* (Rev. Ed.). McGraw-Hill.

Semega, J., Kollar, M., Shrider, E. A., and Creamer. J. F. (2020). Income and poverty in the United States: *Current population reports,* P60–270. Washington, DC: US Census Bureau.

Sen, A. (1999). *Development as freedom.* Anchor Books.

Shermer, M. (2022). *Conspiracy: Why the rational believe the irrational.* Johns Hopkins University Press.

Sidanius, J., & Pratto, F. (1999). *Social dominance: An intergroup theory of social hierarchy and oppression.* Cambridge University Press.

Silow, T. (2010). Embodiment, an ascending and descending development. In S. Esbjörn-Hargens (Ed.), *Integral theory in action* (pp. 79–98). State University of New York Press.

Simard, S. (2022). *Finding the mother tree: Discovering the wisdom of the forest.* Vintage Press.

Skinner, B. F. (2002). *Beyond freedom and dignity.* Hackett Publishing.

Slife, B. D., & Wiggins, B. J. (2009). Taking relationship seriously in psychotherapy: Radical relationality. *Journal of Contemporary Psychotherapy, 39,* 17–24.

Small, D. (2005). *Power, interest and psychology: Elements of a social materialist understanding of distress.* PCCS Books.

Smith, L. (2010). *Psychology, poverty, and the end of social exclusion: Putting our practice to work.* Teachers College Press.

Smucker, J. M. (2017). *Hegemony how-to: A roadmap for radicals.* AK Press.

Soelle, D. (1975). *Suffering* (E. R. Kalin, Trans.). Fortress Press.

Soelle, D. (2001). *The silent cry: Mysticism and resistance* (B. & M. Rumscheidt, Trans.). Fortress Press.

Solomon, S., Greenberg, J., & Pyszczynski, T. (1991). A terror management theory of social behavior: The psychological function of self-esteem and cultural worldviews. In M. P. Zanna (Ed.), *Advances in experimental and social psychology* (Vol. 24, pp. 91–159). Academic Press.

Sperry, L. (2008). The psychologization of spirituality: A compelling case for it has to be made. *The Journal of Individual Psychology, 64*(2), 169–175.

Spicer, J., & Chamberlain, K. (1996). Developing psychosocial theory in health psychology: problems and prospects. *Journal of Health Psychology, 1,* 161–171.

Spiegel, H., & Spiegel, D. (1978). *Trance and treatment: Clinical uses of hypnosis.* Basic Books.

Spinelli, E. (2014). *Practicing existential psychotherapy: The relational world.* (2nd Ed.). London, UK: Sage.

Stanley, J. (2020). *How fascism works: The politics of us and them.* Random House.

Staub, E. (1989). *The roots of evil: The origins of genocide and other group violence.* Cambridge University Press.

Stewart, K. (2019). *The power worshippers: Inside the dangerous rise of religious nationalism.* Bloomsbury Publishing.

Struthers, R., Eschiti, V., & Patchell, B. (2004). Traditional indigenous healing: Part I. *Complementary Therapies in Nursing & Midwifery, 10,* 141–149.

Sue, D. W. (2010). *Microaggressions in everyday life: Race, gender, and sexual orientation.* Wiley.

Sullivan, H. S. (1953). *The interpersonal theory of psychiatry.* Norton.

Suls, J., & Rothman, A. (2004). Evolution of the biopsychosocial model: Prospects and challenges for health psychology. *Health Psychology, 23,* 119–125.

Tart, C. T. (2010). Toward evidence-based spirituality: Some glimpses of an evolving vision. *Subtle Energies & Energy Medicine, 20*(2), 7–37.

Teo, T. (2015). Critical psychology: A geography of intellectual engagement and resistance. *American Psychologist, 70*(3), 243–254.

Teo, T. (2020). Subhumanism: The re-emergence of an affective-symbolic ontology in the migration debate and beyond. *Journal for the Theory of Social Behavior, 28*(5), 581–599.

Teo, T. (2021). Essay of fascist subjectivity. In I. Strasser & M. Dege (Eds.), *The psychology of global crises and crisis politics* (pp. 325–345). Palgrave.

Teo, T. (2023). Subjectivity and work: Critical-theoretical reflections. *Journal of Everyday Activity, 16*(1), 39–59.

Thompson, J. N. (1994). *The coevolutionary process.* University of Chicago Press.

Thorsen, D. E. (2010). The neoliberal challenge. What is neoliberalism? *Contemporary Readings in Law and Social Justice, 2*(2), 188–214.

Tillich, P. (1952). *The courage to be.* Yale University Press.

Tillich, P. (1957). *The dynamics of faith.* Harper & Row.

Tudor, K., & Worrall, M. (2006). *Person-centered therapy: A clinical philosophy.* Routledge.

Umberson, D., & Donnelly, R. (2023). Social isolation: An unequally distributed health hazard. *Annual Review of Sociology, 49,* 379–399.

Underhill, E. (1915). *Practical mysticism.* E. P. Dutton.

Underhill, E. (1961). *Mysticism: A study in the nature and development of man's spiritual consciousness.* E. P. Dutton.

Underhill, E. (1999). *The essentials of mysticism and other essays.* Oneworld.

van Deurzen, E. (1997). *Everyday mysteries: Existential dimensions of psychotherapy.* Routledge.

van Deurzen, E. (2002). *Existential counselling and psychotherapy in practice* (2nd Ed.). Sage.

Victor, S. E., Lewis, S. P., & Muehlenkamp, J. J. (2022). Psychologists with lived experience of non-suicidal self-injury: Priorities, obstacles, and recommendations for inclusion. *Psychological Services, 19*(1), 1–21.

von Eckartsberg, R., & Valle, R. S. (1981). Heideggerian thinking and the Eastern mind. In R. S. Valle and R. von Eckartsberg (Eds.), *The metaphors of consciousness* (pp 286–311). Plenum Press.

von Hayek, F. A. (2007). *The road to serfdom* (B. Caldwell, Ed.). University of Chicago Press.

von Stuckrad, K. (2002). Re-enchanting nature: Modern Western shamanism and nineteenth century thought. *Journal of the American Academy of Religion, 70*(4), 771–800.

Walsh, R. (1996). Shamanism and healing. In B. W. Scotton, A. B. Chinen, & J. R. Battista (Eds.), *Textbook of transpersonal psychiatry and psychology* (pp. 96–103). Basic Books.

Walters, K. (2001). *Rufus Jones: Essential writings.* Orbis Books.

Wampold, B. E., & Imel, Z. E. (2015). *The great psychotherapy debate: The evidence for what makes psychotherapy work* (2nd Ed.). Routledge.

Watkins, M., & Shulman, H. (2008). *Toward psychologies of liberation*. Palgrave Macmillan.

Watts, A. W. (1951). *The wisdom of insecurity*. Vintage Books.

Watts, A. W. (1961). *Psychotherapy east and west*. Pantheon Books.

Watts, A. W. (1963). *The two hands of God: The myths of polarity*. Collier Books.

Watts, A. W. (1966). *The book: On the taboo against knowing who you are*. Collier Books.

Watts, A. W. (1971). *Behold the spirit: A study in the necessity of mystical religion*. Vintage Books.

Watts, A. W. (1972). *The supreme identity: An essay on Oriental metaphysic and Christian religion*. Pantheon.

Watters, E., & Ofshe, R. (1999). *Therapy's delusions: The myth of the unconscious and the exploitation of today's walking worried*. Scribner.

Weber, M. (1993). *The sociology of religion* (E. Fischoff, Trans.). Beacon Press.

Whitaker, R. (2011). *Anatomy of an epidemic: Magic bullets, psychiatric drugs, and the astonishing rise of mental illness in America*. Crown.

Whitaker, R. (2019). *Mad in America: Bad science, bad medicine, and the enduring mistreatment of the mentally ill*. Basic Books.

Whitehead, A. N. (1969). *Process and reality*. Macmillan.

Wickramasekera, I. E. (2013). Hypnosis and transpersonal psychology: Answering the call within. In H. L. Friedman & G. Hartelius (Eds.), *The Wiley-Blackwell handbook of transpersonal psychology* (pp. 492–511). John Wiley & Sons.

Wilber, K. (1977). *The spectrum of consciousness*. Theosophical Publishing House.

Wilber, K. (1980). *The Atman project: A transpersonal view of human development*. The Theosophical Publishing House.

Wilber, K. (1996). *Up from Eden: A transpersonal view of human evolution*. Quest Books.

Wilber, K. (1998). *The marriage of sense and soul: Integrating science and religion*. Random House.

Wilber, K. (1999). An approach to integral psychology. *The Journal of Transpersonal Psychology, 31*(2), 109–136.

Wilber, K. (2000a). *Integral psychology: Consciousness, spirit, psychology, therapy*. Shambhala Press.

Wilber, K. (2000b). *Sex, ecology, spirituality: The spirit of evolution*. Shambhala Press.

Wilber, K., Engler, J., & Brown, D. P. (1986). *Transformations of consciousness: Conventional and contemplative perspectives on development*. Shambala Press.

Wilkinson, R., & Pickett, K. (2009). *The spirit level: Why greater equality makes societies stronger*. Bloomsbury Press.

Wilkinson, R., & Pickett, K. (2018). *The inner level: How more equal societies reduce stress, restore sanity, and improve everyone's well-being*. Penguin Press.

Williams, C. R. (2008). Compassion, suffering and the self: A moral psychology of social justice. *Current Sociology, 56*(5), 5–24.

Wilson, C. (1966). *Introduction to the new existentialism*. Houghton Mifflin.

Winkelman, M. (1990). Shaman and other "magico-religious healers": A cross-cultural study of their origins, nature, and social transformation. *Ethos,18*(3), 308–352.

Winkelman, M. (2000). *Shamanism: The neural ecology of consciousness and healing*. Bergin & Garvey.

Winkelman, M. (2013). Shamanism in cross-cultural perspective. *International Journal of Transpersonal Studies, 31*(2), 4762.

Wright, E. O. (2019). *How to be an anti-capitalist in the 21st century*. Verso.

Wulff, D. M. (2000). Mystical experience. In E. Cardeña, J. Lynn, & S. Krippner (Eds.), *Varieties of anomalous experiences: Examining the scientific evidence* (pp. 397–440). American Psychological Association.

Yalom, I. D. (1980). *Existential psychotherapy*. Basic Books.

Yeh, C. H., Hunter, C. D., Madan-Behel, A., Chiang, L., & Arora, A. K. (2004). Indigenous and interdependent perspectives of healing: Implications for counseling and research. *Journal of Counseling & Development, 82*, 410–419.

Young, I. M. (1990). *Justice and the politics of difference*. Princeton University Press.

Yutang, L. (Trans.) (1948). *The wisdom of Lao Tse.* Random House.

Zerubavel, N., & O'Dougherty Wright, M. (2012). The dilemma of the wounded healer. *Psychotherapy, 49*(4), 482–491.

Index

About the Author

Frank Gruba-McCallister, PhD received his master's and doctoral degree in Clinical Psychology from Purdue University. He is currently retired after having taught and served in academic administration for over thirty-three years at the Illinois School of Professional Psychology-Chicago, Adler University, and the Chicago School of Professional Psychology-Chicago. Prior to teaching, Dr. Gruba-McCallister provided clinical services primarily to individuals in a medical setting and in private practice. While the Vice President of Academic Affairs at Adler, he oversaw the revision of all degree programs to support the newly adopted mission of the school to educate socially responsible practitioners. This innovation was recognized by the Clinical Psychology Doctoral program receiving the 2007 American Psychological Association's Board of Education Affairs Award for Innovative Practices in Graduate Education in Psychology. Dr. Gruba-McCallister has published and given professional presentations in the areas of humanistic/existential psychology, spirituality, health psychology, critical psychology, and the role of psychology in advancing social justice. His book *Embracing Disillusionment: Achieving Liberation Through the Demystification of Suffering,* also published by University Professors Press, explores the significant adverse impact of oppression on physical and psychological well-being, the role of neoliberal ideology in oppression, and the role psychologists must play in exposing and meaningfully addressing the suffering caused by oppression. He also has recently co-edited a book with Jon Hook, *The Revolutionary Psychologist's Guide to Radical Therapy*, a collection of chapters on the theory and practice of diverse forms of radical practice.

www.ingramcontent.com/pod-product-compliance
Lightning Source LLC
Chambersburg PA
CBHW080131270326
41926CB00021B/4436